HARCOURT Science

Harcourt School Publishers

Orlando • Boston • Dallas • Chicago • San Diego

www.harcourtschool.com

School Permissions and Copyrights, Harcourt, Inc.
6277 Sea Harbor Drive
Orlando, FL 32887-6777
Fax: 407-345-2418

Grateful acknowledgment is made to Farrar, Straus and Giroux, LLC for permission to reprint cover illustration from *The Puddle* by David McPhail, jacket design by Filomena Tuosto. Copyright © 1998 by David McPhail.

Printed in the United States of America

ISBN 0-15-323683-3

3 4 5 6 7 8 9 10 073 10 09 08 07 06 05 04 03 02 01

HARCOURT

Science

TEACHER'S EDITION CONTENTS

ABOUT THE PROGRAM

THE UNITS

PUPIL EDITION REFERENCES

TEACHER REFERENCES

Authors

Robert M. Jones, Ed.D. Professor of Education and Environmental Education Affiliate of the Environmental Institute of Houston, he has served at the University of Houston–Clear Lake for 25 years. Dr. Jones has also served on the Board of Directors of the Association for the Education of Teachers in Science and as Director of the Southwest Region of that organization. His areas of interest include aerospace and motion engineering, cooperative learning, and environmental education.

Joyce C. McLeod Visiting Professor, Rollins College, Winter Park, Florida, she has focused on training teachers in how to use the results of brain research to match instructional strategies to the curriculum and to the capabilities and learning styles of their students. As former Harcourt Editor-in-Chief of Science and Mathematics, she guided the development of programs that implemented national standards and reflected the latest research in teaching and learning. Her areas of interest include research on teaching and learning, primary education, teacher professional development, assessment, and connections between science, mathematics, and reading.

Gerald H. Krockover, Ph.D. Professor of Earth and Atmospheric Science Education, he has served as chair of the Elementary Education program area at Purdue University for 10 years. He was a member of the Executive Committee and the Board of Directors of the National Science Teachers Association. He is the coauthor of the two-volume *Creative Sciencing: Ideas and Activities for Primary and Intermediate Teachers and Children.* His areas of interest include earth-space science education, equity in science education, the integration of mathematics and science, and the use of technology and telecommunications in the classroom.

Marjorie Slavick Frank A former member of the adjunct faculty at Hunter, Brooklyn, and Manhattan Colleges, New York, she is a specialist in literacy and language development, as well as a composer and lyricist. Her areas of interest include elementary science and reading instruction, children's literature, and strategies for content-area reading.

Mozell P. Lang Science Education Consultant in the Curriculum Development Program of the Michigan Department of Education, she provides technical assistance and support to schools and organizations for the implementation of professional development in teaching, learning, assessment, and multicultural efforts. She also coordinates statewide recognition programs, such as the Presidential Awards. Her areas of interest include the physical sciences.

Carol J. Valenta Vice President—Exhibits, Education, and Programs at the St. Louis Science Center, she coordinates the Science Center and Outreach Programs with school districts in Illinois and Missouri. She was a classroom teacher, an elementary school principal, and the Coordinator of Science Center Instructional Programs for the Los Angeles Unified School District. Her areas of interest include physical science, integrated curriculum, teacher empowerment and training, video-based instruction, community-based education, family education, and urban education.

Barry A. Van Deman Section Head and Program Director of Informal Science Education at the National Science Foundation, he was an award-winning science teacher, school administrator, university instructor, and leader in science museums. He served as president of the Council for Elementary Science International and board member of the National Science Teachers Association. He is the author of *Nuts and Bolts: A Matter of Fact Guide to Science Fair Projects.* His areas of interest include life sciences, environmental education, museum exhibits, Web-based activities, and teacher professional development.

Dear Educator,

The National Science Education Standards state, "In a world filled with the products of scientific inquiry, scientific literacy has become a necessity for everyone."

Harcourt Science is based on the following principles of scientific literacy:

- All children can investigate and learn science concepts and can experience success in science.
- Children must develop knowledge of and the ability to use the tools and processes of scientific inquiry.
- Children experience success in science when they develop age-appropriate knowledge and understanding of the life, earth, and physical sciences and when they learn about the history and nature of science.
- While engaged in the study of science, children should have the opportunity to build success in other curricular areas.
- Science content should be presented to children in an interesting, comprehensible, and clearly organized format.
- Children's competence in the concepts and processes of science should be assessed through a variety of tools that are consistent, authentic, and fair.

Harcourt Science provides children with the opportunity to

- **Investigate** the natural world,
- **Learn About** interesting, relevant, and exciting science ideas, and
- **Link** science to mathematics, writing, technology, and all other aspects of the elementary curriculum.

Harcourt Science gives you the resources to promote scientific literacy by nurturing in your students a lifelong fascination with the natural world.

Sincerely,

The Authors

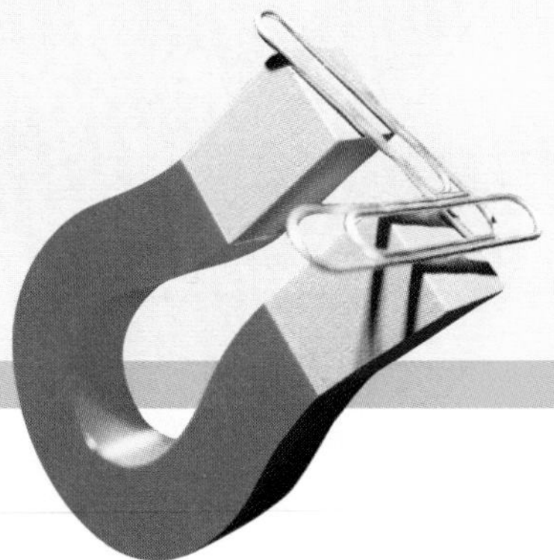

Senior Editorial Advisor

Napoleon Adebola Bryant, Jr.
Professor Emeritus of Education
Xavier University
Cincinnati, Ohio

Program Advisor and Activities Writer

Barbara ten Brink
Science Director
Round Rock Independent School District
Round Rock, Texas

Program Advisors

Michael J. Bell
Assistant Professor of Early Childhood Education
School of Education
West Chester University
West Chester, Pennsylvania

George W. Bright
Professor of Mathematics Education
The University of North Carolina at Greensboro
Greensboro, North Carolina

Pansy Cowder
Science Specialist
Tampa, Florida

Robert H. Fronk
Head, Science/Mathematics Education Department
Florida Institute of Technology
Melbourne, Florida

Bernard A. Harris, Jr.
Physician and Former Astronaut
(STS 55-Space Shuttle *Columbia*, STS 63 Space Shuttle *Discovery*)
President, The Harris Foundation
Houston, Texas

Lois Harrison-Jones
Education and Management Consultant
Dallas, Texas

Kenneth R. Mechling
Professor of Biology and Science Education
Clarion University of Pennsylvania
Clarion, Pennsylvania

Nancy Roser
Professor of Language and Literacy Studies
University of Texas, Austin
Austin, Texas

Dr. Harris invites students to participate in an exciting program that involves them in space exploration. See the article titled "Soaring into Space" on pages T76-77.

Classroom Reviewers and Contributors

Sidney Jay Abramowitz
District Administrator for Mathematics, Science & Technology
Stamford Public Schools
Stamford, Connecticut

Rose G. Baublitz
Director Curriculum and Staff Development
Granville Exempted Village School District
Granville, Ohio

Melcene Beasley
Eastside Elementary School
Douglas, Georgia

Cathy Boles
Sawnee Primary School
Cumming, Georgia

Sharon W. Bowers
Kemps Landing Magnet School
Virginia Beach, Virginia

Susan Busenlehner
Snow Rogers Elementary School
Gardendale, Alabama

Patricia L. Bush
Jesse Stuart Elementary School
Madisonville, Kentucky

Gary Callahan
Goodland Elementary School
Racine, Wisconsin

Edward J. Carroll
Thomas E. Bowe School
Glassboro, New Jersey

Lisa Crooks
Black Bob Elementary School
Olathe, Kansas

Kimberly Gay
Mango Elementary School
Seffner, Florida

Joe E. Hart
Science Lead Teacher
Clayton County Public Schools
Morrow, Georgia

Kathryn Henry
Teacher Trainer
Public School CS 200
New York, New York

Jacqueline Howard
Millard Hensley School
Salyersville, Kentucky

Scott Hudson
Covedale Elementary
Cincinnati, Ohio

Denise Hunt
Cumming Elementary School
Cumming, Georgia

Donna Kavanaugh
Pleasant Hill Elementary School
Cincinnati, Ohio

Faye Kelley
Gardendale Elementary School
Gardendale, Alabama

Kimberly Knause
Brantner Elementary School
Cincinnati, Ohio

Angela Langenkamp
St. Gabriel School
Louisville, Kentucky

Faye McCollum
Instructional Specialist
Muscogee County School District
Columbus, Georgia

Margie H. McCoy
Salyer Elementary School
Salyersville, Kentucky

Marie A. McDermott
Kingsbury School
Waterbury, Connecticut

Leah McGriff
Garrison Elementary School
Savannah, Georgia

Beverly W. McNair
Hollis Hand Elementary School
LaGrange, Georgia

Chester H. Melcher
Supervisor of Curriculum and Instruction—Science
Racine Unified School District
Racine, Wisconsin

Philip J. Natoli
Geneseo Central School
Geneseo, New York

Clyde Partner
Science/Health Curriculum Coordinator
Evanston S.D. #65
Evanston, Illinois

Michael F. Ryan
Educational Technology Specialist
Lake County Schools
Tavares, Florida

Arnold E. Serotsky
Teacher/Science Department Coordinator
Greece Athena Middle School
Rochester, New York

Michelle Bonk Severtson
Olson Elementary
Bloomington, Minnesota

Ann Starek
Memorial School
Natick, Massachusetts

Sandra Seim Tauer
Math/Science Instructional Coordinator
Educational Support Center
Derby, Kansas

Sharon Till
Chattahoochee Elementary School
Cumming, Georgia

Ross A. Vandercook
Principal
Hiawatha Elementary School
Okemos, Michigan

Stanley J. Wegrzynowski
Director of Science
Buffalo Public Schools
Buffalo, New York

Lee Ann White
Morgantown Elementary School
Morgantown, Kentucky

Lynda Wood
Science Coordinator
Southfield Education Center
Southfield, Michigan

Implementing the National Science

At the request of teacher associations, professional societies, and government officials, the National Research Council established a National Committee on Science Education Standards and Assessment to be responsible for the development of national science education standards. The standards were published by the National Academy Press in 1996. The goals for school science that underlie the National Science Education Standards are to educate students so that they are able to

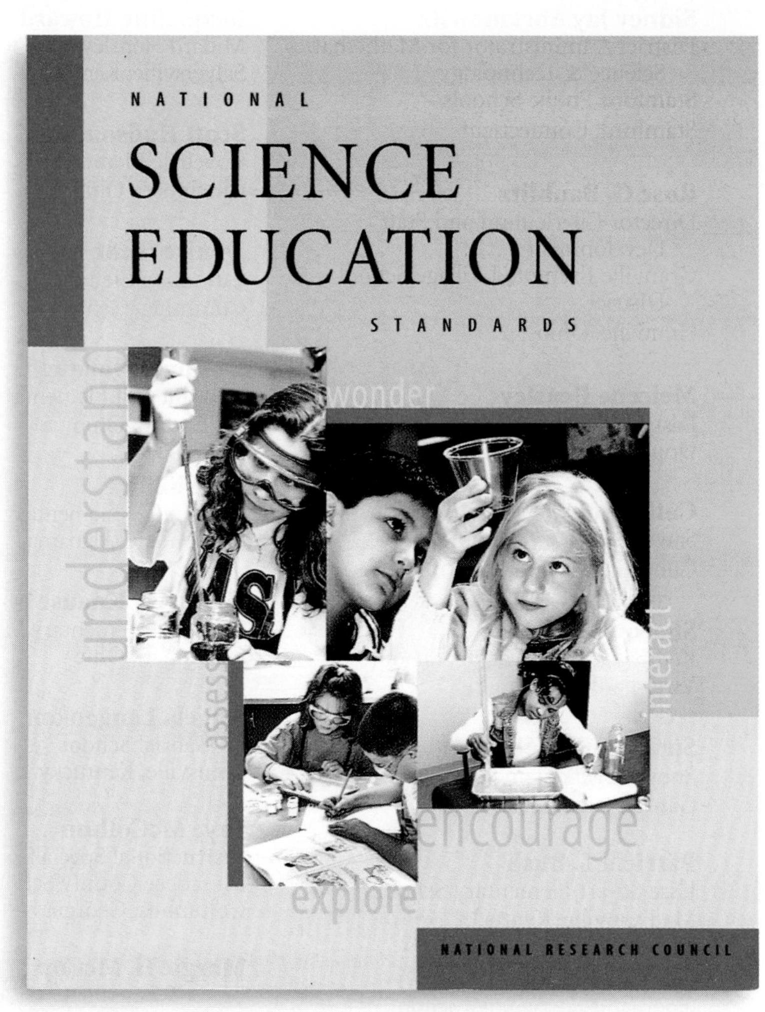

- experience the richness and excitement of knowing about and understanding the natural world;
- use appropriate scientific processes and principles in making personal decisions;
- engage intelligently in public discourse and debate about matters of scientific and technological concern; and
- increase their economic productivity through the use of the knowledge, understanding, and skills of the scientifically literate person in their careers.

"Learning science is something students do, not something that is done to them."

National Science Education Standards

Education Standards

The Science Content and Assessment Standards, which are within the National Science Education Standards, outline what students should know, understand, and be able to do in the natural sciences. They include these categories:

- Unifying concepts and processes in science
- Science as inquiry
- Life science
- Earth and space science
- Physical science
- Science and technology
- Science in personal and social perspective
- History and nature of science
- Assessment that is consistent, fair, and provided in a variety of contexts

Statue of Albert Einstein, Washington, D.C.

Harcourt Science was developed to meet the goals and content objectives of the National Science Education Standards, and it does so in the following ways:

- Standards-based life, earth, and physical science content is provided at each grade.
- Students use the tools and processes of scientific inquiry in every lesson, which always begins with a hands-on investigation.
- Exciting and informative aspects of science and technology are included within the life, earth, and physical science content.
- The history and nature of science and the work of scientists are featured.
- Students are assessed in a variety of ways. (See Assessment Guide.)

A correlation of *Harcourt Science* to the National Science Education Standards is provided in the back of this Teacher's Edition.

Skills for Lifelong Learning

Science Process Skills

Harcourt Science provides many opportunities for students to develop and maintain the essential skills that form the basis for lifelong learning. The science process skills are important inquiry tools and are essential for investigating the natural world. Opportunities for developing the process skills are embedded throughout *Harcourt Science*.

Science Process Skill	Description
Observe	using one or more of the senses to perceive properties of objects and events; can be done directly with the senses or indirectly through the use of simple or complex instruments
Compare	identifying common and distinguishing characteristics among objects or events
Classify/Order	grouping or organizing objects or events into categories based on specific criteria
Gather, Record, Display, or Interpret Data	making observations of objects or events from which to make inferences or predictions; writing down the observations on paper as notes or displaying the data in charts, in tables, or in graphs; making predictions, inferences, and hypotheses from a set of data
Use Numbers	estimating or quantifying data
Communicate	transmitting observable data or ideas visually, orally, or electronically
Plan and Conduct Simple Investigations/Experiments	using one or more of the process skills to find the answer to a question or the solution to a problem
Measure	making quantitative observations using both nonstandard and standard measures
Predict	anticipating outcomes of future events, based on patterns or experience
Infer	using logical reasoning to make conclusions based on observations
Draw Conclusions	interpreting data to make conclusions; the final step of an investigation
Use Time/Space Relationships	estimating the relationships of moving and of nonmoving objects to one another; includes sequencing
Hypothesize	posing a testable explanation for observations or events and stating it as the expected outcome of an experiment
Formulate or Use Models	making a mental or physical representation of a process or structure or using a model that someone else has provided
Identify and Control Variables	stating or controlling factors that affect the outcome of an experiment
Experiment	designing procedures for gathering data to test hypotheses under conditions in which variables are controlled or manipulated

Reading, Writing, and Math Skills

Effective science instruction integrates science content and experiences with all areas of the elementary curriculum. *Harcourt Science* provides students with many opportunities to develop reading, writing, and math skills through meaningful activities and strategies.

Reading Skills

Reading underlies everything students do in school, and many of the reading skills you are teaching are reinforced in *Harcourt Science*. The Pupil Edition helps students become strategic readers by providing

- Grade 1 text that builds in complexity and readability from the first to the last chapters
- highlighted vocabulary
- graphics to support the learning
- clear text structures, such as headings and subheadings
- internal features and questions that guide concept attainment
- lesson and chapter reviews that consolidate learning

Strategies for developing the following reading skills are provided at point of use throughout this Teacher's Edition. Follow-up practice is also provided in the Workbook.

- ☑ use context
- ☑ recall supporting facts and details
- ☑ arrange events in sequence
- ☑ draw conclusions
- ☑ identify the main idea
- ☑ identify cause and effect
- ☑ predict outcomes
- ☑ summarize
- ☑ use graphic sources for information
- ☑ relate pictures to text
- ☑ distinguish between fact and nonfact
- ☑ develop concepts of print
- ☑ build vocabulary

Writing Skills

Opportunities for students to express their ideas in writing are provided throughout *Harcourt Science*. In the Pupil Edition, the writing links in each chapter provide prompts for writing about chapter concepts in interesting and meaningful ways. The prompts include art ideas that make writing fun! Writing Models are provided in the Teaching Resources book.

Math Skills

Opportunities to practice mathematics skills, solve problems, and connect mathematics and science are provided throughout the Pupil and Teacher's Editions. Look for the Math Link in the Pupil Edition at the end of every chapter. Additional Math Links are also provided at point of use in the Teacher's Edition.

Assessment Program

Overview

In *Harcourt Science,* the Assessment Program, like the instruction, is student-centered. By allowing all learners to show what they know and can do, the Assessment Program provides you with ongoing information about each student's understanding of science. The Assessment Program also involves the student in self-assessment, offering you strategies for helping students evaluate their own growth.

The *Harcourt Science* assessment program is based on the following Assessment Model. The model's framework shows the multidimensional aspect of the program, with five assessment components supported by teacher-based and student-based assessment tools. More information about the Assessment Model is provided in the **Assessment Guide**.

Harcourt Science Assessment Model

(**Key:** PE=Pupil Edition; TE=Teacher's Edition; AG=Assessment Guide; WB=Workbook)

Formal Assessment

- **Chapter Review and Test Preparation,** PE
- **Chapter Test,** AG
- **Unit Test,** AG

Ongoing Assessment

- ✓**Questions**, PE
- **Lesson Review**, PE and WB
- **Informal Assessment Strategies**
  - **Observation,** TE
  - **Performance,** TE
  - **Portfolio,** TE
- **Observation Checklist**, AG

Student Self-Assessment

- **Self-Assessment – Investigate**, AG
- **Self-Assessment – Learn About**, AG
- **Experiment/Project Summary Sheet**, AG

Performance Assessment

- **Chapter Review,** PE
- **Chapter Performance Task**, AG
- **Experiment/Project Evaluation Checklist**, AG

Portfolio Assessment

- **Science Experiences Record**, AG
- **Guide to My Science Portfolio**, AG
- **Portfolio Evaluation Checklist,** AG

Formal Assessment

Chapter Review and Test Preparation • Chapter Test • Unit Test

Research into the learning process has shown the positive effects of periodic review. To help you reinforce and assess mastery of chapter objectives, *Harcourt Science* includes both reviews and tests. You will find the Chapter Review and Test Preparation in the Pupil Edition and the Chapter Test and Unit Test in the **Assessment Guide**. Answers to these assessments, including sample responses to open-ended items, are given in the Answer Key.

Performance Assessment

Chapter Review • Chapter Performance Task • Experiment/Project Evaluation Checklist

Science literacy involves more than just what students know. It is also concerned with how they think and how they do things. Performance assessment provides evidence of students' ability to use science process skills and critical thinking skills to complete an authentic problem-solving task. At the chapter level, you will find a performance task included in Chapter Review and Test Preparation. Another is located in the **Assessment Guide,** following each Chapter Test. Each includes teacher's directions and a scoring rubric. Also in the **Assessment Guide** is the Experiment/Project Evaluation Checklist (p. AGxviii), a measure for evaluating students' science projects and unit experiments.

Ongoing Assessment

✓ Questions • Lesson Review • Informal Assessment Strategies • Observation Checklist

There are many opportunities to observe and evaluate student growth during regular classroom instruction in science. *Harcourt Science* supports ongoing informal assessment in three ways. In the Pupil Edition, there are boldface ✓ Questions at the end of sections to help you assess students' immediate recall of information. Then, at the end of each lesson, you will find a Lesson Review to help you find out how well students grasped the concepts taught. The Lesson Review also includes a "test prep" question. In the Teacher's Edition, you will find Informal Assessment Strategies to support classroom observation, performance assessment, and portfolio assessment. In the **Assessment Guide,** you will find yet another assessment tool, the Observation Checklist (pp. AGxiv), on which you can record classroom observations. Ultimately, it is your experienced eye that will provide the most comprehensive assessment of student progress.

Student Self-Assessment

Self-Assessment–Investigate • Self-Assessment–Learn About • Project Summary Sheet

Student self-assessment encourages students to reflect on and monitor changes in their science knowledge, skills, and attitudes. The **Assessment Guide** includes two self-assessment checklists for this purpose, one for use after students complete Investigate (p. AGxvi) and one for use after instruction in Learn About (p. AGxvii). Following the checklists, you will find the Experiment/Project Summary Sheet (p. AGxix), a form on which students can describe and evaluate their efforts on a science project or unit experiment.

Portfolio Assessment

Science Experiences Record • Guide to My Science Portfolio • Portfolio Evaluation Checklist

In *Harcourt Science,* students may create their own portfolios. The portfolio holds self-selected work samples that the student feels are representative of gains in his or her understanding of science concepts and use of science processes. The portfolio may also contain a few required or teacher-selected papers. Support materials are included in the **Assessment Guide** (pp. AGxx–AGxxiv) to assist you and your students in developing portfolios and in using them to evaluate growth in science.

Using Technology

Harcourt Science **includes an array of technology products that**

- bring interactive experiences to the classroom.
- add depth to chapter concepts.
- meet individual needs.

Technology Links—in the Pupil Edition at the end of each lesson for Grades 3–6 and throughout the Teacher's Edition for Grades 1–2—help you integrate technology at the point of its most effective use.

Computer Software

Harcourt Science Instant Readers CD-ROM, Grades K–2

These CD-ROMs are designed to accompany the Harcourt Science Instant Readers. They provide a variety of interactive on-screen activities and reinforce science vocabulary and concepts. Point-of-use references to the Harcourt Science Instant Readers and the CD-ROMs appear in the Teacher's Editions.

Harcourt Science Explorations CD-ROM, Grades 3–6

These engaging CD-ROMs provide interactive, child-centered science explorations. Activities enhance and expand key chapter concepts through simulations and investigations. The activities are designed so that students can complete them with minimal teacher intervention. Multiple outcomes will give students reasons to explore the activities again and again.

Graph Links, Grades 1–6

Graph Links is a tool-based program that enables students to organize, communicate, and interpret data they have collected during their investigations. This software program enables students to make graphs more easily and accurately than they could by hand. Students can compare the different ways data can be represented—by symbols, bars, points on a line, or sections of a circle. They can also customize each graph by changing the font, style, and size of the text or by varying colors or grid lines. Suggestions for using Graph Links appear in the Math Links in the Pupil Edition.

Videos

Harcourt Science Newsroom Videos, Grades 3–6

Harcourt has joined forces with the leaders in news broadcasting—CNN and Turner Learning—to bring timely science news events to your classroom. For each chapter in Grades 3–6, there is a **Harcourt Science Newsroom Video** segment that helps students see the relevance of science to their lives. A CNN news reporter introduces each segment and sets the stage for viewing. The videos also add interesting depth to chapter concepts.

Harcourt Science Activity Videos, Grades 1–6

The Activity Videos show students doing the Investigates for each lesson and can be used to help you prepare for upcoming chapters. The videos can also be used to preview and model the investigation process for students, to review and discuss hands-on experiences, and to help students who may have been absent when hands-on activities were conducted. Students with special needs may also benefit from viewing the videos.

Internet

Smithsonian Institution

Smithsonian Institution®

With *Harcourt Science,* it's easy to make the Smithsonian Institution a part of the science classroom. Through a special agreement, you can visit this Internet site to see correlated links to the Web sites of Smithsonian museums, galleries, and the National Zoological Park. Especially selected by Harcourt to complement textbook lessons, the Web sites include intriguing virtual tours, such as Marine Ecosystems from the National Museum of Natural History, extraordinary on-line exhibits like How Things Fly, from the National Air and Space Museum, and a world of exceptional images and information.

Providing Web access to such resources is a valuable outreach service from the Smithsonian. And helping teachers find and use these resources at precisely the right time—when they are directly relevant to school learning—is a service to classroom teachers from Harcourt. That's why the Pupil Edition at Grades 3–6 includes Smithsonian references in the Technology Links that appear at the end of each lesson. Point-of-use suggestions for teacher background information and activity ideas appear in the Teacher's Editions for Grades 1 and 2.

www.si.edu/harcourt/science

SciLinks

These special Internet links are provided by the National Science Teachers Association (NSTA) in partnership with Harcourt. The SciLinks Web page connects students to Web sites that were specially selected to enhance and enrich Harcourt Science chapter content. With SciLinks, your students will have the best Internet science resources, all selected by NSTA's network of teacher-webwatchers.

www.scilinks.org/harcourt

The Learning Site

The Learning Site, a product of Harcourt, is a user-friendly Web site that provides interactive learning for students, professional development and webliography resources for teachers, and school-home resources. Visit The Learning Site for a world of science resources, including science Expeditions, interactive learning games and activities tied to chapter content, and a multimedia Science Glossary. Point-of-use references to The Learning Site activities appear in the Pupil Edition for Grades 3–6 and the Teacher's Editions for Grades 1–2. But feel free to visit The Learning Site at any time!

www.harcourtschool.com

Curriculum Integration

Harcourt Science is designed to allow you to integrate science into your day through the use of links to all curriculum areas. These ideas promote a broader development of science concepts and skills while showing students examples of how science connects to all parts of their lives. Look for *How to Integrate Your Day* at the beginning of each unit.

Curriculum Integration

Health and Physical Education

Investigating healthful practices encourages students to apply these ideas to their daily lives.

Writing

Writing Links appear in the Pupil Edition at the end of every lesson and chapter. These prompts invite students to apply their science learning in writing as they use the four basic purposes for writing and various types of organizers.

Math

Practice in measurement, data, and computational skills reinforces for students the many connections between math and science. Math Links appear in the Pupil Edition and Teacher's Edition for every lesson and chapter.

Language Arts

Language Arts Links provide varied opportunities for students to communicate their knowledge of science concepts.

Fine Arts

Through music, dance, and drawing, students can express their understandings of the natural world. These Links appear throughout the Pupil and Teacher's Editions.

Literature

Exposure to literature provides ways for students to apply their knowledge of science concepts and to build vocabulary. A list of suggested science trade books is provided for every chapter. Be sure to also consult the Bibliography of Science Trade Books at the back of this Teacher's Edition.

Social Studies

Experience in exploring the ways science is interwoven with history, geography, and culture helps students connect science with the ancient and modern worlds. Suggestions for making these connections are provided throughout the Pupil and Teacher's Editions.

Family Support

A strong partnership between home and school helps students succeed in science. *Harcourt Science* encourages that partnership in a variety of ways.

SCHOOL-HOME CONNECTION

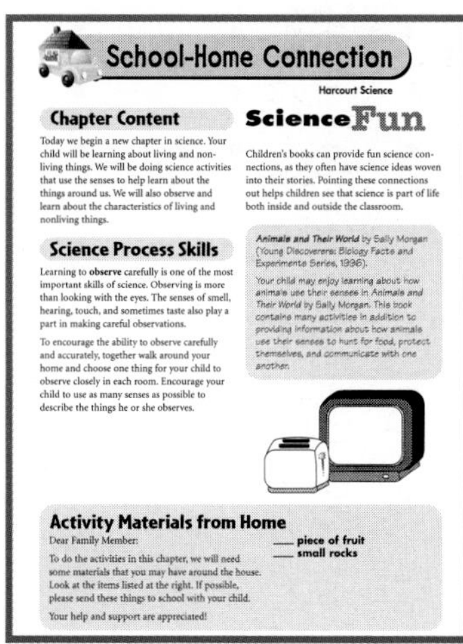

An informative family letter—School-Home Connection—is provided for each chapter. It describes the chapter content, gives tips to parents about science process skills, and includes Science Fun. It also provides a list of materials family members can send to school for the investigations in the student book.

ACTIVITIES FOR HOME AND SCHOOL

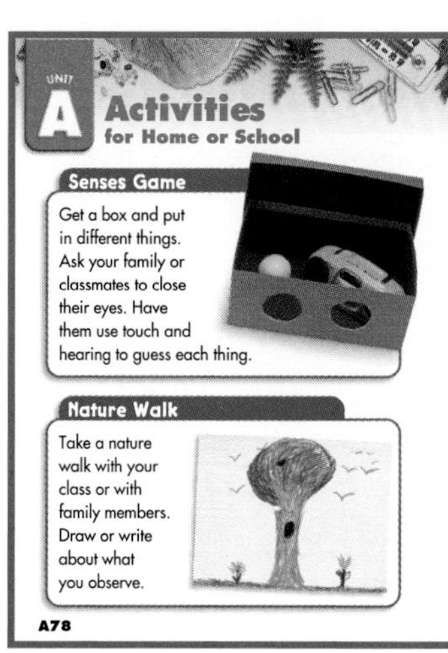

These activities appear in the student book and can be assigned for students to complete at home. Reproducible copies of the activities are provided in the Teaching Resources book.

TAKE-HOME BOOKS

These delightful books are designed to provide additional chapter content and activities. Students can take them home to read with family members. The Take-Home Books can also involve students and their family members in hands-on activities, vocabulary reinforcement, and science fun.

THE LEARNING SITE

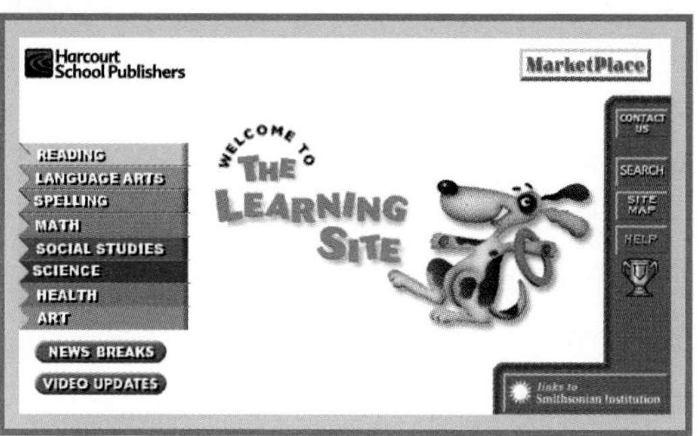

Harcourt's user-friendly web site provides a world of resources for students, teachers, and parents. A clearly organized menu leads family members to interactive learning games, Science News Breaks, and on-line exhibits and virtual tours from the Smithsonian Institution. At the Multimedia Science Glossary, families can see illustrations of *Harcourt Science* vocabulary terms and hear them pronounced. There is also a special page with tips and ideas for parents.

www.harcourtschool.com

Program Components

Harcourt Science Components	1	2	3	4	5	6
Pupil Editions	•	•	•	•	•	•
Teacher's Editions	•	•	•	•	•	•
Unit Big Books	•	•				
Workbook	•	•	•	•	•	•
Workbook, Teacher's Editions	•	•	•	•	•	•
Assessment Guides	•	•	•	•	•	•
Science Instant Readers	•	•				
Science Take-Home Books	•	•	•	•	•	•
Teaching Transparencies	•	•	•	•	•	•
Science Handbook Transparencies	•	•				
Inside Story Transparencies			•	•	•	•
Health Activity Book	•	•	•	•	•	•
Picture Cards	•	•	•			
Teaching Resources	•	•	•	•	•	•
Text on Tape Audiotapes	•	•	•	•	•	•
Science Songs CD	•	•				
Materials Kits	•	•	•	•	•	•

Technology	1	2	3	4	5	6
Activity Videos	•	•	•	•	•	•
Harcourt Science Newsroom Videos—CNN			•	•	•	•
Science Instant Readers CD-ROMs	•	•				
Explorations CD-ROMs			•	•	•	•
Electronic Test System			•	•	•	•
Planning Resources CD-ROM	•	•	•	•	•	•
Smithsonian Links	•	•	•	•	•	•
NSTA SciLinks	•	•	•	•	•	•
The Learning Site Activities and Resources	•	•	•	•	•	•

For Kindergarten

- Big Book
- Teacher's Edition
- Activity Cards
- Picture Cards
- Activity Book
- Teaching Resources
- Science Songs CD
- Planning Resources CD-ROM
- Science Instant Readers
- Science Instant Readers CD-ROMs
- The Learning Site Activities and Resources
- Materials Kit

Materials List

Quantities are indicated for a class of 30 students working individually or in groups of 5, depending on the nature of the activity. Where shared equipment is suggested, a smaller number of items is specified. Quantities are also listed for those materials included in the Materials Kit.

Nonconsumable Materials	Class Quantity Needed	Kit Quantity	Activity Page
aquarium	6	6	E12
ball, plastic	6	6	F8, F12
blocks, wood (1 in. × 1 in. × 1 in.)	6	6	F4
blocks, wood (2 in. × 4 in. × 6 in)	6	6	F12
board, wooden	6		F12, F18
books	36		F1, F22
bottle, 1-L plastic	6		E20, E40
bowl, plastic	12	12	A10, B1, C32, E8
cans, small	6		E46
cap, bottle	6	6	A42
carpet	6 pieces		F42
clock	1*		C32, D38, E34
container, plastic (3L)	6	6	D46
container, plastic (small)	6	6	A42
cups, foam	12	12	D1
cup, measuring	6	6	C8, D1, D16, E1, E8, E40
cups, plastic (clear)	12	1 pkg of 25	A32
cups, plastic (green)	6	1 pkg of 25	A32
cups, plastic (12 oz)	18	1 pkg of 50	C32, D34, E1, E8, E16
egg, plastic	6	6	F8
film canister	12	12	B34
flashlight with batteries	6	6	D30, E42, E46
globe	1*		D30
granite	6 pieces	6 pieces	C4
hand lens	6	6	A10, A28, C4, D26
jar with lid	6	6	D16
jar, plastic	6	6	E8
limestone	6 pieces	6 pieces	C4

*Student groups should share this equipment.

Nonconsumable Materials	Class Quantity Needed	Kit Quantity	Activity Page
lunchbox, metal	6		F42
magnet, bar	6	6	F32, F38, F42, F46
marbles, glass	18	1 pkg of 20	C32, E4
meterstick	6		F1, F18
paint brushes	6 sets		E4, E24
paper clips	42	1 box of 100	B30, F38, F42, F46
paper punch	1*		C1, E34
picture cards	6 sets of each	See TR	A58, A70, B14, B38, C12
quartzite	6 pieces	6 pieces	C4
rocks	12	12	A10, A42, E4, E16
rubber bands	24	1 bag	B34, C32, E34, E46
ruler	6		E34
sandstone	6 pieces	6 pieces	C4
schist	6 pieces	6 pieces	C4
scissors	6		A54
shells	6	30	C8
spring toy	2*	2	F8
sock, wool	6	6	B1
spoons, measuring	6	6	C1, E1
spoons, plastic	12	1 pkg of 24	C32
spray bottle	6	6	D34
stapler	1*		D38
thermometer	6	6	D1, D8, D38, E34
timer or watch	6		B4, E1
truck, toy	6	6	F1, F8, F18, F22

Consumable Materials	Class Quantity Needed	Kit Quantity	Activity Page
adding machine tape	6 rolls	6 rolls	F1
aluminum foil	1 roll	1 roll	E34
animals, small soil	12	coupon for 30	A42
apples	6		D42
bag, plastic	18	1 box of 50	C12
bag, plastic produce	30		C28
bag, plastic self-sealing	18	1 pkg of 80	D42, D46
balloons	6	1 pkg of 35	E20, E46
balls, Styrofoam	18	36	A54, B10
beans, dried	6 pkg	6 pkg	E46
bran meal	1 pkg	1 pkg	A10
butterfly garden kit (box, 3-5 caterpillars)	1 kit	1 kit	A64
cardboard	6 pieces		F42
carrot	6		A22
chenille sticks	56	1 pkg of 70	A54, E4
clay, cream modeling	2 boxes	2 boxes	E12
clay, red modeling	1 box	1 box	E4
cloth, cotton	6 small pieces	1 large piece	E4
cloth, wool	6 small pieces	1 large piece	D46
cotton balls	100	1 pkg of 300	A1, B10, D46
craft sticks	6	1 pkg of 30	E16, F4
crayon, dark	30		B26
crayon, red	6		D8
cups, paper	24	1 pkg of 25	C32
foam peanuts	30	1 pkg of 200	D46
fruit, small pieces	6 sets		A4
glitter	6 bottles		E24
gloves, plastic	30 pair	1 pkg of 50 pair	A4, A42
glue	1 bottle		B10, C8, E24
ice cubes	55		B1, D16
index cards	24	1 pkg of 100	E24

Consumable Materials	Class Quantity Needed	Kit Quantity	Activity Page
markers	6 sets		D4, D34
mealworms	6	coupon for 100	A10
newspaper	3		B1, C36, D46
objects, everyday magnetic	18		F32
objects, everyday nonmagnetic	18		F32
paints	6 sets		E4, E24
pan, aluminum foil	6	6	C8
paper	500 sheets		A22, A48, A58, A64, B4, B26, C4, C22, D4, D8, D24, D38, D42, E4, E8, E12, E16, E24, F4, F8, F18, F32, F38, F42
paper towels	1 roll		A1, B30, D34
paper triangle	6		D12
paper, colored	24 sheets		D30, D38
paper, wax	1 roll	1 roll	A54, B30
paper, yellow construction	12 sheets		E4, E40
pencil	6		A22, A48, A58, A64, B4, B26, C4, C22, C36, D8, D24, D38, D42, E4, E8, E12, E16, E24, E46, F1, F4, F8, F18, F32, F38
petroleum jelly	1 jar	1 jar	C1, C8
plant with flower	6		A22
plastic wrap	1 roll	1 roll	B34, C32
plates, small foam	24	25	C1
salt	1 box	1 box	C32, E1, E16
sand	2 bags	2 bags	C8, C32, E16
sand paper	6 small sheets	2 large sheets	B10

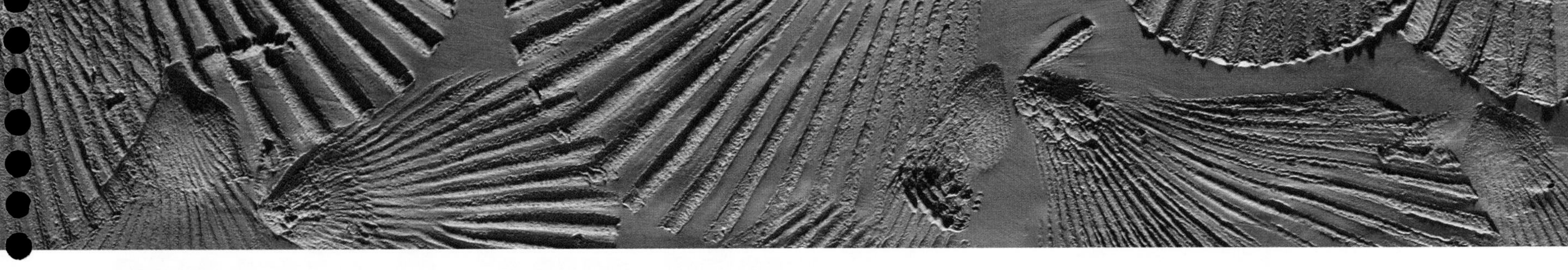

Consumable Materials	Class Quantity Needed	Kit Quantity	Activity Page
seeds	1 pkg	1 pkg	B34
seeds, bean	1 pkg	1 pkg	A28, D34
seeds, pea	1 pkg	1 pkg	A32
seeds, radish	1 pkg	1 pkg	A1
soda, baking	1 can	1 can	E16
soil, loam	1 bag	1 bag	A42
soil, potting	1 bag	1 bag	A32
straws, plastic	12	1 pkg of 50	D12, F4
string	1 roll	1 roll	B4, C1, D42, F4
sugar	1 bag	1 bag	E1
swab, cotton	30	1 box of 72	C32
tape, masking	1 roll		F12, F22
tape, transparent	1 roll		C36, D12, D30, D34
toothpicks	56	1 pkg of 250	A54, D12
tube, cardboard	6		E34
twig	6		A42
Velcro	6 pieces	1 strip	B10

Additional kit options are available. Contact your sales representative for details.

Conducting Live-Animal Activities

Several Investigates and Activities within *Harcourt Science* require the use of live animals, such as mealworms and butterflies. You may wish to keep these animals in the classroom after the conclusion of the activities for students' continued observations. Instructions for the care of these animals are included in the directions that accompany them when they arrive from the scientific supply house.

If animals are no longer needed or wanted in the classroom, they must be dealt with in an environmentally responsible manner. Any animals that have been collected locally may be released. It is, however, best to consider the season and its effects on the animal before release. Most animals ordered from supply houses are not native species and ***must not*** be released into the environment. These animals may not be able to survive in your area and would needlessly suffer before they died. Other non-native species can survive and reproduce. Their existence in a new environment may threaten native species or cause environmental damage. Oftentimes, these animals can be given to a pet store as a source of food for store animals. Otherwise, the animals must be euthanized. Please consult the instructions that accompanied these animals for advice on how to deal with these issues.

UNIT A LIFE SCIENCE

Plants and Animals All Around

UNIT B LIFE SCIENCE

Living Together

5

UNIT C EARTH SCIENCE

About Our Earth

★6

EARTH SCIENCE

Weather, the Sky, and Seasons

UNIT E

PHYSICAL SCIENCE

Matter and Energy

★8

UNIT F PHYSICAL SCIENCE

Forces

How Scientists Work

INVESTIGATING

Harcourt Science provides children with many opportunities for scientific inquiry, including unit experiments, lesson investigations, activities for home or school, and science fair projects. Help your children plan their investigations by discussing the steps of the scientific method, shown on the *Pupil Edition* pages.

The following materials are needed if children choose to do the experiment on pages *10–*11:

- **2 toy cars**
- **1 weight**
- **meter stick**
- **board**
- **several books**

Scientific Method Children should use these steps or steps like these as they plan and conduct their experiments.

- ▶ **Observe, and ask a question.** Invite children to think of questions they might ask about how the weight of a car affects how far it rolls. For example: "Which car will roll farther?"
- ▶ **Form a hypothesis.** Ask children to form a hypothesis to answer their question. The hypothesis should be phrased as a statement. For example: "The blue car will roll farther because it is heavier."

How Scientists Work

Investigating

This plan will help you work like a scientist.

STEP 1 — Observe and ask a question.

Which car will roll farther?

STEP 2 — Form a hypothesis.

The blue car will roll farther because it is heavier.

STEP 3 — Plan a fair test.

I'll start each car at the same spot.

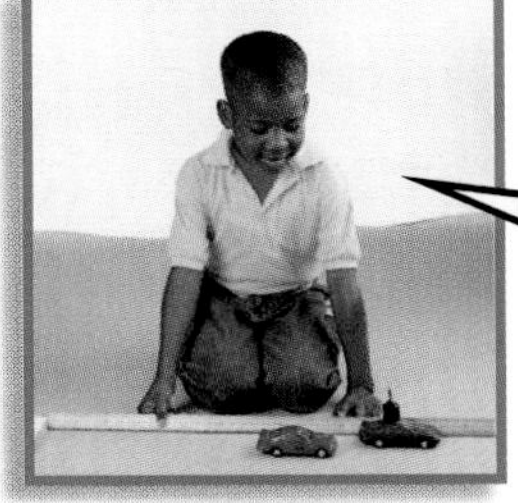

STEP 4 — Do the test.

I'll measure how far each car rolls.

STEP 5 — Draw conclusions. Communicate results.

My hypothesis was correct. The red car did not roll as far as the blue car.

Investigate More

I wonder if the height of the ramp will make a difference.

★11

PARTICIPATING IN A SCHOOL SCIENCE FAIR

These reproducible pages, which appear in the **Teaching Resources** book, provide helpful information for children and their families.

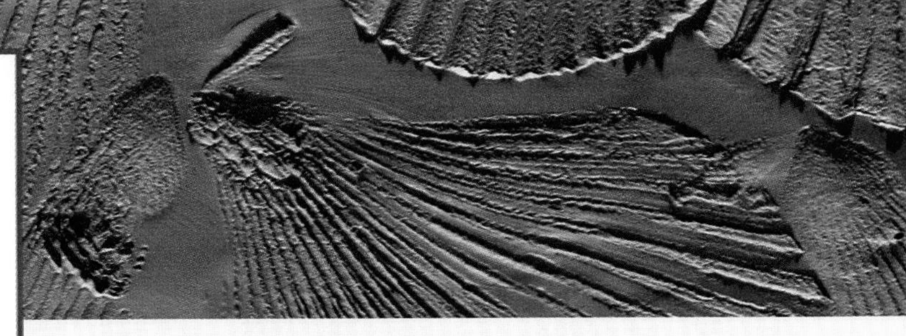

How Scientists Work

INVESTIGATING

- **Plan a fair test.** Ask children to plan a way to test their hypothesis. They should write down the steps they intend to use. Lead them to an understanding of a fair test—that is, a test that takes into account one or more variables and has a way to control the variables. In the case of the sample investigation, variables are controlled by starting each car at the same spot.
- **Do the test.** Let children test their hypothesis according to their plan. They should follow the steps they wrote, record what they observe, and organize their data so that they can study it before drawing a conclusion.
- **Draw conclusions and communicate results.** Tell children that when they draw a conclusion, they compare the results of their test with their hypothesis. They decide whether their hypothesis was correct or incorrect. They write their conclusion and describe the test and the results.

Suggest to children that what they learn during their experiment might help them think of other questions to ask, or it might help them think of ways to change their experiment. Encourage them to continue the experiment in any way they choose.

Experimenting Further Here are some questions your children might enjoy investigating independently.

- **What color of construction paper will fade most in the sun?**
- **Do people feel things equally well with each of their fingers?**
- **Are in-line skates faster than regular roller skates?**
- **Does the color of a jacket affect how warm it will keep you?**
- **Would sow bugs rather eat potatoes, leaves, meat, or paper?**
- **Which brand of paper towel is strongest in water?**
- **Can I blow square bubbles if my bubble wand is square?**

How Scientists Work

USING SCIENCE SKILLS

Science process skills are important inquiry tools and are essential for investigating the natural world. Opportunities for developing process skills are provided throughout *Harcourt Science.* You may wish to use pages *12–*17 at the beginning of the school year to introduce children to the processes. Children may also refer to these pages throughout the year as they conduct unit experiments and lesson investigations.

Each lesson investigation in *Harcourt Science* also develops the science processes by providing a Science Skill Tip on the *Pupil Edition* page. You can use the Science Skill Tip as a springboard for a lesson that focuses on that skill. A mini-lesson for teaching the process skill appears in the *Teacher's Edition* beneath the corresponding *Pupil Edition* page. An overhead transparency is provided for the mini-lesson, and an opportunity for practicing the process skill is provided in the *Workbook.*

Observe

- ▶ **How does the leaf look?** green, big, jagged edges
- ▶ **What can you see with a hand lens?** I can see details that I might not see with my eyes alone.
- ▶ **What is a tool a scientist uses to observe things that are too small to see with the eyes?** microscope

Compare

- ▶ **How are the two leaves the same?** both have lines (veins) and stems; both have jagged edges
- ▶ **How are the two leaves different?** color, size, shape

How Scientists Work

Using Science Skills

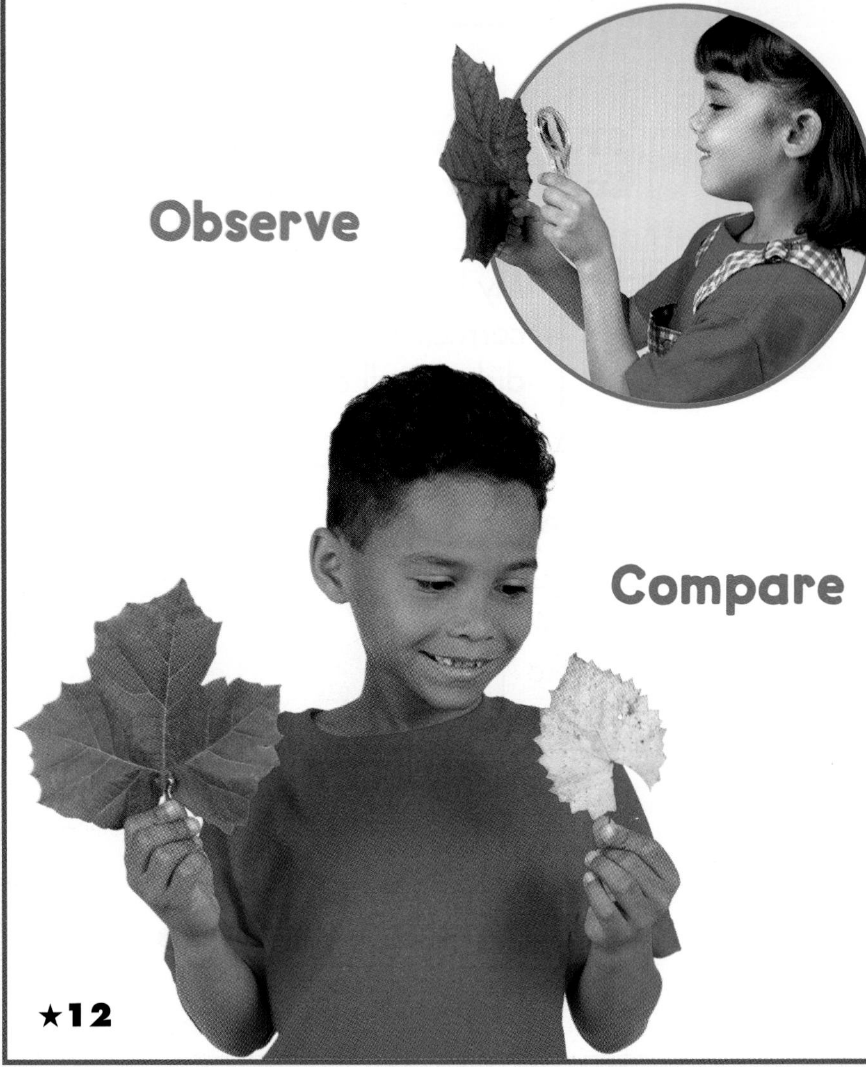

★12

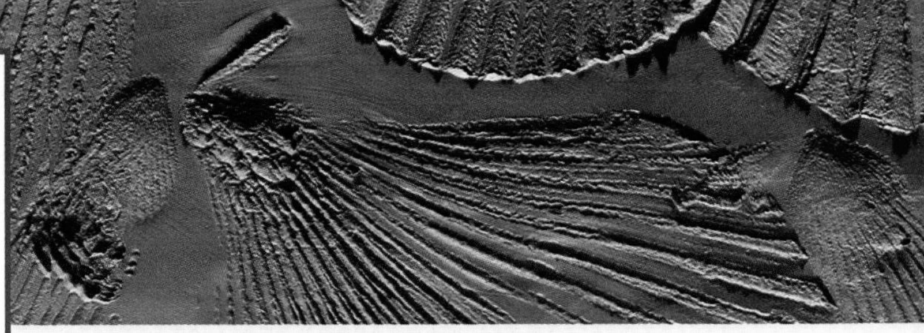

Sequence

Classify

★13

How Scientists Work

USING SCIENCE SKILLS

Sequence

- **What order should you put the plants in to show how they grow?** smallest to largest; shortest to tallest; 8 days, 22 days, 35 days
- **How do the number of days help you learn about plant growth?** as the number of days grows, so do the plants

Classify

- **How can you sort the apples into groups that are the same?** by color
- **What is another way to sort the apples?** by size; with or without a stem; by other variations in size, color, or shape

How Scientists Work

USING SCIENCE SKILLS

Infer

Tell children that when we use observations to explain how or why something happens, we are using the process of **inferring**.

- **What will happen to the ball when the girl drops it in the tube?** It will slide down the path and come out the bottom.
- **How will the ball move down through the tubes?** It will follow the path the tubes make and come out the bottom. **How do you know?** It reminds me of what happens when I go down a slide.

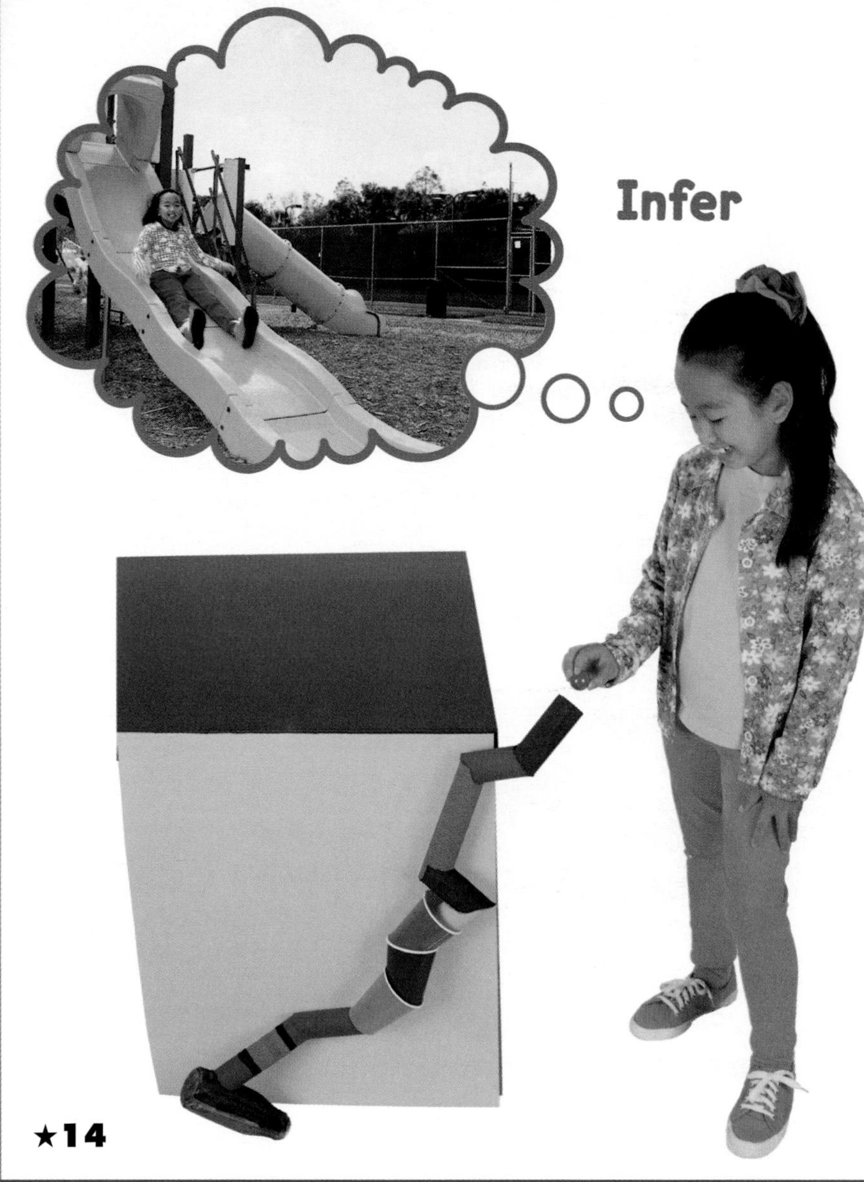

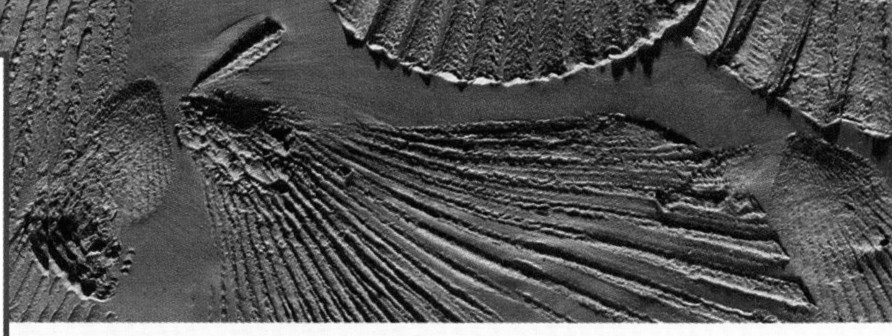

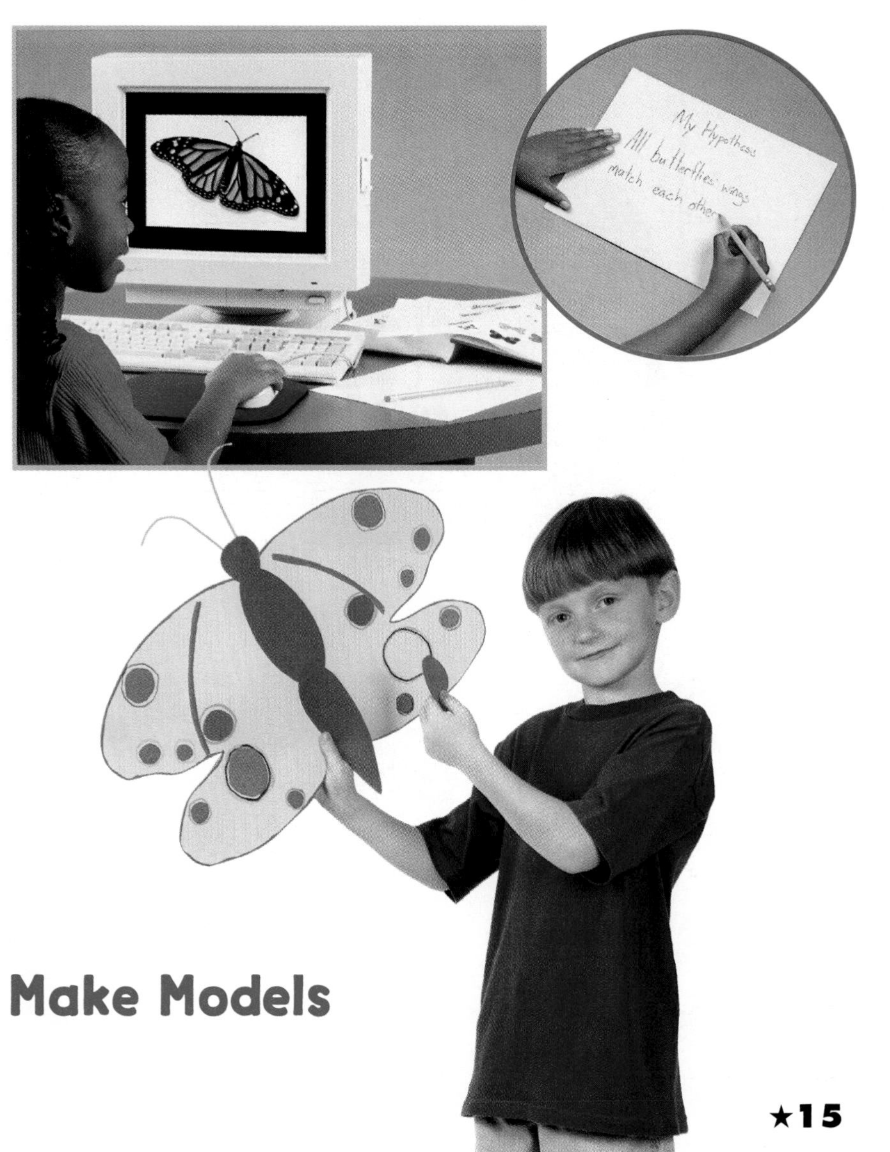

How Scientists Work

USING SCIENCE SKILLS

Form a Hypothesis

Introduce children to the word *hypothesis*. Explain that **forming a hypothesis** is important to the work of a scientist. A hypothesis is a statement that tells how or why you think something happens. A hypothesis has to be tested with an experiment before you can be sure the hypothesis is true.

- ▶ **Based on what you know about butterflies, form a hypothesis about butterflies' wings.** All butterflies' wings match each other.
- ▶ **How could you test your hypothesis to see if it is true?** I could observe and compare the wings of several butterflies.
- ▶ **Look at where butterflies land. Form a hypothesis about how butterfly wings help butterflies.** different colors and shapes help butterflies hide in leaves and flowers

Make Models

- ▶ **How could you make a model to show what you know about butterfly wings?** I could read about butterfly wings and make a model out of paper to show what I know.
- ▶ **How does making a model help you understand science ideas?** It helps me explain things to others I have learned. When I explain things, it helps the ideas become clearer to me.

How Scientists Work

USING SCIENCE SKILLS

Measure

▶ **What is the girl using to measure the plant?** her hands

▶ **Will her measurement be the same as other students'?** not if their hands are different sizes

▶ **What tool can you use to measure a plant?** ruler; meterstick

▶ **What are other measuring tools you might use in a science investigation?** balance, weight scale, measuring tape, measuring cup, thermometer

Predict

Explain to children that in order to **make a prediction** in science, we think about patterns or things we may have observed before. Direct children's attention to the picture of the plant that the boy has drawn.

▶ **What has the boy predicted will happen to the plant?** the blooms on the plant will open into two flowers with red petals and a yellow center

▶ **Why do you think the boy has predicted this?** He may have seen these flowers before; he has seen how flowers bloom.

▶ **What do *you* predict will happen to the plant?** Accept all reasonble responses.

Measure

Predict

★16

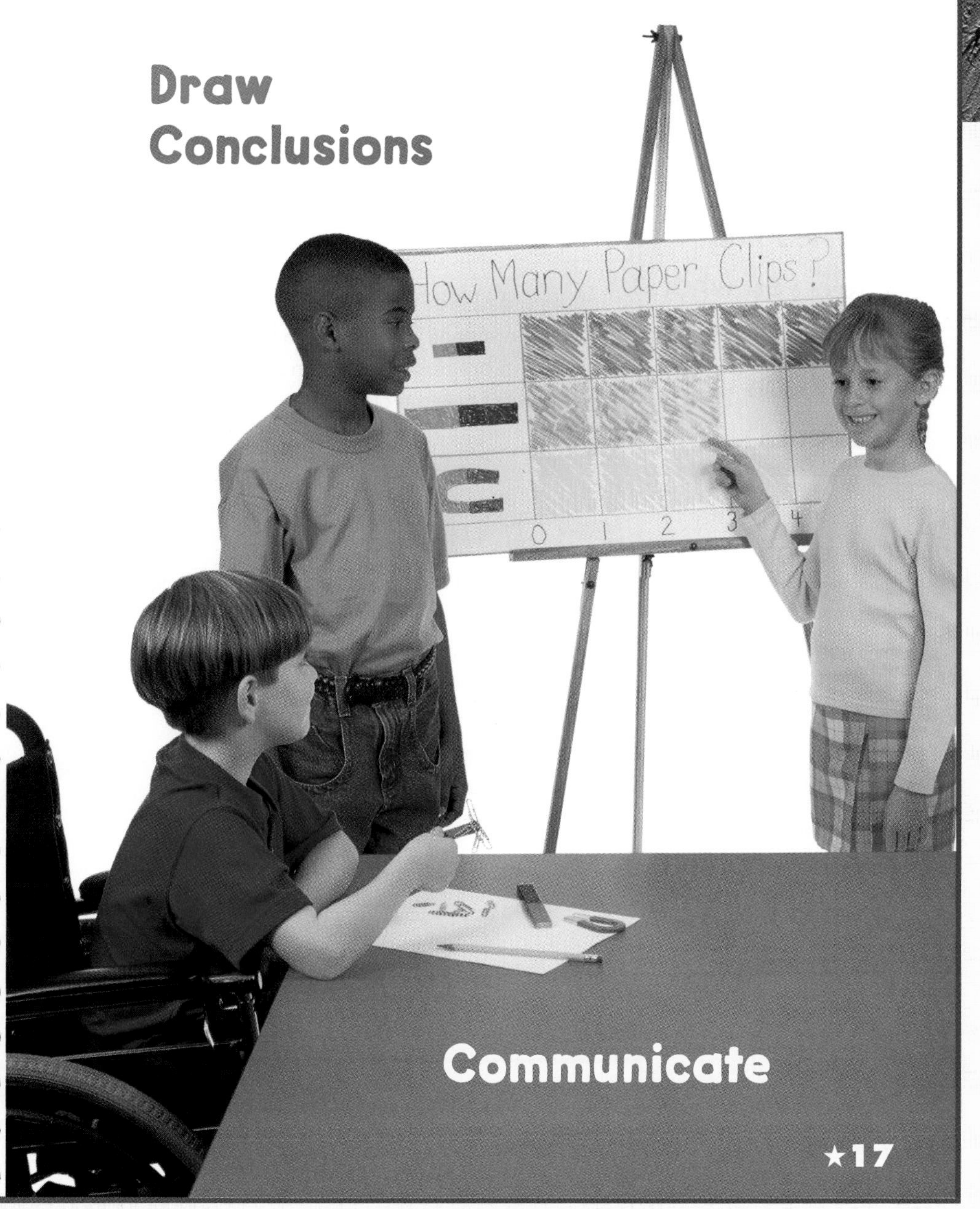

How Scientists Work

USING SCIENCE SKILLS

Draw Conclusions

Explain that a **conclusion** is what we learn from an investigation.

▶ **Which magnet attracted the most paper clips?** the small bar magnet

▶ **Which magnet attracted the least paper clips?** the large bar magnet

▶ **What conclusion can you draw about the three magnets?** The small bar magnet is the strongest because it picked up the most paper clips. The large bar magnet is the weakest.

Communicate

▶ **What is another way the children could have shown the results of their investigation?** They could have used tally marks instead of a bar graph; They could have written a number next to each magnet.

▶ **Why is a bar graph a good way to show others what happened in an investigation?** It is easy to see what happened.

How Scientists Work

READING

Discuss with children how scientists use reading in their work.

- **Why is having good reading skills important to a scientist?** Scientists need to read to find out about things they are investigating.
- **What kinds of work-related materials do you think scientists read?** Possible responses: encyclopedias, scientific journals and magazines, newspapers, reports on the Internet, reports from other scientists, letters from other scientists

Use pages *18-*20 to discuss with children reading strategies they can use.

- **Why is it important to preview titles and headings in a lesson?** They help me know what I will be reading about.
- **How does a caption help you?** It helps me understand what I see in a picture.
- **What are ways you can preview the vocabulary terms?** I can read the definition on the page when I see the yellow highlight. I can look up the vocabulary terms in the Glossary to find out their meanings. Glossary pictures help me understand what the terms mean.

How Scientists Work

Reading

A heading tells you what a section of a lesson is about.

A caption helps you understand what is in a picture.

A highlighted word helps you learn science vocabulary.

Ways Animals Begin Life

Rabbits are small when they are born. Their eyes are closed. They can not walk or hop until they are older.

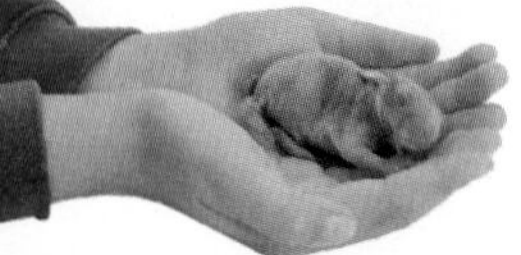

just born

8 days old

■ **How do the chick and the rabbit change in different ways?**

Chicks **hatch**, or break out of eggs. Their eyes are open. Soon they can walk and peck for food.

just hatched

8 days old

A60

★18

A picture helps you see what a lesson is about.
8 weeks old
adult
8 weeks old
adult
A label tells you what is in a picture.
A61

★19

How Scientists Work

READING

- **How do pictures help you?** They give examples of the science ideas and help make the text interesting.
- **Why is a label important?** A label tells you what a picture is showing.

Harcourt Science provides many opportunities for children to develop science vocabulary. The following is a list of additional vocabulary features in the program.

- **Vocabulary Preview** on the first page of each chapter in the *Pupil Edition*
- **Develop Science Vocabulary** throughout the *Teacher's Edition*, such as on page A12
- **Vocabulary Strategies and Activities** in the *Teaching Resources* book
- **Vocabulary Cards** in the *Teaching Resources* book
- **Vocabulary Review** for each chapter, in the *Workbook*

How Scientists Work

READING

- **How do Think About It questions help you?**
  Answering these questions helps me think about the main ideas of a lesson and helps me prepare for reviews and tests.

Harcourt Science provides many opportunities for children to become strategic readers and to practice and apply reading skills. The following features in *Harcourt Science* help children become better science readers.

- Consistent support for reading via text features, such as highlighted vocabulary words, Think About It lesson review questions, and Chapter Reviews
- **Graphic Organizer for Chapter Concepts** for each chapter, in the *Workbook*, and on an overhead transparency
- **Reading Mini-Lessons**, one for each chapter, in the *Teacher's Edition*, with an accompanying overhead transparency
- **Reading Skills Practice** for each chapter, in the *Workbook*
- **Reading Organizers**, including K-W-L and prediction charts, in the *Teaching Resources* book

How Scientists Work

Some animals stay close to their young to keep them warm. Others keep their young warm in pouches.

Think About It
These questions help you make sure you understand the important ideas of a lesson.

Think About It

1. What are two ways that animals begin life?
2. How do all young animals change as they grow?

A63

★20

Writing

Links
Movement/Drama Link
Move Like a Frog
These children think about a time in a frog's life. Then they move to show what that time is like.
Write
Find an open space on the floor. Show what a frog does as an egg, a tadpole, or an adult frog. Then write about how frogs change.
A74
Write Scientists write about what they learn. When you work like a scientist, you will do different kinds of writing. You will describe what you are learning and doing.

★21

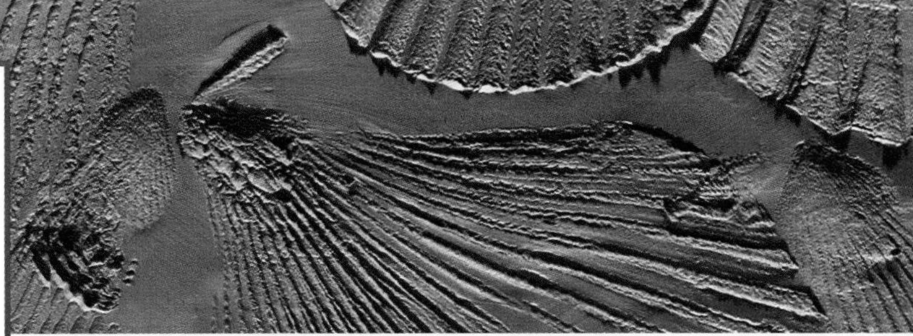

How Scientists Work

WRITING

Discuss with children how scientists use writing in their work.

- ▶ **Why is having good writing skills important to a scientist?** Scientists need to be able to tell others about the results of their work.

Use page *21 to discuss with children writing strategies they can use.

- ▶ **How can you use good writing skills to work like a scientist?** I can write sentences, stories, poems, and story problems to describe what I am learning and doing.

Harcourt Science provides many opportunities for children to develop and apply writing skills. The following is a list of features in the program that address writing skills.

- ▶ **Writing Link** for each chapter, in the *Pupil Edition*
- ▶ **Writing Practice** for each chapter, in the *Workbook*
- ▶ **Writing Models** in the *Teaching Resources* book

How Scientists Work

USING NUMBERS

Use page *22 to discuss with children how scientists use measuring in their work.

- **What kinds of measuring tools do scientists use in their work?** Possible responses: thermometers, clocks, metersticks, rulers, balances, measuring cups, and clocks
- **Why is it important to measure accurately while gathering data?** If measurements are not accurate, you cannot draw accurate conclusions based on your data.

Remind children to look on pages R2–R6 for more information about how to use measuring tools. You may also want to point out to them the Measurements chart on page R8.

How Scientists Work

Using Numbers

Scientists use numbers when they collect and show data.

Measuring

Scientists measure as they gather data. They use many different kinds of measuring tools.

For more information about measuring tools, see pages R2–R6.

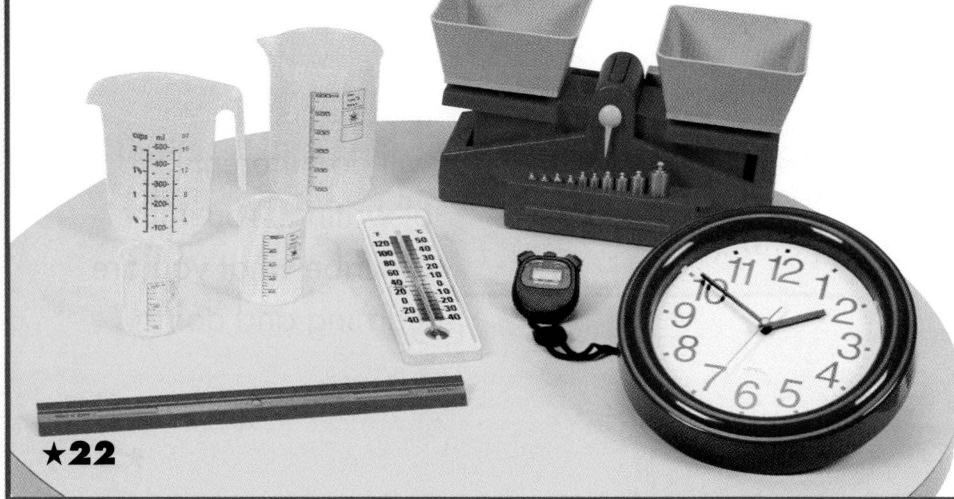

★22

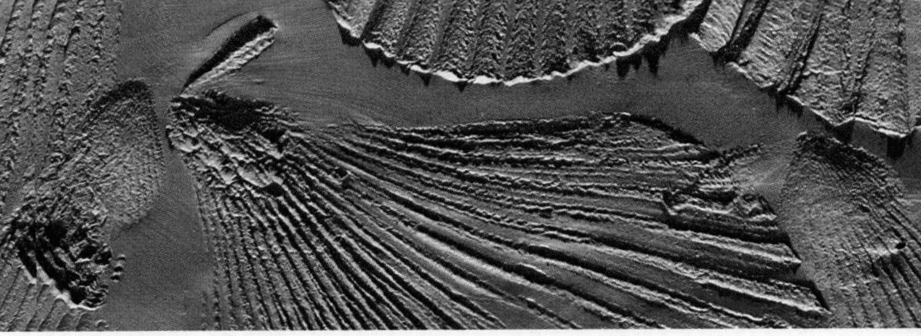

Interpreting Data

Scientists collect data. Tables, charts, and graphs are good ways to show data so the data can be interpreted by others.

You can read the data in tables, charts, and graphs.

How Much Rain?
Winter
Spring
Summer
Fall

inches 0 1 2 3 4 5 6 7 8 9 10 11

centimeters 5 10 15 20 25

You can also make your own tables, charts, and graphs.

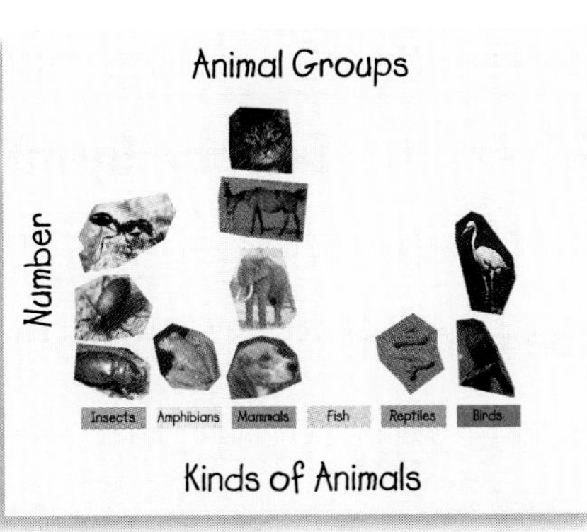

★23

How Scientists Work

USING NUMBERS

Use page *23 to discuss with children how to interpret data.

▶ **Why are tables, charts, and graphs important to the work of a scientist?** Discuss how they can be used to display data in ways that make the data easier to interpret. They can show patterns and relationships.

Harcourt Science provides many opportunities for children to develop and apply mathematics skills. Many of the unit experiments, lesson investigations, and other activities involve using numbers to do things such as take measurements and record data.

Numerous charts and graphs appear throughout the program for children to interpret. A Math Link is also provided at the end of each chapter.

How Scientists Work

SCIENCE SAFETY

When children first begin science explorations, it is important for them to develop a sense of what is and what is not appropriate in the laboratory. Beginning these lessons at this grade level, in which experiments are relatively safe, will prepare children for experiments in upper grades, when safety rules must be observed more closely and the potential dangers are greater. Emphasize to children that as they study science they will be working like scientists, and that it is important for scientists to work safely.

The most important rule for children at this level is to behave appropriately in the laboratory. Emphasize that children must not run, push others, throw objects, or engage in any other behavior that might cause accidents.

Help children become familiar with the safety signs and caution statements that appear where they are needed throughout *Harcourt Science.* Discuss each safety rule and ask children to predict what can happen if a rule is not followed.

A copy of the Science Safety page and a Safety Checklist are provided in the *Workbook.*

Science Safety

Think ahead.

Be neat and clean.

Be careful.

Do not eat or drink things.

Safety Symbols
CAUTION
Be careful!
CAUTION
Sharp!
CAUTION
Be careful!
CAUTION
Wear an apron.
CAUTION
Wear goggles.

★24

UNIT E

Unit Overview

Unit Theme Everything in the physical universe is made of matter. Heat and light energy can change matter.

CHAPTER 1

Matter can be observed, described, and classified. Matter exists as a solid, liquid, or gas and can change from one form to another. When matter changes form, no mass is gained or lost.

CHAPTER 2

Everything you hear is a sound. Sound is all around you. Some sounds are quiet, and some are loud. Some sounds are high, and others are low. Many of these sounds can be made by musical instruments.

Skills for Lifelong Learning

Science Process Skills

The Science Process Skills are important inquiry tools and are essential for investigating the natural world. Opportunities for developing process skills are provided throughout *Harcourt Science*. The pages shown in this chart indicate where the process skills receive special emphasis.

Science Process Skill	Skill Tip and Mini-Lesson	Skills Practice (Workbook)	Reinforcement
Observe			E1j, E22, E37, E38, E56
Compare			E6, E10, E14, E18, E22, E26, E37, E43, E48, E56
Classify/Order	E4	WB108	
Gather, Record, Display, or Interpret Data	E12	WB112	E1j, E31
Use Numbers	E8, E40	WB110, WB126	E53
Communicate			E1j
Plan and Conduct Simple Investigations	E24, E34	WB118, WB124	E1j
Measure			E1j
Predict			
Infer			E42
Draw Conclusions	E20	WB116	E1j, E54, E55
Use Time/Space Relationships			
Formulate or Use Models			
Form a Hypothesis	E16, E46	WB114, WB128	E1j

Reading, Writing, and Math Skills

Effective science instruction integrates science content and experiences with all areas of the elementary curriculum. *Harcourt Science* provides students with many opportunities to develop reading, writing, and math skills via meaningful activities and strategies built into every lesson in this unit.

Reading Skills Checklist

Strategies for developing the following reading skills are provided in this unit.

- ☑ **use context** E18
- ☑ **recall supporting facts and details** E9, E35, E42
- ☐ **arrange events in sequence**
- ☑ **draw conclusions** E10
- ☑ **identify the main idea** E5, E13, E17, E18, E21, E25, E35, E36, E41, E42, E43, E44, E47, E48
- ☑ **identify cause and effect** E13, E22, E26
- ☑ **predict outcomes** E10, E22, E41
- ☑ **summarize** E7, E11, E15, E19, E23, E27, E39, E45, E49
- ☑ **use graphic sources for information** E6, E10
- ☑ **relate pictures to text** E2, E6, E9, E21, E32, E35, E36, E38, E41, E42, E47
- ☐ **distinguish between fact and nonfact**
- ☑ **develop concepts of print** E5
- ☑ **build vocabulary** E5, E6, E9, E10, E13, E14, E17, E18, E21, E22, E25, E26, E35, E36, E41, E44, E47, E48

Writing Links

Prompts that provide opportunities for students to express their ideas in writing are provided in every chapter in this unit.

Mixing Objects to Make Art E28

Writing About Science E31, E53

Sounds from Around the World E50

Math Links

Opportunities to practice math skills, solve problems, and connect math and science are provided in every chapter.

Counting Solids E6

Measure and Compare E18

Estimate How Much Ships Can Carry E29

Math Music E48

Measure How Far a Whisper Travels E51

UNIT E

How to Integrate Your Day

Use these topics to help you integrate science into your daily planning.

Curriculum Integration

Fine Arts

Floaters and Sinkers Collage E14
Make a Rock Animal E26
Mixing Objects to Make Art E28
Water Bells E28
Paint Bubbling Volcanoes E29
It's All in the Voice E38
Make Panpipes E44
A Scale Song E50
The Art of Sound E51

Health

Three-Liquid Salad Dressing E10
Make Fruit Gelatin E29
The Sounds of Emergency Vehicles E38
Too Loud E42
Red Light, Green Light E51

Math

Counting Solids E6
Measure and Compare E18
Estimate How Much Ships Can Carry E29
Math Music E48
Measure How Far a Whisper Travels E51

Writing

Mixing Objects to Make Art E28
Writing About Science E31, E53
Sounds from Around the World E50

Language Arts

What Am I? E28
The Sounds of English E37
Communicating Through Claps E43
Musical How-To E50
Tab Book E55

Literature

Mushroom in the Rain E7
Very Last First Time: An Inuit Tale E7
Solids and Liquids E11
A Raindrop Hit My Nose E11
Sink or Float? E15
Sunken Treasure E15
Lemonade for Sale E19
Grandpa's Soup E19
The Grumpalump E23
Balloons: Building and Experimenting with Inflatable Toys E23
Heat Changes Things E27
Paper, Paper Everywhere E27
Hearing Sounds E39
Thump, Thump, Rat-a-Tat-Tat E39
Big Band Sound E45
Sounds All Around E45
Max Found Two Sticks E49
Song and Dance Man E49

Social Studies

The Big Balloon Race E22
Sounds from Around the World E50

UNIT E

Science in Centers

Science Center

Matter and Energy

Ongoing Center Activity Place these items in your science center, which children can use to investigate on an ongoing basis:

- aquarium, water table, or other container of water for float or sink exploration
- samples of solids, colored water and other liquids
- measuring cup, balance, and ruler
- scissors, paper, glue, markers, crayons, old magazines
- book box of related books. See recommended books listed at the beginning of each chapter on the "Providing More Depth" pages.

Center Management Tip As you begin each lesson, place the lesson investigation or a copy of it and needed materials in the science center.

Bulletin Board Idea Separate the bulletin board into sections for solids, liquids, and gases. Encourage children to draw pictures of the samples in the activity center as well as cut out pictures from old magazines and place them in the correct section of the bulletin board. Have them think of and add their own examples.

Art Center

Changing-Matter Flip Books

Materials blank index cards (5 per child), crayons, pencils

Center Activity Have children make a flip book showing what happens to a substance when heat is added or taken away. Help the class brainstorm ideas, such as an ice cream cone melting in the sun or water freezing into ice. Help children assemble the index cards in order and staple their flip books. Display children's flip books in the center.

Unit Technology

Look for these technology links referenced throughout the lessons in your Teacher's Edition.

Smithsonian Institution®

Visit this special Internet site for correlated links to virtual tours, on-line exhibits, and hands-on investigations from the Smithsonian Institution. **www.si.edu/harcourt/science**

Harcourt Science Instant Readers CD-ROM These CD-ROM programs reinforce science vocabulary and concepts and provide a variety of on-screen activities.

Harcourt Science Activity Video These videos show children doing the investigations for each lesson.

The Learning Site Visit the Harcourt Learning Site for a world of science resources, including News Breaks, interactive learning games, and an animated Science Glossary. **www.harcourtschool.com**

NSTA

NSTA SciLinks Internet links provided by the National Science Teachers Association in partnership with Harcourt. **www.scilinks.org/harcourt**

UNIT E

Reaching All Learners

Strategies for Multi-Age Classrooms

Develop Science Process Skills

- In this unit, children will be asked to use a measuring cup and a thermometer, which older children will have already had some experience using. Have older or more advanced children model using measuring tools.

Build Science Concepts

- Group short-term for intensive instruction in the different lessons that introduce solids, liquids, and gases. Share photographs from the different texts to provide additional illustrations and build concepts.
- After both younger and older children complete an activity or investigation involving problem solving, such as when Grade 1 children investigate sounds (p. E34), have volunteers share their problem-solving strategies with classmates.

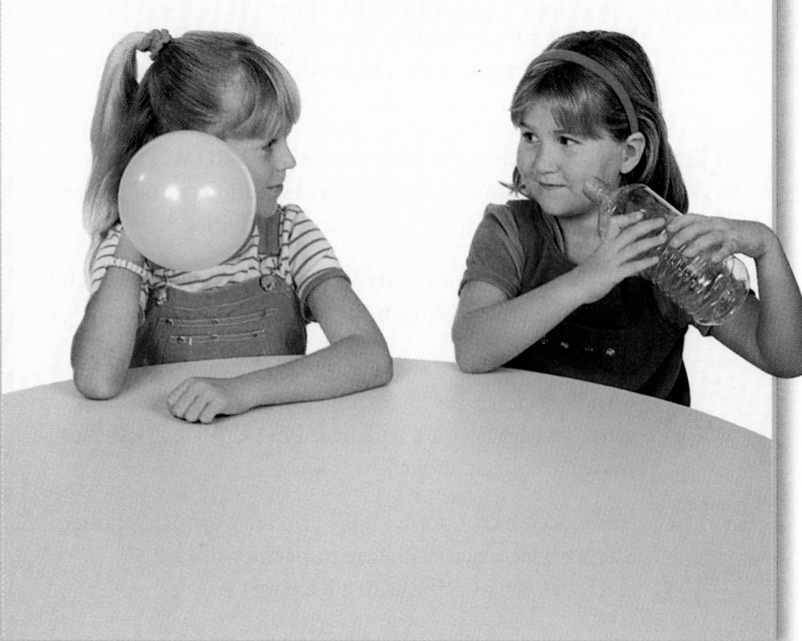

Strategies for ESL Students

Build Concepts

Use charts such as these to help children build and review lesson concepts.

solid	liquid	gas

sink	float

Develop Oral Language

Game Children may enjoy playing a game in which small groups work together to come up with clues that name a specific solid, liquid, or gas. Children write and then read a clue in sentence frames. For example, a child might say, "I am thinking of a liquid. It is white." Once a child in another group correctly guesses the object, that child's group takes a turn giving clues for a new object for others to guess.

Reread Have small groups reread sections, discuss them, and then choose a concept to demonstrate for classmates. For example, children may want to tell about and show objects that sink or float, demonstrate how liquids take the shape of their containers, or show how a gas fills the shape of its container.

ESL Activities

Point-of-use ESL activities are provided in the lessons throughout the unit.

Strategies for Special Needs Students

Learning Difficulties

Modify the instruction for children who need extra support by writing sentence frames in which children can fill in key words. Examples:

A solid is matter that keeps its shape.

Matter that flows and takes the shape of what it is poured into is a liquid.

Visually Impaired

To build self-esteem and independence, provide unique opportunities for these children to express their ideas or share a completed activity with the class. In this unit, using senses other than sight to observe matter provides these children with the chance to share what they observe about solids, liquids, and gases by using touch, smell, and hearing.

These children may also benefit from listening to the lesson audiotapes.

Hearing Impaired

Provide for additional repetition of skills such as in measuring liquids. When modeling lesson activities and investigations, break down tasks into smaller steps and repeat as necessary.

Strategies for Advanced Learners

The following are strategies to allow advanced learners to study the content of the unit in greater depth.

Chapter 1 Investigate Matter

To extend the learning, children may enjoy planning and organizing a class "matter party" that extends basic concepts. Children can form committees for food, decorations, and signs. Help them brainstorm ideas, gather supplies to make decorations, and write invitations. Examples of things to do might include the following:

- **Decorations:** Cut and tape colorful paper chains (cutting matter) and blow up balloons (gases).
- **Food:** Make trail mix or fruit punch (mixing) or float apples in a bucket of cold water (float and sink).
- **Signs:** Write labels for the different "matter concepts" demonstrated at the party and write and decorate invitations and signs.

Chapter 2 Making Sound

To extend learning about sound, children may enjoy finding out how their ears detect sounds. Help children set up a simple activity to demonstrate this concept. Stretch a piece of plastic tightly over a bowl. Secure it with a rubber band. Tape the plastic down to keep it taut. Then have children sprinkle a few grains of rice on top of the "drum". Have them hold a saucepan near the drum and hit the pan sharply with a wooden spoon. Ask the children to observe the grains of rice jump up and down. Encourage children to explain what causes the rice to do this. When the pan is hit, it vibrates. The sound travels through the air to the drum, which also vibrates. The vibrations cause the rice to jump.

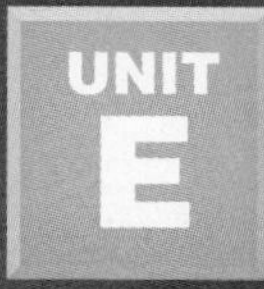

Unit Materials List

Quantities are indicated for a class of 30 students working individually or in groups of 5, depending on the nature of the activity. Where shared equipment is suggested, a smaller number of items is specified. Quantities are also listed for those materials included in the Materials Kit.

Nonconsumable Materials	Class Quantity Needed	Kit Quantity	Activity Page
aquarium	6	6	E12
bottle, 1-L plastic	24		E20, E40
bowl, plastic	6	6	E8
can, small	6		E46
cup, measuring	6	6	E1, E8, E40
cup, plastic (300 mL)	30	1 pkg of 50	E1, E8, E16
jar, plastic	6	6	E8
marble, glass	6	6	E4
paint brushes	6 sets		E4, E24
paper punch	1*	1	E34
rubber bands	6	1 pkg	E34, E46
rocks, small	12	12	E4, E16
ruler	6		E34
spoons, measuring	6	6	E1
timer	1*		E1

*Student groups should share this equipment.

Consumable Materials	Class Quantity Needed	Kit Quantity	Activity Page
aluminum foil	1 roll	1 roll	E34
baking soda	1 can	1 can	E16
balloons	6	1 pkg of 35	E20, E46
beans, dried	1 bag	1 bag	E46
chenille sticks	6	1 pkg of 20	E4
clay, cream modeling	2 boxes	2 boxes	E12
clay, red modeling	1 box	1 box	E4
cloth, cotton	6 small pieces	1 large piece	E4
craft sticks	6	30	E16
glitter	6 bottles		E24
glue	1 bottle		E24
index cards	24	1 pkg of 100	E24
paints	6 sets		E24
paper, notebook	360 sheets		E4, E8, E12, E16, E24
paper, yellow construction	12 sheets		E4, E40
pencil	6		E4, E8, E12, E16, E24, E46
sand	1 bag	1 bag	E16
salt	1 box	1 box	E1, E16
sugar	1 bag	1 bag	E1
tube, cardboard	6		E34

Additional kit options are available. Contact your sales representative for details.

UNIT E PHYSICAL SCIENCE

Matter and Energy

UNIT EXPERIMENT

Solids in Water

How does water temperature change the way solids dissolve? Plan and do a test to find out.

Informal Assessment

Research shows that informal assessment is an effective way to monitor and evaluate children's progress. Performance assessment and teacher observation are particularly useful for assessing projects and other similar tasks.

Performance Develop a rubric that will be used to evaluate children's completed projects. Use Developing Your Own Rubric on page AGxi of the Assessment Guide.

Classroom Observation You can gain insight into children's learning by observing how they use scientific processes, plan investigations and projects, collect and record information, and select and use appropriate tools to implement their project. While children are working on their projects, use the Project Evaluation Checklist on page AGxviii of the Assessment Guide for ongoing assessment.

UNIT E EXPERIMENT

Objectives

- **Promote scientific inquiry.**
- **Use a scientific method to plan and conduct a long-term investigation.**
- **Design an experiment to learn how water temperature affects how solids dissolve.**

A lesson plan for guiding children through the Unit Experiment is provided on pages E1i–E1j.

Science Fair Project Ideas

In addition to the Unit Experiment, you may wish to allow children to plan and carry out these science fair projects related to the chapters in Unit E. Children can use the framework on pages *10–17 to help them plan and conduct experiments.

Chapter 1 Candy Race Have children investigate what variables could affect the rate at which candy dissolves. Children should put a piece of candy in a plastic cup of water to use as a control test. Have them measure the temperature and the amount of water. Children should record how long it takes for the candy to dissolve. Then have children design an experiment that will cause the same kind of candy to dissolve more quickly in water. Children should think about what might be done to change the rate of dissolving such as breaking the piece of candy or if the water was warmer or colder than the test water. Have children run the tests and make posters to compare the results. Children should communicate conclusions that can be made using the results. Challenge children to tell what they should do if they don't want their candy to dissolve quickly.

Chapter 2 A Smorgasbord Band Have children bring in "sound makers" such as horns and any other item that they are sure will make sound. Then children can graph what makes the loudest sound, what makes the softest sound, what is the highest-pitched sound, and what is the lowest-pitched sound. Have children decide what these items have in common and how they are different. Challenge children to conduct an experiment to determine which pitch can be heard from the greatest distance. Ask one child to make the lowest-pitched sound at one end of the hall. Ask another child to walk away from the sound until he or she can no longer hear it. Repeat the experiment with the other higher-pitched sound-makers. Record and compare the distances.

UNIT E EXPERIMENT

Solids in Water

Choose from these options to help children complete the unit experiment.

Option 1 Independent Inquiry Assign the experiment for children to complete independently or with the help of an adult at home. (SAFETY NOTE: Supervise children closely during use of hot water.) Have children use the prompt as a springboard for writing their own questions and designing their own experiment. They can write a hypothesis, plan a fair test, select materials, and conduct the test. Children can refer to pages *10–17 in the Pupil Edition for guidance.

Option 2 Guided Inquiry Suggest that children use the prompt and the Experiment Log (Workbook pp. WB175–177) to help them plan their experiment. The Experiment Log pages shown here appear in the Workbook, but without answers. Children can write or draw their responses.

Option 3 Structured Inquiry Have children complete the experiment by testing the hypothesis and using the procedure that have been provided on the overhead transparency. You may wish to display the overhead transparencies shown here (or provide photocopies from the transparency package) and have children copy the hypothesis, variables, and procedure onto their Experiment Log (Workbook pp. WB175–177). You might prefer to copy the steps for conducting the experiment onto chart paper. Use the Experiment Lesson Plan to guide children as they complete the experiment.

BACKGROUND

Webliography GO ONLINE
Keyword changes in matter
www.harcourtschool.com

Water Solutions Water is a substance in which many solids dissolve easily, including salt and sugar. The particles in solids are held together by chemical bonds. Some solids have bonds that are strong and difficult to break. Solids that dissolve in water have relatively weak bonds. In general, the higher the water temperature, the faster such solids dissolve, due to the increased motion of the water molecules when water is heated. Stirring also adds to the motion of the molecules, increasing the rate of dissolving.

LESSON PLAN

Resources

Experiment Log, Unit E, Workbook pp. WB175–177

Experiment Transparencies, Unit E

Time 30–45 minutes

Expected Results Children should determine that salt and sugar dissolve faster in hot or warm water than in cold water.

Suggested Materials

- <u>**4 clear plastic cups or jars**</u>
- <u>**2 spoons***</u>
- <u>**measuring cups**</u>
- **marker**
- **hot water**
- **cold water**
- <u>**sugar**</u>
- <u>**salt**</u>
- **timer**

[* NOTE: If measuring spoons are used, have children use the teaspoon measure. The experiment will work using simple plastic spoons, however.]

<u>Underlined items</u> above are provided in the equipment kits (available separately).

Preparation Tips CAUTION: **Supervise children closely while using hot water.** As an alternative, use warm water instead. In this case, the difference in dissolving times will be less pronounced, as warm water will slow the rate at which solids dissolve. Use a fresh spoon to stir each container to avoid mixing some different solids in the same container.

Transparency Exp E, p. 1
Workbook p. WB175

Solids in Water

Observe and ask a question.

1. What can you ask about the way that solids dissolve in water of different temperatures?
   How does water temperature change the way solids dissolve? Which solids dissolve more easily in warm water than in cold water?

Form a hypothesis.

2. What could be true about how water temperature changes the way salt and sugar dissolve?
   Water temperature does not change the way salt and sugar dissolve in water.

Plan a fair test.

3. What things will you keep the same in the test? Write or draw them here.
   I will use the same amount of water and solid each time. Both the hot and cold water should be

1 Observe and Ask a Question

Have children discuss the prompt. Write the question on chart paper, or suggest that children record it in the Experiment Log, item 1.

2 Form a Hypothesis

Guide children in forming a testable hypothesis and recording it in the Experiment Log, item 2.

- **Look at the question we are going to investigate. What do you predict will be the answer to this question?** Possible answer: Solids will dissolve just as fast in hot water as in cold water.
- **Use your answer to form a statement. Your statement should be something you think will happen when you do your experiment. This statement will be your hypothesis.** Possible answer: Water temperature does not affect the way salt and sugar dissolve in water.

3 Plan a Fair Test

Remind children that an experiment is a fair test of a hypothesis. Discuss the concept of "fair test." This is also known as *controlling variables.*

- **Suppose you put more than one solid in the same container of water. Would this be fair?** Possible answer: No; with the solids mixed, it is impossible to tell how fast each one dissolves.
- **We want to keep most things the same for each test. What is the one thing that will be different in each test?** The water temperature will be different.

Have children record the plans for conducting a fair test in the Experiment Log, items 3–6, or write the plans on the board or on chart paper.

4 Do the Test

Children can record their data in the Experiment Log, item 7. They should enter sugar and salt under the Solids column, then write what they observed as well as the time it took for each solid to dissolve.

Common Error Alert Point out the importance of filling the measuring cup to the same level each time, and of filling the spoons with the same amounts of solid each time.

5 Draw Conclusions and Communicate Results

Guide children in interpreting the data they have recorded. Children should conclude that hot or warm water will dissolve both salt and sugar faster than cold water will. Note that salt water will appear cloudier than sugar water, and that the salt may not completely dissolve.

Discuss whether the test supported the hypothesis.

- **How do our results compare to our hypothesis?** Possible answer: We found that water temperature affects the way sugar and salt dissolve; hot water makes both substances dissolve faster. Therefore, our hypothesis was not correct. It was not supported by our data.

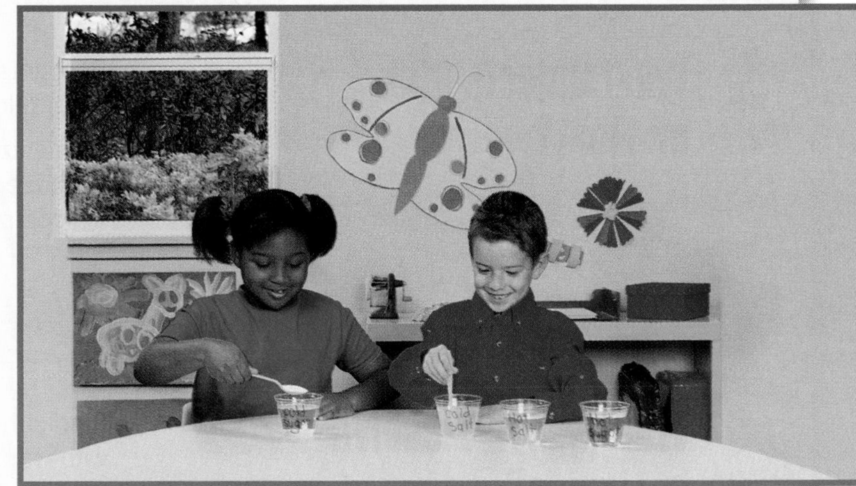

Transparency Exp E, p. 2 Workbook p. WB176

about the same temperature each time. I will stir at about the same speed each time.

4. What is one thing you will change in the test?
   I will change only the water temperature.
5. What objects will you need to do the test? Write or draw them here.
   plastic cups, spoons, measuring cups, marker, hot water, cold water, sugar, salt, timer, thermometer
6. What steps will you take to do the test?
   a. Label 4 containers: "COLD SALT," "HOT SALT," "COLD SUGAR," "HOT SUGAR."
   b. Measure hot tap water into two of the containers.
   c. Measure cold tap water into the other two containers.
   d. Stir a spoonful of sugar into the "HOT SUGAR" container. Time how long it takes the crystals to dissolve completely. Write what happens.
   e. Do the same thing for "HOT SALT."
   f. Do the steps again with the sugar and salt for the cold containers.

Transparency Exp E, p. 3 Workbook p. WB177

Do the test.

7. Record your data in the chart.

How Does Water Temperature Change the Way Solids Dissolve?

Name of Solid	Cold Water	Hot Water
	Dissolving time: ____ seconds	Dissolving time: ____ seconds
	Dissolving time: ____ seconds	Dissolving time: ____ seconds

Draw conclusions. Communicate results.

8. What are your results? How can you communicate your results to others?

Investigate Further Encourage children to build on this experiment to explore in greater depth how solids dissolve. For example, will the results change if a greater amount of solid is added? Is there a point at which no more solid will dissolve? What other solids will dissolve in water? What kinds of solids will not dissolve?

Planning Guide Investigate Matter

LESSON	PACING	OBJECTIVES	MATERIALS
1 What Can We Observe About Solids? E4–7	2 days	▶ Recognize that everything around us is matter. ▶ Observe and describe the properties of solids.	**Investigate** objects, paper, pencil
2 What Can We Observe About Liquids? E8–11	2 days	▶ Recognize that liquid is matter that flows. ▶ Observe and describe the properties of liquids.	**Investigate** 3 containers, measuring cup, water, paper, pencil
3 What Objects Sink or Float? E12–15	2 days	▶ Recognize that some objects sink and others float in water. ▶ Recognize that objects can be described in terms of their floating and sinking properties.	**Investigate** ball of clay, water, aquarium, paper, pencil
4 What Solids Dissolve in Liquids? E16–19	2 days	▶ Predict how a solid acts when mixed with water. ▶ Classify solids into those that will dissolve in water and those that will not.	**Investigate** solids to test, 4 cups, water, paper and pencil, stirring stick

PROCESS SKILLS	VOCABULARY	RESOURCES AND TECHNOLOGY	REACHING ALL LEARNERS
Process Skill Tip classify **Other Process Skills** compare	**matter** **solid**	**Workbook,** pp. WB107–109 **Vocabulary Cards,** pp. TR145–150 **Transparency** E1-1 **Harcourt Science Activity Video** **Internet Site**	**Advanced Learners,** p. E1g **ESL Activity,** p. E6 **Informal Assessment,** p. E7
Process Skill Tip use numbers **Other Process Skills** compare	**liquid**	**Workbook,** pp. WB110–111 **Transparency** E1-2 **Harcourt Science Activity Video**	**Informal Assessment,** p. E11
Process Skill Tip gather and record data **Other Process Skills** compare	**float** **sink**	**Workbook,** pp. WB112–113 **Transparency** E1-3 **Harcourt Science Activity Video** **Harcourt Science Instant Readers CD-ROM** **Internet Site**	**Investigation Challenge,** p. E14 **Informal Assessment,** p. E15
Process Skill Tip form a hypothesis **Other Process Skills** compare	**dissolve**	**Workbook,** pp. WB114–115 **Transparency** E1-4 **Harcourt Science Activity Video**	**ESL Activity,** p. E17 **Investigation Challenge,** p. E18 **Informal Assessment,** p. E19

LESSON	PACING	OBJECTIVES	MATERIALS
5 What Can We Observe About Gases? E20–23	2 days	▶ Recognize that gas is matter that fills and takes the shape of the container it is in. ▶ Observe and describe the properties of gases.	**Investigate** balloon, plastic soft drink bottle
6 How Can We Change Objects? E24–27	2 days	▶ Recognize that things can be done to solid matter to change its properties. ▶ Observe and describe the behavior of solid matter when we do things to change it.	**Investigate** 4 cards with slits, paints and brushes, glitter, glue, paper, pencil
End of Chapter E28–31 **Art Link: Mixing Objects to Make Art** **Math Link: Estimate How Much Ships Can Carry** **Chapter Review and Test Preparation**		▶ Recognize that knowledge about science is used in art. ▶ Determine how shape and weight make an object sink or float. ▶ Review chapter concepts.	

PROCESS SKILLS	VOCABULARY	RESOURCES AND TECHNOLOGY	REACHING ALL LEARNERS
Process Skill Tip draw a conclusion **Other Process Skills** observe, compare	**gas**	**Workbook,** pp. WB116–117 **Transparency** E1-5 **Harcourt Science Activity Video**	**ESL Activity,** p. E21 **Kinesthetic Learners,** p. E22 **Informal Assessment,** p. E23
Process Skill Tip conduct an investigation **Other Process Skills** compare	**change**	**Workbook,** pp. WB118–122 **Transparency** E1-6 **Harcourt Science Activity Video**	**Investigation Challenge,** p. E26 **Informal Assessment,** p. E27
		Take-Home Book, pp. TH35–36 *Jeff's Present* **Take-Home Book,** pp. TH37–38 *Mike Measures Matter* **Activities for Home or School,** pp. TR106–107 **Chapter Test,** pp. AG71–74 **Science Songs,** Track 14	**Informal Assessment,** p. E28 **Performance Assessment,** p. AG75 **Portfolio Evaluation,** p. AGxxiv

Prepare for Activities

Use this page to help you organize and prepare materials for the Investigations, which begin each lesson of this chapter.

LESSON INVESTIGATION	MATERIALS

1 Solid Objects
E4

PURPOSE Observe solid objects and classify them according to their properties.

PREPARATION TIPS Select objects that have different colors, sizes, shapes, textures, hardness, and flexibility for children to choose from and sort.

TIME 20 minutes

EXPECTED RESULTS Children recognize that solid objects have observable properties by which they can be classified.

MATERIALS

- objects: red chenille stick, yellow cloth, red marble, red modeling clay, yellow paper, and small rock painted yellow
- paper and pencil

2 Liquids in Bottles
E8

PURPOSE Observe that the same amount of water takes different shapes depending upon the container it is poured into.

PREPARATION TIPS Prepare 3 plastic containers of different shapes and sizes ahead of time with exactly the same amount of water in each. Have paper towels on hand for spills.

TIME 20 minutes

EXPECTED RESULTS Children use numbers to observe that each container has the same amount of water, even though the water takes a different shape in the container.

MATERIALS

- 3 differently shaped containers
- measuring cup
- water
- paper and pencil

3 Shapes That Sink or Float
E12

PURPOSE Recognize that the same material may sink or float depending upon its shape.

PREPARATION TIPS Fill the aquarium almost to the top with water. Have paper towels on hand for children to dry the clay and their hands as needed before recording. Use golf-ball-size clay balls.

TIME 20–25 minutes

EXPECTED RESULTS Children gather and record data as they discover that most bowl- or boat-like shapes formed from a thin layer of clay will float. Compact masses of clay will sink.

MATERIALS

- ball of clay
- water
- aquarium
- paper and pencil

Prepare for Activities Continued

LESSON INVESTIGATION	MATERIALS

4 Solids in Water
E16

PURPOSE Observe that some solids dissolve in water and others do not.

PREPARATION TIPS You may wish to use a spoon to add the salt, baking soda, and sand to the water. Make copies of the data sheet (p. TR166) or provide blank paper.

TIME 20 minutes

EXPECTED RESULTS Children discover that salt and baking soda dissolve in water while sand and rocks do not.

- solids to test: salt, sand, rocks, baking soda
- cups
- water
- paper and pencil
- stirring stick

5 Air In a Bottle
E20

PURPOSE Observe that air is a form of matter that takes up space.

PREPARATION TIPS Use easy-to-inflate round, rather than oblong, balloons. Use clean, 1-liter plastic soft drink bottles. Encourage children having difficulty with Step 2 to put the balloon over the top of the bottle and then poke it in.

TIME 15 minutes

EXPECTED RESULTS Children discover that they cannot blow up the balloon when it is in the bottle because there is air in the bottle that takes up space and cannot escape.

- balloon
- plastic soft drink bottle

6 Changing Paper
E24

PURPOSE Investigate ways to change the properties of paper.

PREPARATION TIPS Cut half-inch slits, one in each end and two on each side of the cards ahead of time. Arrange all materials in an area spread with newspaper before children begin decorating.

TIME 20-25 minutes

EXPECTED RESULTS Children discover different ways to change how their papers look and feel.

- four 3 x 5-in. cards (with $\frac{1}{2}$ in. slits on ends and sides)
- paints and brushes
- glitter
- glue
- paper and pencil

Harcourt Science Activity Videos

The Activity Video for this unit shows children doing the Investigations. You may wish to view the video for classroom management ideas. The video can also be used to model the investigation process for children.

Equipment Kits

Underlined items above are provided in the equipment kits (available separately).

. . . with More Activities

. . . with the Take-Home Books

Jeff's Present
pages TH35–36, *Take-Home Books*

Mike Measures Matter
pages TH37–38, *Take-Home Books*

These take-home books provide reinforcement of science concepts and vocabulary presented in the chapter and provide an activity. See p. E31.

Jeff's Present

Jeff's dad gives him a birthday present. He wants Jeff to guess what is inside the box.

. . . with the Harcourt Science Instant Readers

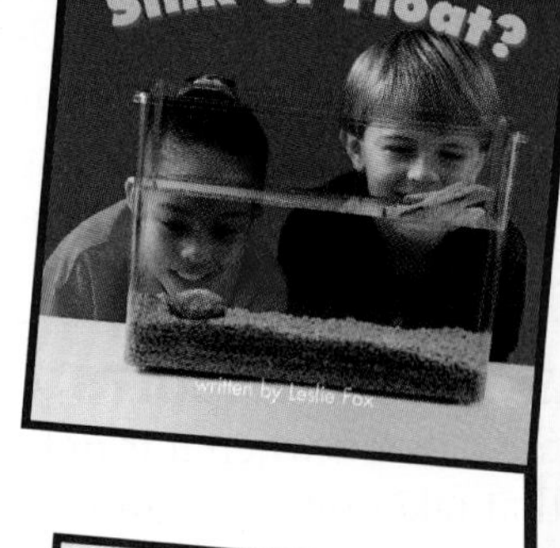

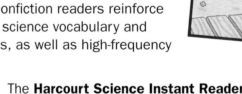

Sink or Float? by Leslie Fox identifies objects that will float or sink. See p. E15.

Heat Changes Things by Michael Medearis shows what happens when different solids, such as butter and chocolate chips, and liquids, such as water and soup, are heated. See p. E27.

These nonfiction readers reinforce chapter science vocabulary and concepts, as well as high-frequency words.

The **Harcourt Science Instant Readers** are also available on **CD-ROM**, which includes science activities and investigations.

. . . with Trade Books

These books provide in-depth information about our senses and living and nonliving things.

Balloons: Building and Experimenting with Inflatable Toys by Bernie Zubrowski (William Morrow, 1990) tells how to use inflatable balloons to power toys.

The Big Balloon Race by Eleanor Coerr (Harpercrest, 1992) tells of a historic flight of balloonist Carlotta Myers.

Cars and Trucks and Other Vehicles by Claude Delafosse (Cartwheel Books, 1996) provides information on parts of cars and other vehicles.

Grandpa's Soup by Eiko Kadono (Eerdmans Books for Young Readers, 1999) tells about the making of Grandpa's soup and the sharing of it with friends.

The Grumpalump by Sarah Hayes (Clarion, 1990) tells what a small group of animals do to inflate the Grumpalump to change it into a hot-air balloon.

Lemonade for Sale by Stuart J. Murphy (HarperCollins, 1998) tells how the Elm Street Kids' Club makes lemonade to make money. This book can also be used as a springboard to discuss math concepts such as graphing.

Machines We Use by Sally Hewitt (Children's Press, 1998) provides information about simple machines and experiments for children to try.

Mushroom in the Rain by Mirra Ginsburg (Aladdin, 1997) explains how a mushroom can shelter many woodland creatures after it rains. *ALA Notable*

Paper, Paper Everywhere by Gail Gibbons (Voyager, 1997) explains how paper is made. *Children's Choice*

A Raindrop Hit My Nose by Ray Butrum (Multnomah, 1998) explains where the raindrop came from and where it is going.

Solids and Liquids by David Glover (Kingfisher Books, 1993) looks at the make-up of solids and liquids and includes experiments.

Sunken Treasure by Gail Gibbons (HarperCollins, 1988) looks at why ships sink and explores ways to recover them as well as their cargo.

Very Last First Time: An Inuit Tale by Jan Andrews (Simon & Schuster, 1998) tells how an Inuit girl explores a cave of sea ice formed at low tide.

What is the World Made Of? All About Solids, Liquids, and Gases by Kathleen Weidner Zoelfeld (HarperCollins, 1998) provides hands-on examples to show how matter can change.

Trade book titles are current at time of publication but may go out of print without notice.

Visit The Learning Site for related links, activities, and resources.

www.harcourtschool.com

Assessment Options ✔ Chapter 1

Formal Assessment

- **Chapter Review and Test Preparation,** PE pp. E30–31
- **Chapter Test,** pp. AG71–74

Performance Assessment

- **Chapter Review and Test Preparation**, PE p. E31
- **Chapter Performance Task**, pp. AG75–76

Project Evaluation Checklist, p. AGxviii

Ongoing Assessment

- **✔Questions**, PE pp. E5–7, E9–11, E13–15, E17–19, E21–23, E25–27
- **Lesson Review**, PE pp. E7, E11, E15, E19, E23, E27
- **Informal Assessment**
  - **Classroom Observation,** TE p. E11
  - **Performance,** TE pp. E7, E19, E27
  - **Portfolio,** TE pp. E15, E23, E28
- **Observation Checklist,** AGxiv

Student Self-Assessment

- **Self-Assessment – Investigate**, p. AGxvi
- **Self-Assessment – Learn About**, p. AGxvii
- **Project Summary Sheet**, p. AGxix

My Work Portfolio Assessment

- **Science Experiences Record**, p. AGxxii
- **Guide to My Science Portfolio**, p. AGxxiii
- **Portfolio Evaluation,** p. AGxxiv

Chapter Test AG71

Investigate Matter

Part I Vocabulary 4 points each

Write the letter of the word that best completes the sentence.

A change	**C** gas	**E** liquid	**G** sink
B floats	**D** matter	**F** dissolve	**H** solid

The air that fills the tube is a **1.** C.
The tube keeps its shape, so it is a **2.** H.
The tube **3.** B on the top of a **4.** E.
The goggles **5.** G to the bottom.
Salt can **6.** F in water.
Everything in the picture is **7.** D
You can **8.** A an object by bending it.

Chapter Test AG72

Part II Science Concepts and Understanding

Circle the letter of the best answer. 6 points each

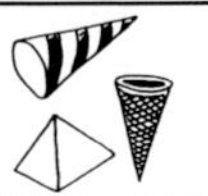

9. How are these solids sorted?

Ⓐ by shape
B by sound
C by color

10. What is a way to measure liquids?

F by color
G by shape
Ⓗ by amount

11. Which liquids do **NOT** mix?

A vinegar and water
Ⓑ oil and water
C milk and water

12. Which object will float?

F an anchor
Ⓖ a cork
H a ball of clay

13. What is inside a beach ball that helps it float?

a gas

Chapter Test AG73

Draw a line to what will happen.

14. If you fill a jar with water, •
15. If you fill a jar with marbles, •
16. If you fill a jar with gas, •

• it will fill up the space in in the jar.
• it will take the shape of the jar.
• they will keep their shape.

17. Write two ways to classify these objects.

by shape by size

Chapter Test AG74

Part III Process Skills Application 7 points each

Process skills: collect and record data, draw conclusions

18. Put an ***X*** below the words that tell what does **NOT** mix.

warm water and cold water	warm water and ice cubes	oil and water
___	___	X

19. Look at the bottles. Make a tally mark for each bottle.

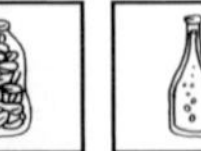

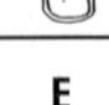

A B C D E

Matter

	A	B	C	D	E	Total
Solid	I	I				2
Liquid			I		I	2
Gas	I	I	I	I	I	5

Performance Assessment AG75

PERFORMANCE TASK

Mix and See

Materials

1 marble, 1 toothpick, 1 cotton ball, 1 paper clip, water, paper, clear plastic container

1. You will put four things into water.
2. Tell what you think will happen to each.
3. Put each thing in the water. Then write ***yes*** or ***no*** to show what happened.

The Water Test

	Keeps Shape	Loses Shape	Sinks	Floats
Cotton Ball				
Marble				
Toothpick				
Paper Clip				

Performance Assessment AG76

PERFORMANCE TASK

Teacher's Directions

Mix and See

Materials marbles, toothpicks, cotton balls, paper clips, water, paper, clear plastic containers

Time 20–30 minutes

Suggested Grouping pairs

Science Processes predict, record data

Preparation Hints Set up one area where children can come to get water. Assemble other materials.

Introduce the Task Elicit the different things that can happen when objects are put into water (for example, life preservers float; anchors sink; paper things may lose their shape). Tell children that they will make some predictions about what will happen to some things when they put them into water. Distribute Performance Task sheets and materials. Ask children to read the directions silently. Then have volunteers explain the directions so that children can confirm or correct their understanding.

Promote Discussion When children finish, ask them to share their task results with a partner. Have children tell whether or not their predictions were correct.

Scoring Rubric

Performance Indicators

_____ Writes a prediction about what will happen to the four items.
_____ Follows through on directions for immersing the four items.
_____ Records results accurately.
_____ Articulates clearly both predictions and results of immersing items.

Observations and Rubric Score

3 2 1 0

Workbook Support

Process Skills Practice WB108

Classify

1. Group the objects that are the same. Draw your groups in the chart.

My Groups	
Group 1	**Group 2**
marbles	present
beach ball	book
grapes	blocks

2. Tell why you grouped the objects as you did.

Most children will group the materials by shape—those that are round or have corners.

Lesson Concept Review/Assessment WB109

What Can We Observe About Solids?

1. Draw something that is matter.
Children can draw any object—solid, liquid, or gas.

2. Color the solids **red**.

Everything except the spilled milk and air should be colored.

3. How is this man changing a solid?

He is carving the wood and changing its shape.

Process Skills Practice WB110

Use Numbers

1. Circle the container you think has more water.
Accept any response; most children will indicate Container B.

A B

2. Circle the tool you could use to measure the water.

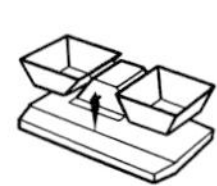

3. Jill measured the water in each container. Both containers had 12 ounces. Circle the words that tell about the containers.

Container A ____.

a. has more water than Container B

b. has the same amount of water as Container B

c. has less water than Container B

4. Why does B look as if it has more water than A?

Container B is taller.

Lesson Concept Review/Assessment WB111

What Can We Observe About Liquids?

1. Draw liquids in the containers.
Children should show liquids taking the shape of each container.

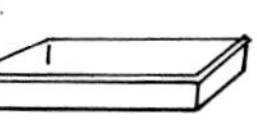

2. Circle the liquid that does not mix with water.

3. Circle the things that are liquid.

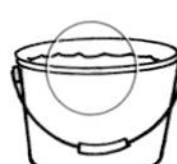

Workbook Support Continued

Process Skills Practice WB112

Gather and Record Data

1. Observe the picture. Record in the chart the liquids and solids.

Matter	
Liquids	**Solids**
Children may write or draw fountain spray, fountain water, and spilled soft drink.	Children may write or draw bench, bush, tree, ball, soft drink can, and rocks.

2. How many solids are there? 6
3. How many liquids are there? 3

Lesson Concept Review/Assessment WB113

What Objects Sink or Float?

Circle **float** or **sink** for each picture.

1.  float (sink)
2.  (float) sink
3. 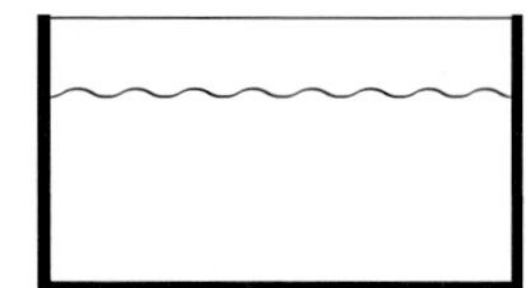 (float) sink
4. float (sink)

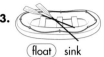

5. Draw something that floats and something that sinks. Color the object that floats **red**. Color the object that sinks **blue**.

Process Skills Practice WB114

Form a Hypothesis

Use terms from the box to help you form a hypothesis. Write it.

1. A tea bag is placed in a cup of hot water.

water	dissolve	tea

The tea will dissolve in the water.

2. A rock is dropped into a container of water.

rock	water	sink

The rock will sink in the water.

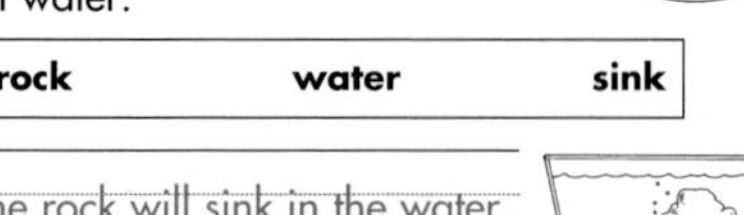

3. A chef stirs a cup filled with vinegar and water.

mix	water	vinegar

The vinegar will mix with water.

Lesson Concept Review/Assessment WB115

What Solids Dissolve in Liquids?

1. Circle the solids that dissolve in water.

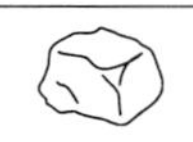  

2. Circle the solids that do not dissolve in water.

  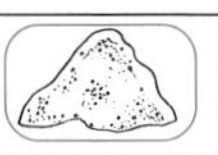

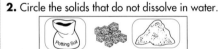

3. In what temperature of a liquid will solids dissolve faster?

(hot) cold

4. Complete the sentence below.
A solid dissolves in a liquid when the solid mixes completely with the liquid.

Process Skills Practice WB116

Draw a Conclusion

1. These spoons had different liquids on them. Why is one liquid still on the spoon?

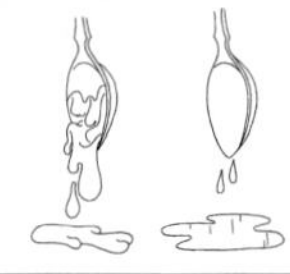

It is thicker and takes more time to run off the spoon.

2. The boy has the same balloon in both pictures. Why does the balloon look different in the second picture?

It has air in it.

3. What happened to the clay?

It was molded into a ball.

Lesson Concept Review/Assessment WB117

What Can We Observe About Gases?

1. There is gas in each container. Color the space the gas takes up.

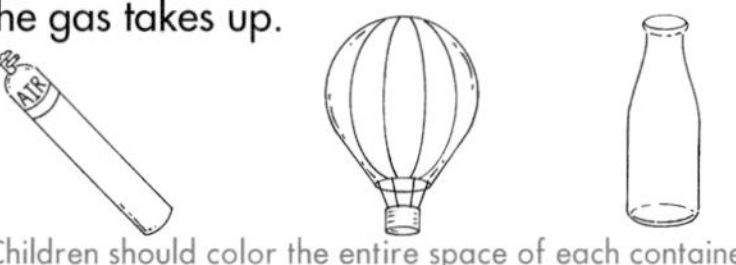

Children should color the entire space of each container.

2. Color where the gas is in this liquid.

Children should color the bubbles.

3. You can not see air.
How do you know it is here?

Possible answer: Wind is blowing the balloon.

Process Skills Practice WB118

Investigate

1. These pictures are not finished. Finish each picture a different way.

2. These pictures are the same. Color each picture to make it look different.

Lesson Concept Review/Assessment WB119

How Can We Change Objects?

1. This toy is made of wire. Draw how you could bend it to make it look different.

Figure should be changed to look different from the starting picture.

2. You could change this paper with scissors. Draw how it would look after you cut it.

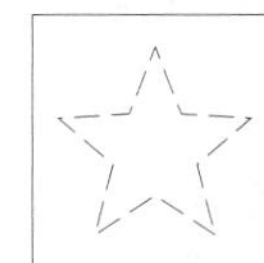

Drawing should be star shaped.

3. Finish the sentence. Circle the best word.

____ changes liquid juice to a frozen ice pop.

Melting (Freezing) Mixing

Vocabulary Review WB120

Matter

Write your answer. Use the words in the box.

gas	liquid	matter

1. I am all around you. What am I? matter or gas
2. I take up the shape of my container. What am I? gas or liquid
3. I can flow fast or slow. What am I? a liquid

Match the word to the picture that tells about it.

4. solids
5. sink
6. float
7. change
8. dissolve

Reading Skills Practice WB121

Use Graphic Sources for Information

How Objects React on Water

Use the chart to answer the questions.

Objects That Sink	Objects That Float
marble	beach ball
rock	driftwood
anchor	toy boat
	plastic cup

1. How many objects float? 4 How many sink? 3
2. Circle the object that you might find at the bottom of a pond.
3. Which objects would be best used in a fish tank? Circle your answers.

Writing Practice WB122

Write to Compare and Contrast

A. Draw a container of a thin liquid and a container of a thick liquid that you like to drink. Label your pictures.

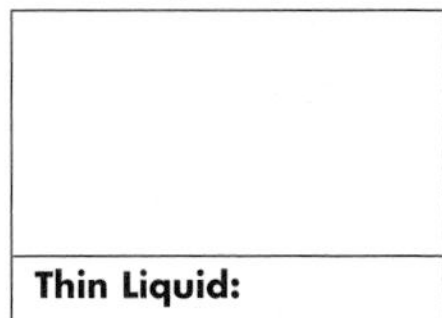

Thin Liquid:	Thick Liquid:

B. Write about how these liquids are alike.

Answers will vary but should describe how the liquids are alike.

C. Write about how these liquids are different.

Answers will vary but should include that one liquid is thin and the other liquid is thick.

Chapter 1

Investigate Matter

Generate Questions

Did You Know?/*Fast Facts*

Talk about floating and sinking before children open their books. Ask:

- ▶ **What are some things that float?** Accept things that float in liquids as well as things that float in air.
- ▶ **What are some things that sink?** Accept things that sink down through liquids as well as things like feathers that appear to "sink" through air.

Tell children to open their books to page E2. Ask volunteers to read aloud the text.

Discuss the photographs. Ask questions such as these to help children **relate pictures to text**:

- ▶ **Which boat is in salt water?** the one that floats higher
- ▶ **What liquid do you see sinking here?** chocolate syrup

Encourage children's questions. Write children's questions on the board, or have them write or draw in their journals.

PUPIL'S EDITION OR BIG BOOK

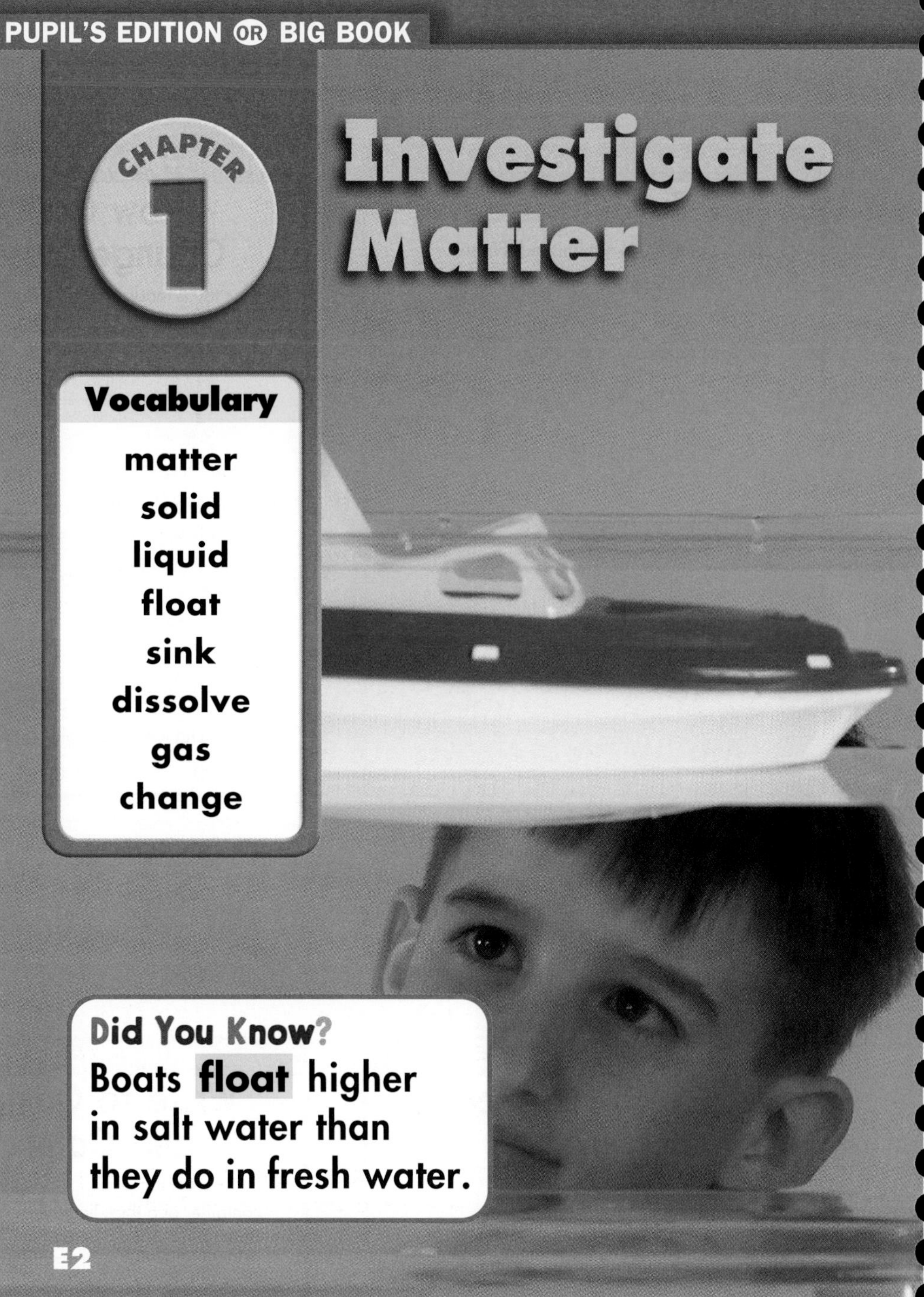

CHAPTER 1

Investigate Matter

Vocabulary
matter
solid
liquid
float
sink
dissolve
gas
change

Did You Know?
Boats **float** higher in salt water than they do in fresh water.

E2

Reading Skills Checklist

Strategies for developing the following reading skills are provided in this chapter.

- ☑ use context *p. E18*
- ☑ recall supporting facts and details *p. E9*
- ❑ arrange events in sequence
- ❑ follow directions
- ☑ draw conclusions *p. E10*
- ☑ identify the main idea *pp. E5, E13, E17, E18, E21, E25*
- ☑ identify cause and effect *pp. E13, E22, E26*
- ☑ predict outcomes *p. E10, E22*
- ☑ summarize *pp. E7, E11, E15, E19, E23, E27*
- ☑ use graphic sources for information *p. E6, E10*
- ☑ relate pictures to text *pp. E2, E6, E9, E21*
- ❑ distinguish between fact and nonfact
- ☑ develop concepts of print *p. E5*
- ☑ build vocabulary *pp. E5, E6, E9, E10, E13, E14, E17, E18, E21, E22, E25, E26*

School-Home Connection

Distribute copies of the School-Home Connection, p. TR19.

Follow Up Have volunteers compare the results of the activity they did at home. Additional School-Home connections are provided by the **Activities for Home or School** (pp. E54–E55) and the **Take-Home Book** (p. E2g).

Teaching Resources, p. TR19

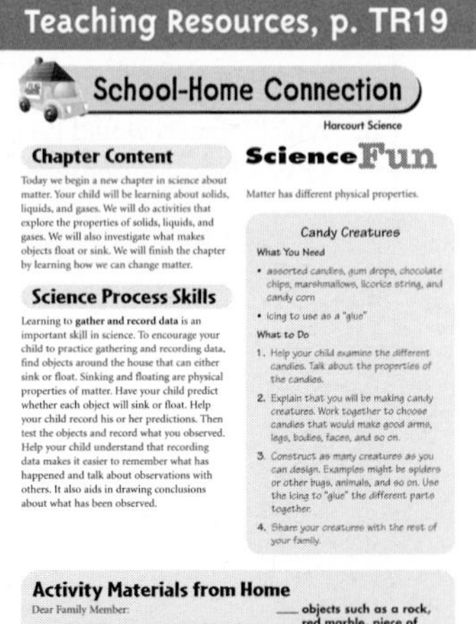

School-Home Connection

Harcourt Science

Chapter Content

Today we begin a new chapter in science about matter. Your child will be learning about solids, liquids, and gases. We will do activities that explore the properties of solids, liquids, and gases. We will also investigate what makes objects float or sink. We will finish the chapter by learning how we can change matter.

Science Process Skills

Learning to **gather and record data** is an important skill in science. To encourage your child to practice gathering and recording data, find objects around the house that can either sink or float. Sinking and floating are physical properties of matter. Have your child predict whether each object will sink or float. Help your child record his or her predictions. Then test the objects and record what you observed. Help your child understand that recording data makes it easier to remember what has happened and talk about observations with others. It also aids in drawing conclusions about what has been observed.

Science Fun

Matter has different physical properties.

Candy Creatures

What You Need

- assorted candies, gum drops, chocolate chips, marshmallows, licorice string, and candy corn
- icing to use as a "glue"

What to Do

1. Help your child examine the different candies. Talk about the properties of the candies.
2. Explain that you will be making candy creatures. Work together to choose candies that would make good arms, legs, bodies, faces, and so on.
3. Construct as many creatures as you can design. Examples might be spiders or other bugs, animals, and so on. Use the icing to "glue" the different parts together.
4. Share your creatures with the rest of your family.

Activity Materials from Home

Dear Family Member:

To do the activities in this chapter, we will need some materials that you may have around the house. Please note the items at the right. If possible, please send these things to school with your child.

Your help and support are appreciated!

___ **objects such as a rock, red marble, piece of yellow fabric**
___ **different-size plastic containers**
___ **balloon**
___ **plastic soft drink bottle**

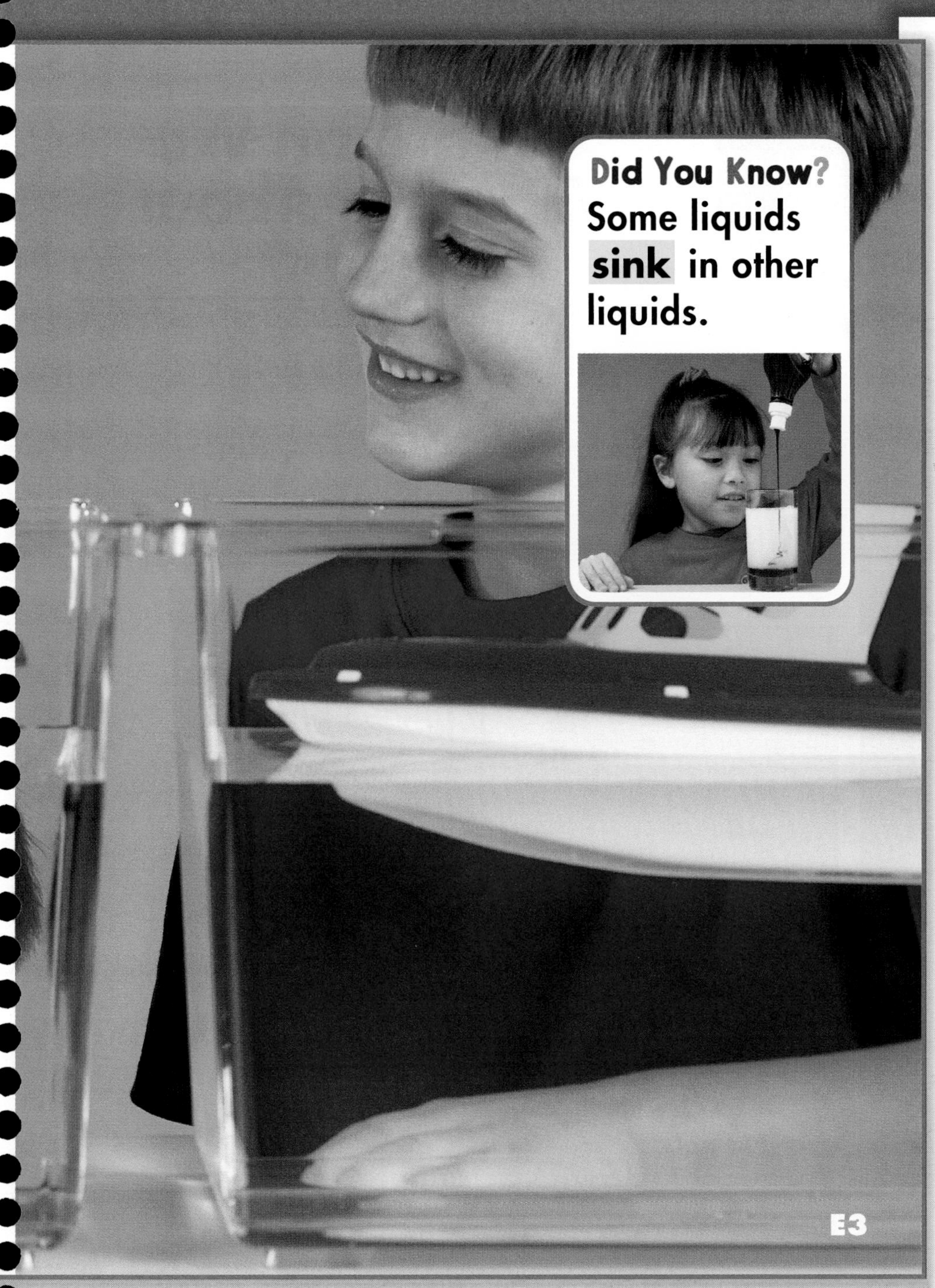

Did You Know?
Some liquids sink in other liquids.
E3

Graphic Organizer for Chapter Concepts

Transparency E1 • Workbook, p. WB107

Unit E, Chapter 1 Investigate Matter

LESSON 1 What Can We Observe About Solids?	LESSON 2 What Can We Observe About Liquids?	LESSON 3 What Objects Sink or Float?
1. Everything around us is matter. 2. Solids are matter that keep their shape. 3. Solids can be sorted in many ways.	1. Matter that flows is called a liquid. 2. Liquids take the shape of what they are poured into. 3. Some liquids mix with water, but oil does not.	1. Some objects float and some objects sink. 2. Changing the shape of an object helps it sink or float.
LESSON 4 What Solids Dissolve in Liquids?	**LESSON 5 What Can We Observe About Gases?**	**LESSON 6 How Can We Change Objects?**
1. Some solids dissolve in liquids. 2. Soil and sand do not dissolve in water.	1. Gas spreads out and takes the shape of its container. 2. You can not see gases but you can see what they do.	1. You can change objects by rolling or bending them. 2. You can change objects by freezing or mixing them.

Prereading Strategies

Preview the Chapter

Do a walk-through of the chapter. Read aloud the main headings for each lesson and have volunteers suggest answers. Keep track of any questions that come up during discussion.

Preview the Photographs

Have children look at the photos in the lessons. Ask which ones interest them most and discuss why. Use this as a beginning to find out what children know and want to know about the lesson.

Preview the Vocabulary

Write the vocabulary words from page E2 on the board. Read aloud the list and ask children to tell about the words they know and don't know. Tell them that they will learn about these words throughout the lessons.

DEFINITIONS

matter everything around us

solid matter that keeps its shape

liquid matter that flows and takes the shape of the container it is poured into

float to stay in or on top of a liquid

sink to drop to the bottom of a liquid

dissolve to mix with liquid completely

gas matter that spreads out to fill and take the shape of the container it is in

change to make different

VOCABULARY CARDS AND ACTIVITIES

Children can use the Vocabulary Cards to make their own graphic organizers or to add to an ongoing file of science terms. The Vocabulary Cards and a variety of strategies and activities are provided beginning on p. TR110 in the **Teaching Resources** book.

GRAPHIC ORGANIZER FOR CHAPTER CONCEPTS

Children can use the graphic organizer to record key concepts and ideas from each lesson. See **Workbook p. WB107** and **Transparency E1**. A completed graphic organizer is also shown on page E30.

LESSON 1

What Can We Observe About Solids?

Objectives

- ▶ Recognize that everything around us is matter.
- ▶ Observe and describe the properties of solids.

Motivate

Talk About Objects Have children examine different objects in the classroom. Ask them to describe them and discuss what these objects have in common.

Investigate

Time 20 min **Grouping** individuals

Process Skill classify

Preparation Tips and Expected Results See page E2e.

Center Activity Option Place this investigation or a copy of the Investigation, page TR62, in your science center.

Activity Tips

- ▶ If children select their own objects, invite them to identify and pick different properties such as color, shape, and size.
- ▶ Brainstorm with children different ways to record on paper how they classified their objects.

Children can place their recording papers in their science journals.

Activity Questions

- ▶ What properties such as size, color, or shape did you use to classify your objects?
- ▶ What more would you like to know about solid objects?

When Minutes Count . . .

As a whole-class activity, use pictures of different objects or use Picture Cards 21–30, *Teaching Resources*, pp. TR91–93. Have children identify three properties such as size, color, and shape. Then have them compare and sort the objects accordingly.

PUPIL'S EDITION OR BIG BOOK

LESSON 1

What Can We Observe About Solids?

Investigate

Solid Objects

You will need

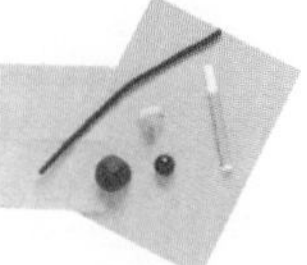

objects

paper and pencil

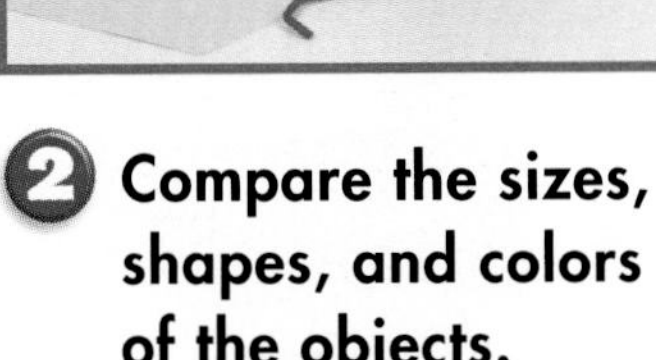

1. Observe each object.
2. Compare the sizes, shapes, and colors of the objects.
3. Think of three ways to classify the objects. Draw or write them on your paper.

Science Skill

To classify the objects, find ways they are the same and group them.

E4

Science Skills

Process Skill: Classify Display Process Skill Tip Transparency E1-1. Have children observe each solid. Ask volunteers to help you list words that tell about each object's shape, size, and flexibility. Then have children fill in the chart to group the solids. Have them tell how the objects are the same.

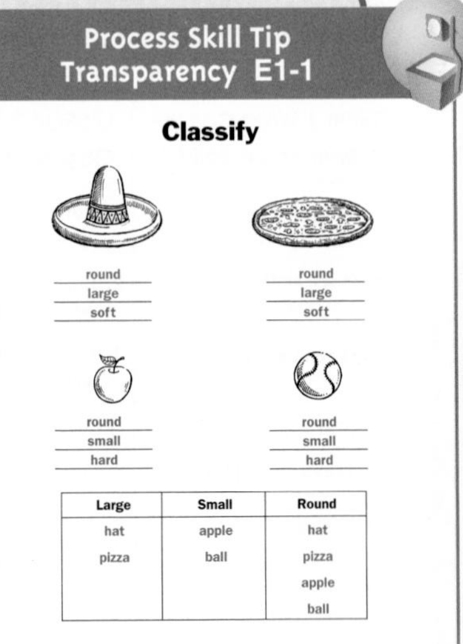

Process Skill Tip Transparency E1-1

Classify

round / large / soft

round / large / soft

round / small / hard

round / small / hard

Large	Small	Round
hat	apple	hat
pizza	ball	pizza
		apple
		ball

PROCESS SKILLS PRACTICE

To practice and apply process skills, see **Workbook p. WB108.**

Learn About

Matter and Solids

Everything around you is **matter**.
Toys and blocks are matter. You are, too!

- **What matter do you see?**
  Accept all reasonable answers.

E5

1 Before Reading

PREVIEW/SET PURPOSE

Have children preview pages E5–E7. Make a web. Explain that children will help you fill in examples of matter and solids as the lesson progresses.

2 Guide the Learning

SCIENCE IDEAS

Ask a volunteer to read aloud page E5 to **identify the main idea: Everything around you is matter.**

- **What do you feel when you wave your hand?**
  air
- **What examples of matter do you see in the classroom?** Answers will vary.

DEVELOP READING SKILLS

Develop Concepts of Print Have children read the question on page E5. Point out and name the question mark. Ask why this punctuation is used. Then point out and name the exclamation mark at the end of the paragraph. Discuss how it is different from the question mark.

BACKGROUND

Webliography GO ONLINE
Keyword states of matter
www.harcourtschool.com

Matter For the purposes of discussion with first graders, defining matter as everything around you is generally considered appropriate. Matter should not be confused with energy, which is also all around you but is not considered matter. Matter is anything that occupies space and has mass. It is made up of atoms and generally exists in three states: solid, liquid, and gas. Plasma is considered by scientists to be a fourth state of matter. Matter has physical properties, such as color, odor, taste, density, and solubility. Unlike liquid and gases that have no shape of their own, solids have definite shape.

SCIENCE WORD WALL

Matter and Solids Put word cards with the words *matter* and *solids* on the Word Wall. Have children write or draw examples of matter and solids.

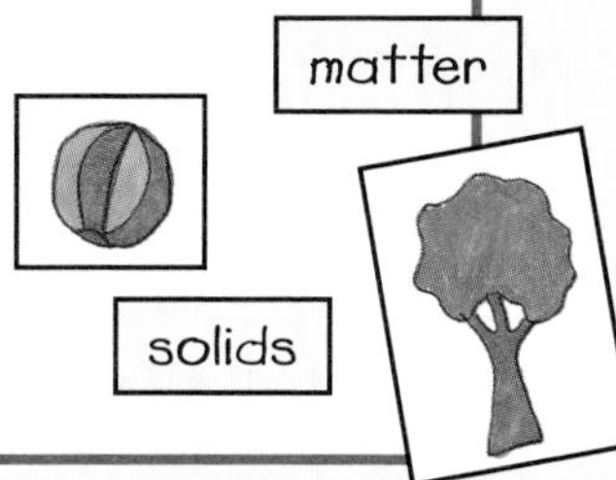

GO ONLINE Technology Link

Visit the Harcourt Learning Site for related links, activities, and resources.
www.harcourtschool.com

Guide the Learning continued

SCIENCE IDEAS

Have children read aloud pages E6–E7. Help them **relate pictures to text** by observing the photo.

- ▶ **What other examples of solid matter can you think of?** anything not a liquid or a gas

Critical Thinking Encourage children to consider different types of solids.

- ▶ **Is sugar a solid? Explain.** Yes. Sugar crystals are very small solids that hold their shape.

Children can use a hand lens to look at sugar crystals to observe their solid properties.

ANALYZE AND INTERPRET DATA

Have children **use the graph for information.**

- ▶ **What do you see in the graph?** different colors of the toys
- ▶ **Which color has the most?** green **Which color has the fewest?** blue
- ▶ **What does the graph show?** how many toys of each color are in the box

USE PROCESS SKILLS

Compare Have children gather and compare solid objects on their own. Have them group the objects and tell which properties they used to sort them.

DEVELOP SCIENCE VOCABULARY

matter Have children paste pictures of different types of matter in a "matter book."

solids Have children list words that describe the properties of solids.

PUPIL'S EDITION OR BIG BOOK

Observing Solids

Some matter is solid. A **solid** is matter that keeps its shape. It keeps its shape even when you move it.

■ **How do you know these toys are solids?**
Each one keeps its shape.

E6

ESL ACTIVITY

Have pairs of children make a *solids* display. Have them draw solid objects and make word cards to label and tell about the objects.

Make this an ongoing activity with children adding word cards for *liquids* and *gases* as they continue through the chapter.

Math Link

Counting Solids Have children make large number cards for the numbers one to ten and place them in order on the floor to make the horizontal axis of a floor graph. Then have them find solid objects in the classroom to correspond to the numbers. For example, 1 plant, 2 chalkboard erasers, 3 crayon boxes, and so on. Have them place the objects in vertical columns above the numbers.

Science Songs

The Science Songs CD provides original children's songs that can be used to reinforce chapter concepts. Use **Track 14** with this chapter.

Sorting Solids

You can sort solids in many ways. You can sort toys by color. This graph shows how many toys of each color there are.

green	■	■	■	■	
yellow	■	■			
red	■	■	■		
blue	■				

■ **What other ways could you sort the toys in the toy box?**
By size, texture, hardness; accept all reasonable answers.

Think About It

1. What is matter?
2. What is a solid?

Literature Connections

Read Alouds

Mushroom in the Rain by Mirra Ginsburg, Aladdin, 1997.

Very Last First Time: An Inuit Tale by Jan Andrews, Simon & Schuster, 1998.

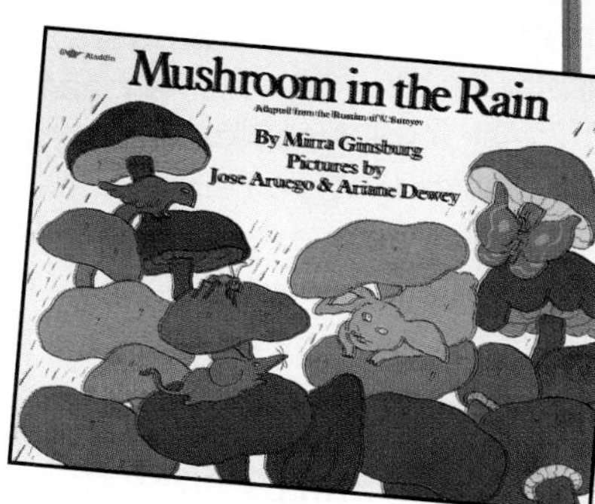

3 Wrap Up and Assess

SUMMARIZE

Have children **summarize** what they have learned. Ask children to help complete the web begun on page E5. Have children fill in different examples of solids and then examples of matter that are not solids.

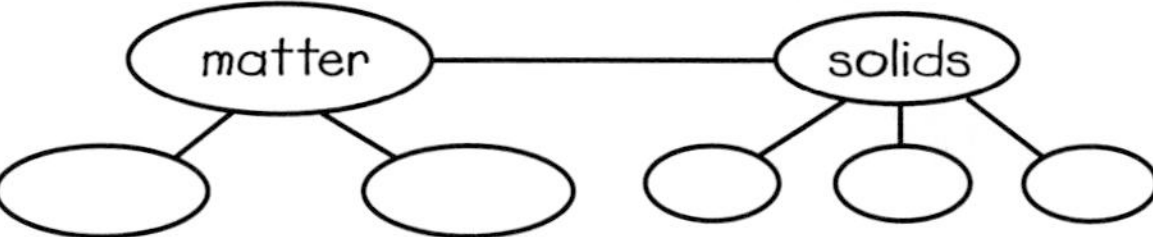

THINK ABOUT IT

1. Matter is everything around us.
2. A solid is a form of matter that keeps its shape when it is moved.

Informal Assessment

Performance Provide children the opportunity to tell you orally or in writing what matter and solids are, and to name some examples. They may want to put their written work in their science journals.

LESSON CONCEPT REVIEW/ASSESSMENT

Children can use **Workbook p. WB109** to review the lesson concepts.

LESSON 2

What Can We Observe About Liquids?

Objectives

- ▶ **Recognize that liquid is matter that flows.**
- ▶ **Observe and describe the properties of liquids.**

Motivate

Play a Game Give one or two clues about a liquid you drank at lunch such as thin or thick, what you poured it into, and the color, and then have children guess what it was. Discuss some liquids that have different properties such as honey, milk, water, and molasses.

Time 20 min **Grouping** individuals

Process Skill use numbers

Preparation Tips and Expected Results See page E2e.

Center Activity Option Place this investigation or a copy of the Investigation, page TR63, in your science center.

Activity Tips

- ▶ Fill the containers with water ahead of time.
- ▶ Model for children how to read a measuring cup. See Science Handbook page T45.

Children may add their recording papers to their science journals.

Activity Questions

- ▶ How much water is in each container?
- ▶ How did your prediction compare with what you found out?

When Minutes Count . . .

As a whole-class activity, fill an 8-oz measuring cup with water. Show children an empty salad dressing bottle and ask them to draw what shape the water will become when you pour it into the bottle. Pour the water and discuss what happened.

PUPIL'S EDITION OR BIG BOOK

LESSON 2

What Can We Observe About Liquids?

Investigate

Liquids in Bottles

You will need

3 containers

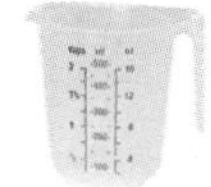

measuring cup

paper and pencil

1. Draw the shape of the water in each container.
2. Which container do you think has the most water?
3. Measure the water. Write a number for each container. Use the numbers to tell what you found out.

Science Skill

You can write numbers when you measure. Use the numbers to compare the things you measured.

E8

Science Skills

Process Skill: Use Numbers

Display Process Skill Tip Transparency E1-2. Ask a volunteer to name the three liquids that are being compared. Read aloud the questions with children and record their answers on the lines provided.

PROCESS SKILLS PRACTICE

To practice and apply process skills, see **Workbook p. WB110.**

Process Skill Tip Transparency E1-2

Use Numbers

Liquid	Amount	Weight
water	2 tablespoons	15 grams
salad oil	2 tablespoons	30 grams
ketchup	2 tablespoons	40 grams

How much of each liquid was measured? 2 tablespoons

How much does each liquid weigh?

liquid	weight
water	15 grams
salad oil	30 grams
ketchup	40 grams

How are the liquids the same? They all have the same amount.

How are they different? Some weigh more than others.

Which liquid is the heaviest? ketchup

Which liquid is the lightest? water

Learn About

Liquids

Matter that flows is called a **liquid**. A liquid does not have a shape of its own. It takes the shape of the container you pour it into.

E9

Learn About

1 Before Reading

PREVIEW/SET PURPOSE

Have children preview pages E9–E11. Draw a web as shown below. Tell children they will help you fill in other properties as the lesson progresses.

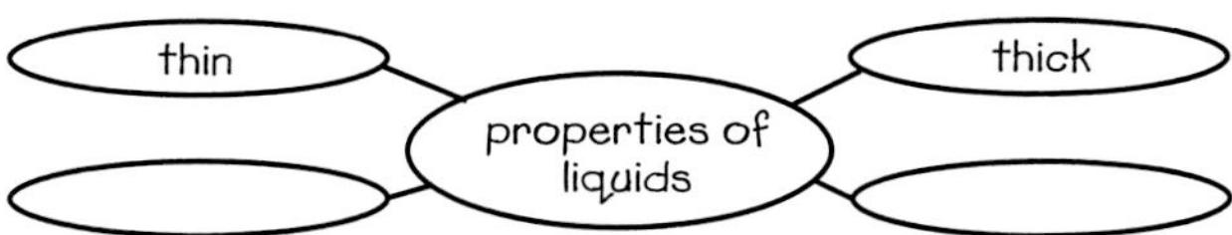

2 Guide the Learning

SCIENCE IDEAS

Have children read page E9. Discuss what they have already learned about matter. Help them **recall supporting facts and details.**

- ▶ **What type of matter is a liquid?** matter that flows
- ▶ **What is the shape of a liquid?** It has no shape of its own. It takes the shape of whatever it is poured into.

DEVELOP READING SKILLS

Relate Pictures to Text Have children observe and describe what happens to the water that is being poured into the containers in the photo.

BACKGROUND

Webliography GO ONLINE
Keyword states of matter
www.harcourtschool.com

Liquids are a state of matter. Unlike solids, they have no form of their own. A liquid fits the shape of any container because its molecules move about freely. When heated, liquids can become gases such as water becoming water vapor, and when cooled, they may become solid such as water becoming ice. Different liquids have different boiling and freezing points.

Water is the most familiar liquid to children, and its properties, such as color, taste, smell, and temperature, can be compared to that of other liquids such as salad oil, honey, dishwashing detergent, and milk.

Liquids can also be compared in terms of their thickness, or *viscosity*, and how they react to water. Oil will not mix with water, for example, while honey eventually will. Honey sinks in water while oil floats.

SCIENCE WORD WALL

Liquids Make a word card for *liquids*. Have children think of different liquids such as water and milk and make word cards for these words. Children can post their word cards and use them in writing as the lesson progresses.

liquids

water

milk

Guide the Learning continued

SCIENCE IDEAS

Read pages E10 and E11. Encourage children to **draw conclusions**.

- ▶ **Where is the milk on page E10? How do you know?** near the right; it's white
- ▶ **Which liquids are thin like milk?** water, juice

USE PROCESS SKILLS

Compare Invite children to brainstorm other thick and thin liquids and compare them to the liquids shown on page E10. Ask them to tell about the thickest and thinnest liquids they know.

VISUAL LEARNING

Have children look at the liquids on page E10 and **predict** and describe how each will act when mixed in water. They can test their predictions by shaking a small amount of each in a jar of water and waiting to see if the liquid separates out.

DEVELOP SCIENCE VOCABULARY

liquid Have children make a list of liquids.

PUPIL'S EDITION OR BIG BOOK

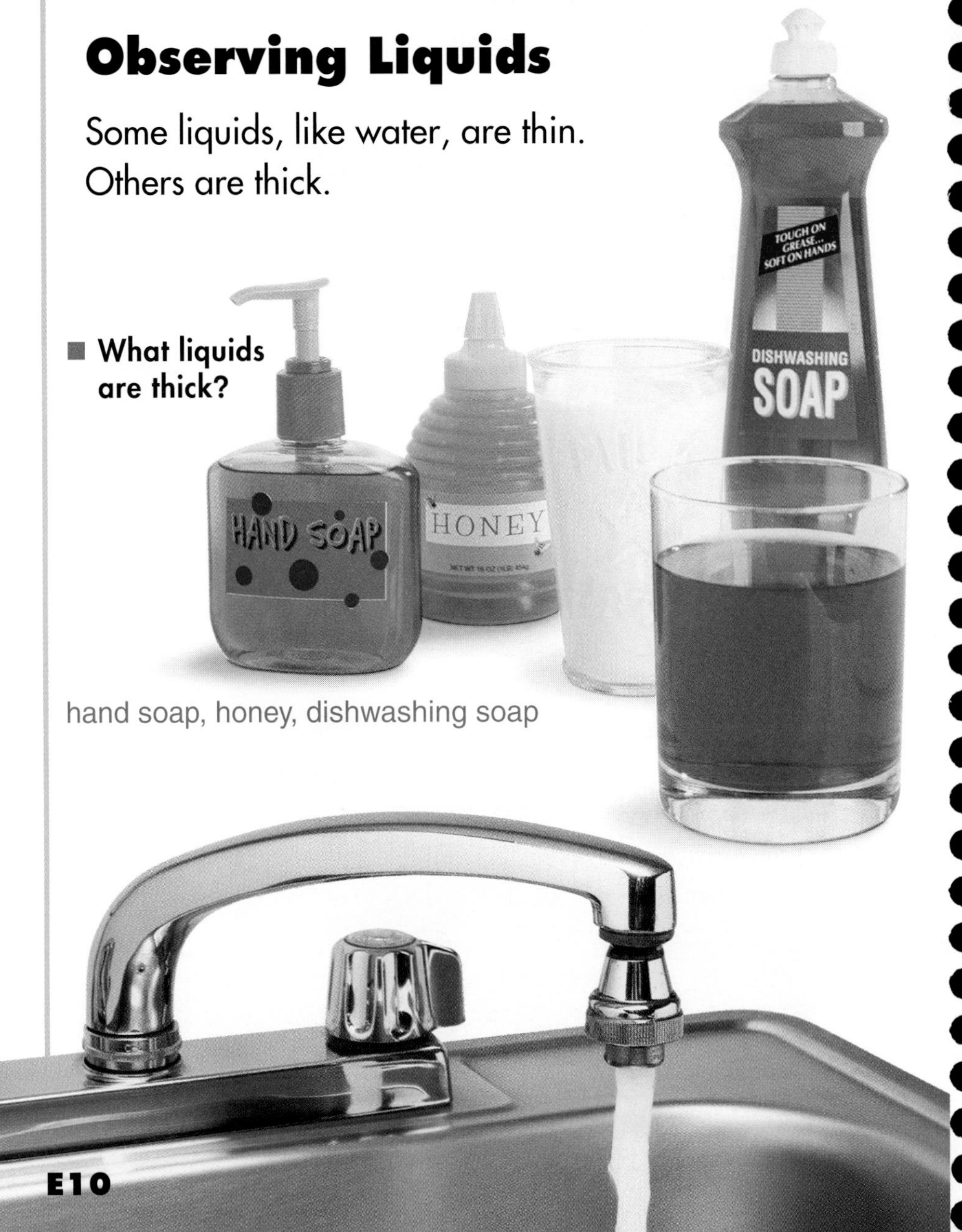

Observing Liquids

Some liquids, like water, are thin. Others are thick.

■ **What liquids are thick?**

hand soap, honey, dishwashing soap

E10

Health Link

Three-Liquid Salad Dressing Children can observe how different liquids interact when they make this salad dressing. In a pint jar with a lid, have them mix $\frac{1}{4}$ cup vinegar with 2 tablespoons lemon juice and describe what happens. Measure and add $\frac{1}{2}$ teaspoon sugar, $\frac{1}{2}$ teaspoon mustard, and a teaspoon of dried herbs. Shake and have children describe how these materials interact. Add $\frac{1}{2}$ cup salad oil and guide children to observe how the oil stays separate. Shake the dressing to distribute the oil. Discuss how oil is a form of fat and should be used sparingly. Explain that shaking the salad dressing before using it helps to mix the oil with the other ingredients.

Reading Mini-Lesson

Use Graphic Sources for Information Read again the text on page E11. Display the transparency and guide children to use the text and photos to answer the questions.

READING SKILLS PRACTICE

To practice and apply this reading skill, see **Workbook p. WB121**.

Reading Mini-Lesson Transparency E1

Use Graphic Sources for Information

1. Which liquid mixes with water? vinegar
2. Which liquid doesn't mix with water? oil

Some liquids mix with water. Vinegar mixes with water. Oil does not mix with water.

Think About It

1. What is a liquid?
2. What can we observe about liquids?

3 Wrap Up and Assess

SUMMARIZE

Have children **summarize** what they have learned. Complete the web started on page E9. Help children list words that tell about the properties of liquids.

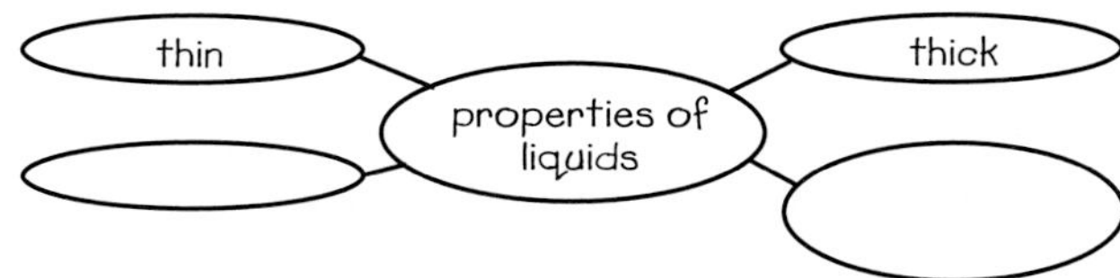

THINK ABOUT IT

1. A liquid is a form of matter that takes the shape of whatever it is poured into.
2. We can observe the color, smell, and thickness of liquids, as well as whether or not they mix with water.

Informal Assessment

Classroom Observation To assess children's understanding of the lesson content, give each child an opportunity to observe and describe different liquids. Note the number of different properties they can identify and describe.

LESSON CONCEPT REVIEW/ASSESSMENT

Children can use **Workbook p. WB111** to review the lesson concepts.

Literature Connections

Read Alouds

Solids and Liquids by David Glover, Kingfisher Books, 1993.

A Raindrop Hit My Nose by Ray Butrum, Multnomah, 1998.

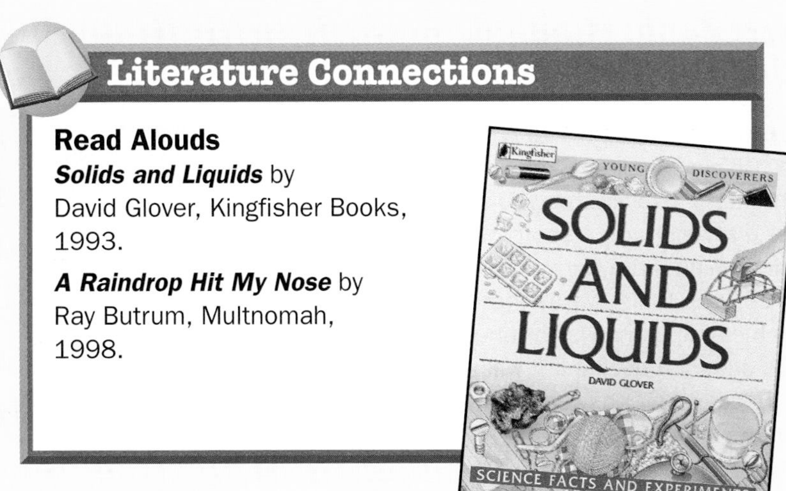

LESSON

3 What Objects Sink or Float?

Objectives

- ▶ **Recognize that some objects sink and others float in water.**
- ▶ **Recognize that objects can be described in terms of their floating and sinking properties.**

Motivate

What Would Happen If . . . Hold up several objects such as a marble, sponge, and pencil eraser and ask what would happen if you put them in water. Challenge children to name three objects that would stay on top of the water and three objects that would not.

Time 20–25 min **Grouping** individuals or pairs

Process Skill gather and record data

Preparation Tips and Expected Results See page E2e.

Center Activity Option Place this investigation or a copy of the Investigation, page TR64, in your science center.

Activity Tips

- ▶ Model how you want children to record their data ahead of time so they include the shape they tried and what happened.

Children may put their record sheets in their science journals.

Activity Questions

- ▶ Which shapes float? Which shapes sink?
- ▶ What is your explanation for why some shapes float?

When Minutes Count . . .

As a whole-class activity, have children brainstorm different shapes that might float and record what happens on chart paper or the board.

PUPIL'S EDITION OR BIG BOOK

LESSON 3

What Objects Sink or Float?

Investigate

Shapes That Sink or Float

You will need

ball of clay

aquarium with water

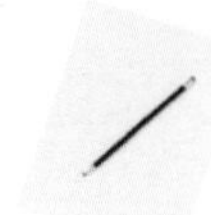

paper and pencil

1. Gather data about shapes that sink or float. Put the clay ball in the water.
2. Record data about what happens.
3. Make the clay into different shapes. Do they sink or float? Record.

Science Skill

When you gather data, you observe things. When you record data, you write and draw what you observe.

E12

Science Skills

Process Skill: Gather and Record Data Display Process Skill Tip Transparency E1-3. Explain that you will gather and record data about objects and determine if they sink or float. Invite children to list words that tell about the shape and weight of each object, and then decide if it will sink or float. Record their answers to the questions on the lines.

Process Skill Tip Transparency E1-3

Gather and Record Data

Object	Shape	Weight (heavy or light)	Sink or Float?
1.	round	heavy	sink
2.	flat	light	float
3.	rectangular, flat	heavy	sink
4.	oval, flat	light	float
5.	flat, rectangular	light	float
6.	long	heavy	sink

Which objects are flat? boat, book, leaf, piece of paper

How are all the objects that float the same?

They are flat and light.

PROCESS SKILLS PRACTICE

To practice and apply process skills, see **Workbook p. WB112**.

Learn About

Objects That Sink or Float

Some objects **float**, or stay on top of a liquid. Others **sink**, or drop to the bottom of a liquid. You can change the shape of some objects to make them float or sink.

E13

Learn About

1 Before Reading

PREVIEW/SET PURPOSE

Have children preview pages E13–E15. Draw two charts. Tell children they will fill in the charts with objects that sink and float and list their properties, such as shape and size.

Objects That Sink	
Name	Properties

Objects That Float	
Name	Properties

2 Guide the Learning

SCIENCE IDEAS

Read aloud page E13. **Identify the main idea: Some objects float in liquid, others sink.**

- ▶ **What does *float* mean?** to stay on top of a liquid
- ▶ **What does *sink* mean?** to drop to the bottom of a liquid

DEVELOP READING SKILLS

Identify Cause and Effect Ask children to observe and describe the objects in the photo that are floaters and sinkers. Ask:

- ▶ **What can you do to floaters to make them sinkers?** change their shape, add mass
- ▶ **What can you do to sinkers to make them floaters?** change their shape, take away mass

BACKGROUND

Webliography GO ONLINE
Keyword properties of matter
www.harcourtschool.com

Objects That Sink or Float Solid objects can be described in terms of whether they stay near the top of water, or drop below the surface of the water. Changing an object's shape can change whether it sinks or floats. This is because the amount of space an object occupies, relative to its mass, affects how much water can push up on it. A lump of clay the size of a Ping Pong ball will sink, but flatten the lump, roll up the sides a bit, and the clay floats.

Archimedes, a Greek scientist, found that the buoyant, or lifting, force on an object is the same as the weight of the liquid that the object displaces. If an object and the displaced liquid weigh the same, the object floats. So, you could weigh yourself by entering a completely full pool and measuring the water that spills out.

SCIENCE WORD WALL

Float and Sink Add the words *float* and *sink* to the Word Wall.

float

sink

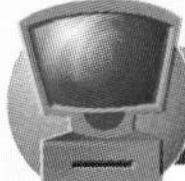

Technology Link

Children can learn more about sinking or floating in *Sink or Float?* by Leslie Fox on **Harcourt Science Instant Readers CD-ROM.**

Learn more about sinking and floating by visiting the National Air and Space Museum Internet Site. **www.si.edu/harcourt/science**

Guide the Learning continued

SCIENCE IDEAS

Have children read pages E14 and E15. Have them find objects and guess which will float and which will sink. Encourage them to find objects they are not sure about. Then have them plan and conduct a simple investigation to test their guesses.

Critical Thinking Ask children to tell about objects they guessed would be floaters but were sinkers (or the other way around). Ask:

- **Why did you think it would float (or sink)?** Answers will vary. **Why do you think it did the opposite?** Encourage all responses.

VISUAL LEARNING

Help children list the objects shown. Have them sort the list into those that float and those that sink. Then have them write words to describe properties that make them that way.

USE PROCESS SKILLS

Compare Have children identify objects that have the same shape, but which are floaters or sinkers such as marbles and rubber balls. Have them compare the objects and think about other properties that might make them float or sink.

DEVELOP SCIENCE VOCABULARY

float and **sink** To help children recognize that *float* and *sink* are properties that can be used to describe matter besides solids, float some oil on water.

PUPIL'S EDITION OR BIG BOOK

Floaters and Sinkers

Some objects have shapes that help them float. Others have shapes that make them sink.

You can not always guess which objects will float. You must test them to find out.

E14

Investigation Challenge

Hands-On Activity: Observe How Water Pushes Up

Challenge children to observe how water pushes up on objects to help make them float. Use a string tied to the center of a ruler to make a simple balance, and attach two identical sinkers, such as weights or pennies wrapped in foil, to the ends of the ruler as shown. The sinkers should balance. Slowly lower the balance so that one of the sinkers drops into a bowl of water. Children will see the water push up (exert a force) on the sinker and tip the balance.

Art Link

***Floaters and Sinkers* Collage** Have children collect pictures of things that float and sink, as well as actual objects that they can glue on construction paper to make a collage. Have them design their collage to sort the floaters from the sinkers, and label each group. Display the collages.

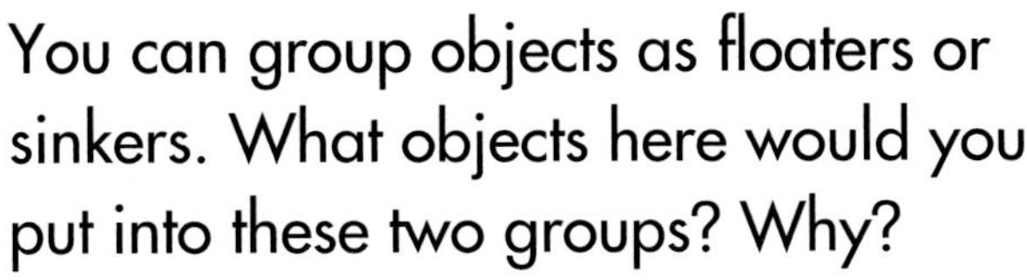

You can group objects as floaters or sinkers. What objects here would you put into these two groups? Why?

Float: driftwood, beach ball, and boat.

Sink: rock, shell, and anchor.

Think About It

1. What do *float* and *sink* mean?
2. What helps an object sink or float?

3 Wrap Up and Assess

SUMMARIZE

Have children **summarize** what they have learned. Return to the charts begun on page E13 and have children write the names of floaters and sinkers and their properties.

Objects That Sink	
Name	Properties

Objects That Float	
Name	Properties

THINK ABOUT IT

1. To float is to stay on top of a liquid. To sink is to drop to the bottom.
2. Changing the shape of an object helps it sink or float.

Informal Assessment

Portfolio Assess children's understanding of floating and sinking by having them divide a sheet of paper into two parts. They can label one part *Float* and the other part *Sink*. Then have them draw, cut out and glue, or list objects for each category. They may add their work to their portfolios.

LESSON CONCEPT REVIEW/ASSESSMENT

Children can use **Workbook p. WB113** to review the lesson concepts.

Literature Connections

Harcourt Science Instant Reader

Sink or Float?

by Leslie Fox.

Also available on CD-ROM.

Read Aloud

Sunken Treasure

by Gail Gibbons,

HarperCollins, 1988.

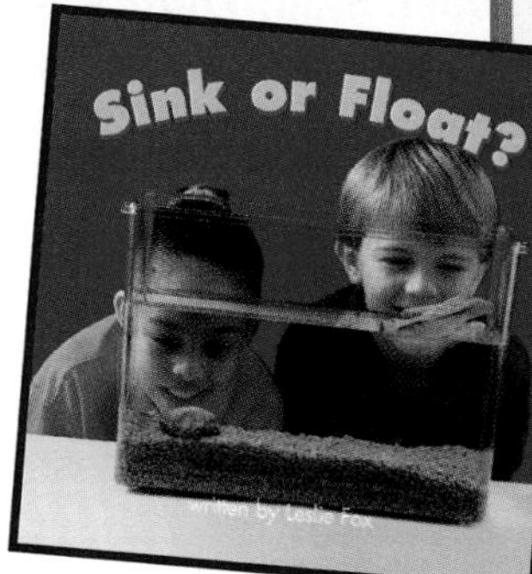

LESSON 4

What Solids Dissolve in Liquids?

Objectives

- ▶ Predict how a solid acts when mixed with water.
- ▶ Classify solids into those that will dissolve in water and those that will not.

Motivate

Observe a Cup of Water Display a cup of water. Ask children if anything else is or could be in the water. Write children's ideas on the board.

Investigate

Time 30 min **Grouping** pairs or small groups

Process Skill form a hypothesis

Preparation Tips and Expected Results See page E2f.

Center Activity Option Place this investigation or a copy of the Investigation, page TR65, in your science center.

Activity Tips

Safety Tip Caution children to use the stirring sticks *only* for their intended purpose in order to avoid accidents.

- ▶ Prepare the cups prior to the activity. The water should be at room temperature in order for the salt and baking soda to dissolve easily.
- ▶ Model how to make the chart on page TR166, and fill it in.

Children can make the chart in their science journals.

Activity Questions

- ▶ Which solids dissolved in the water?
- ▶ What other solids could you test with water?

When Minutes Count . . .

Invite one student to lead the class through the steps of the Investigate. If you wish, have a different student test each solid.

PUPIL'S EDITION OR BIG BOOK

What Solids Dissolve in Liquids?

Investigate

Solids in Water

You will need

stirring stick

paper and pencil

solids to test

4 cups of water

1. What do you think these solids will do in water? Form a hypothesis for each one.
2. Put a solid into water. Stir for a minute. When the water stops swirling, observe.
3. Can you see the solid in the water? Record what you observe. Repeat for the other solids.

Solids in Water

	My hypothesis		My results	
	Will dissolve	Will not dissolve	Did dissolve	Did not dissolve
salt				
sand				
rocks				
baking soda				

Science Skill

When you form a hypothesis you choose and test a possible answer.

Science Skills

Process Skill: Form a Hypothesis

Display Process Skill Transparency E1-4. Read the title. Have students recall the hypotheses they formed as they did the Investigate. Invite them to form hypotheses about the solids named on the transparency. Record children's ideas. Guide them to construct a plan for testing their hypotheses.

Process Skill Tip Transparency E1-4

Form a Hypothesis

Solids in Water

	My Hypothesis	
	Will Dissolve	Will Not Dissolve
Soil		x
Sugar	x	
Pepper		x

PROCESS SKILLS PRACTICE

To practice and apply process skills, see **Workbook p. WB114**.

Solids in Liquids

Some solids do not mix well with a liquid. They do not **dissolve**, or mix with the liquid completely. Soil and sand do not dissolve in water.

soil in water

E17

1 Before Reading

PREVIEW/SET PURPOSE

Have children preview pages E17–E19. Make a chart as shown. Tell children that they will help fill in the names of solids that do and do not dissolve in water.

Solids That Dissolve in Water	Solids That Do Not Dissolve in Water

2 Guide the Learning

SCIENCE IDEAS

Read aloud page E17. **Identify the main idea: Some solids do not mix well with a liquid. They do not dissolve, or mix with the liquid completely.**

- ▶ **What is the child in the photo doing with the soil?** mixing it with the water
- ▶ **Is soil a solid that does or does not dissolve in water?** does not
- ▶ **How do you know that the soil has not dissolved?** It is not mixed in completely.

DEVELOP READING SKILLS

Build Vocabulary Direct attention to the photos one at a time. Have children use the word *dissolve* in sentences that describe each photo.

BACKGROUND

Webliography
Keyword properties of matter
www.harcourtschool.com
GO ONLINE

Solutions When one substance dissolves completely in another, the result is a solution. Carbonated water is a solution of a gas, carbon dioxide, and a liquid, water. Coffee, tea, and powdered drinks are solutions made up of a solid dissolved in a liquid. The consistency and composition of a solution is uniform throughout; the substances that form a solution cannot be separated by filtration.

Dissolving Liquids in Liquids Some liquids, such as vinegar and alcohol, dissolve in water. Other liquids, such as oil, do not dissolve in water. Similarly, oil does not dissolve in vinegar or in alcohol.

Suspensions When tiny particles of one substance are suspended in another substance, the result is a colloidal suspension. Paint is an example of a suspension. A chief difference between suspensions and solutions is the size of the particles.

SCIENCE WORD WALL

Solids That Do and Do Not Dissolve Make a word card for the word *dissolve* and phrase cards that say *Dissolves in Water* and *Does Not Dissolve in Water.* Have children post pictures of solids that do and do not dissolve in water.

dissolve

ESL ACTIVITY

In discussing the lesson concepts, create a word diagram, such as the one shown below, for children to use as a reference.

Sugar in Hot Tea → Dissolves Quickly

Sugar in Cold Tea → Dissolves Slowly

Guide the Learning continued

SCIENCE IDEAS

Have children read aloud pages E18–E19. Help children **identify the main idea**: **Some solids you use at home dissolve in water.** Ask:

- ▶ **How are solids different?** some dissolve in water; some do not

USE PROCESS SKILLS

Compare Have children compare the photos of the child mixing the drink mix on page E18.

- ▶ **What happened to the solid?** It dissolved in the liquid.

VISUAL LEARNING

To help children **use context,** direct their attention to the photos. Have children use picture clues to determine whether the tea is hot or cold. Ask:

- ▶ **How does the temperature of the tea affect what happens to the sugar?** Sugar dissolves quickly in hot tea, but slowly in cold tea.

Critical Thinking Guide children to construct a plan for testing other solids in hot and cold liquids. Ask:

- ▶ **How could you find out if salt dissolves faster in hot water than in cold water?** Put the solid in hot and cold water and observe.

DEVELOP SCIENCE VOCABULARY

dissolve Have children list solids that dissolve in water and solids that do not dissolve in water.

PUPIL'S EDITION OR BIG BOOK

Observing Solids That Dissolve

Some solids you use at home dissolve in water. Sugar and salt dissolve in water. Baking soda dissolves in water. Many kinds of drink mixes also dissolve in water.

E18

Investigation Challenge

Hands-On Activity: Do Liquids Dissolve in Liquids?
Set up three clear plastic cups of water and one cup of vinegar, one cup of cooking oil, and one cup of rubbing alcohol. Use food coloring to give the vinegar and rubbing alcohol an observable color. Ask children to form a hypothesis about what will happen if you pour some vinegar into the water. Write their hypothesis on the board. Call on a volunteer to test the hypothesis. Ask children to summarize the results of the test in a sentence. Write the sentence on the board.

Repeat the procedure with the other liquids. Vinegar and rubbing alcohol dissolve in water; cooking oil does not. Read aloud the sentences children have generated. Ask a volunteer to suggest a sentence that states the main idea: Some liquids dissolve in water, and some do not.

Math Link

Measure and Compare Have children measure and pour 240 ml (one cup) of cold water into a glass and 240 ml of warm water into another glass. Call on a volunteer to measure, pour, and stir 15 ml (1 tablespoon) of sugar into the warm water until it is dissolved while another child uses a stop watch to determine the time it takes for the sugar to dissolve. Repeat the process with the cold water. Guide children to compare the results:

- **How can we find out how much longer it took for the sugar to dissolve in the cold water than in the warm water?** subtract the time for the warm water from the time for the cold water

Guide children in setting up the math problem and calculating the answer.

Some solids dissolve faster in a hot liquid than in a cold liquid. Salt dissolves quickly in hot water but slowly in cold water.

- **What happens when you put sugar into liquids at different temperatures?** Sugar dissolves quickly in hot tea; sugar dissolves slowly in cold tea.

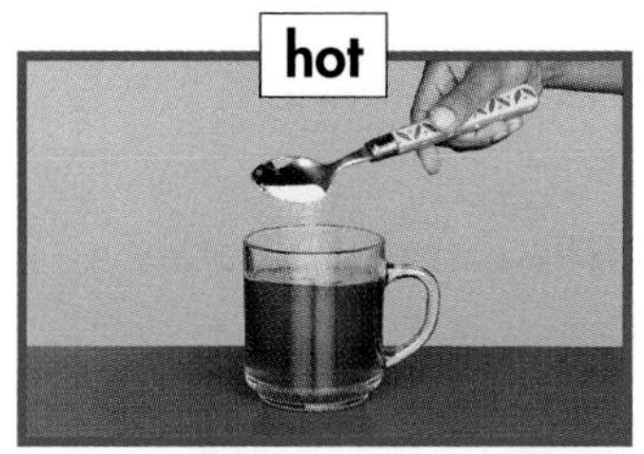

Think About It

1. What happens when a solid dissolves in a liquid?
2. When do some solids dissolve faster in a liquid?

Literature Connections

Read Alouds

Lemonade for Sale by Stuart J. Murphy, HarperColllins, 1998.

Grandpa's Soup by Eiko Kadono, Eerdmans Books for Young Readers, 1999.

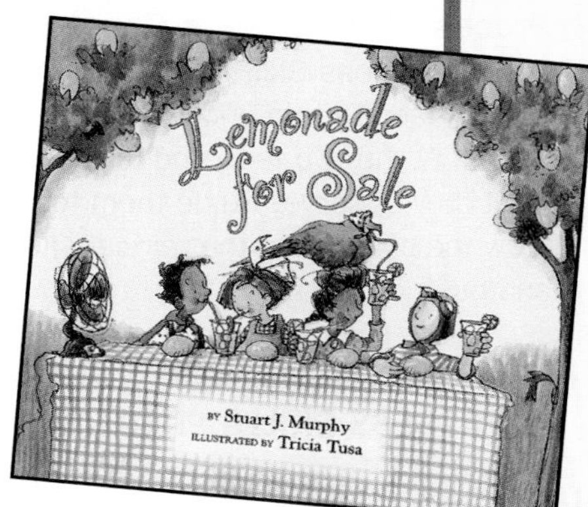

3 Wrap Up and Assess

SUMMARIZE

Have children **summarize** what they have learned. Refer back to the web you began on page E17. Have children help you list the different solids that do and do not dissolve in water.

Solids That Dissolve in Water	Solids That Do Not Dissolve in Water

THINK ABOUT IT

1. It mixes with the liquid completely.
2. when the liquid is warm or hot

Informal Assessment

Performance Provide children with the option of retelling the key concepts in this lesson orally or in writing. Some children may prefer to demonstrate their understanding by forming a hypothesis and then conducting a test to see whether a solid does or does not dissolve in water.

LESSON CONCEPT REVIEW/ASSESSMENT

Children can use **Workbook p. WB115** to review the lesson concepts.

Reaching All Learners

Kinesthetic Learners Children who learn best kinesthetically may find the lesson concepts easier to understand if they test the various examples themselves and observe the results.

LESSON 5

What Can We Observe About Gases?

Objectives

- ▶ Recognize that gas is matter that fills and takes the shape of the container it is in.
- ▶ Observe and describe the properties of gases.

Motivate

Dramatize Blow some bubbles for children to observe. Then ask what is inside a bubble that makes it round. Explain that when you blow, your breath is a gas that fills the bubble.

Investigate

Time 15 min **Grouping** individuals

Process Skill draw a conclusion

Preparation Tips and Expected Results See page E2f.

Center Activity Option Place this investigation or a copy of the Investigation, page TR66, in your science center.

Activity Tips

Safety Tip Warn children not to share balloons because of germs. Caution them to be careful with balloons to avoid choking.

- ▶ Guide children to reuse or recycle the bottles, if possible, and to dispose of the balloons by putting them in the trash.

Children may draw pictures in their science journals to show what happens when they try to blow up the balloon.

Activity Questions

- ▶ Why can't you blow up the balloon when it is inside the bottle?
- ▶ What would happen if you made a hole in the bottle and tried to blow up the balloon?

When Minutes Count . . .

As a whole-class activity, have a volunteer first blow up the balloon, then try to blow it up in the bottle.

What Can We Observe About Gases?

Investigate

Air in a Bottle

You will need

balloon

plastic soft drink bottle

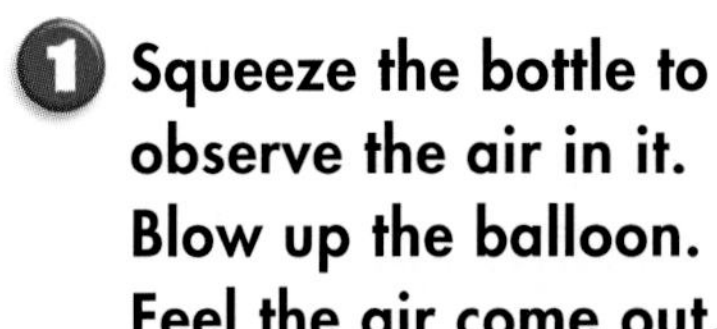

1. Squeeze the bottle to observe the air in it. Blow up the balloon. Feel the air come out.
2. Put the balloon in the bottle. Pull the end over the top.

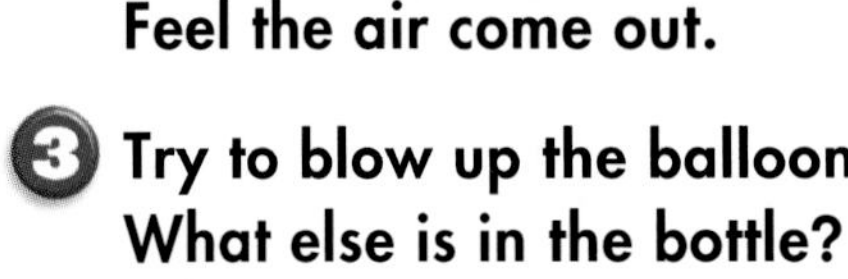

3. Try to blow up the balloon. What else is in the bottle? Draw a conclusion.

Science Skill

To draw a conclusion about what happened, think about what you observed.

Science Skills

Process Skill: Draw a Conclusion

Display Process Skill Tip Transparency E1-5. Read the title and ask children to look at the two fans and tell you what they observe. Guide them to draw the conclusion that air can blow and push on things.

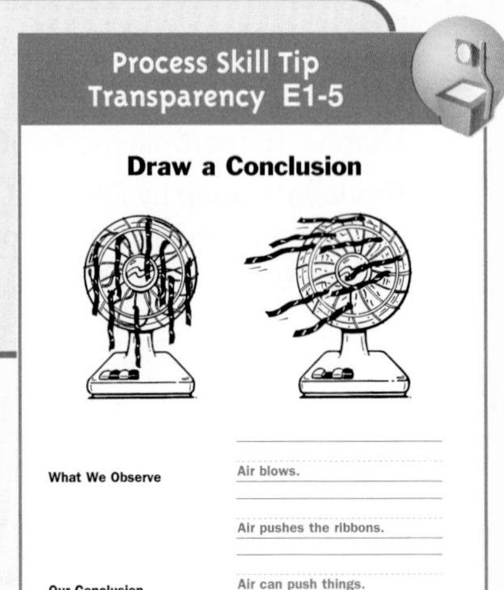

Process Skill Tip
Transparency E1-5
Draw a Conclusion
What We Observe
Air blows.
Air pushes the ribbons.
Our Conclusion
Air can push things.
Air blows.

PROCESS SKILLS PRACTICE

To practice and apply process skills, see **Workbook p. WB116.**

Learn About

Gases

Gases are matter. A **gas** does not have a shape of its own. It spreads out to fill its container and take its shape.

E21

Learn About

1 Before Reading

PREVIEW/SET PURPOSE

Have children preview pages E21–E23. Make a web as shown. Tell children that they will help you fill in the different properties of gases.

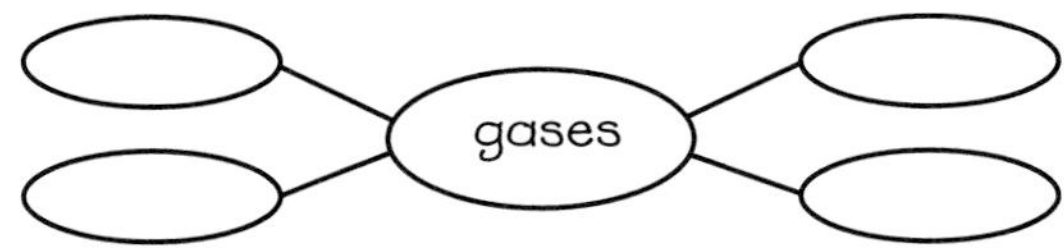

2 Guide the Learning

SCIENCE IDEAS

Read aloud page E21. **Identify the main idea: Gases are matter with no shape of their own.**

- ▶ **What are gases?** matter
- ▶ **What are some properties of gases or ways they act?** no shape of their own, spread out to fill containers and take their shape

Critical Thinking To help children compare gases and liquids, ask:

- ▶ **How are gases different from liquids?** Gases spread out to fill whatever space they are in, while liquids do not.

DEVELOP READING SKILLS

Relate Pictures to Text Have children identify where gases are present in the photo.

BACKGROUND

Webliography

GO ONLINE

Keyword changes in matter

www.harcourtschool.com

Gases Like solids and liquids, gases are a form of matter with properties that can be observed and described. Gases spread out to fill whatever empty space they occupy, from balloons and bubbles to rooms, or Earth's atmosphere.

Water vapor, oxygen, and carbon dioxide are some gases that children have experience with. They can see carbon dioxide bubbles in soda water, oxygen bubbles on the *elodea* plant in fish tanks, and observe water evaporate and become invisible as water vapor. These gases are odorless and colorless, but others can smell like rotten eggs or swampy muck. Children can experience how gases act when they squeeze an inflated balloon, open a bottle of soda water, or stand in front of a fan.

SCIENCE WORD WALL

What Gas Can Do Make a word card for the word *gas*. Then as the lesson continues, have children make word cards for terms that tell what gas can do.

gas

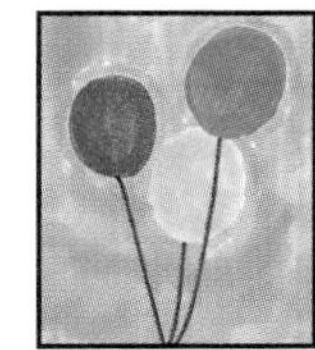

ESL Activity Children can cut pictures from magazines or draw their own pictures to show what gas can do. Have them add the pictures to the Word Wall.

Guide the Learning continued

SCIENCE IDEAS

Have children read aloud pages E22 and E23. Help them **identify cause and effect** by asking them to tell what gases are doing in each picture.

USE PROCESS SKILLS

Observe and Compare Have children observe the photo of the inverted glass in the bowl of water. Ask them to compare the air in the glass with the air in the bottle when they tried to blow up the balloon.

Critical Thinking Have children observe the boy with the balloons and ask how the helium, which is the gas inside the balloons, makes the balloons float in the air.

▶ **Is helium heavier or lighter than air?** lighter **How do you know?** It makes the balloons float.

VISUAL LEARNING

Help children **predict outcomes** by having them look at each photo and tell what would happen if the gases escaped or disappeared.

DEVELOP SCIENCE VOCABULARY

gas Help children think of places where gases might be found, such as gas stoves, clothes dryers, car and bicycle tires, containers of gas for outdoor barbecues, rising from a tea kettle, and scuba divers' air tanks. Suggest that children draw pictures or cut out scenes showing where gases might be found.

PUPIL'S EDITION OR BIG BOOK

Observing Gases
Gases are all around you. Air is made up of different gases. You can not see most gases, but you can see what they do.
A gas fills up the space inside a balloon. A fan makes air blow your hair.
E22

Reaching All Learners

Kinesthetic Learners Have children blow soap bubbles since bubbles contain air or gas, stand in front of a fan to feel air blow on them, and open a bottle of soda water to see gas bubbles. Then ask them to tell what gases can do.

Social Studies Link

The Big Balloon Race In 1882, balloonist Carlotta Myers entered a balloon race and discovered that her young daughter had stowed away on the flight. Have children read *The Big Balloon Race* by Eleanor Coerr (Harpercrest, 1992), make illustrations of the historic flight, and write captions.

THE QUESTIONS KIDS ASK!

What gas do I put in a balloon when I use my breath to blow it up?

Address Misconceptions When you breathe out, your breath is mostly carbon dioxide, a gas your body releases through your lungs. So when you blow up a balloon, or into a paper bag, the gas you put inside is carbon dioxide. This is the same gas used to put bubbles in soda water. Provide children with small paper bags. Ask them to observe what happens when they blow in it. Invite them to discuss what filled the paper bags. **CAUTION: To avoid suffocation, tell children not to cover both their nose and mouth when blowing into the bag.**

Some gases, like the gas in this soft drink, can mix with water. You can see bubbles in the soft drink as the gas comes out.

Like all matter, gases take up space. Air takes up space in this cup, so no water can come in.

Think About It

1. What are gases?
2. What can we observe about gases?

E23

3 Wrap Up and Assess

SUMMARIZE

Have children **summarize** what they have learned. Refer back to the web you began on page E21. Have children help you fill in the different properties of gases.

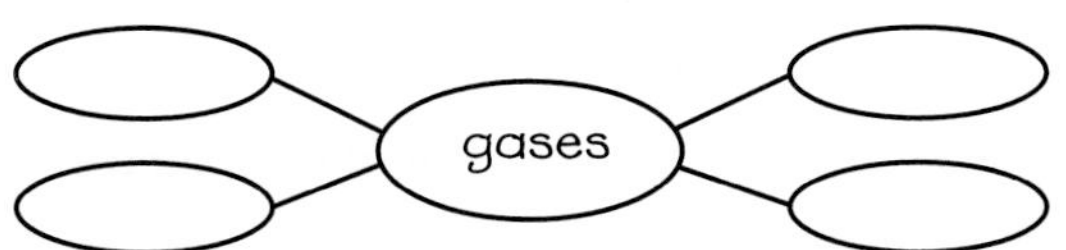

THINK ABOUT IT

1. Gases are a form of matter that spread out to fill and take the shape of whatever container they're in.
2. We can observe what gases do, such as take up space inside bottles, fill balloons and bubbles, or push on things.

Informal Assessment

Portfolio Assess children's understanding of gases by having them draw pictures that show what gases can do. Have them write captions to tell what they know. They may put their work in their portfolios.

LESSON CONCEPT REVIEW/ASSESSMENT

Children can use **Workbook p. WB117** to review the lesson concepts.

Literature Connections

Read Alouds

The Grumpalump by Sarah Hayes, Clarion, 1990.

Balloons: Building and Experimenting with Inflatable Toys by Bernie Zubrowski, Morrow, 1990.

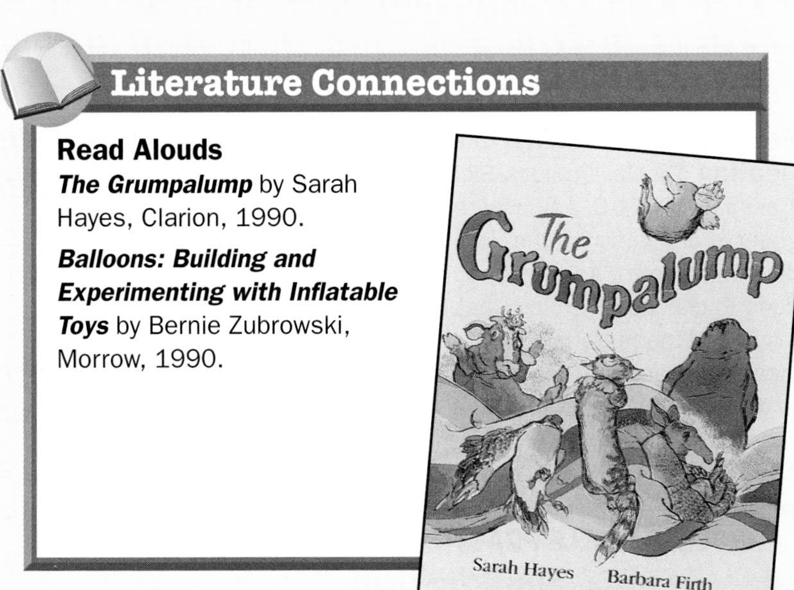

LESSON 6

How Can We Change Objects?

Objectives

- Recognize that things can be done to solid matter to change its properties.
- Observe and describe the behavior of solid matter when we do things to change it.

Motivate

Play a Game Give each child a small piece of foil and ask him or her to change it. Wait a few seconds and then ask volunteers to tell what they did.

Safety Tip Tell children not to put foil or glitter in their mouths, eyes, ears, or noses.

Investigate

Time 20–25 min **Grouping** individuals

Process Skill conduct an investigation

Preparation Tips and Expected Results See page E2f.

Center Activity Option Place this investigation or a copy of the Investigation, page TR67, in your science center.

Activity Tips

- Model how to use the slits to assemble a structure.
- Model ways to record the changes so children can use their data to communicate what they did.

Children may add their recorded data or pictures of their structures to their science journals.

Activity Questions

- How do your cards look and feel?
- How are your cards the same as they were when you started? How are they different?

When Minutes Count . . .

Use the Activity Video to preview and model ways to change the cards. Discuss ways the cards are the same and different after the investigation.

PUPIL'S EDITION OR BIG BOOK

How Can We Change Objects?

Investigate

Changing Paper

You will need

4 cards with slits

paints and brushes

glitter

glue

paper and pencil

1. Observe the cards. Record how they look and feel.
2. How could you change the way the cards look and feel? Investigate your ideas.
3. Record how you change the cards.

Science Skill

To investigate, think of changes you could make, and then try them out.

E24

Science Skills

Process Skill: Conduct an Investigation Display Process Skill Tip Transparency E1-6. Ask children to observe and describe the doll-like object as shown. Ask what could be done to change it. Explain that they might use the materials shown. Write ideas for changes. Then ask for words to describe the object after the changes have been made.

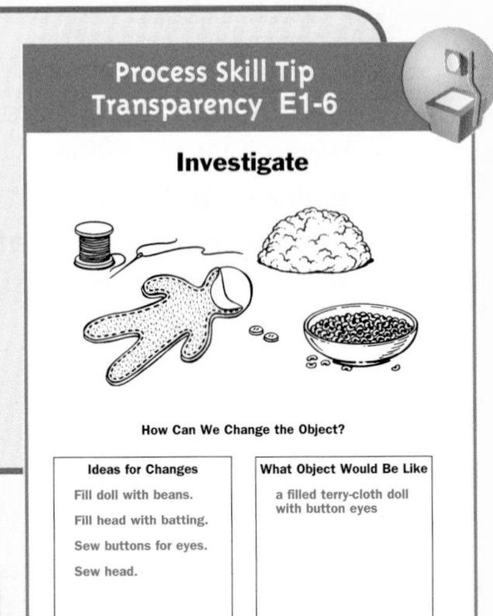

Process Skill Tip Transparency E1-6

Investigate

How Can We Change the Object?

Ideas for Changes	What Object Would Be Like
Fill doll with beans. Fill head with batting. Sew buttons for eyes. Sew head.	a filled terry-cloth doll with button eyes

PROCESS SKILLS PRACTICE

To practice and apply process skills, see **Workbook p. WB118.**

Learn About

Changing Objects

You can **change** objects, or make them different. You can change their shape, size, color, or texture.

E25

Learn About

1 Before Reading

PREVIEW/SET PURPOSE

Have children preview pages E25–E27. Make a chart as shown. Invite children to name objects, tell ways to change objects, and describe how each object would be changed. Tell them that they will help you fill in the chart as the lesson progresses.

Object	Ways to Change Objects	How Object Was Changed

2 Guide the Learning

SCIENCE IDEAS

Read aloud page E25 with children. **Identify the main idea: You can change objects.**

- **What are the children in the photo doing to change the paper?** cutting, folding, pasting
- **How is the paper changing?** size, shape

DEVELOP READING SKILLS

Build Vocabulary Write the word *change* on the board. Discuss ways to use the word, such as *make change, a change of clothes, change how something looks.* Have them write sentences, using the word to give directions. Children can exchange their sentences and have a partner follow their directions.

BACKGROUND

Webliography GO ONLINE
Keyword states of matter
www.harcourtschool.com

Changing Matter Things can be done to materials to change their properties, but not all materials respond the same way. You can change the shape, size, color, or texture of an object by cutting, painting, or adding something to it. When finished, you have changed its properties without having changed the basic material from which it was made.

Different forms of matter act differently when they interact. When sugar, a solid, mixes with water, a liquid, the sugar dissolves. It breaks down in the water and you can't see it anymore. When you mix cornstarch with water, you discover new properties not present in either before mixing. But when you mix sand with water, the sand does not interact with the water because neither substance changes.

Substances can also be changed by heating or cooling them. Water changes from a solid to a liquid or a gas with the application of heat.

SCIENCE WORD WALL

Change Have children make a word card for the word *change.* Then have them make word cards for things they can do to objects to change them. Post the cards on the Word Wall.

change

Guide the Learning continued

SCIENCE IDEAS

Have children read aloud pages E26–E27. Guide them to **identify cause and effect** by having them point to each example and describe what was done to each object to change it. Ask how the properties of the object are the same and different.

USE PROCESS SKILLS

Compare Have children compare the two photos of the boy making frozen ice pops on page E26.

▶ **What form of matter is the juice in the first picture?** liquid **How can you tell?** It flows out of the cup.

▶ **What form of matter is the juice in the second picture?** solid **How can you tell?** It holds its shape.

Critical Thinking Use this question to help reinforce ways objects can be changed.

▶ **How could you change a lump of bread dough into a pretzel?** roll it, bend it, twist it, sprinkle salt on it, put butter on it, bake it

VISUAL LEARNING

Give children a lump of clay and have them find ways to change it. Have them measure with paper clips and record the changes they make, and communicate what they did.

DEVELOP SCIENCE VOCABULARY

change Make sure children understand that *change* in this lesson means "to make different." Have them use the word in sentences.

PUPIL'S EDITION OR BIG BOOK

Observing Changes

You can change objects in different ways. You can roll or bend some objects to change their shape.

■ **How can you change clay from a lump into coils that stack?**

Roll the clay to make the coils. Bend to stack.

You can change some liquids by freezing them. Freezing changes fruit juice into a frozen ice pop.

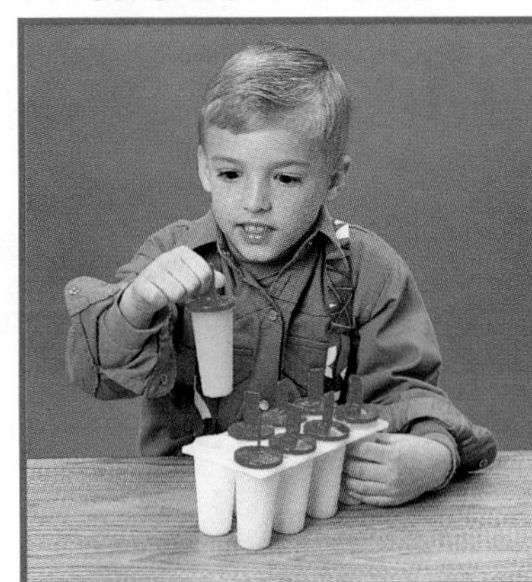

E26

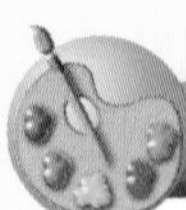

Art Link

Make a Rock Animal Have children bring in rocks and use paints, glue, cotton balls, and other materials to make rock animals. Have them record the changes they made and how the materials changed as they put them together to make the animal.

Investigation Challenge

Hands-On Activity: Mixing Cornstarch with Water

Have children observe and describe cornstarch and water separately. Then mix two parts cornstarch with one part water and have children observe and describe the mixture. Challenge them to classify the mixture as a solid or liquid. Point out that it can be described as either.

You can change an object by mixing it with other things. You might make a rock animal for fun. It might be a mix of the rock, paint, and other things.

■ **How did someone change this rock to look like a spider?**

painted it and glued pom poms, plastic eyes, and chenille sticks to it

Think About It

1. What are some things you can change about objects?
2. What are three things you can do to objects to change them?

E27

Literature Connections

Harcourt Science Instant Reader
Heat Changes Things
by Michael Medearis.
Also available on CD-ROM.

Read Aloud
Paper, Paper Everywhere
by Gail Gibbons,Voyager, 1997.

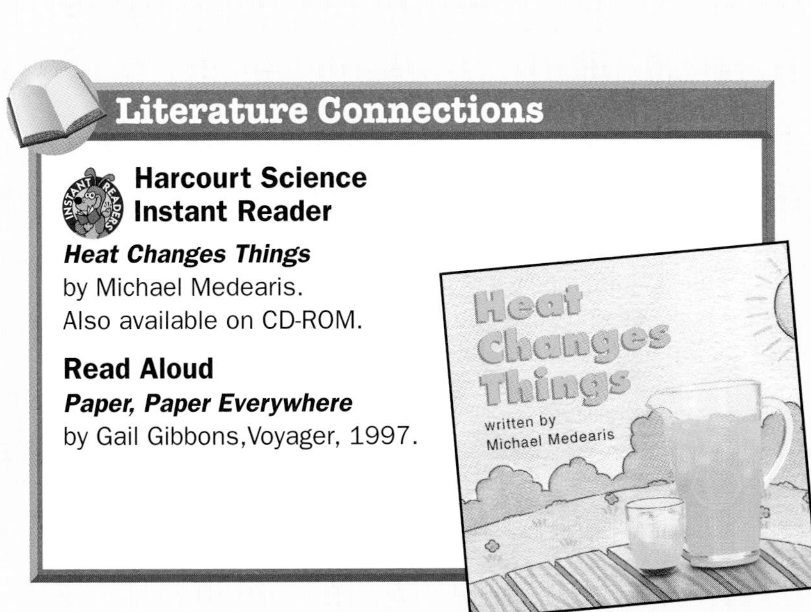

3 Wrap Up and Assess

SUMMARIZE

Have children **summarize** what they have learned. Refer back to the chart begun on page E25. Have children help you fill in different things you can do to objects to change them. Then have them write words that tell how properties of objects change as you do things to them.

Object	Ways to Change Objects	How Object Was Changed

THINK ABOUT IT

1. You can change an object's shape, size, color, and texture.
2. You can roll, freeze, and mix objects with other things to change them.

Informal Assessment

Performance Provide children with the opportunity to tell you about things they can do to objects to change them and how the objects' properties change. They can tell you orally or in writing. Some may prefer to show you by actually changing an object.

LESSON CONCEPT REVIEW/ASSESSMENT

Children can use **Workbook p. WB119** to review the lesson concepts.

VOCABULARY REVIEW

Children can use **Workbook p. WB120** to review the chapter vocabulary.

Chapter 1 Links

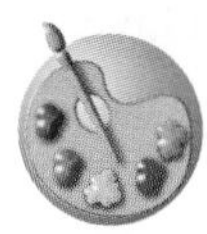

Art Link
Mixing Objects to Make Art

Link Objective Recognize that knowledge about science is used in art.

Talk about the photographs. Ask children to tell what makes the sculpture look like a bull's head. shape of the seat and handlebars Ask children to give their opinions of the art.

Read aloud the text. Explain that Pablo Picasso (1881–1973) is considered one of the greatest artists of the twentieth century because he introduced and perfected new styles in both painting and sculpture, which other artists soon copied. He made this bronze cast of bicycle parts in 1943. The sculpture is a little more than 16 inches high.

WRITE

Collect various objects ahead of time. Have children write a plan for putting objects together to make something new and then follow their plan.

Informal Assessment

Portfolio Children may want to add pictures of their sculptures to their portfolios.

PUPIL'S EDITION OR BIG BOOK

Links

Art Link

Mixing Objects to Make Art

A Spanish artist named Pablo Picasso made this sculpture. He used two everyday objects to show something new. Look at the bicycle seat and handlebars.

- **How does this art look like a bull's head?**

Bull's Head by Pablo Picasso

Write

Choose two or three objects in your classroom. Write about a way to put them together to show something new. Then follow your plan.

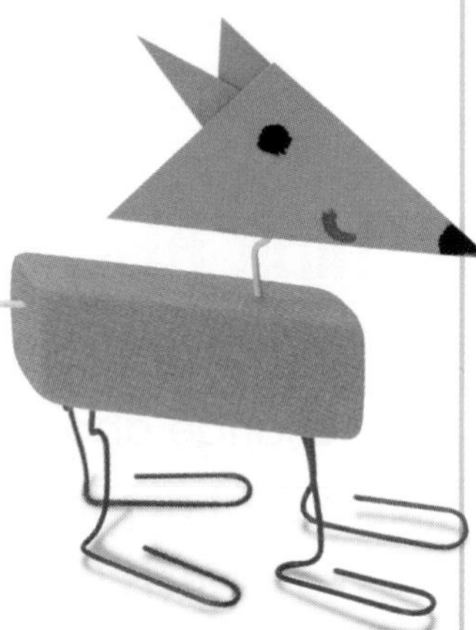

E28

More Link Options . . .

Language Arts Link

What Am I? Have children write riddles that begin with *I am an object made of. . . .* Have them list several parts that make the object work and then end with *What am I?* They can write their answers upside down or on the backs of their papers. Have them swap riddles and identify the objects from their parts.

Music Link

Water Bells Prepare five drinking glasses that are at least 6 inches tall with the following heights of water: one inch, two inches, three inches, four inches, and five inches. Order the glasses and number them from one to five. Tap each with a metal spoon and ask children to identify the glasses with the highest and lowest pitches. Allow time for children to tap tunes on the glasses, adding or removing water as needed.

Estimate How Much Ships Can Carry

Big ships can carry heavy cargo. On the left you see a ship with no cargo. The red line shows that it is floating high in the water. On the right you see a ship loaded with cargo. You can not see the red line. The ship is floating lower in the water.

Think and Do

Make a foil boat. Put it in the water. Estimate how many pennies your boat can carry. Try it. Check your estimate.

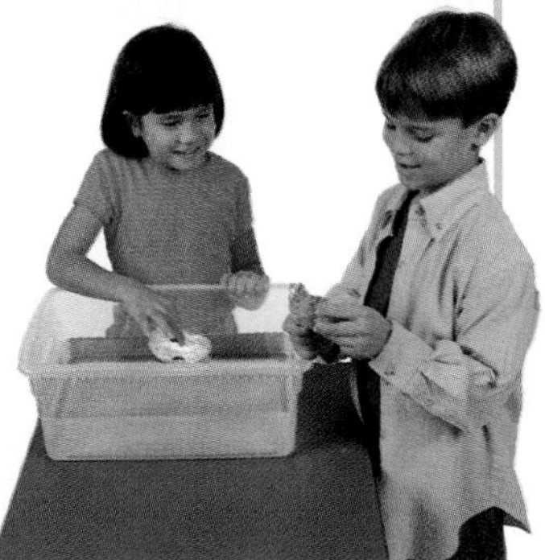

E29

Math Link
Estimate How Much Ships Can Carry

Link Objective Determine how shape and weight make an object sink or float.

Talk about the photographs. Ask children to compare water marks as indicated by the lines on the ships' hulls. Discuss how huge, heavy ships like this one can float because it is displacing a greater weight of water than its own weight.

Read aloud the text. Explain that, as heavy cargo is added, the ship sinks lower and lower in the water. If enough cargo is added, the ship will drop low enough in the water to sink. Ships have lines on their hulls so that people can avoid overloading them.

THINK AND DO

Give children ten-inch lengths of foil to make their boats. Put 50 or more pennies in a bowl for them to use as masses. Have them record their estimates and how many pennies they actually load before the boat sinks. Challenge them to change their boat design so the boat holds more.

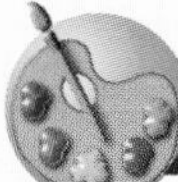

Art Link

Paint Bubbling Volcanoes Make a paste using baking soda and water. Have children use crayons to draw pictures of cone-shaped volcanoes. Have them paint lava on the mountains with the baking soda paste. Mix red food coloring with a little vinegar and have children use brushes to splash the red vinegar onto their baking soda lava. Have them observe what happens when the two substances mix. Have them allow drying time before displaying.

Health Link

Make Fruit Gelatin Help children make fruit gelatin for a snack. Have them observe and describe the gelatin and water before mixing. Have them observe and describe the mixture after mixing, after cooking, and after cooling. Have them write about the changes in their science journals while enjoying their snack. **CAUTION: Check for food allergies before children eat any food.**

Chapter 1

Review and Test Preparation

Tell What You Know

SUMMARIZE/RETELL

1. Have children tell about the pictures. Use these concepts to assess their understanding.

- ▶ A solid is matter that keeps its shape.
- ▶ A liquid is matter that flows and takes the shape of whatever container it is in.
- ▶ A gas is matter that spreads out to fill its container and takes its shape.

TEST PREP Test-Taking Tips

Model this strategy with children to help them use the words to tell about the pictures:

To use the word to tell about the picture, first I look at the word to see what it describes. I find clues in the picture that go with the word. Then I make up a sentence.

Vocabulary

REVIEW SCIENCE VOCABULARY

Children review chapter vocabulary by using each word to tell about the picture.

2. **Matter is everything around us.**
3. **Some objects float on water.**
4. **Some objects sink to the bottom.**
5. **Some things change when you cool them.**
6. **Some solids dissolve in liquids.**

GRAPHIC ORGANIZER FOR CHAPTER CONCEPTS

Children can use the graphic organizer to review the key concepts and ideas from each lesson. See **Workbook p. WB107** and **Transparency E1**.

PUPIL'S EDITION OR BIG BOOK

CHAPTER 1 REVIEW

Tell What You Know

1. Use the word *solid, liquid,* or *gas* to tell about each picture.

Vocabulary

Use each word to tell about the picture.

2. 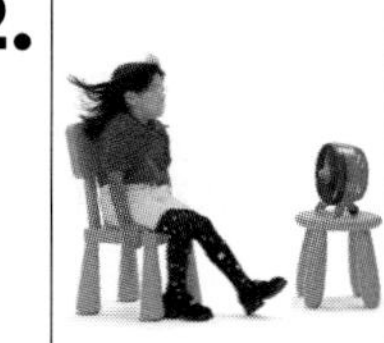
matter

3. 
float

4. 
sink

5. 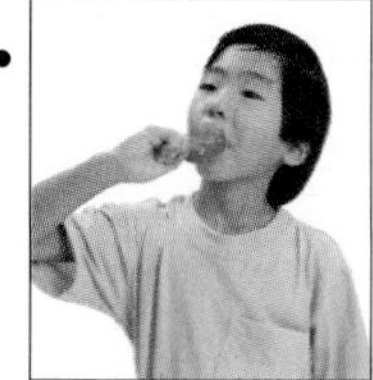
change

6. 
dissolve

E30

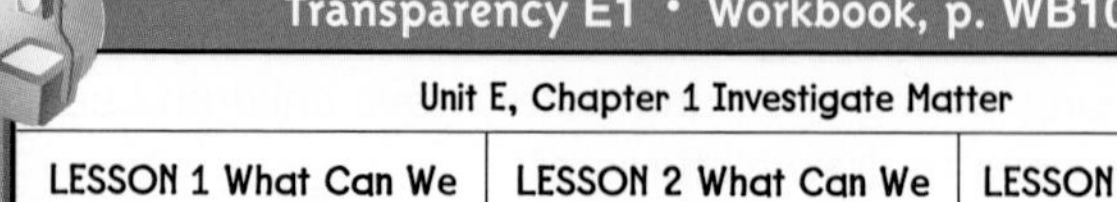

Graphic Organizer for Chapter Concepts

Transparency E1 • Workbook, p. WB107

Unit E, Chapter 1 Investigate Matter

LESSON 1 What Can We Observe About Solids?	LESSON 2 What Can We Observe About Liquids?	LESSON 3 What Objects Sink or Float?
1. Everything around us is matter. 2. Solids are matter that keep their shape. 3. Solids can be sorted in many ways.	1. Matter that flows is called a liquid. 2. Liquids take the shape of what they are poured into. 3. Some liquids mix with water, but oil does not.	1. Some objects float and some objects sink. 2. Changing the shape of an object helps it sink or float.
LESSON 4 What Solids Dissolve in Liquids?	**LESSON 5 What Can We Observe About Gases?**	**LESSON 6 How Can We Change Objects?**
1. Some solids dissolve in liquids. 2. Soil and sand do not dissolve in water.	1. Gas spreads out and takes the shape of its container. 2. You can not see gases but you can see what they do.	1. You can change objects by rolling or bending them. 2. You can change objects by freezing or mixing them.

Using Science Skills

7. Gather and Record Data
Make a chart to gather and record data about liquids. Put one drop of water and one drop of oil on wax paper.

Liquids				
	Makes a Round Drop	Makes a Flat Drop	Can Be Dragged	Can Not Be Dragged
Water				
Oil				

Observe each drop. Use a toothpick to drag each one. Try other liquids and add them to the chart.

8. Draw a Conclusion Think about what makes these cars roll. Draw a conclusion about why one car rolled farther.

E31

Using Science Skills

REVIEW PROCESS SKILLS

7. **Gather and Record Data** Help children make the chart or have a duplicate prepared ahead of time. Give each child a piece of wax paper and a toothpick. **Caution: Remind them to be careful with the toothpick because it is sharp.**

   Put a drop of water and a drop of oil on each piece of wax paper and have children record data about each liquid. Have children try other liquids such as milk and hand cream and record their observations. Have them use the chart to identify which of the liquids they observed behave more like water and which behave more like oil. Then have them make predictions about how liquids like suntan oil and juice will behave, based on their experiences with the liquids they observed.

PERFORMANCE ASSESSMENT

8. **Draw a Conclusion** Provide two cars, one with four wheels, the other with two removed, so that children can draw a conclusion based on their own experiences. Ask children why one car rolled farther than the other. Then ask them to explain their thinking. An acceptable response should include: because it had all four wheels, and the other only had two; because a car needs all four wheels to roll.

WRITING ABOUT SCIENCE

Have children write a composition that involves writing for a specific purpose. You may wish to use the prompt that is provided in the Workbook. The prompt is accompanied by a graphic organizer that will help children organize their ideas before writing. Models for writing are provided in the **Teaching Resources** book. You may wish to reproduce those for children or display them on a transparency.

WRITING PRACTICE

A chapter writing prompt and a prewriting activity are provided on **Workbook p. WB122**.

CHAPTER TEST

See **Assessment Guide pages AG71–74** for the Chapter Test. Assessment Options are provided on p. E2i.

TAKE-HOME BOOK

Use the **Take-Home Books** (described on p. E2g) to provide more chapter content and activities.

Planning Guide Making Sound

LESSON	PACING	OBJECTIVES	MATERIALS
1 What Are Sounds? E34–39	3 days	▶ Demonstrate how sounds are made. ▶ Observe and compare different sounds.	**Investigate** cardboard tube, ruler, pencil, foil, rubber band, paper punch
2 How Are Sounds Different? E40–45	2 days	▶ Describe different kinds of sounds. ▶ Compare sounds.	**Investigate** 4 bottles, labels, water, measuring cup
3 What Sounds Do Instruments Make? E46–49	2 days	▶ Describe the part of a musical instrument that vibrates. ▶ Compare musical instruments.	**Investigate** small can, beans, balloon, rubber band, pencil with eraser
End of Chapter E50–53 **Social Studies Link: Sounds from Around the World** **Math Link: Measure How Far a Whisper Travels** **Chapter Review and Test Preparation**		▶ Recognize that similar types of instruments are used in various cultures. ▶ Measure the distance a whisper can be heard. ▶ Review chapter concepts.	

PROCESS SKILLS	VOCABULARY	RESOURCES AND TECHNOLOGY	REACHING ALL LEARNERS
Process Skill Tip investigate **Other Process Skills** observe and compare	**sound** **vibrate**	**Workbook,** pp. WB123–125 **Vocabulary Cards,** pp. TR149–152 **Transparency** E2-1 **Harcourt Science Activity Video** **Internet Site**	**Advanced Learners,** p. E1g **ESL Activity,** p. E35 **Hearing Impaired,** p. E36 **Investigation Challenge,** p. E36 **Informal Assessment,** p. E39
Process Skill Tip use numbers **Other Process Skills** compare	**pitch**	**Workbook,** pp. WB126–127 **Transparency** E2-2 **Harcourt Science Activity Video**	**ESL Activity,** p. E41 **Investigation Challenge,** pp. E43, E44 **Informal Assessment,** p. E45
Process Skill Tip form a hypothesis **Other Process Skills** compare	**musical instrument**	**Workbook,** pp. WB128–132 **Transparency** E2-3 **Harcourt Science Activity Video**	**ESL Activity,** p. E47 **Informal Assessment,** p. E49
		Take-Home Book, pp. TH39–40 *Emma's Music* **Activities for Home or School,** pp. TR106–107 **Chapter Test,** pp. AG77–80	**Informal Assessment,** p. E50 **Performance Assessment,** p. AG81 **Portfolio Evaluation,** p. AGxxiv

Prepare for Activities

Use this page to help you organize and prepare materials for the Investigations, which begin each lesson of this chapter.

LESSON INVESTIGATION	MATERIALS

1 Sounds
E34

PURPOSE Use a cardboard tube to observe how different sounds can be made.

PREPARATION TIPS Provide small, precut pieces of foil to cover the tubes. Prepunch holes in the tubes with the paper punch and model how to attach the foil with a rubber band.

TIME 20–30 min

EXPECTED RESULTS Children discover that the humming sound changes as holes are made in the cardboard tube or as foil covers the end of the tube.

MATERIALS
- cardboard tube
- ruler
- paper punch
- foil
- rubber band

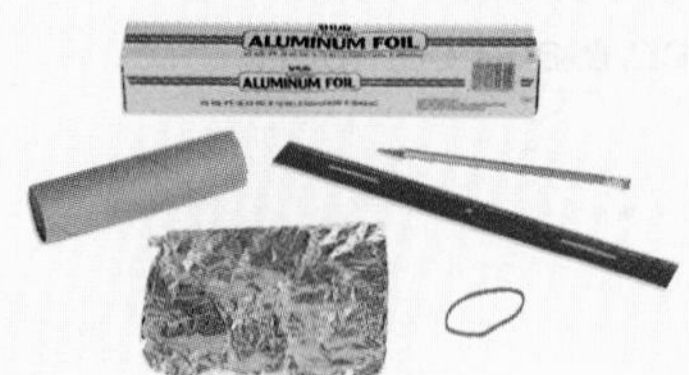

2 Some Different Sounds
E40

PURPOSE Observe that different amounts of water in same-shaped bottles affect the sound.

PREPARATION TIPS Provide a pitcher of water and a measuring cup for each group. You may wish to demonstrate how to blow across the top of a bottle to produce a sound.

TIME Steps 1 and 2: 20 min; Step 3: 20 min

EXPECTED RESULTS Children discover that the sound has a higher pitch when there is more water in the bottle.

MATERIALS
- 4 plastic bottles
- labels
- water
- measuring cup

3 Making Your Own Drum
E46

PURPOSE Make a model of a musical instrument to observe the different sounds it produces and compare variations in sounds.

PREPARATION TIPS Cut the tops off the uninflated balloons. Model how to stretch the rubber band over the balloon to cover the open end of the can.

TIME 20 min

EXPECTED RESULTS Children discover that different sounds can be produced from their drums depending on the parts that vibrate.

MATERIALS
- small can
- beans
- balloon
- rubber band
- pencil with eraser

Harcourt Science Activity Videos

The Activity Video for this unit shows children doing the Investigations. You may wish to view the video for classroom management ideas. The video can also be used to model the investigation process for children.

Equipment Kits

Underlined items above are provided in the equipment kits (available separately).

. . . with Trade Books

These books provide in-depth information about sound.

Big Band Sound by Harriet Diller (Boyds Mills, 1996) tells how a young girl makes her own drum set from recycled materials.

Hearing Sounds by Gary Gibson (Aladdin Books, 1994) explains interesting sounds facts and suggests easy scientific activities.

Max Found Two Sticks by Brian Pinkney (Simon & Schuster, 1997) finds a young boy responding to questions by drumming on various objects.

Song and Dance Man by Karen Ackerman (Knopf, 1992) tells of the relationship between children and their grandfather, a former vaudevillian. *ALA Notable*

Sounds All Around by Wendy Pfeffer (HarperCollins, 1999) explains how sound waves travel through the air and are picked up by tiny bones in the ear.

Thump, Thump, Rat-a-Tat-Tat by Gene Baer (HarperCollins, 1989) has the sounds of a distant marching band growing larger and louder as it approaches.

Trade book titles are current at time of publication but may go out of print without notice.

Visit The Learning Site for related links, activities, and resources.

www.harcourtschool.com

. . . with the Take-Home Book

Emma's Music
pages TH39–40, *Take-Home Books*

This take-home book provides reinforcement of science concepts and vocabulary presented in the chapter and provides an activity. See p. E53.

Emma's Music

Emma and her sister are eating a snack after school. Emma taps her water glass with her spoon by mistake. It makes a ringing sound. She likes the sound, so she taps it again and makes the same sound.

. . . with More Activities

Assessment Options ✓ Chapter 2

Formal Assessment

- **Chapter Review and Test Preparation**, PE pp. E52–53
- **Chapter Test,** pp. AG77–80

Ongoing Assessment

- **✓Questions**, PE pp. E35–39, E41–45, E47–49
- **Lesson Review**, PE pp. E39, E45, E49
- **Informal Assessment**
  - **Performance,** TE pp. E39, E49
  - **Portfolio,** TE pp. E45, E51
- **Observation Checklist,** AGxiv

Student Self-Assessment

- **Self-Assessment – Investigate**, p. AGxvi
- **Self-Assessment – Learn About**, p. AGxvii
- **Project Summary Sheet**, p. AGxix

Performance Assessment

- **Chapter Review and Test Preparation**, PE p. E53
- **Chapter Performance Task**, pp. AG81–82
- **Project Evaluation Checklist**, p. AGxviii

Portfolio Assessment

- **Science Experiences Record**, p. AGxxii
- **Guide to My Science Portfolio**, p. AGxxiii
- **Portfolio Evaluation,** p. AGxxiv

Chapter Test AG77

Making Sound

Part I Vocabulary 4 points each

Write the letter of the best choice.

D 1. Something used to make music
B 2. Something you hear
A 3. How high or low a sound is
C 4. Moves back and forth very fast

A pitch
B sound
C vibrates
D musical instrument

Part II Science Concepts and Understanding

Circle the best answer to each question. 6 points each

5. What must a rubber band do to make sound?
   stretch (vibrate)
6. What word describes a dog that has a loud, low bark?
   (big) small

Chapter Test AG78

7. Which bell makes a higher sound?
   (small bell) big bell
8. A whistle makes a sound with a high pitch. How fast do its parts vibrate?
   (fast) slow
9. Which one often makes a softer sound?
   (kitten) cat
10. Which makes a louder sound?
   (shout) whisper
11. Draw a musical instrument you pluck to make a sound. stringed instrument

Chapter Test AG79

12. Draw a musical instrument you beat to make sound. drum

Part III Process Skills Application 6 points each

Process skills: investigate, use numbers, form a hypothesis

Write the letter that best describes the amount of water in each bottle.

13. A
14. C
15. B

A. about $\frac{1}{4}$ cup
B. about $\frac{1}{2}$ cup
C. about 1 cup

Chapter Test AG80

16. Circle the letter for the bottle that makes the highest sound when you blow across its top.
   A B (C)
17. Draw a small bell. Then draw one that is a little larger and one that is a lot larger.
18. Color the bell that makes the lowest sound.
   The largest bell should be colored.

Performance Assessment AG81

PERFORMANCE TASK

Sound Test

Materials

rubber bands (two different widths) · box lid · pencil · paper

1. Stretch a thin and a wide rubber band across the lid of a box.
2. Predict which rubber band will make the highest sound and which will make the loudest sound.
3. Pluck each rubber band and compare the sounds they make.
4. On the chart below, record what kind of sound each one makes.

Sound		
Rubber Bands	Loud-Soft	High-Low
1. thin	soft	high
2. wide	loud	low

5. Compare what you predicted with what you found out.

Performance Assessment AG82

PERFORMANCE TASK

Teacher's Directions

Sound Test

Materials rubber bands (two different widths), box lid, pencil, paper

Time 20–30 minutes

Suggested Grouping individuals, pairs, or small groups

Science Processes predict, investigate, compare

Preparation Hints Group the rubber bands by width. Have a sample lid for the children to observe. Have the other materials ready.

Introduce the Task Hold up the sample lid and pluck one rubber band. Ask children to describe the sound. Using this experience, encourage children to predict the characteristics of the sounds from the other rubber bands.

Promote Discussion Have children compare their predictions with their results and tell what they learned from the Sound Test.

Scoring Rubric

Performance Indicators

_____ Makes a prediction relating rubber band width and pitch.
_____ Makes a prediction relating rubber band width and loudness.
_____ Compares the prediction with the results.
_____ Explains what was learned from the investigation.

Observations and Rubric Score

3 2 1 0

Workbook Support

Process Skills Practice WB124

Investigate

1. This guitar makes sound. Color the part that vibrates to make sound.

guitar strings should be colored

Match the sound to the thing that makes it.

2. ring
3. boom
4. shhh

Lesson Concept Review/Assessment WB125

What Are Sounds?

1. Mark an X on all the things that are making sounds.

Circle the word that best finishes each sentence.

2. Sound is made when things ________.
   stand still   (vibrate)
3. When strings on a violin stop vibrating, the sound ________.
   (stops)   gets louder

Process Skills Practice WB126

Use Numbers

Each bottle has a different pitch.

high pitch

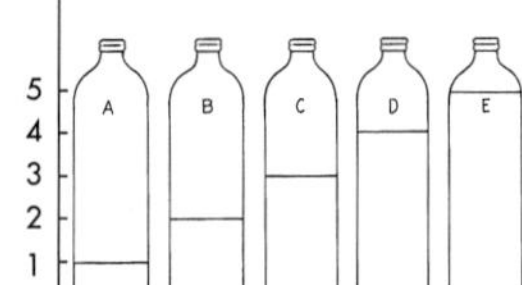

low pitch

Circle the best answer to each question.

1. Which bottle has the highest pitch when you blow across its top?

   Bottle A Bottle C (Bottle E)

2. Which bottle has the lowest pitch when you blow across its top?

   (Bottle A) Bottle C Bottle E

Lesson Concept Review/Assessment WB127

How Are Sounds Different?

1. Circle the things that make loud sounds. Mark an **X** over the things that make soft sounds.

2. Write the word that best finishes the sentence.

loud	**low**

The pitch is how high or low the sound is.

Workbook Support Continued

Process Skills Practice WB128

Form a Hypothesis

1. What kinds of sounds do these instruments make? Draw a line to the word in the box that tells your answer.

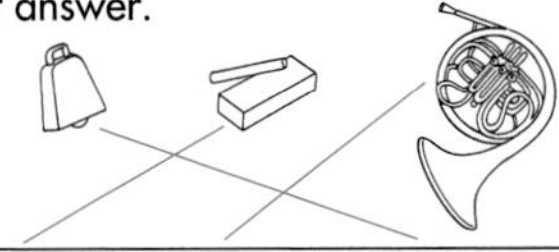

tap honk ding

2. What part of this instrument is missing? Draw what is missing.

Children should draw the strings.

3. Write a sentence about how you can make the banjo make noise.

The sentences should indicate that plucking or picking strings makes them vibrate.

Lesson Concept Review/Assessment WB129

What Sounds Do Instruments Make?

1. Color the part of the instrument that vibrates to make sound. The following should be colored: drum head, triangle, strings on violin.

These children are making music.

Write a sentence that tells how the musical instruments are different.

Sentences should indicate that the instruments sound different from one another and are played differently.

Vocabulary Review WB130

Making Sound

These sentences are false. Change the underlined word to make the sentence true.

1. To move back and forth very fast is to hum.

vibrate

2. Music is how high or low a sound is. Pitch

Circle the word that best finishes the sentence.

3. Everything you hear is ______.

loud (sound) soft

4. A ______ is something used to make music.

(musical instrument) loud pitch

Look at the picture.
X the part that vibrates.

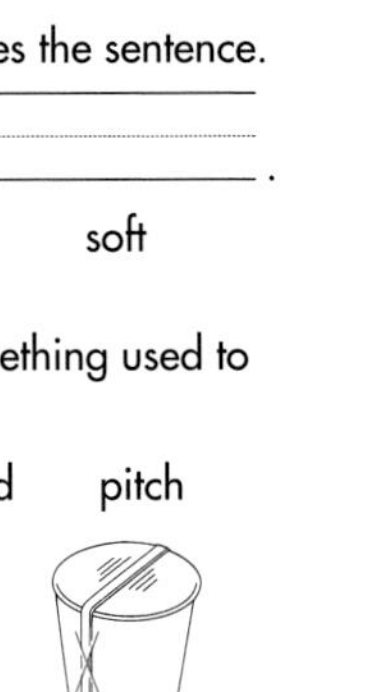

Reading Skill WB131

Recall Supporting Facts and Details

Read the story below. Then answer the questions.

Max likes to make his guitar sound right. Before he plays it, he always tunes it. To do this, he has to turn the keys. Turning the keys one way makes the strings get tighter. The sound goes higher. Turning the keys the other way makes the sound go lower. The strings get looser. Max can make his guitar sound right by changing the way the strings sound.

What is the main idea?

Max likes to make his guitar sound right.

Draw a line under some ways Max makes his guitar sound good.

Writing Skill WB132

Write to Describe

A. Make up a musical instrument. Draw a picture of your instrument. Give your instrument a name.

My musical instrument is called a ______.

B. Write about your musical instrument. Describe how it sounds. Describe its pitch.

Chapter 2

Making Sound

Generate Questions

Did You Know?/*Fast* Facts

Play an instrument guessing game. Call on one volunteer to pantomime playing a musical instrument. Have others name the instrument and describe the sound it makes. Comment on all the different sounds instruments can make.

Discuss the photographs. Explain that the picture shows a musical instrument not made totally by people. To help children **relate pictures to text**, ask:

- **What is the instrument in the photo?** an organ
- **Where is the organ?** in a cave

Explain that the organ pipes are made from mineral deposits that hang from the ceiling of the cave in Luray, Virginia.

- **What helps a rabbit hear sounds that warn of danger?** its long ears

Have children cup their hands behind their ears and listen for sounds to see if increasing the size of their ears helps them hear better.

Encourage children's questions. Write children's questions on the board, or have them write or draw in their journals.

PUPIL'S EDITION OR BIG BOOK

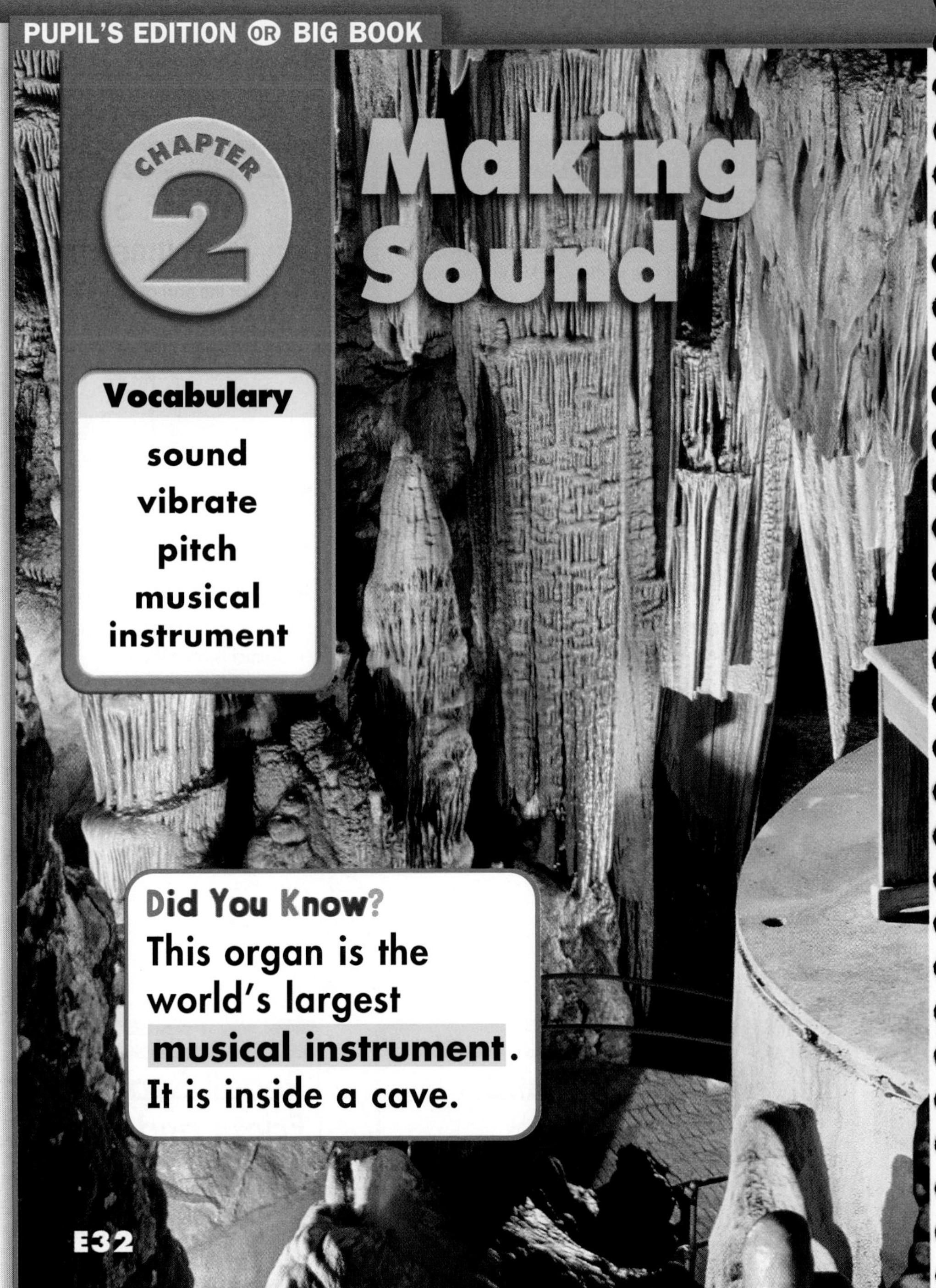

CHAPTER 2
Making Sound
Vocabulary
sound
vibrate
pitch
musical instrument
Did You Know?
This organ is the world's largest musical instrument.
It is inside a cave.
E32

Reading Skills Checklist

Strategies for developing the following reading skills are provided in this chapter.

- ☐ use context
- ☑ recall supporting facts and details *pp. E35, E42*
- ☐ arrange events in sequence
- ☐ draw conclusions
- ☑ identify the main idea *pp. E35, E36, E41, E42, E43, E44, E47, E48*
- ☐ identify cause and effect
- ☑ predict outcomes *p. E41*
- ☑ summarize *pp. E39, E45, E49*
- ☐ use graphic sources for information
- ☑ relate pictures to text *pp. E32, E35, E36, E38, E41, E42, E47*
- ☐ distinguish between fact and nonfact
- ☐ develop concepts of print
- ☑ build vocabulary *pp. E35, E36, E41, E44, E47, E48*

School-Home Connection

Distribute copies of the School-Home Connection, p. TR21.

Follow Up Have volunteers compare the results of the activity they did at home. Discuss reasons children think they saw different results.

Teaching Resources, p. TR21

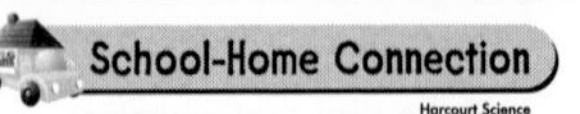

Chapter Content

ScienceFun

Science Process Skills

Activity Materials from Home

cardboard tube
foil
small coffee can
beans
balloon

Did You Know?
Rabbits hear sound with their long ears. Sounds may warn them of danger.
E33

Prereading Strategies

Preview the Chapter

Do a walk-through of the chapter. Read aloud the main headings for each lesson and have volunteers suggest answers. Keep track of any questions that come up during the discussion.

Preview the Photographs

Have children look at the photos throughout the chapter. Ask which ones interest them most and discuss why. Use this as a beginning to find out what children know and want to know about the lessons in the chapter.

Preview the Vocabulary

Write the vocabulary words from page E32 on the board. Read aloud the list and ask children to tell about the words they know and don't know. Tell them that they will find out more about these words as the lesson progresses.

DEFINITIONS

sound everything you hear
vibrate to move back and forth very fast
pitch how high or low a sound is
musical instrument something used to make music

VOCABULARY CARDS AND ACTIVITIES

Children can use the Vocabulary Cards to make their own graphic organizers or to add to an ongoing file of science terms. The Vocabulary Cards and a variety of strategies and activities are provided beginning on p. TR110 in the **Teaching Resources** book.

GRAPHIC ORGANIZER FOR CHAPTER CONCEPTS

Children can use the graphic organizer to record key concepts and ideas from each lesson. See **Workbook p. WB123** and **Transparency E2.** A completed graphic organizer is also shown on page E52.

Graphic Organizer for Chapter Concepts

Transparency E2 • Workbook, p. WB123

Unit E, Chapter 2 Making Sound

LESSON 1 What Are Sounds?	LESSON 2 How Are Sounds Different?	LESSON 3 What Sounds Do Instruments Make?
1. Sound is made when objects vibrate. 2. You hear sounds all around you.	1. Sounds are different. 2. Sounds can be quiet or loud. 3. The pitch of a sound is how high or low the sound is.	1. Musical instruments make sound when a part vibrates. 2. Each instrument has its own sound.

LESSON 1

What Are Sounds?

Objectives

- ▶ **Demonstrate how sounds are made.**
- ▶ **Observe and compare different sounds.**

Motivate

Play a Memory Game Use your voice to make a short beeping sound. Have children do the same. Then make a short and a long beeping sound. Again, have children repeat. Continue this pattern making a longer string of beeps each time. See how many beeps children can remember in the correct sequence.

Investigate

Time 20–30 min **Grouping** individuals or pairs

Process Skill investigate

Preparation Tips and Expected Results See page E32c.

Center Activity Option Place this investigation or a copy of the Investigation, page TR68, in your science corner.

Activity Tips

Safety Tip Remind children to use the cardboard tube only for its intended purpose.

- ▶ Suggest that children test each change by listening carefully to the humming sound before exploring their next idea.
- ▶ To change the tube, suggest that children bend it up or down, shorten it, or add holes.

Children can draw pictures of the changes they made and write about the effect each change had on the humming sound.

Activity Questions

- ▶ What effect did changing the tube have?
- ▶ What are some other ways sounds can change?

When Minutes Count . . .

Have each pair of children work on a different modification and then compare results. Or, have volunteers demonstrate the effect of different changes for the whole class.

PUPIL'S EDITION OR BIG BOOK

LESSON 1 What Are Sounds?

Investigate

Sounds

You will need

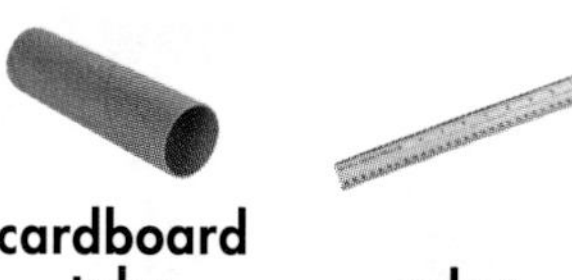

cardboard tube | ruler | pencil | foil | rubber band

1. Hum into the cardboard tube. Listen to the sound.
2. Punch a hole that is 2 centimeters from one end of the tube. Use the rubber band to hold foil over the other end.
3. Hum and listen again. Now investigate this problem. How can you change the foil or the tube to change the humming sound?

Science Skill

To investigate a problem, you test different ideas.

E34

Science Skills

Process Skill: Investigate Display Process Skill Tip Transparency E2-1. Explain that the children are talking to each other through a string telephone. Have children describe and compare the cans in the different pictures. Discuss why the children might be changing the size and shape of the cans. to find out which size and shape work better When the investigation is completed, the string should be taut.

Process Skill Tip Transparency E2-1

Investigate

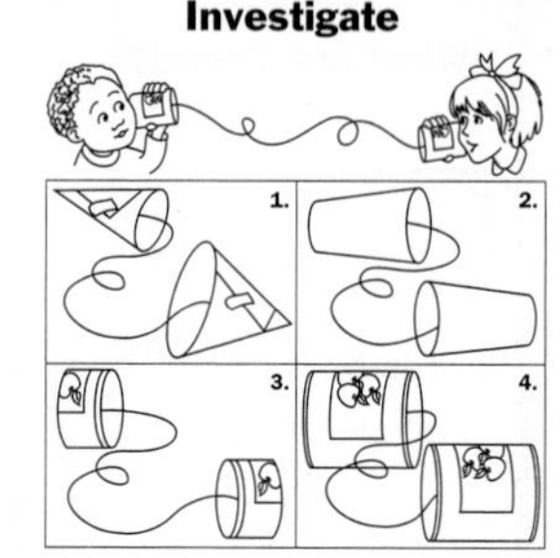

1. What problem are the children investigating?
how the size and shape of a can affects sound
2. What are they doing to investigate the problem?
changing the size and shape of the can in their string telephone

PROCESS SKILLS PRACTICE

To practice and apply process skills, see **Workbook p. WB124.**

Learn About

Sound

Everything you hear is **sound**. You might hear the beating of a drum. You might hear the call of an elephant. You might also hear the voice of a friend. Sound is all around you.

E35

Learn About

1 Before Reading

PREVIEW/SET PURPOSE

Have children preview pages E35–E39. Make a K-W-L chart as shown. Have children fill in what they know and want to know about sound.

K-W-L Chart		
What I Know	What I Want to Know	What I Learned

2 Guide the Learning

SCIENCE IDEAS

Read aloud page E35 with children. Help reinforce the **main idea: Sound is everything you hear.** Ask:

▶ **What is sound?** everything you hear

▶ **Where is sound?** all around you

Lead children to **recall supporting facts and details.** Ask:

▶ **What are examples of sound mentioned in the text?** the beating of a drum, the call of an elephant, the voice of a friend

DEVELOP READING SKILLS

Relate Pictures to Text Have children observe the photo and name sounds they might hear if they were watching the parade live. Children should mention the sounds of the various musical instruments and the sounds of the crowd.

BACKGROUND

Webliography GO ONLINE
Keyword sound
www.harcourtschool.com

Sound All sounds, whether they are high or low, loud or soft, are made by a vibration. When an object vibrates, it causes the air around it to vibrate. The vibrations travel away from their point of origin in all directions. The vibrations can travel through air, liquids, and solids.

Sounds Humans Make Humans produce sound in a section of the throat called the larynx. Two folds of tissue, called the vocal cords, cross the larynx. Between the vocal cords is an opening, or slit. When the vocal cords are relaxed, air rushes through the slit causing little or no vibration. When the vocal cords are tight, such as during speech, the rushing air causes the vocal cords to vibrate, which, in turn, causes the sound. The tighter the vocal cords, the faster the vibration and the higher pitched the sound.

SCIENCE WORD WALL

sound

Sound Off! Make a word card for the word *sound.* Invite children to draw or cut out pictures of objects that make sounds. Post the pictures on the Word Wall.

ESL Activity Encourage children to name the pictures they drew or cut out and describe or demonstrate the sounds the objects make.

Technology Link

Visit the Harcourt Learning Site for related links, activities, and resources.
www.harcourtschool.com

Guide the Learning continued

SCIENCE IDEAS

Read aloud page E36 with children. Help children understand the **main idea: A sound is made when something vibrates.** Ask:

- ▶ **What two things happen when you pluck a stretched rubber band?** The rubber band vibrates; a sound is made.
- ▶ **When does the sound stop?** when the vibrating stops

VISUAL LEARNING

Help children observe the photo and **relate pictures to text** in order to make inferences. Ask:

- ▶ **Do you think the child is hearing a sound?** Children's responses should demonstrate an understanding of the connection between vibration and sound.

DEVELOP SCIENCE VOCABULARY

sound, **vibrate** Invite children to demonstrate the meaning of vibrate by moving their hands back and forth quickly. Have pairs of children work with a rubber band to make sound. Have one child stretch the rubber band while the other child plucks it. Ask children to find out what happens when the rubber band is held slack and then plucked. It doesn't vibrate, and no sound is heard.

PUPIL'S EDITION OR BIG BOOK

How Sounds Are Made

If you pluck a stretched rubber band, you may hear a sound. You may also see the rubber band move back and forth very fast. To move back and forth very fast is to **vibrate**.

When the rubber band stops vibrating, the sound stops.

E36

Investigation Challenge

Hands-On Activity: What Causes Sound?

Guide pairs of children to make sound with a ruler. Have children wear safety goggles. Then have one child lay the ruler on a desk with half of it extended over the edge and hold it in place. Have the other child pull up on the free end, release it, and tell what happened. The ruler vibrates and makes a sound until the vibration stops. Allow time for children to change the position of the ruler so that more and then less is extended over the edge of the desk and observe the effect on the sound. Ask:

- ▶ **What happened each time the vibration stopped?** The sound stopped.

Reaching All Learners

Hearing Impaired Children who are hearing impaired may not be able to hear the sound made by a vibrating object. Allow them to hold the object as it is being made to vibrate so they can both see and feel the vibrations.

Cultural Connection

Sounds from Many Languages Encourage native speakers of languages other than English to explore the sounds of their native language as suggested in the Language Arts Link on page E37. Invite them to demonstrate and share the results with their classmates.

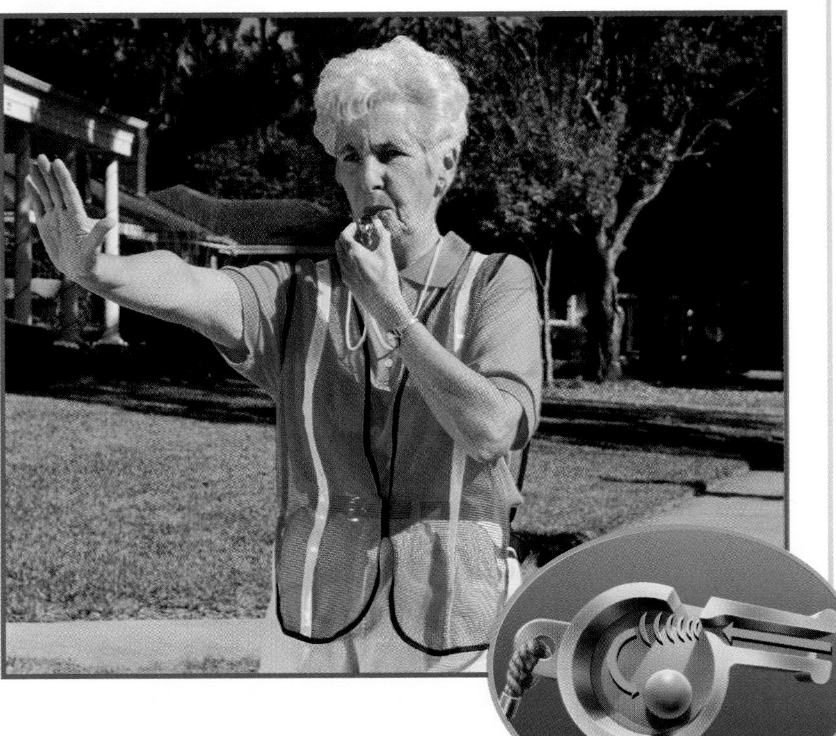

Sound is made when things vibrate. A ball vibrates inside a whistle. You can feel it vibrate.

Gently touch your throat while you hum. Then stop humming. Something in your throat vibrates and then stops. Tell what it feels like.

SCIENCE IDEAS

Read aloud page E37 with children. Suggest they gently touch their neck just below the chin and slowly say the word *zoo*. Ask:

▶ **What do you feel on your neck when you say *zoo*?** vibration

USE PROCESS SKILLS

Observe and Compare Have children feel the difference when they utter a *z* and an *s* sound. Lead them to use their sense of touch by asking:

▶ **What do you feel when you say a *z* sound? An *s* sound?** Children should report that they feel vibration when they say a *z* sound but not when they say an *s* sound.

Explain that vocal cords are in the throat. Vocal cords are like rubber bands. They become taut and vibrate to make the sound of the letter *z*. They are slack and do not vibrate to make an *s* sound.

Stretch and then release a rubber band to demonstrate the difference between taut and slack.

VISUAL LEARNING

Direct attention to the photo of the whistle. Have children point to the part that vibrates. Point out that blowing air into the whistle starts the ball vibrating.

THE QUESTIONS KIDS ASK!

Why do I hear something even when my vocal cords are not vibrating?

Address Misconceptions The human vocal tract includes the throat, tongue, teeth, lips, and mouth, as well as the larynx and vocal cords. Many parts of the vocal tract vibrate during speech even when the vocal cords are quiet. For example, air rushing under and around the tongue vibrates when an *s* sound is uttered. A burst of air between the tongue and roof of the mouth causes vibration when a *t* sound is made. Air passing between the teeth and lips vibrates when a *v* sound is made. A burst of air between the lips causes vibration when a *p* sound is made. To help children experience the effect of vibration in these quiet sounds, have them make the sound while holding their breath and then while exhaling.

Language Arts Link

The Sounds of English Have children explore the sounds of English by determining what part of the vocal tract vibrates to make each sound. Have them use the alphabet as a reference. Make a chart such as the one shown. Have them record the source of vibration as they make each sound. Two examples are provided.

Letter/Sound	Vibration
a as in at	air passing through vocal chords
b as in bat	air passing through vocal chords and between lips

Guide the Learning continued

SCIENCE IDEAS

Have children read aloud pages E38 and E39. To help children **relate pictures to text**, ask:

- **How are the microphone and the megaphone changing each person's voice?** They are making the voice louder.

Critical Thinking To help children use analogy to deepen their understanding, ask them to judge which is more like cupping hands around the mouth, using a megaphone or a microphone. using a megaphone

USE PROCESS SKILLS

Observe Have children observe the photo of an ocean scene and name things that would make a sound. Ask:

- **Which of these are pleasant sounds?** Accept children's feelings about the different sounds.

VISUAL LEARNING

Have children name the sounds they might hear in the street scene. Discuss whether each sound is pleasant or harsh.

Direct attention to the emergency vehicle and demonstrate the sound it would make. Ask:

- **Is this a pleasant sound or a harsh sound?** harsh
- **What is the meaning of the sound?** The sound tells pedestrians, drivers, and bicyclists to get out of the way so the vehicle can hurry to its destination and help people in need.
- **Why do emergency vehicles make harsh sounds?** so people will pay attention to them

PUPIL'S EDITION OR BIG BOOK

Sounds You Hear

You can hear the sound of your own voice. You can whisper and shout. You can laugh and cry. You can cover your mouth to make your voice quiet. You can cup your hands around your mouth to make your voice loud.

microphone

megaphone

- **What are these people using to change the sound of their voices?** microphone, megaphone

E38

Drama Link

It's All in the Voice Encourage children to explore the drama of their voices. Point out that a single word can show many emotions. Have volunteers demonstrate how they feel about something by saying "hello" in different ways, for example, to show love, fear, and excitement. Follow up by inviting children to practice and read aloud a familiar story, using their voice to dramatize the feelings the story evokes.

Health

The Sounds of Emergency Vehicles Help children develop a list of emergency vehicles, including police, fire, and ambulance, on chart paper under a heading such as Emergency Vehicles. Have them draw or cut out a picture of each vehicle and display it next to its name. Point out that each type of emergency vehicle has a different siren sound. Call on volunteers to demonstrate the different sounds. Discuss what pedestrians, bicyclists, and drivers should do when they hear the sound of a siren. Pedestrians should get onto the sidewalk immediately. Bicyclists and drivers should pull over to the right so the emergency vehicle can pass.

Some sounds are nice to hear, like the sound of waves crashing against rocks. Other sounds, like sirens blowing, are not so nice. The more carefully you listen, the more sounds you can hear.

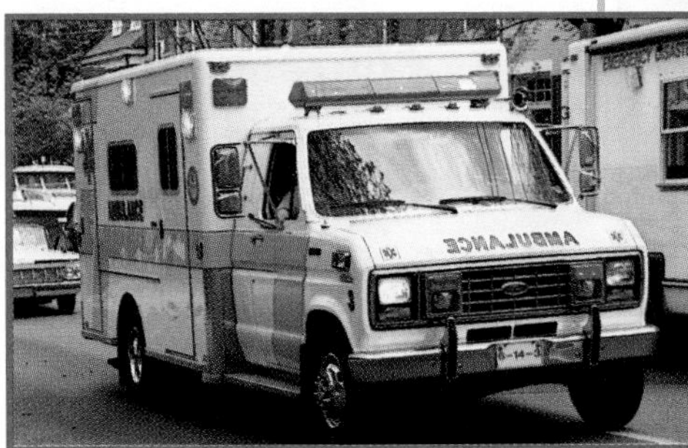

Think About It

1. How are sounds made?
2. What happens when something stops vibrating?

3 Wrap Up and Assess

SUMMARIZE

Have children **summarize** what they have learned. Have them fill in what they have learned on the K-W-L chart begun on page E35. Review any questions that remain unanswered and develop strategies for finding out more.

K-W-L Chart		
What I Know	What I Want to Know	What I Learned

THINK ABOUT IT

1. Sounds are made when things vibrate.
2. Sound stops.

Informal Assessment

Performance To assess children's understanding of what causes sound, have them use pictures or words to show what happens when something, such as a rubber band or a ruler, is made to vibrate. Call on volunteers to name and demonstrate different sounds in the environment.

LESSON CONCEPT REVIEW/ASSESSMENT

Children can use **Workbook p. WB125** to review the lesson concepts.

Literature Connections

Read Alouds

Hearing Sounds
by Gary Gibson, Aladdin Books, 1994.

Thump, Thump, Rat-a-Tat-Tat
by Gene Baer, HarperCollins, 1989.

LESSON 2

How Are Sounds Different?

Objectives

- Describe different kinds of sounds.
- Compare sounds.

Motivate

Have volunteers use their voices to make high, low, loud, and soft sounds as you request. Talk about when each type of voice might be used. Explain that children will learn more about different types of sounds in this lesson.

Time Steps 1 and 2: 20 min; Step 3: 20 min

Grouping pairs or small groups

Process Skill use numbers

Preparation Tips and Expected Results See page E32c.

Center Activity Option Place this investigation or a copy of the Investigation, page TR69, in your science center.

Activity Tips

Safety Tip Only one child in the group should blow across the bottles. Other children should stand back because the bottle could damage a tooth if knocked against it.

- Read aloud the fractions with children. Discuss their meaning. Use color-coded tape markings to help children distinguish among them.

Children can draw the bottles in order according to how much water they contain and write a description of how the sound changed from bottle to bottle.

Activity Questions

- What was the sound when there was one cup of water in the bottle? When there was $\frac{1}{4}$ cup?
- How did the amount of water in a bottle affect the sound?

When Minutes Count . . .

Prepare the labels, and measure and pour the water ahead of time.

PUPIL'S EDITION OR BIG BOOK

How Are Sounds Different?

Investigate

Some Different Sounds

You will need

4 bottles

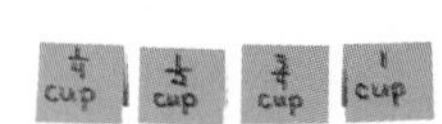

labels

water

measuring cup

1. Make labels. Put each one in front of a bottle.
2. Measure and pour the right amount of water into each bottle.
3. Blow across the top of each bottle. Tell about the sounds you make. Use numbers to tell about the bottles for the different sounds.

Science Skill
You can use numbers to tell how the amount of water changes sound.

E40

Science Skills

Process Skill: Use Numbers
Display Process Skill Tip Transparency E2-2. Have children listen to and describe the sound of one classmate clapping. Follow the same procedure for three classmates and then for the whole class clapping. Discuss how the number of people clapping affects the sound made.

Process Skill Tip Transparency E2-2

Use Numbers

Which picture shows the softest sound being made? picture 1

How many children are clapping? 1

Which picture shows the loudest sound being made? picture 3

How many children are clapping? 8

How does the number of children clapping change the sound being made? The more children clapping, the louder the sound.

PROCESS SKILLS PRACTICE

To practice and apply process skills, see **Workbook p. WB126.**

Learn About

Different Sounds

There are many kinds of sounds. A big train makes a loud, low sound. A small train makes a higher, quieter sound. You may be able to infer how big a train is just by listening to its sound.

E41

Learn About

1 Before Reading

PREVIEW/SET PURPOSE

Have children preview pages E41–E45. Make a web on the board or on chart paper. Tell children they will fill in the web as they learn about different sounds.

2 Guide the Learning

SCIENCE IDEAS

Have children read page E41. Help children **identify the main idea** by asking:

- ▶ **How are sounds different from one another?** Some are quiet; some are loud. Some are high; some are low.

DEVELOP READING SKILLS

Relate Pictures to Text Help children **predict** the different sound each type of train would make. Ask:

- ▶ **Which train would make a loud, low sound?** the large train engine
- ▶ **What kind of sound would the other train make?** a higher, quieter sound

BACKGROUND

Webliography
Keyword sound
www.harcourtschool.com
GO ONLINE

Different Sounds In general, sounds are distinguished by pitch or intensity.

Pitch The pitch of a sound, how high or low it is, is a function of the number of sound waves an object gives off per second. The human ear hears a fairly narrow range of pitches. Dolphins, bats, dogs, and cats, for example, can hear sounds at a higher pitch than humans.

Intensity The intensity, or loudness, of a sound is a measure of energy. Louder sounds, those with greater intensity, have more energy than quieter, less intense, sounds.

SCIENCE WORD WALL

Different Sounds Have children make a word card for the word *pitch* and for words that describe different pitches. Ask volunteers also to make cards for words that describe other ways in which sounds are different. Post the word cards on the Word Wall as each one is discussed.

ESL Activity Have children name and demonstrate sounds described by the words on the Word Wall. Encourage them to draw or cut out pictures of things that make sounds described by those words.

Guide the Learning continued

SCIENCE IDEAS

Read page E42 with children. Help children **identify the main idea** of the text on this page. Ask:

- ▶ **What two kinds of sounds are described?** loud sounds and quiet sounds

DEVELOP READING SKILLS

Infer Direct attention to the photos of water. Have children describe each photo and infer which one shows water that makes a loud sound. Ask:

- ▶ **What can you infer about the sound of the waterfall?** It is loud.

Tell children that the waterfall in the photo is Niagara Falls, a famous waterfall at the border between the United States and Canada. Point out that one reason the water makes a loud sound is that it falls about 50 meters (about 163 feet) to the river below.

VISUAL LEARNING

Have children **relate pictures to text.**

- ▶ **Which animal often makes a quiet sound?** kitten
- ▶ **Which animal often makes a loud sound?** tiger

To reinforce variations in sound, encourage children to make sounds like these animals and explain how they are different.

PUPIL'S EDITION OR BIG BOOK

Quiet and Loud Sounds

Some sounds are quiet, and some sounds are loud. A small stream makes a quiet sound. A big waterfall makes a loud sound.

A kitten often makes a quiet sound. A tiger often makes a loud sound.

E42

Health Link

Too Loud! Call on children to name the loudest sound they can think of. Tell children that standing close to very loud sounds can harm their ears. Point out that factory and outdoor construction workers often wear earplugs to protect their ears from loud sounds. Have children cut out magazine pictures of machines or situations in which the sounds may be so loud as to damage the ear. Suggest they post the pictures on a bulletin board under a heading such as "Wear Earplugs for Safety."

Reading Mini-Lesson

Recall Supporting Facts and Details Direct children's attention to the first paragraph on page E42. Point out that the first sentence contains the main idea. The other sentences state facts and details to support the main idea. Display the transparency. Ask children to locate the main idea in the first paragraph on page E43. Then have children identify supporting facts and details from the text.

Reading Mini-Lesson Transparency E2

Recall Supporting Facts and Details

Main Idea

Some things can make both loud sounds and quiet sounds.

Supporting Facts and Details

When you shout, your voice makes a loud sound. When you whisper, it makes a quiet sound.

READING SKILLS PRACTICE

To practice and apply this reading skill, see **Workbook p. WB131.**

Some things can make both loud sounds and quiet sounds. When you shout, your voice makes a loud sound. When you whisper, you make a quiet sound.

Drums can make loud and quiet sounds, too. When a drummer hits a drum hard, it makes a loud sound. With gentle taps, the drum makes a quiet sound.

E43

SCIENCE IDEAS

After children read page E43, help them identify the main idea: **Some things can make both loud sounds and quiet sounds.** Ask:

- ▶ **How do you make a loud sound on a drum?** hit the drum hard
- ▶ **How do you make a quiet sound with your voice?** whisper

USE PROCESS SKILLS

Compare To help children compare sounds, have them whisper and shout. Ask:

- ▶ **What did you notice when you whispered?** possible answers: It was easier; it was harder to hear.

VISUAL LEARNING

Have children describe the sound the drum in each picture probably makes. Ask:

- ▶ **Which shows the drum that makes a louder sound?** the one with the boy who has his sticks far away to hit the drum hard

Encourage children to share their experiences with drums.

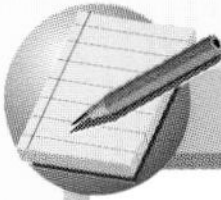

Language Arts Link

Communicating Through Claps Have children practice clapping their hands loudly and then quietly. Point out that claps can be used to communicate feelings and actions. Demonstrate how to use loud and quiet claps to communicate different types of footsteps, for example, quick, quiet claps to denote a child running; alternating soft-loud, soft-loud claps to denote skipping. Challenge pairs of children to work together to develop an interesting pattern of their own. Allow time for children to demonstrate their pattern while their classmates guess what feeling or action it is intended to communicate.

Investigation Challenge

Hands-On Activity: Exploring Sound and Solids Point out that most of the sound children hear is sound that has traveled through air. Explain that sound also travels through solids, such as plastic and wood. Have children work in pairs taking turns listening to sound traveling through a solid. Suggest that one child have his or her ear on a desk or tabletop and, with eyes closed, listen to the rhythm the other child gently taps out. After the listener duplicates the rhythm to "prove" it was heard, have the children change places and repeat.

Guide the Learning continued

SCIENCE IDEAS

Read page E44 with children. Help them understand the **main idea** of the text: **Sounds have different pitches.** Ask:

- ▶ **We know that sounds can be loud or quiet. How else are sounds different from one another?** Sounds can be high or low; they can have different pitches.

Call on volunteers to demonstrate a sound with a high pitch and then with a low pitch.

VISUAL LEARNING

Have children look at the photos on pages E44–E45. Ask:

- ▶ **Which dog makes a low-pitched bark?** the big dog

Follow a similar procedure with the remaining pairs of photos. Point out that the children are playing chimes and the big bell which is called a gong. The chimes make a higher-pitched sound than the gong. A boy's voice is higher-pitched than a man's voice.

DEVELOP SCIENCE VOCABULARY

pitch Call on individuals to make as low-pitched a sound and as high-pitched a sound as they can. Invite children to name other high-pitched sounds, such as the whistle of a tea kettle and the squeak of chalk on the board. Discuss other low-pitched sounds such as the rumble of a train and a lion's roar.

PUPIL'S EDITION OR BIG BOOK

High and Low Sounds

Some sounds are high, and some sounds are low. The **pitch** of a sound is how high or low the sound is. A big dog's bark has a low pitch. A big bell has a low pitch, too. A man's voice also has a low pitch.

E44

Music Link

Make Panpipes Tell children that they can use air to make a musical instrument work. Have them make simple panpipes by cutting plastic straws to different lengths and taping them side by side as shown. To play the pipe, have them blow across the top of the staws as they would blow across the mouth of a bottle. As the air columns vibrate, children will hear different pitches. Ask:

- ▶ Which straw has the highest sound? the shortest Which has the lowest? the longest

Record children's responses on a chart.

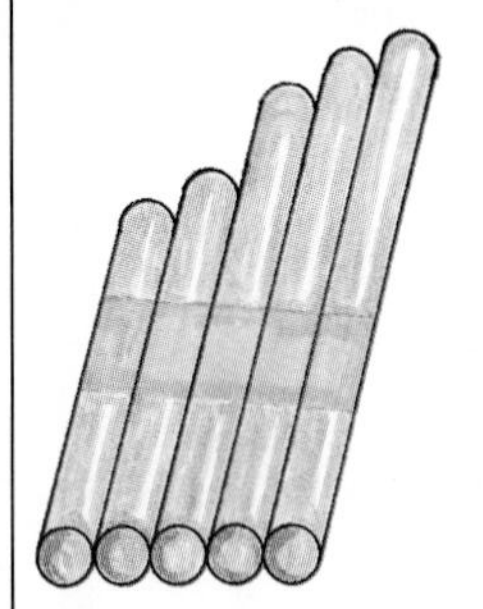

Investigation Challenge

Hands-On Activity: Exploring Pitch with Rubber Bands Have children work in pairs to discover different-pitched sounds rubber bands can make. Give each pair of children a thick and a thin rubber band. Have one child stretch the rubber band while the other child plucks it. Have children pluck each rubber band twice, once when it is stretched as far as possible and once when it is stretched only slightly. Lead children to observe that the thicker rubber band makes a lower sound than the thinner rubber band, and that both rubber bands make a lower sound when they are not stretched tightly than when they are stretched.

The bark of a small dog and ringing chimes have high pitches. A boy´s voice has high pitch, too.

Think About It

1. How is the sound of a kitten different from the sound of a tiger?
2. What is the pitch of a sound?

Literature Connections

Read Alouds

Big Band Sound by Harriett Diller, Boyds Mills Press, 1996.

Sounds All Around by Wendy Pfeffer, HarperCollins, 1999.

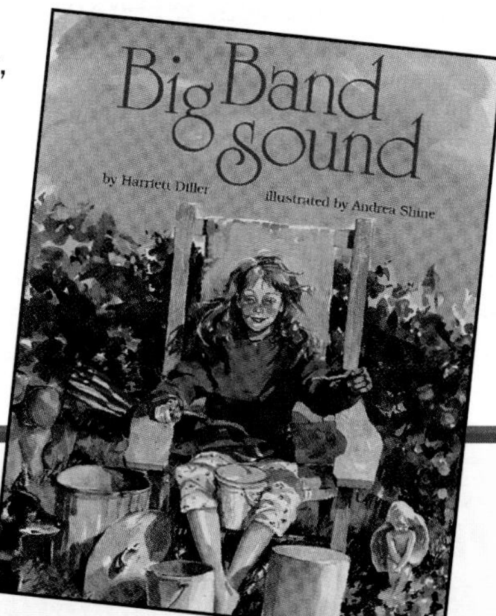

3 Wrap Up and Assess

SUMMARIZE

Have children **summarize** what they have learned as they help you complete the web begun on page E41. Guide them to think of words that describe ways in which sounds are different from one another.

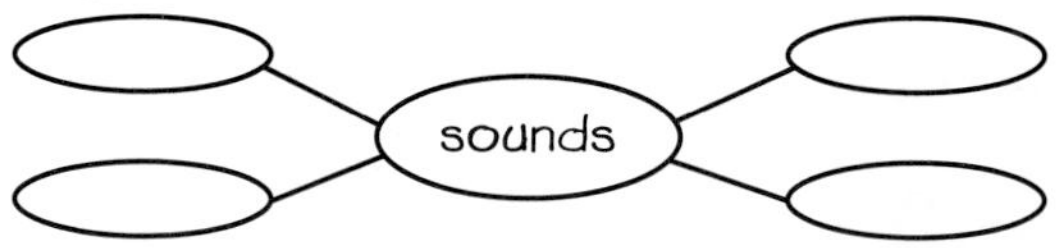

THINK ABOUT IT

1. A kitten often is quiet; a tiger often is loud.
2. how high or low the sound is

Informal Assessment

Portfolio Give each child the opportunity to describe a kind of sound. Have them fold a piece of paper into four sections and label each section with a word that describes sound: high, low, loud, quiet. Have them draw pictures or write the name of an object that makes the sound described in each section.

LESSON CONCEPT REVIEW/ASSESSMENT

Children can use **Workbook p. WB127** to review the lesson concepts.

LESSON 3

What Sounds Do Instruments Make?

Objectives

- ▶ Describe the part of a musical instrument that vibrates.
- ▶ Compare musical instruments.

Motivate

Challenge children to name as many musical instruments as they can. Ask children to suggest different ways to group the instruments. At the end of the lesson, invite children to suggest additional groupings based on lesson concepts.

Investigate

Time 20 min **Grouping** individuals

Process Skill form a hypothesis

Preparation Tips and Expected Results See page E32c.

Center Activity Option Place this Investigation or a copy of the Investigation, page TR70, in your science center.

Activity Tips

Safety Tip To avoid injury, have children use an unsharpened pencil.

- ▶ Guide children to select the hypothesis that most closely resembles their observations after children beat the drums.
- ▶ Have children demonstrate the sound their drums make and compare the sound with that of a classmate's drum.

Children may want to write their hypothesis and the results of the test in their science journal.

Activity Questions

- ▶ How are all the drums alike? How are they different?
- ▶ What makes the sounds different?

When Minutes Count . . .

Use the Activity Video to preview and model how the drum is made and the sound it makes when struck.

PUPIL'S EDITION OR BIG BOOK

What Sounds Do Instruments Make?

Investigate

Making Your Own Drum

You will need

a small can

beans

balloon

rubber band

pencil with eraser

1. Put the beans into the can. Stretch the balloon over the top. Put the rubber band on.
2. Form a hypothesis about your drum. What kind of sound will it make? What will vibrate?
3. Test your hypothesis. Use the pencil to beat the drum. Listen for the sounds.

Science Skill

When you form a hypothesis, you choose and test a possible answer.

E46

Science Skills

Process Skill: Form a Hypothesis

Display Process Skill Tip Transparency E2-3. Have children follow the visual instructions to make the harmonica. Before playing the harmonica, have children predict the sound it will make and the part that will vibrate. Record children's ideas on the transparency. After testing the harmonica, invite children to revise their hypothesis as needed.

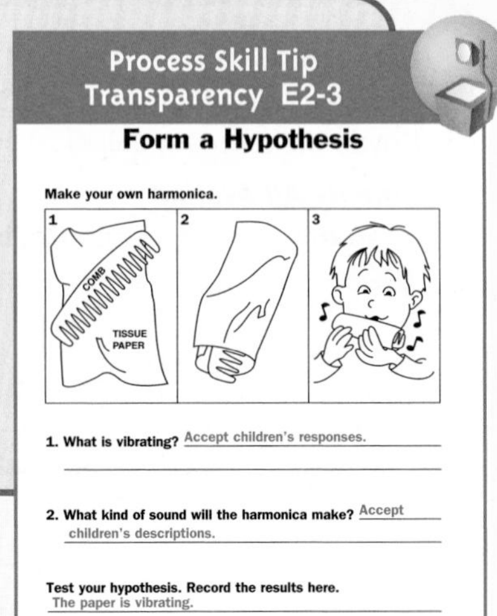

Process Skill Tip Transparency E2-3

Form a Hypothesis

Make your own harmonica.

1. What is vibrating? Accept children's responses.

2. What kind of sound will the harmonica make? Accept children's descriptions.

Test your hypothesis. Record the results here.
The paper is vibrating.

PROCESS SKILLS PRACTICE

To practice and apply process skills, see **Workbook p. WB128.**

Learn About

Instrument Sounds

The boys and girls are making music together. Each person is playing a **musical instrument**, something used to make music. Each instrument has its own sound.

E47

Learn About

1 Before Reading

PREVIEW/SET PURPOSES

Have children preview pages E47–E49. Make a K-W-L chart. Have children fill in what they know and want to know about musical instruments.

K-W-L Chart		
What I Know	What I Want to Know	What I Learned

2 Guide the Learning

SCIENCE IDEAS

Read aloud page E47 with children. To help reinforce the **main idea**, ask:

- **What is a musical instrument?** something used to make music
- **What is special about each kind of instrument?** Each instrument makes it own sound.

DEVELOP READING SKILLS

Relate Pictures to Text Have children look at the photo and describe what they see. Ask:

- **What are the children doing?** making music together
- **If you were listening to the music, do you think you would hear just one sound or many sounds?** many sounds

BACKGROUND

Webliography
GO ONLINE
Keyword sound
www.harcourtschool.com

Musical Instruments Musical instruments have either a string, a thin piece of metal or wood, or some other part that vibrates when set in motion. In western culture instruments are divided into strings, woodwinds, percussion, and keyboard.

Stringed Instruments, like the violin, harp, and guitar, produce sound when one or more strings vibrate when plucked or bowed.

Wind Instruments are of two types—woodwinds, which include the the clarinet and the saxophone; and brass instruments, which include the trumpet. Both types produce sound via a column of vibrating air.

Percussion Instruments, such as drums and maracas, are played by shaking or striking them with a stick or mallet.

Keyboard Instruments, such as the piano, produce sound when a key is struck, which causes a string to vibrate.

SCIENCE WORD WALL

The Sound of Music Make a word card for the term *musical instrument*. Have children make word cards for different instruments. As a class, decide how to group the instrument word cards. Then have children post them on the Word Wall accordingly.

musical instrument
violin
guitar
piano

ESL Activity Have children draw or cut out pictures of the musical instruments named. Post each picture next to the corresponding word card.

Guide the Learning continued

SCIENCE IDEAS

Have children read pages E48 and E49. Have children find and read aloud the sentence on each page that states the **main idea**. Then ask:

- ▶ **What instruments make a high-pitched sound?** instruments with parts that vibrate very fast
- ▶ **What are two ways instruments are played?** Some instruments are plucked; a drum is beaten or hit.

VISUAL LEARNING

Direct attention to the top pair of photos on page E48. Explain that the person is playing a guiro, a South American instrument made from a gourd. When scraped with a stick, the guiro gives off a raspy sound. Ask:

- ▶ **What is the child using as a homemade musical instrument?** a bottle with a ridged side

USE PROCESS SKILLS

Compare Direct attention to the photos, pair by pair. Point out that each pair of photos shows a manufactured instrument and a homemade instrument. For each pair of photos, ask:

- ▶ **How are the instruments alike?** in how they are played and in the part of the instrument that vibrates

DEVELOP SCIENCE VOCABULARY

musical instrument Have children revisit pages E47–E49 and name the musical instruments shown. Invite them to tell about other instruments they have heard or have played.

PUPIL'S EDITION OR BIG BOOK

Listen to Instrument Sounds

A musical instrument makes sound when part of it vibrates. Some instruments have parts that vibrate very fast. These instruments make a sound with a high pitch. Other instruments have parts that vibrate more slowly. These make a sound with a low pitch.

E48

Math Link

Math Music Sing a familiar song with children and have them clap the beat with you. Explain that most music has a basic beat similar to the one they just experienced. Point out that a beat may be divided in parts. Demonstrate by clapping out a slow, four beat rhythm, putting emphasis on the first of each four beats. Have children count the beats as you clap them. Ask children to clap and count a rhythm in which each basic beat is divided into two quicker beats. How many times did they clap? eight Experiment with dividing each beat into three and then four quicker beats. Children should clap 12 times and 16 times, respectively. Point out that much music is based on rhythmic and number relationships like these.

THE QUESTIONS KIDS ASK!

What is the difference between music and noise?

Address Misconceptions Music is organized and pleasing sound. It consists primarily of two elements—melody and rhythm. Noise is a random mixture of sounds. It is most often made by objects sending out irregular vibrations at irregular intervals. Machines, other human-made objects, and natural events, such as thunder and earthquakes, all create noise.

Instruments are played in different ways. A drummer beats a drum to make its covering vibrate. Players sometimes pluck the strings of an instrument to make them vibrate.

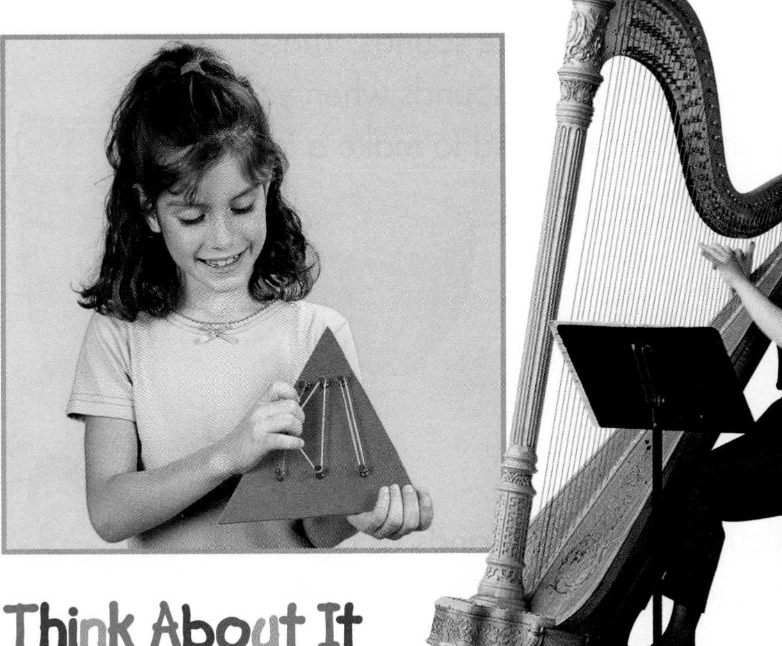

Think About It

1. In what way are all musical instruments the same?
2. How are musical instruments different?

E49

Literature Connections

Read Alouds

Max Found Two Sticks by Brian Pinkney, Simon & Schuster, 1997.

Song and Dance Man by Karen Ackerman, Knopf, 1992.

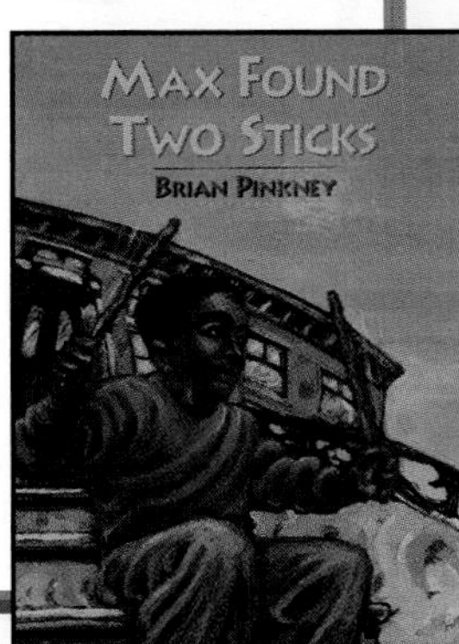

3 Wrap Up and Assess

SUMMARIZE

Have children **summarize** what they have learned. Have them fill in what they have learned on the K-W-L chart begun on page E47. Review any questions that remain unanswered, and develop strategies for finding out more.

K-W-L Chart		
What I Know	What I Want to Know	What I Learned

THINK ABOUT IT

1. Every instrument makes sound when part of it vibrates.
2. They make different sounds and are played differently.

Informal Assessment

Performance Provide children with the opportunity to retell key concepts in this lesson about musical instruments. Some may want to demonstrate their understanding by showing how different musical instruments are played.

LESSON CONCEPT REVIEW/ASSESSMENT

Children can use **Workbook p. WB129** to review the lesson concepts.

VOCABULARY REVIEW

Children can use **Workbook p. WB130** to review the chapter vocabulary.

Chapter 2 Links

Social Studies Link
Sounds from Around the World

Link Objective Recognize that similar types of instruments are used in various cultures.

Talk about the photograph. Explain that the instruments shown are used in cultures from all over the world. Encourage children to describe what they all have in common. Each is played by striking or hitting some part of it.

Read aloud the text. Point out that the instruments shown belong to a group called membranophones. Musicians tap the stretched skin or membrane with sticks or their hands. Have children describe other instruments played the same way.

WRITE

Have children work in pairs to develop a rhythm they want to share with classmates. Offer them pots or pans to use as instruments. Then have children write several sentences about which type of sound they like best. Ask:

- **Which makes a harsher sound, pots and pans or hands clapping?** pots and pans
- **Which makes a more pleasant sound?** hands clapping

PUPIL'S EDITION OR BIG BOOK

Links

Social Studies Link

Sounds from Around the World

People all over the world use musical instruments to make sounds. These instruments make sounds when you hit them. They are used to make a beat.

Write

You can use your hands as a musical instrument. Clap to make a beat. Then change the beat. Listen to the sounds you make. Pots and pans can make sounds like instruments, too. Write about which of these sounds you like better.

E50

More Link Options . . .

Music Link

A Scale Song Tell children that a musical scale is made up of eight notes and that each note has a lyrical name. Write the names of the notes on the board and read them aloud with children. (do, re, mi, fa, so, la, ti, do) To help children remember the notes, teach them the lyrics to the well-known song, "Do-Re-Mi."

Language Arts Link

Musical How-To Provide children with materials such as paper cups and plates, cardboard tubes and boxes, rubber bands, dried beans, masking tape, paints, colored paper, and glue. Encourage children working in pairs to use the materials to make a musical instrument. After the instrument is made, have them work together to write directions so that someone else could make the instrument. Invite volunteers to demonstrate how their instruments are played and read aloud the instructions for making them. Display children's finished work on a "musical" tabletop.

Measure How Far a Whisper Travels

A whisper is a quiet sound. It can not be heard from far away. You can measure how far a whisper travels.

Think and Do

Make a long tape line on the floor. Measure and mark every meter with an **X**. Stand one meter from a classmate. Can you hear a whisper? Move farther away, one meter at a time. Find out how far the sound of a whisper travels.

E51

Math Link
Measure How Far a Whisper Travels

Link Objective Measure the distance a whisper can be heard.

Talk about the photograph. Have children describe the sound being made by the child who is talking. Ask them if someone standing far away could hear the sound.

Read aloud the text. Ask children how to measure the distance a whisper travels. Discuss factors needed for a fair measurement. The volume and setting of the whisper should remain the same.

THINK AND DO

After tape has been laid on the floor and marked with Xs at meter intervals, have children observe the distances. Ask them to predict how far away the sound of a whisper will be heard. Then have children record the results.

Investigate the effect of louder and softer whispers. Have children record the results of these whispers.

Informal Assessment

Portfolio Have children add to their portfolios the results they recorded about how far whispers travel.

Physical Education Link

Red Light, Green Light Have children play a game of "Red Light, Green Light" in which you give the commands in a whisper. After several minutes, change your voice to a normal speaking voice, and then to a shout. Afterward, talk about how the loudness of your voice affected the game.

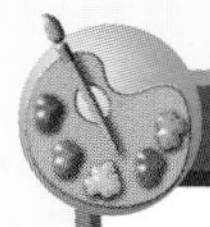

Art Link

The Art of Sound Talk about the feelings children may experience as they hear different sounds or music. Some sounds or music may make them feel happy; others may make them feel sad or excited. Provide children with paper and drawing or painting materials. Then play some music. Encourage children to paint a picture that shows how the music makes them feel. Invite volunteers to tell about their work. Display the pictures on a bulletin board under a title such as "How Music Makes Us Feel."

Chapter 

Review and Test Preparation

Tell What You Know

SUMMARIZE/RETELL

1. Children can use the photos to tell what they know about sound. Check for the following concepts in their responses.

- ▶ Vibration causes sound.
- ▶ Sound may be quiet or loud, high or low.

TEST PREP Test-Taking Tips

Model this strategy with children to help them use the word to tell about the picture.

To use the word to tell about the picture, first I think about the meaning of the word. Then I look for clues in the picture that go with the word. Then I make up a sentence.

Vocabulary

REVIEW SCIENCE VOCABULARY

Children review chapter vocabulary by using each word to tell about the picture.

2. The rubber bands vibrate and make a sound.
3. The microphone makes the sound of the ring-master's voice louder.
4. The boy's voice has a higher pitch than the man's voice.

GRAPHIC ORGANIZER FOR CHAPTER CONCEPTS

Children can use the graphic organizer to record key concepts and ideas from each lesson. See **Workbook p. WB123** and **Transparency E2.**

PUPIL'S EDITION OR BIG BOOK

Tell What You Know

1. Tell what you know about each musical instrument.

Vocabulary

Use each word to tell about the picture.

2. 
vibrate

3. 
sound

4. pitch

E52

Graphic Organizer for Chapter Concepts

Transparency E2 • Workbook, p. WB123

Unit E, Chapter 2 Making Sound

LESSON 1 What Are Sounds?	LESSON 2 How Are Sounds Different?	LESSON 3 What Sounds Do Instruments Make?
1. Sound is made when objects vibrate. 2. You hear sounds all around you.	1. Sounds are different. 2. Sounds can be quiet or loud. 3. The pitch of a sound is how high or low the sound is.	1. Musical instruments make sound when a part vibrates. 2. Each instrument has its own sound.

Using Science Skills

5. Use Numbers Make four shakers by putting dried beans inside plastic cups taped together. The numbers in the chart tell how many dried beans to put in each shaker. How does the number of dried beans change the sound a shaker makes? Record your ideas.

Number of Dried Beans	2	10	20	40
Sound the Shaker Makes				

6. Form a Hypothesis Hold a bell by the handle at the top. Use a spoon to strike the side of the bell. Listen for the sound. Then hold the bell by the side. Form a hypothesis about the sound the bell will make now. Test your hypothesis.

E53

Using Science Skills

REVIEW PROCESS SKILLS

5. Use Numbers Divide the class into four groups. Have each group make a shaker with 2, 10, 20, or 40 beans. Write the following instructions on the board for children to follow:

Step 1: Take the number of beans you need.
Step 2: Put the right number of beans in a cup.
Step 3: Tape the two cups together.

Call on a volunteer from each group to demonstrate the sound the instrument makes by shaking it. Discuss how the sound changes from one shaker to the next. Remind children that the primary difference in sound is caused by the difference in the number of beans. Allow time for children to record their conclusions about the experience in writing.

PERFORMANCE ASSESSMENT

6. Form a Hypothesis For a clear sound and the greatest contrast, use a metal spoon or a mallet to strike the bell. Before striking the bell while holding it from the side, call on volunteers to form a hypothesis about the sound it will make. Encourage children to explain their thinking. Write the hypotheses on the board. An acceptable hypothesis is: The sound will be softer because the bell, held by the side, will not be able to vibrate very much.

WRITING ABOUT SCIENCE

Have children write a composition that involves writing for a specific purpose. You may wish to use the prompt that is provided in the Workbook. The prompt is accompanied by a graphic organizer that will help children organize their ideas before writing. Models for writing are provided in the **Teaching Resources** book. You may wish to reproduce those for children or display them on a transparency.

WRITING PRACTICE

A chapter writing prompt and a prewriting activity are provided on **Workbook p. WB132**.

CHAPTER TEST

See **Assessment Guide pages AG77–80** for the Chapter Test. Assessment Options are provided on p. E32e.

TAKE-HOME BOOK

Use the **Take-Home Book** (described on p. E32d) to provide more chapter content and activities.

Activities
for Home or School

Make Juice Bars

Objective

▶ **Observe how matter can change.**

Suggested Time 5 minutes plus 3-hour wait

Hints

▶ To prevent the toothpicks from falling out, cover the fruit-juice-filled tray with aluminum foil; then stick the toothpicks in through the foil.

▶ Children should note the state of the juice before and after it is frozen.

Safety Tip Warn children to be careful when handling the toothpicks because they have sharp points.

Draw Conclusions Children observe that liquids can change to solids.

Investigate Further Under adult supervision, children can place in the freezer plastic cups filled respectively with water, salt water, and oil. Every hour children observe the state of the substance in each cup.

Floating Drops

Objective

▶ **Conduct a simple investigation to observe the density of different liquids.**

Suggested Time 10 minutes

Hints

▶ You may need to demonstrate how to use a dropper before children do this activity.

▶ You may wish to add water to the jar after children have observed what happens when they put drops of food coloring in the oil.

Safety Tip Make sure children close the lid tightly before they tip the jar.

Draw Conclusions Children observe that the drops of food coloring sink to the bottom of the oil and infer that they are heavier.

UNIT E

Activities
for Home or School

Make Juice Bars

Change liquid juice into a solid by making juice bars.

1. Have a family member help you pour fruit juice into an ice cube tray.
2. Put a toothpick into each part of the tray. *Be careful. Toothpicks are sharp.*
3. Freeze and eat!

Floating Drops

1. Fill a jar with salad oil.
2. Put two or three drops of food coloring into the oil. Put the lid on the jar.
3. Tip the jar. What happens to the colored drops? Talk about what floats and why.

E54

School-Home Connection

These activities provide an excellent opportunity to assign hands-on activities for the children and their families. The materials are often easy to obtain and are safe to work with. For those activities that you do not wish to do in the classroom, encourage children to complete them at home. Remind them that communicating their results is always important, but especially so for home activities since you will not be there to observe their activities. Ask children to use sketches, graphs, or even photographs to show their results.

Listen for Sounds

1. Close your eyes and sit quietly for one minute. Do not speak or move.
2. Listen carefully for sounds.
3. Draw pictures to show the sounds you heard.
4. Compare with a classmate or family member. Which sounds did both of you hear?

Find the Sound

1. All players close their eyes.
2. One player is "it" and rings a bell softly.
3. The other players guess where the sound is coming from.
4. The player who locates "it" makes the next sound.

E55

Language Arts Link

Tab Book Have children complete the following prompt.

On separate sheets of paper, write about solids, liquids, and gases. Add a label to each page. Put your pages together to make a book.

Listen for Sounds

Objective

- **Observe and identify sounds heard during the course of one minute.**

Suggested Time 1 minute to observe sounds; 15 minutes to draw pictures of sounds and compare with classmates

Hints

- Remind children to listen for indoor and outdoor sounds.
- Children may list the sounds instead of drawing pictures if they wish.

Safety Tip Remind children not to move while their eyes are closed in order to avoid an accident.

Draw Conclusions Children observe that the quieter they are and the more closely they listen, the more sounds they hear. Not everyone hears the same sounds.

Investigate Further Children may want to try the listening activity in a different location to see whether the sounds they hear are similar or different from those heard in the first location.

Find the Sound

Objective

- **Observe the direction from which a sound is coming.**

Suggested Time 5 minutes per "round"

Hints

- The player who is "it" should tiptoe so as not to give away the location from which the sound of the bell will be coming.
- To avoid giving away the sound's location, be sure the player who rings the bell returns to his or her seat before the other players open their eyes.

Safety Tip To avoid possible harm to another person's hearing, tell children not to ring the bell next to someone's ear.

Draw Conclusions Children discover that they are able to determine the direction from which a sound is coming by using only their sense of hearing.

ACTIVITIES FOR HOME OR SCHOOL

Reproducible copies of these activities are provided in the **Teaching Resources** book.

UNIT E Expeditions

Objectives

- Observe how sound has been used through the invention of the telephone.
- Compare telephone technology of the past with technology used today.

Hints

A field trip to the Georgia Rural Telephone Museum or a similar destination may not be feasible for your class. If so, consider visiting The Learning Site on the Internet. This site provides links to sites appropriate for student learning.

www.harcourtschool.com

UNIT E

Expeditions

Georgia Rural Telephone Museum, Leslie, Georgia

At this museum, you can learn about the telephone. You can learn how sound travels long distances. You can also see how the telephone has changed over time.

Plan Your Own Expedition

Visit a museum near you. Or log on to The Learning Site.

www.harcourtschool.com

E56

UNIT TEST

See **Assessment Guide pp. A83–86** for the Unit Assessment. The Unit Assessment includes items for all the chapters in this Unit.

UNIT F

Unit Overview

Unit Theme A force (push or pull) interacts with an object and causes the object to move. Magnetic attraction is a force that affects the motion of an object.

Skills for Lifelong Learning

Science Process Skills

The Science Process Skills are important inquiry tools and are essential for investigating the natural world. Opportunities for developing process skills are provided throughout *Harcourt Science.* The pages shown in this chart indicate where the process skills receive special emphasis.

Science Process Skill	Skill Tip and Mini-Lesson	Skills Practice (Workbook)	Reinforcement
Observe			F1j, F10, F16, F20, F44, F48, F56
Compare			F6, F10, F24, F34, F56
Classify/Order	F8	WB136	
Gather, Record, Display, or Interpret Data	F32	WB148	F1j
Use Numbers			
Communicate			F1j
Plan and Conduct Simple Investigations	F4, F42	WB134, WB152	F1j, F40
Measure	F18	WB140	F1j, F29
Predict	F12	WB138	F36, F40
Infer	F38	WB150	F53
Draw Conclusions	F22, F46	WB142, WB154	F1j, F24, F54, F55
Use Time/Space Relationships			
Formulate or Use Models			
Form a Hypothesis			F1j

Reading, Writing, and Math Skills

Effective science instruction integrates science content and experiences with all areas of the elementary curriculum. *Harcourt Science* provides students with many opportunities to develop reading, writing, and math skills via meaningful activities and strategies built into every lesson in this unit.

Reading Skills Checklist

Strategies for developing the following reading skills are provided in this unit.

- ☑ **use context** F35
- ☑ **recall supporting facts and details** F9, F13
- ☐ **arrange events in sequence**
- ☑ **draw conclusions** F15, F16, F23, F24, F44, F48
- ☑ **identify the main idea** F5, F9, F13, F19, F23, F33, F39, F43, F47
- ☑ **identify cause and effect** F2, F15, F16, F20, F40, F44
- ☑ **predict outcomes** F6, F14, F24, F40, F44, F48
- ☑ **summarize** F7, F10, F11, F17, F21, F25, F37, F41, F45, F49
- ☑ **use graphic sources for information** F20, F37
- ☑ **relate pictures to text** F2, F5, F6, F9, F13, F19, F24, F30, F33, F35, F36, F43, F47
- ☐ **distinguish between fact and nonfact**
- ☐ **develop concepts of print**
- ☑ **build vocabulary** F5, F6, F9, F10, F13, F14, F19, F20, F23, F24, F33, F34, F39, F40, F43, F44, F47, F48

Writing Links

Prompts that provide opportunities for students to express their ideas in writing are provided in every chapter in this unit.

Add Pushes for Points F27
Writing About Science F29, F53
Measure Magnetic Force F50

Math Links

Opportunities to practice math skills, solve problems, and connect math and science are provided in every chapter.

How Many Wheels? F24
Add Pushes for Points F27
Count the Pages F44
Measure Magnetic Force F50
Magnetic Ants Go Marching F50

UNIT F

How to Integrate Your Day

Use these topics to help you integrate science into your daily planning.

Fine Arts

Paper Pop-Ups F10
Designing with Clay F26
Feel the Tickle F26
Rowing with Music F27
Guess What I'm Pushing, Guess What I'm Pulling F27
Make a Magnet Animal F48
Magnetic Ants Go Marching F50
Sail the Boat F51

Physical Education

Using Friction to Crabwalk F20
Rowing with Music F27
A Magnetic Version of Musical Chairs F40

Math

How Many Wheels? F24
Add Pushes for Points F27
Count the Pages F44
Measure Magnetic Force F50
Magnetic Ants Go Marching F50

Writing

Add Pushes for Points F27
Writing About Science F29, F53
Measure Magnetic Force F50

Literature

Push It or Pull It? F7
Train Song F7
The Wheeling and Whirling-Around Book F11
Forces and Movement F11
The Science Book of Motion F17
Doctor DeSoto F17
Mrs. Toggle's Zipper F21
Inclined Planes F21
Wheels and Axles F25
The Wheels on the Bus F25
Jeff's Magnet F37
Experiments with Magnets F37
Magnetism F41
What Magnets Can Do F41
Science With Magnets F45
Magnets and Sparks F45
The Science Book of Magnets F49
Electricity and Magnetism F49

Language Arts

Concrete Poetry: Bumps and Bounces F16
Silly Magnetic Sentences F51
Accordion Book F55

Social Studies

Putting Pushes and Pulls to Work F6
An Architect Plans Buildings F26
Sorting Trash F34
Original Magnets F36
Compass Points F50
Compass Readings F51

UNIT F

Science in Centers

Science Center

Forces

Ongoing Center Activity Place these items in your science center, which children can use to investigate on an ongoing basis:

- pictures of people and things in motion
- paper, pencil, magnets, marbles, paper clips, balls, toys with wheels, ramps, tubes, wind-up toys
- book box of related books. See recommended books listed at the beginning of each chapter on the "Providing More Depth" pages.

Center Management Tip As you begin each lesson, place the lesson investigation or a copy of it and needed materials in the science center.

Bulletin Board Idea Label the bulletin board "How We Move Things." Invite children to draw or cut out pictures of people using forces to move objects. After pictures are pinned up, encourage children to label the pictures according to the type of force shown.

Game Center

Races and Mazes

Materials marbles, magnets, blocks, masking tape, cardboard tubes, rulers, books

Center Activity Divide the class into small groups. Have each group design a tabletop maze or racetrack using blocks, masking tape, tubes, and rulers. Children can navigate the path either by pushing a marble or using one magnet to pull another.

Have groups devise rules for playing their tabletop game. Help them write their rules in sequence. Then post the rules in the center.

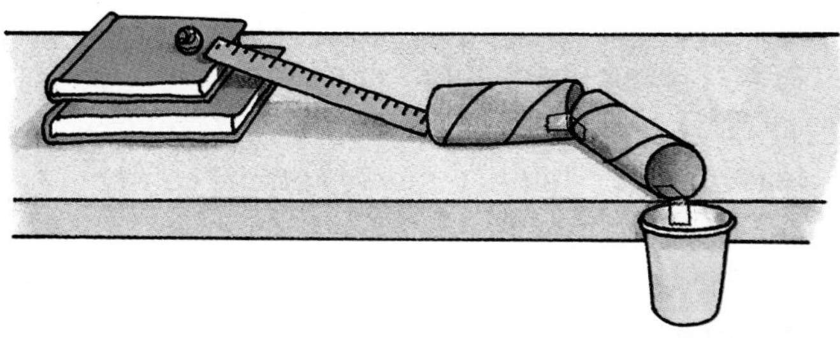

Unit Technology

Look for these technology links referenced throughout the lessons in your Teacher's Edition.

Smithsonian Institution®

Visit this special Internet site for correlated links to virtual tours, on-line exhibits, and hands-on investigations from the Smithsonian Institution. **www.si.edu/harcourt/science**

Harcourt Science Instant Readers CD-ROM These CD-ROM programs reinforce science vocabulary and concepts and provide a variety of on-screen activities.

Harcourt Science Activity Video These videos show children doing the investigations for each lesson.

The Learning Site Visit the Harcourt Learning Site for a world of science resources, including News Breaks, interactive learning games, and an animated Science Glossary. **www.harcourtschool.com**

NSTA SciLinks Internet links provided by the National Science Teachers Association in partnership with Harcourt. **www.scilinks.org/harcourt**

UNIT F

Reaching All Learners

Strategies for Multi-Age Classrooms

Develop Science Process Skills

- Pair children who are using a ramp, meterstick, and different textures to investigate motion and friction with older children who are investigating different ways to measure motion. Children can work together and benefit from examining different surfaces while gaining practice in measuring distance.

Build Science Concepts

- Build and reinforce the concepts of push and pull by grouping children short-term for intensive instruction. Have more advanced children help younger children understand the concept of changing motion by demonstrating it in a visual or kinesthetic way—such as by using a paddle to deflect a ping-pong ball or by drawing an illustration with motion lines showing the curved path a train may make.
- Younger, less-advanced children may benefit from hearing others tell what they learned in their investigations of forces and motion, how they found out, and why they think what they learned is important.

Strategies for ESL Students

Build Concepts

Use webs to help children build and review lesson concepts.

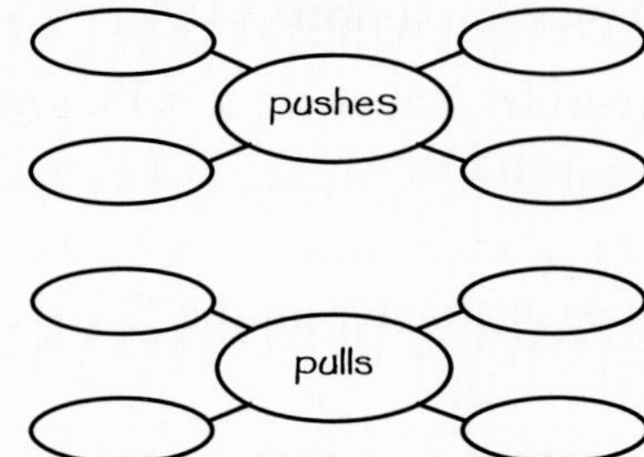

Develop Oral Language

Game Children may enjoy playing a game in which they take turns demonstrating a push or pull and then having a partner guess which force it is. To extend the activity, have children use the word *push* or *pull* in a sentence to tell what is being moved.

Reread Have small groups reread sections of lessons, discuss them, and then choose a concept to demonstrate for classmates. For example, children may want to demonstrate curving motion or friction in Chapter 1 lessons and magnetic force or magnetizing an object in Chapter 2 lessons.

ESL Activities

Point-of-use ESL activities are provided in the lessons throughout the unit.

Strategies for Special Needs Students

Learning Difficulties

To provide extra support while reinforcing vocabulary and concepts, have children read and discuss the Take-Home Books in class before taking them home to share.

Visually Impaired

Empower children during investigations that examine the effect of friction on motion by having them feel and select different materials to test. To aid children in reading measurements on a meterstick, provide them with a hand lens.

Children may also benefit from listening to the lesson audiotapes.

Hearing Impaired

Provide for additional repetition of skills, such as in measuring distance. Also, when modeling lesson activities and investigations, break down tasks into smaller steps and repeat as necessary.

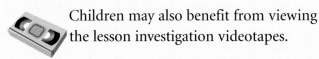

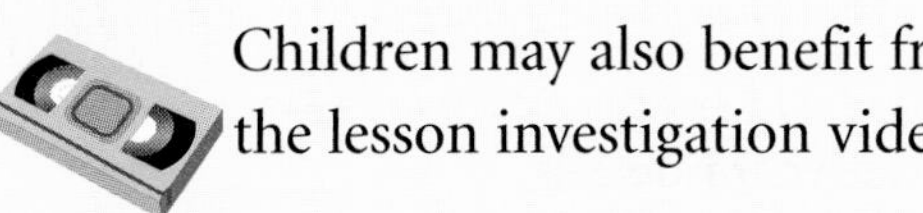

Children may also benefit from viewing the lesson investigation videotapes.

Strategies for Advanced Learners

The following are strategies to allow advanced learners to study the content of the unit in greater depth.

Chapter 1 Pushes and Pulls

- Since many children enjoy games and sports, have them investigate three of their favorite sports and determine how a key push or pull is used in each one. Children then make a chart with labels and pictures to show how push or pull is used in each sport. Encourage children to share their charts and compare the information in them.

Chapter 2 Magnets

Children might enjoy an activity that combines their knowledge of magnets with other forms of force or motion. Have them plan and make a model of a new toy or other object that uses both a magnet and another form of push or pull, such as rollers. Children might first discuss what they have learned in small groups and then brainstorm ideas for their toy and how they want it to work. Encourage exploration of ideas.

Unit Materials List

Quantities are indicated for a class of 30 students working individually or in groups of 5, depending on the nature of the activity. Where shared equipment is suggested, a smaller number of items is specified. Quantities are also listed for those materials included in the Materials Kit.

Nonconsumable Materials	Class Quantity Needed	Kit Quantity	Activity Page
ball, plastic	6	6	F8, F12
blocks, wood (1 in. x 1 in. x 1 in.)	6	6	F4
blocks, wood (2 in. x 4 in. x 6 in)	6	6	F12
board, wooden	6		F1, F12, F18
books	36		F1, F22
carpet	6 pieces		F42
egg, plastic	6	12	F8
lunchbox, metal	6		F42
magnet, bar	6	6	F32, F38, F42, F46
meterstick	6		F1, F18
paper clips	30	1 box of 100	F38, F42, F46
rubber bands	6	1 bag	F4
spring toy	2*	2	F8
truck, toy	6	6	F1, F8, F18, F22

*Student groups should share this equipment.

Consumable Materials	Class Quantity Needed	Kit Quantity	Activity Page
cardboard	6 pieces		F42
craft sticks	6	1 pkg of 30	F4
objects, everyday magnetic	18		F32
objects, everyday nonmagnetic	18		F32
paper, notebook	360 sheets		F4, F8, F18, F32, F38, F42
pencil	24		F1, F4, F8, F18, F22, F32, F38
straws, plastic	6	1 pkg of 50	F4
string	1 roll	1 roll	F4
tape, adding machine	6 rolls	6 rolls	F1
tape, masking	1 roll		F12, F22

Additional kit options are available. Contact your sales representative for details.

UNIT F PHYSICAL SCIENCE

Forces

UNIT EXPERIMENT

Height and Distance

How will the height of a ramp change the distance a car travels? Plan and do a test to find out.

F1

Informal Assessment

Research shows that informal assessment is an effective way to monitor and evaluate children's progress. Performance assessment and teacher observation are particularly useful for assessing projects and other similar tasks.

Performance Develop a rubric that will be used to evaluate children's completed projects. Use Developing Your Own Rubric on page AGxi of the Assessment Guide.

Classroom Observation You can gain insight into children's learning by observing how they use scientific processes, plan investigations and projects, collect and record information, and select and use appropriate tools to implement their project. While children are working on their projects, use the Project Evaluation Checklist on page AGxviii of the Assessment Guide for ongoing assessment.

UNIT F EXPERIMENT

Objectives

- **Promote scientific inquiry.**
- **Use a scientific method to plan and conduct a long-term investigation.**
- **Design an experiment to learn how the height of a ramp affects the distance a car can go.**

A lesson plan for guiding children through the Unit Experiment is provided on pages F1i–F1j.

Science Fair Project Ideas

In addition to the Unit Experiment, you may wish to allow children to plan and carry out these science fair projects related to the chapters in Unit F. Children can use the framework on pages *10–17 to help them plan and conduct experiments.

Chapter 1 Demolition Derby Have children investigate how a toy car can be changed to make it push a wood block a greater distance. Have children set up a control by running a toy car down a ramp into a wood block. Children should mark the starting point on the ramp and run this experiment three times to compare the distance the block is pushed each time. Have children record their results on a poster. Then have children make a change to the car to make it push the block farther. For example, children might add more weight to the car, add rubber bands to the wheels to improve traction, or launch the car backwards. Have children test each variable and measure and record the distance the wood block travels. Suggest that children test what would happen if the car stayed the same, but the ramp was altered. Have them make changes in the ramp such as angle, surface, and a change in starting point. Then have children make a bar graph to compare their results.

Chapter 2 Magnet Mania Have children investigate how various conditions affect the strength of a magnet. For example, children can obtain three identical magnets and test their strengths by recording how many paper clips each can pick up. Then have children place one magnet in a freezer, place another in water, and leave another as is. Children can then test each magnet again to see if the varied conditions affect the magnet's ability to pick up paper clips. Guide children in suggesting their own conditions for testing a magnet's strength.

UNIT F EXPERIMENT

Height and Distance

Choose from these options to help children complete the unit experiment.

Option 1 Independent Inquiry Assign the experiment for children to complete independently or with the help of an adult at home. Children should use the prompt as a springboard for writing their own questions and designing their own experiments. They can write a hypothesis, plan a fair test, select materials, and conduct the test. Children can refer to pages *10–17 in the Pupil Edition for guidance.

Option 2 Guided Inquiry Suggest that children use the prompt and the Experiment Log (Workbook pp. WB178–180) to help them plan their experiment. The Experiment Log pages shown here appear in the Workbook, but without answers. Children can write or draw their responses.

Option 3 Structured Inquiry Have children complete the experiment by testing the hypothesis and using the procedure that have been provided on the overhead transparency. You may wish to display the overhead transparencies shown here (or provide photocopies from the transparency package) and have children copy the hypothesis, variables, and procedure onto the Experiment Log (Workbook pp. WB178–180). You might also prefer to copy the steps for conducting the experiment onto chart paper. Use the Experiment Lesson Plan to guide children as they complete the experiment.

BACKGROUND

Webliography GO ONLINE
Keyword motion
www.harcourtschool.com

Gravity When a force acts on an object, it pushes or pulls on it. This can cause a change in an object's speed, direction, or both. In this experiment, the force of gravity pulls downward on a truck, making it roll down a board ramp. Each time the upper end of the ramp is raised, increasing its height, the truck rolls downhill faster. The faster its speed, the greater the distance it rolls after leaving the ramp. Eventually, the force of friction between the wheels of the truck and the surface they are rolling on acts to slow and stop the truck. The smoother the surface, the less friction, and the farther the truck will roll.

LESSON PLAN

Resources

Experiment Log, Unit F, Workbook pp. WB178–180

Experiment Transparencies, Unit F

Time 30–45 minutes

Expected Results Children should find that the toy truck rolls a greater distance each time the ramp height is increased.

Suggested Materials

- board (thin cardboard works best)
- meterstick
- 4–6 books
- toy truck
- adding machine tape
- pencil

Underlined items above are provided in the equipment kits (available separately).

Preparation Tips To enable the truck to roll smoothly between the ramp and the flat surface, tape a folded sheet of paper to the bottom of the ramp. Make sure the truck has a smooth surface to run on after it leaves the board.

Have children use metersticks to measure the height of the ramp. They should roll the adding machine tape out to the distance traveled, tear off the paper where the truck stopped, and write the height of the ramp for that run on the same piece of paper.

Transparency Exp F, p. 1
Workbook p. WB178

Height and Distance

Observe and ask a question.

1. What can you ask about the way height affects distance?

   How does the height of a ramp change how far a toy truck will go?

Form a hypothesis.

2. What could be true about the way a change in height changes the distance a toy truck will go?

   Making one end of a ramp higher will make a toy truck go farther.

Plan a fair test.

3. What things will you keep the same in the test? Write or draw them here.

   I will use the same toy truck, the same board, and the same rolling surface each time. I will start the truck at the same place each time.

1 Observe and Ask a Question

Have children discuss the prompt. Write the following question on chart paper, or suggest that children record it in the Experiment Log, item 1.

2 Form a Hypothesis

Guide children in forming a testable hypothesis and recording it in the Experiment Log, item 2.

- **Look at the question we are going to investigate. What do you predict will be the answer to this question?** Possible answer: If a ramp is made higher, a toy truck will roll farther.
- **Use your answer to form a statement. Your statement should be something you think will happen when you do the test. This statement will be your hypothesis.** Possible statement: The higher a ramp is, the farther a toy truck will roll after it leaves the ramp.

3 Plan a Fair Test

Remind children that an experiment is a fair test of a hypothesis. Discuss the concept of "fair test." This is also known as *controlling variables.*

- **What things should you keep the same in order to make the test fair?** Possible answers: I should use the same toy truck and ramp each time. The truck needs to start at the same spot and roll on the same surface each time it leaves the ramp.
- **Suppose you added weight to the truck when you changed the height of the board, or used a heavier truck. Would this be fair?** Possible answer: No, adding weight might change the speed at which the truck rolls.
- **We are keeping many things the same. What is the one thing that will be different in the test?** the ramp height

Have children record their plans for conducting a fair test in the Experiment Log, items 3–6, or write the plans on the board or on chart paper.

4 Do the Test

Children can record their data in the Experiment Log, item 7, by recording the measured ramp height and the distance traveled from the ramp. Children may wish to use metersticks to measure and record the length of the adding machine tape, or they may describe the distances traveled using comparative phrases such as "not far," "farther," and "farthest."

Common Error Alert Make sure children position the truck at the same spot at the top of the ramp each time before letting it roll. You might suggest that they line up the back of the truck with the end of the board. Tape the ramp down so it doesn't move.

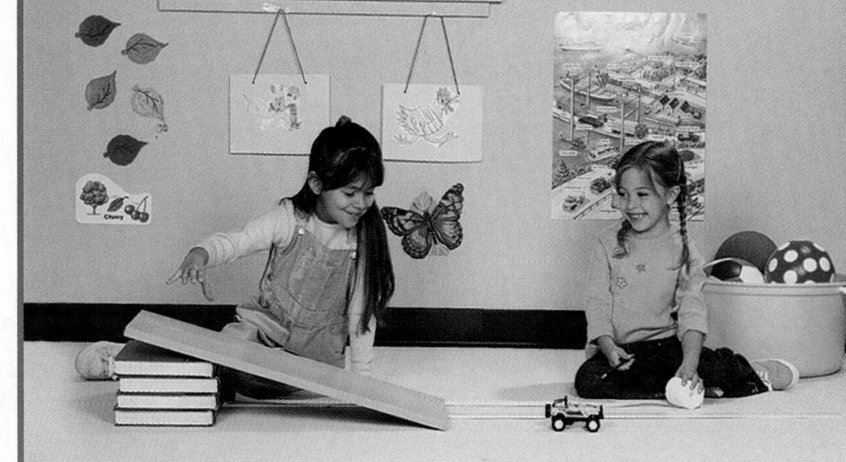

5 Draw Conclusions and Communicate Results

Guide children in interpreting the data they have collected. Children should conclude that the truck travels a greater distance each time the ramp is raised. This is due to the increased speed of the truck.

Discuss whether the test supported the hypothesis.

- **How do our results compare to our hypothesis?** Possible answer: We found that the truck travels a greater distance when the ramp is made higher, so our hypothesis is correct. The data from our experiment supports our hypothesis.

Transparency Exp F, p. 2
Workbook p. WB179

4. What is one thing you will change in the test?
I will change the height of the ramp.

5. What objects will you need to do the test? Write or draw them here.
I will use a toy truck, board, books, meterstick, roll of paper, and pencil.

6. What steps will you take to do the test?
a. Put one end of a board on one or two books. Measure the height of the ramp.
b. Put a toy truck at the top. Let it roll down the ramp.
c. Use the roll of paper to measure how far the toy truck rolled after leaving the ramp.
d. Repeat these steps three times. Raise the ramp each time by adding more books.

Transparency Exp F, p. 3
Workbook p. WB180

Do the test.

7. Record your data in the chart.

How Does the Height of a Ramp Change How Far a Toy Truck Will Go?

Height of Ramp (Board)	Distance the Truck Rolls

Draw conclusions. Communicate results.

8. What are your results? How can you communicate your results to others?

Planning Guide Pushes and Pulls

LESSON	PACING	OBJECTIVES	MATERIALS
1 What Makes Things Move? F4–7	2 days	▶ Recognize that a force is a push or a pull. ▶ Observe and describe what pushes and pulls can do.	**Investigate** small block, things to make the block move, paper, pencil
2 What Are Some Ways Things Move? F8–11	2 days	▶ Recognize that objects move in different ways. ▶ Observe and describe different kinds of movement.	**Investigate** objects, paper, pencil
3 Why Do Things Move the Way They Do? F12–17	3 days	▶ Recognize that motion involves moving from one place to another. ▶ Recognize that the amount of a change in motion is related to the strength of the push or the pull.	**Investigate** ramp, plastic ball, tape, block

PROCESS SKILLS	VOCABULARY	RESOURCES AND TECHNOLOGY	REACHING ALL LEARNERS
Process Skill Tip plan an investigation **Other Process Skills** compare	**force** **push** **pull**	**Workbook,** pp. WB133–135 **Vocabulary Cards,** pp. TR151–156 **Transparency** F1-1 **Harcourt Science Activity Video** **Harcourt Science Instant Readers CD-ROM**	**Advanced Learners,** p. F1g **Investigation Challenge,** p. F6 **Informal Assessment,** p. F7
Process Skill Tip classify **Other Process Skills** observe, compare	**curve**	**Workbook,** pp. WB136–137 **Transparency** F1-2 **Harcourt Science Activity Video** **Internet Site**	**ESL Activity,** p. F9 **Visually Impaired or Kinesthetic Learners,** p. F10 **Informal Assessment,** p. F11
Process Skill Tip predict **Other Process Skills** observe	**motion** **speed**	**Workbook,** pp. WB138–139 **Transparency** F1-3 **Harcourt Science Activity Video**	**ESL Activity,** p. F14 **Investigation Challenge,** p. F14 **Informal Assessment,** p. F17

Planning Guide Pushes and Pulls

LESSON	PACING	OBJECTIVES	MATERIALS
4 How Do Objects Move on Surfaces? F18–21	2 days	▶ Recognize that friction is a force that makes it harder to move things. ▶ Observe that the motion of objects can be changed by the amount of friction acting upon them.	**Investigate** ramp, toy truck, meterstick, paper, pencil
5 How Do Wheels Help Objects Move? F22–25	2 days	▶ Recognize that a wheel is a roller that turns on an axle. ▶ Recognize that rollers and wheels can be used to make things easier to push or pull.	**Investigate** rollers, heavy book, toy truck, tape
End of Chapter F26–29 **Social Studies/Career Link: An Architect Plans Buildings** **Math Link: Add Pushes for Points** **Chapter Review and Test Preparation**		▶ Recognize how understanding forces is necessary in some careers. ▶ Recognize how pushing and pulling can be used to score points in a game. ▶ Review chapter concepts.	

PROCESS SKILLS	VOCABULARY	RESOURCES AND TECHNOLOGY	REACHING ALL LEARNERS
Process Skill Tip measure **Other Process Skills** observe	**surface** **friction**	**Workbook,** pp. WB140–141 **Transparency** F1-4 **Harcourt Science Activity Video**	**ESL Activity,** p. F19 **Informal Assessment,** p. F21
Process Skill Tip draw a conclusion **Other Process Skills** compare	**wheel**	**Workbook,** pp. WB142–146 **Transparency** F1-5 **Harcourt Science Activity Video**	**Informal Assessment,** p. F25
		Take-Home Book, pp. TH43–44 *Carmina Plays on the Swings* **Activities for Home or School,** pp. TR108–109 **Chapter Test,** pp. AG87–90 **Science Songs,** Track 17	**Informal Assessment,** p. F26 **Performance Assessment,** p. AG91 **Portfolio Evaluation,** p. AGxxiv

Prepare for Activities

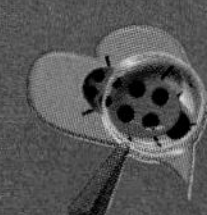

Use this page to help you organize and prepare materials for the Investigations, which begin each lesson of this chapter.

LESSON INVESTIGATION	MATERIALS

1 Pushes and Pulls
F4

PURPOSE Investigate different ways to push or pull an object to make it move.

PREPARATION TIPS Provide rubber bands, craft sticks, pencils, string, straws, and so on, for children to choose from.

TIME 20 minutes

EXPECTED RESULTS Children recognize that objects can be pushed or pulled in different ways.

MATERIALS
- small wooden block
- things to make the block move: rubber band, craft stick, string, and plastic straw
- paper and pencil

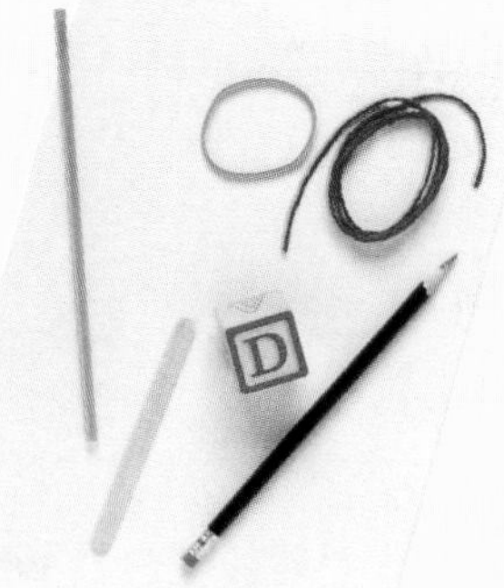

2 Moving Objects
F8

PURPOSE Observe and classify different ways that objects can be moved.

PREPARATION TIPS Provide objects that roll, wobble, slide, vibrate back and forth, and move in other ways for children to try. A rubber band, paper tube, spinning top, ball, and toy truck can be used. Include several of each kind for grouping.

TIME 20–30 minutes

EXPECTED RESULTS Children discover that different objects move in different ways and can be grouped by how they move.

MATERIALS
- objects: plastic ball, plastic egg, spring toy, and toy truck
- paper and pencil

3 Predicting Motion
F12

PURPOSE Observe the motion of an object to predict where it will move when a force is used to change its direction.

PREPARATION TIPS Use a wooden ramp with an incline about three inches high. You may also use a game board or other stiff card-board and two or three books to make a ramp. Set up the ramp on a wood or linoleum floor.

TIME 20–25 minutes

EXPECTED RESULTS Children make predictions and observe how far the ball rolls unobstructed, and how far it rolls after a force is used to change its direction.

MATERIALS
- ramp
- plastic ball
- tape
- wooden block or books

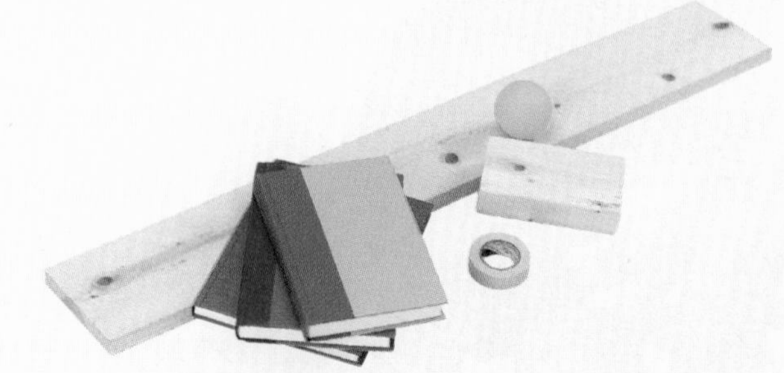

LESSON INVESTIGATION	MATERIALS

4 Smooth and Rough Surfaces
F18

PURPOSE Measure and compare the distances an object rolls on smooth and rough surfaces.

PREPARATION TIPS Prepare the same ramp setup as used for Lesson 3, first on a linoleum floor, then on a carpeted floor. Use a toy truck or car that rolls easily.

TIME 20–25 minutes

EXPECTED RESULTS Children discover that changing the surface affects the distance an object will roll.

- ramp
- toy truck
- meterstick
- paper and pencil

5 Rollers
F22

PURPOSE Conclude that rollers and wheels make objects easier to move.

PREPARATION TIPS Use round pencils for the rollers, and a toy truck or car with wheels that move easily.

TIME 20 minutes

EXPECTED RESULTS Children observe and conclude that rollers and wheels make things easier to push or pull.

- rollers (round pencils)
- heavy book
- toy truck
- tape

Harcourt Science Activity Videos

The Activity Video for this unit shows children doing the Investigations. You may wish to view the video for classroom management ideas. The video can also be used to model the investigation process for children.

Equipment Kits

Underlined items above are provided in the equipment kits (available separately).

. . . with More Activities

. . . with the Take-Home Book

Carmina Plays on the Swings
pages TH43–44, *Take-Home Books*

This take-home book reinforces science concepts and vocabulary presented in the chapter and provides an activity. See p. F29.

Carmina Plays on the Swings

Carmina and her friends want to play together at recess. They love to play on the swings.

. . . with the Harcourt Science Instant Reader

Push It or Pull It? by Rozanne Lanczak Williams looks at objects in everyday life to examine how a push or a pull can be used to make movement. This nonfiction reader reinforces chapter science vocabulary and concepts, as well as high-frequency words. See p. F7.

The **Harcourt Science Instant Reader** is also available on **CD-ROM,** which includes science activities and investigations.

. . . with Trade Books

These books provide in-depth information about how pushes and pulls make things move.

Doctor DeSoto by William Steig (Farrar Straus Giroux, 1990) explains how to use simple machines to do dental work on larger patients when you are a mouse.

Forces and Movement by Peter D. Riley (Franklin Watts, 1998) tells about pushing and pulling forces that make things start, stop, slow down, stick, and slip.

Inclined Planes by Michael S. Dahl (Bridgestone Books, 1996) uses photos and simple text to show different examples of inclined planes and how they help things move.

Mrs. Toggle's Zipper by Robin Pulver (Aladdin, 1993) tells how Mrs. Toggle's zipper gets stuck and traps her inside her coat.

The Science Book of Motion by Neil Ardley (Harcourt, 1992) offers a variety of different activities that help explore how things move.

Train Song by Diane Siebert (HarperCollins, 1993) provides a nostalgic look at trains. *ALA Notable*

Wheels and Axles by Michael S. Dahl (Bridgestone Books, 1996) describes uses of wheels.

The Wheeling and Whirling-Around Book by Judy Hindley (Candlewick, 1996) explains the things in our world that go 'round and 'round.

The Wheels on the Bus by Maryann Kovalski (Little Brown & Co., 1990) discusses moving parts.

Trade book titles are current at time of publication but may go out of print without notice.

Visit The Learning Site for related links, activities, and resources.

www.harcourtschool.com

Assessment Options ✓ Chapter 1

Formal Assessment

- **Chapter Review and Test Preparation,** PE pp. F28–29
- **Chapter Test,** pp. AG87–90

Performance Assessment

- **Chapter Review and Test Preparation,** PE p. F29
- **Chapter Performance Task,** pp. AG91–92
- **Project Evaluation Checklist,** p. AGxviii

Ongoing Assessment

- ✓**Questions,** PE pp. F5–7, F9–11, F13–17, F19–21, F23–25
- **Lesson Review,** PE pp. F7, F11, F17, F21, F25
- **Informal Assessment**
  - **Classroom Observation,** TE p. F21
  - **Performance,** TE pp. F11, F17, F25
  - **Portfolio,** TE pp. F7, F26
- **Observation Checklist,** AGxiv

Student Self-Assessment

- **Self-Assessment – Investigate,** p. AGxvi
- **Self-Assessment – Learn About,** p. AGxvii
- **Project Summary Sheet,** p. AGxix

Portfolio Assessment

- **Science Experiences Record,** p. AGxxii
- **Guide to My Science Portfolio,** p. AGxxiii
- **Portfolio Evaluation,** p. AGxxiv

Chapter Test AG87

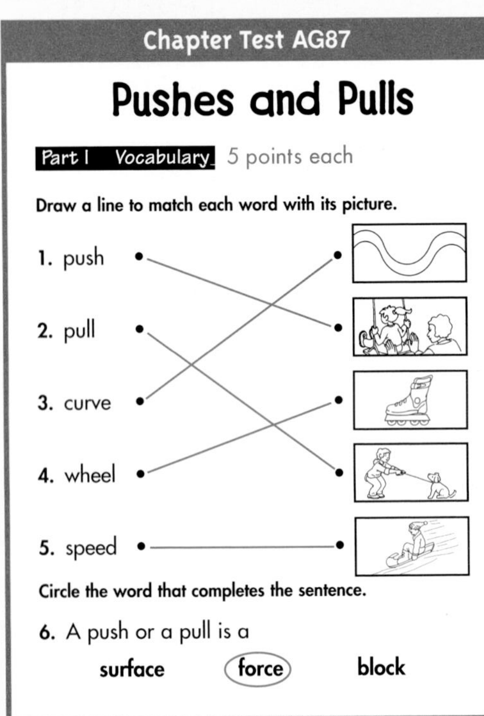

Pushes and Pulls

Part I Vocabulary 5 points each

Draw a line to match each word with its picture.

1. push
2. pull
3. curve
4. wheel
5. speed

Circle the word that completes the sentence.

6. A push or a pull is a

surface (force) block

Chapter Test AG88

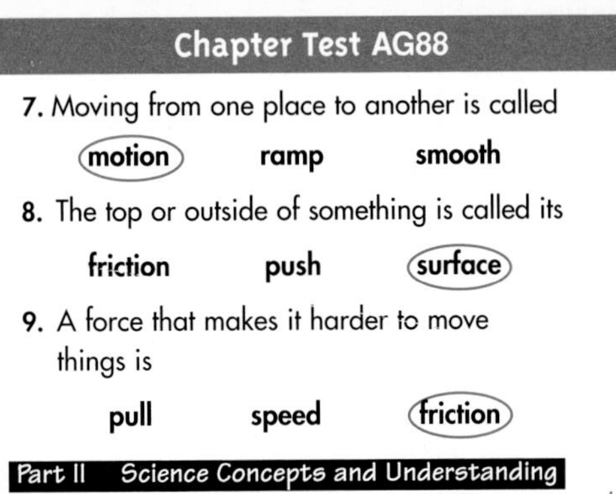

7. Moving from one place to another is called

(motion) ramp smooth

8. The top or outside of something is called its

friction push (surface)

9. A force that makes it harder to move things is

pull speed (friction)

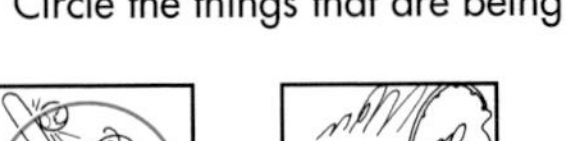

Part II Science Concepts and Understanding 8 points each

10. Circle the things that are being pushed.

Chapter Test AG89

11. Put an *X* under the animal that is moving faster.

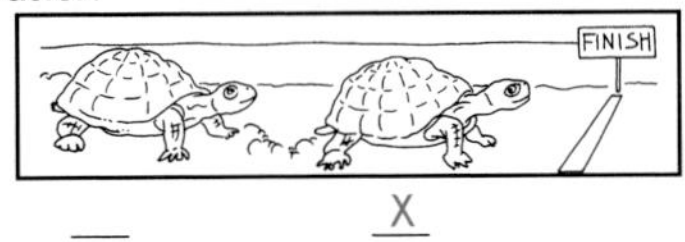

X

Circle the letter of the correct answer.

12. A path that changes directions is a

A miss (B) curve C hit

13. A ball rolls farther on a

F rough surface
(G) smooth surface
H bumpy surface

14. Circle the surface that has more friction.

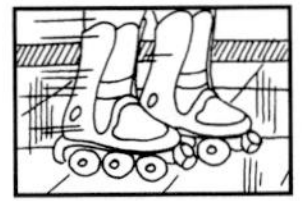

Chapter Test AG90

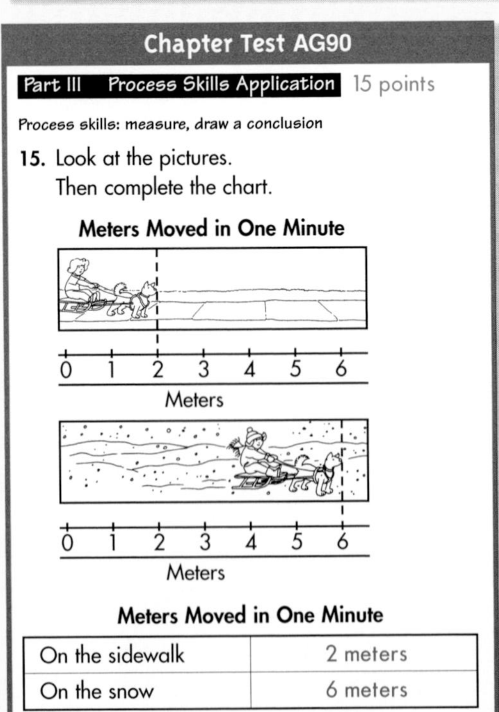

Part III Process Skills Application 15 points

Process skills: measure, draw a conclusion

15. Look at the pictures. Then complete the chart.

Meters Moved in One Minute

Meters Moved in One Minute

On the sidewalk	2 meters
On the snow	6 meters

Performance Assessment AG91

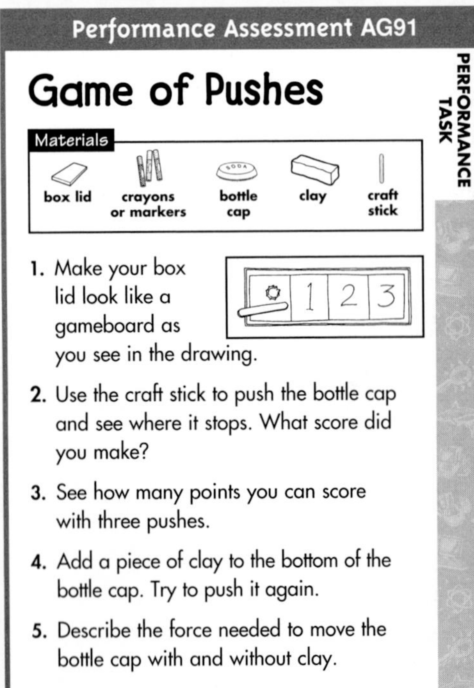

PERFORMANCE TASK

Game of Pushes

Materials

1. Make your box lid look like a gameboard as you see in the drawing.
2. Use the craft stick to push the bottle cap and see where it stops. What score did you make?
3. See how many points you can score with three pushes.
4. Add a piece of clay to the bottom of the bottle cap. Try to push it again.
5. Describe the force needed to move the bottle cap with and without clay.

Performance Assessment AG92

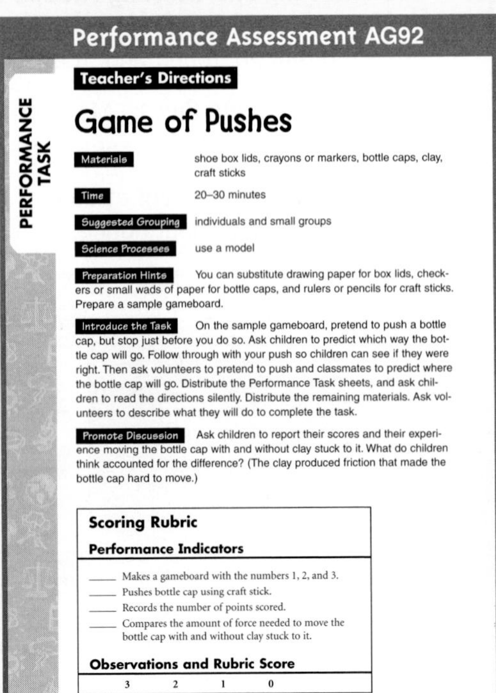

PERFORMANCE TASK

Teacher's Directions

Game of Pushes

Materials shoe box lids, crayons or markers, bottle caps, clay, craft sticks

Time 20–30 minutes

Suggested Grouping individuals and small groups

Science Processes use a model

Preparation Hints You can substitute drawing paper for box lids, checkers or small wads of paper for bottle caps, and rulers or pencils for craft sticks. Prepare a sample gameboard.

Introduce the Task On the sample gameboard, pretend to push a bottle cap, but stop just before you do so. Ask children to predict which way the bottle cap will go. Follow through with your push so children can see if they were right. Then ask volunteers to pretend to push and classmates to predict where the bottle cap will go. Distribute the Performance Task sheets, and ask children to read the directions silently. Distribute the remaining materials. Ask volunteers to describe what they will do to complete the task.

Promote Discussion Ask children to report their scores and their experience moving the bottle cap with and without clay stuck to it. What do children think accounted for the difference? (The clay produced friction that made the bottle cap hard to move.)

Scoring Rubric

Performance Indicators

_____ Makes a gameboard with the numbers 1, 2, and 3.
_____ Pushes bottle cap using craft stick.
_____ Records the number of points scored.
_____ Compares the amount of force needed to move the bottle cap with and without clay stuck to it.

Observations and Rubric Score

3 2 1 0

Workbook Support

Process Skills Practice WB134

Investigate

These logs need to be moved from the pile to the campfire.

1. Circle the things that could help you move the logs.

2. Tell how you could move a pencil across a desk.

Answers will vary but should include pushing it with a hand.

Lesson Concept Review/Assessment WB135

What Makes Things Move?

Tell how each thing is being moved. Write **push** or **pull**.

1. pull 2. pull 3. push

4. Show what the ball will do when the girl kicks it. Draw an arrow. Arrow should indicate the ball being kicked to a defensive player.

Process Skills Practice WB136

Group

1. Circle the toys you push. Make an **X** on the toys you pull.

2. Mark an **X** on objects that move easily with a gentle push.

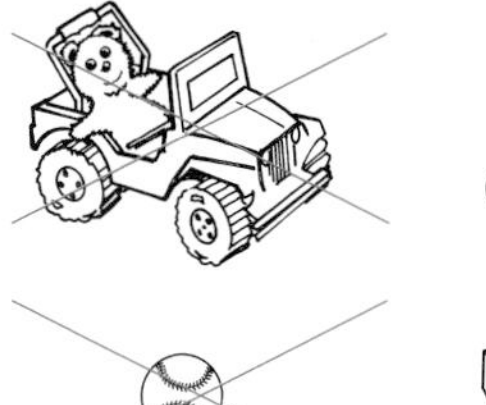

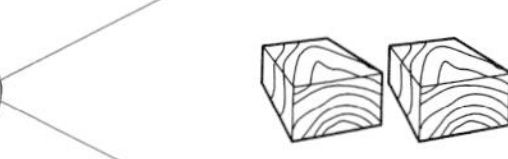

Lesson Concept Review/Assessment WB137

What Are Some Ways Things Move?

Match the objects to the words that tell how each moves.

1. straight
2. fast
3. slow
4. zigzag
5. round and round
6. back and forth

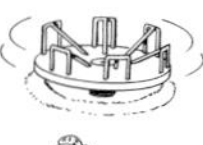

Process Skills Practice WB138

Predict

Kathy made a ramp. She put a marble at the top of her ramp.

1. What will happen when Kathy lets go of the marble? Draw a line to show where it will go.

Children should draw a line straight down the ramp.

2. This ramp is curved. Draw a line to show where Kathy's marble will go.

Children should draw a line that follows the curve of the ramp.

Lesson Concept Review/Assessment WB139

Why Do Things Move the Way They Do?

1. Circle the push that will make a toy car go a short way.

hard push

gentle push

2. Show how the soccer ball might change direction on the playing field. Draw arrows.

Arrows will vary but should indicate changing directions.

3. What will happen when the balls bump together? Write or draw your ideas.

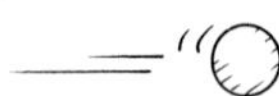

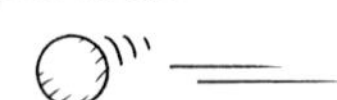

They will bounce back.

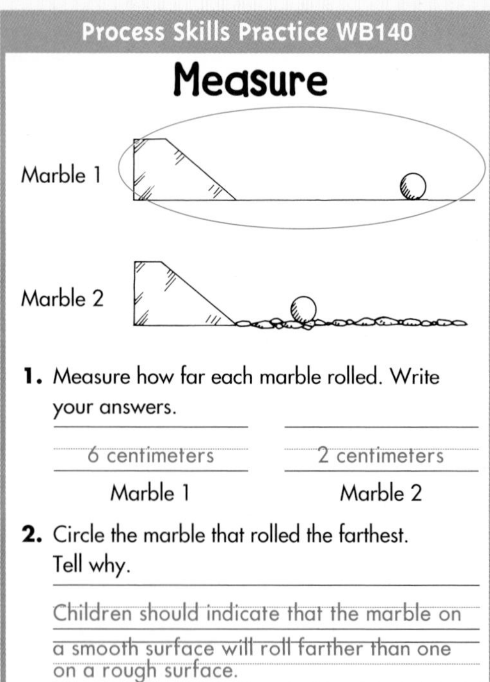

Process Skills Practice WB140

Measure

Marble 1

Marble 2

1. Measure how far each marble rolled. Write your answers.

6 centimeters	2 centimeters
Marble 1	Marble 2

2. Circle the marble that rolled the farthest. Tell why.

Children should indicate that the marble on a smooth surface will roll farther than one on a rough surface.

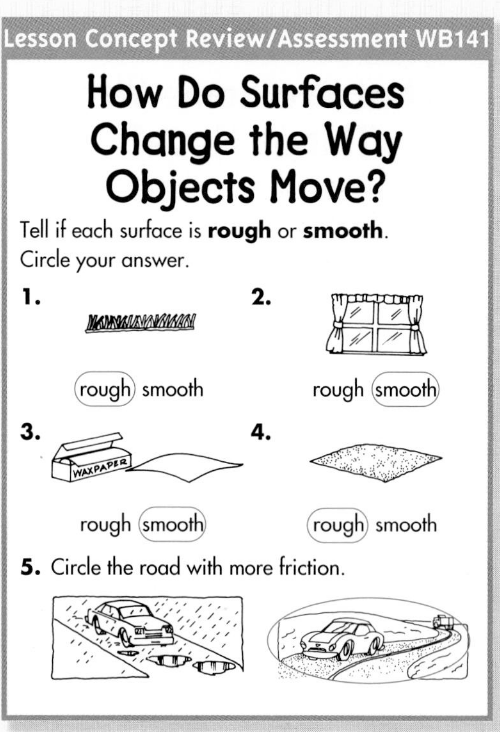

Lesson Concept Review/Assessment WB141

How Do Surfaces Change the Way Objects Move?

Tell if each surface is **rough** or **smooth**. Circle your answer.

1. rough smooth
2. rough smooth
3. rough smooth
4. rough smooth

5. Circle the road with more friction.

Process Skills Practice WB142

Draw a Conclusion

Mike and Jenny rode on different paths.

1. Circle the child that would be more tired after the ride. Tell why.

   Mike was riding on a rough surface, which made it harder to pedal.

2. Joyce made this toy. Draw something that you could add to make it easier to move.
   Children should add wheels to the boxes.

Lesson Concept Review/Assessment WB143

How Do Wheels Make Objects Easier to Move?

1. Draw wheels on the things that need wheels to move. Children should add wheels to the cart and bus.

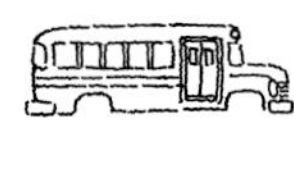

2. Circle the thing that will make the refrigerator move the easiest.

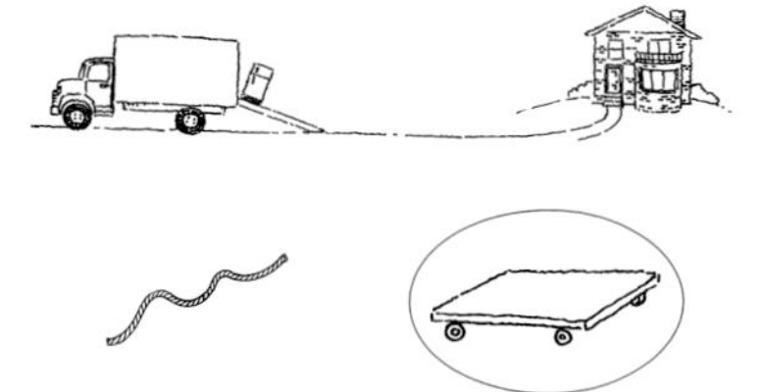

Vocabulary Review WB144

Pushes and Pulls

Circle the word that best finishes each sentence.

1. When you ____ something, you tug it closer to you.
   A wheel   B push   (C) pull
2. A ____ is a push or a pull.
   A surface   (B) force   C zigzag
3. When you ____ something, you press it away from you.
   (A) push   B pull   C motion
4. When two surfaces rub together, it is called ____.
   A motion   B zigzag   (C) friction
5. Moving from one place to another is called ____.
   (A) motion   B friction   C surface

Reading Skills Practice WB145

Identify Cause and Effect

Why Things Move the Way They Do

Susan and her classmates were playing volleyball. When the ball came to Susan, she hit it over the net. The other team members hit it back over. One time, the ball hit the pole on the net and bounced out of bounds. Another time, someone hit the ball very hard. The ball bounced high off the ground.

Finish the chart.

Cause	Effect
The ball came to Susan.	She hit the ball over the net.
The ball hit the pole on the net.	The ball bounced out of bounds.
Someone hit the ball very hard.	The ball bounced high off the ground.

Writing Practice WB146

Write to Explain

A. Draw a picture of your favorite sport or game. Be sure to show pushes and pulls.

B. Draw circles around the pushes in the picture. Draw squares around the pulls in the picture.

C. Write about how your favorite sport or game uses pushes and pulls.

Chapter 1

Pushes and Pulls

Generate Questions

Did You Know?/*Fast* Facts

Before children open their books, guide them in a discussion about different kinds of movement. Ask:

▶ **What are some ways that things move?** fast, slow, jump, fly, slide, crawl, roll, curve

Tell children to open their books to pages F2–F3. Ask volunteers to read aloud the text.

Discuss the photographs. Guide children to **relate pictures to text.**

▶ **What animal curls up to roll like a wheel?** golden wheel spider

Explain that the golden wheel spider lives on sand dunes in the African Namib Desert. It curls up and rolls when it senses danger.

Ask questions such as this one to help children think about how tree roots can push rocks and **identify cause and effect:**

▶ **What happened to the tree roots that made them push this rock up?** They grew.

Encourage children's questions. Write children's questions on the board, or have them write or draw in their journals.

PUPIL'S EDITION OR BIG BOOK

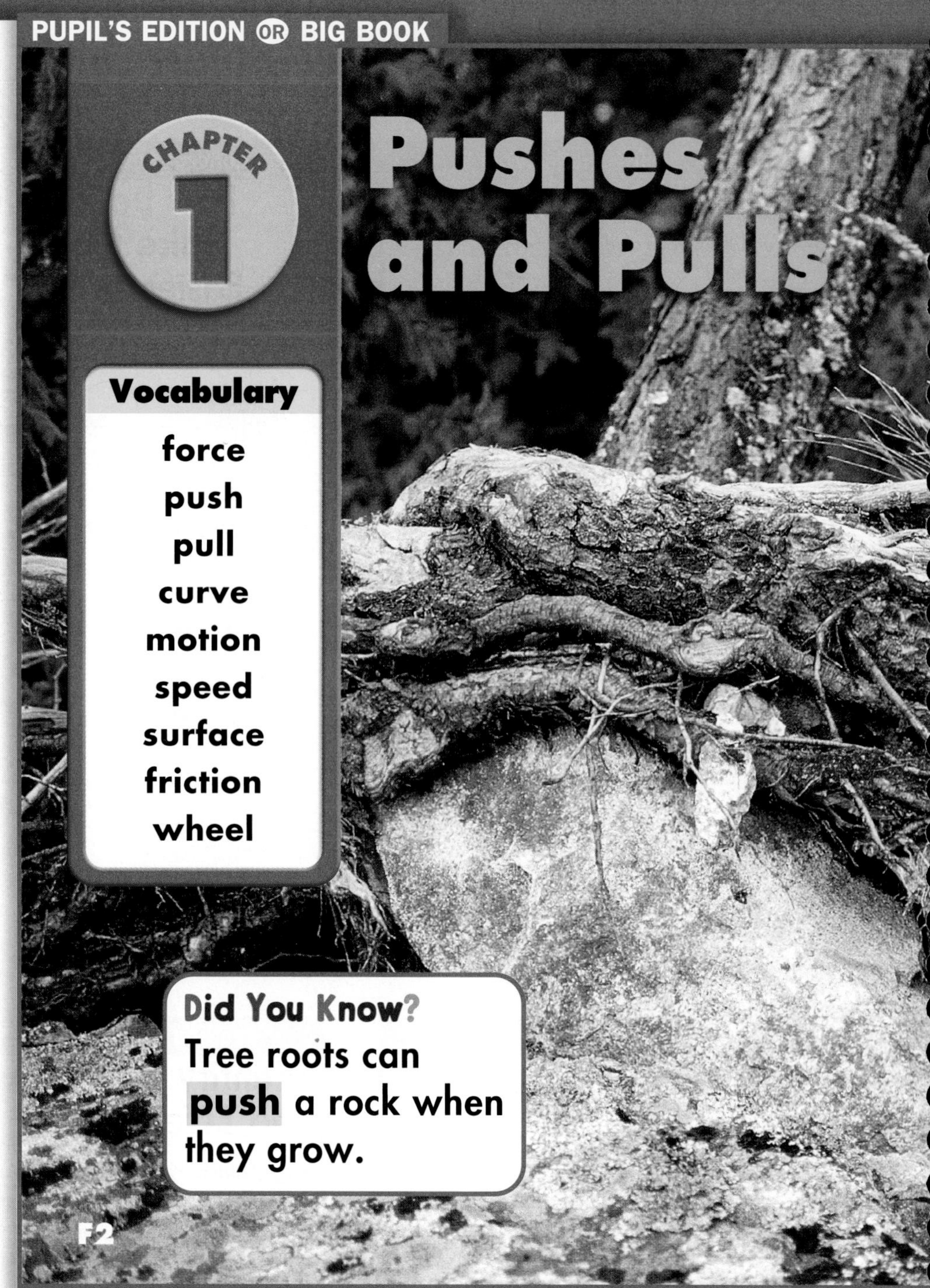

CHAPTER 1
Pushes and Pulls
Vocabulary
force
push
pull
curve
motion
speed
surface
friction
wheel
Did You Know?
Tree roots can push a rock when they grow.
F2

Reading Skills Checklist

Strategies for developing the following reading skills are provided in this chapter.

- ❑ use context
- ☑ recall supporting facts and details *pp. F9, F13*
- ❑ arrange events in sequence
- ☑ draw conclusions *pp. F15, F16, F23, F24*
- ☑ identify the main idea *pp. F5, F9, F13, F19, F23*
- ☑ identify cause and effect *pp. F2, F15, F16, F20*
- ☑ predict outcomes *pp. F6, F14, F24*
- ☑ summarize *pp. F7, F10, F11, F17, F21, F25*
- ☑ use graphic sources for information *p. F20*
- ☑ relate pictures to text *pp. F2, F5, F6, F9, F13, F19, F24*
- ❑ distinguish between fact and nonfact
- ❑ develop concepts of print
- ☑ build vocabulary *pp. F5, F6, F9, F10, F13, F14, F19, F20, F23, F24*

School-Home Connection

Distribute copies of the School-Home Connection, p. TR23.

Follow Up Have volunteers compare the results of the activity they did at home. Additional School-Home Connections are provided by the **Activities for Home or School** (pp. F54–F55) and the **Take-Home Book** (p. F2g).

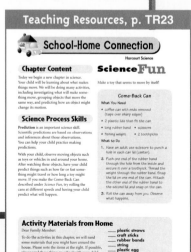

Teaching Resources, p. TR23

School-Home Connection

Chapter Content

Science Fun

Science Process Skills

Activity Materials from Home

Did You Know?
The golden wheel spider can roll like a wheel.
F3

Prereading Strategies

Preview the Chapter

Have children look through the chapter. Read aloud the main question titles for each lesson and give children time to suggest answers.

Preview the Photographs

Have children look at the photos in each lesson and use them to tell what they think the chapter will be about.

Preview the Vocabulary

Write the vocabulary words on page F2 on the board. Have children identify words they don't know or would like to know more about.

DEFINITIONS

force a push or a pull
push a pressing force
pull a tugging force
curve bend
motion moving from one place to another
speed rate of motion
surface the top or outside of something
friction a force that makes it harder to move things
wheel a roller on an axle

VOCABULARY CARDS AND ACTIVITIES

Children can use the Vocabulary Cards to make their own graphic organizers or to add to an ongoing file of science terms. The Vocabulary Cards and a variety of strategies and activities are provided beginning on p. TR110 in the **Teaching Resources** book.

GRAPHIC ORGANIZER FOR CHAPTER CONCEPTS

Children can use the graphic organizer to record key concepts and ideas from each lesson. See **Workbook p. WB133** and Transparency F1. A completed graphic organizer is also shown on page F28.

Graphic Organizer for Chapter Concepts

Transparency F1 • Workbook, p. WB133

Unit F, Chapter 1 Pushes and Pulls

LESSON 1 What Makes Things Move?	LESSON 2 What Are Some Ways Things Move?	LESSON 3 Why Do Things Move the Way They Do?
1. A force is a push or a pull.	1. Things move in many different ways.	1. Motion changes when you push or pull something.
2. When you push something, you press it away.	2. One way to tell how a thing moves is by the path it makes.	2. A hard push will move something quickly.

LESSON 4 How Do Objects Move on Surfaces?	LESSON 5 How Do Wheels Help Objects Move?
1. Friction makes it harder to move objects.	1. A wheel is a roller that turns on an axle.
2. A rough surface makes more friction than a smooth surface.	2. Wheels and rollers make things easier to push and pull.

LESSON

1 What Makes Things Move?

Objectives

- Recognize that a force is a push or a pull.
- Observe and describe what pushes and pulls can do.

Motivate

Talk About Force Ask children to give examples of times they might use a force to make something move. Make a list of their ideas. Note their questions and what they already know about forces.

Time 20 min **Grouping** individuals

Process Skill plan an investigation

Preparation Tips and Expected Results See page F2e.

Center Activity Option Place this investigation or a copy of the Investigation, page TR71, in your science center.

Activity Tips

- Before beginning the investigation, ask children to explain the problem in their own words.
- Have children use their plans to communicate what they did to move the block.

Children can put their investigation plans in their science journals.

Activity Questions

- What did you use to move the block?
- Was it a push or a pull that moved it?

When Minutes Count . . .

Use the Activity Video to preview and model different ways to make the block move.

PUPIL'S EDITION OR BIG BOOK

What Makes Things Move?

Investigate

Pushes and Pulls

You will need

small block

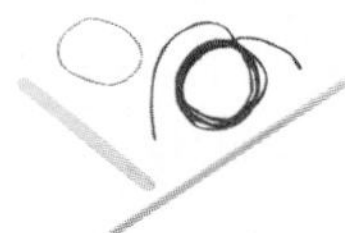

things to make the block move

paper and pencil

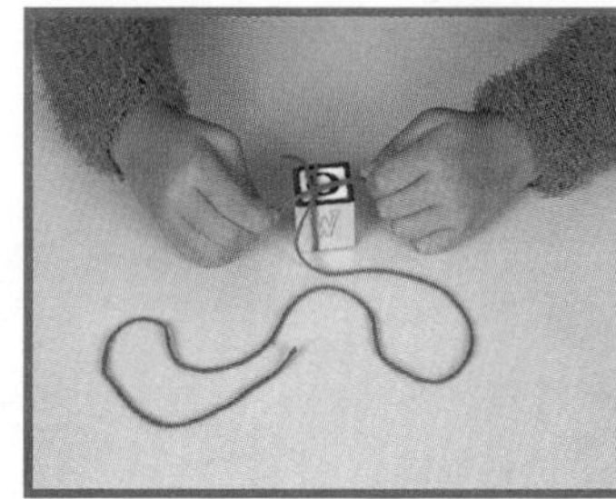

1. What could you do to push or pull the block?
2. Write a plan to investigate your ideas. Then follow your plan.
3. Tell what you used to move the block. Use the word *push* or *pull*.

Science Skill

You investigate by thinking of ideas and trying them out.

F4

Science Skills

Process Skill: Plan an Investigation Display Process Skill Tip Transparency F1-1, covering the bottom half. Ask children to suggest ways they could make the block swing back and forth. give it a push or a pull Record their ideas. Then uncover the bottom half of the transparency and ask children to describe what is happening in each picture. Record their responses.

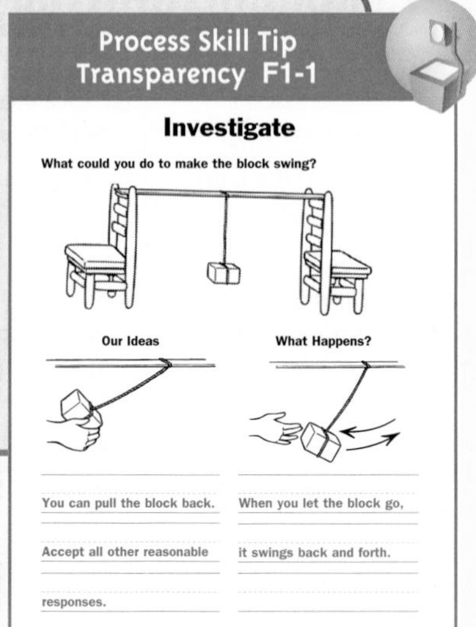

Process Skill Tip
Transparency F1-1
Investigate
What could you do to make the block swing?
Our Ideas
What Happens?
You can pull the block back.
Accept all other reasonable
responses.
When you let the block go,
it swings back and forth.

PROCESS SKILLS PRACTICE

To practice and apply process skills, see **Workbook p. WB134.**

Learn About

Making Things Move

A **force** is a push or a pull. When you **push** something, you press it away. When you **pull** something, you tug it closer.

Learn About

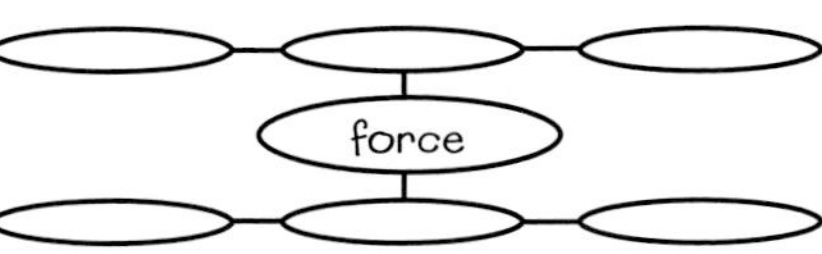

1 Before Reading

PREVIEW/SET PURPOSE

Have children preview pages F5–F7. Then make a web on the board or on chart paper. Explain to children that they will help you fill in examples of forces and what the forces can do as the lesson progresses.

force

2 Guide the Learning

SCIENCE IDEAS

Ask a volunteer to read aloud page F5. Be sure children understand these **main ideas**:

- ▶ **A force is a push or pull.**
- ▶ **To make something move, a force is needed.**

DEVELOP READING SKILLS

Relate Pictures to Text Have children use the photo to point out examples of pushes and pulls that make the sleds move up and down the hill.

BACKGROUND

Webliography GO ONLINE
Keyword motion
www.harcourtschool.com

What Makes Things Move A force is needed to make something move or stop moving. A force is always a push or a pull, whether it be gravity, friction, magnetism, or electricity. We use pushes and pulls to change the position and motion of objects.

When you throw a ball, for example, your push sets the ball on a path. The ball may begin its path on a straight line, but that soon changes as the force of gravity pulls it down. The ball drops to Earth and the force of friction soon makes it roll to a stop. If you could escape from Earth's gravity and throw the same ball, the ball's straight path could be endless. With no forces acting upon it, the ball would never stop. Things in the universe tend to stay in motion unless forces act upon them.

SCIENCE WORD WALL

Push, Pull, and Force Have children make word cards for *push*, *pull*, and *force* to post on the Word Wall. Children may want to draw pictures to show machines that use pushes or pulls to do work.

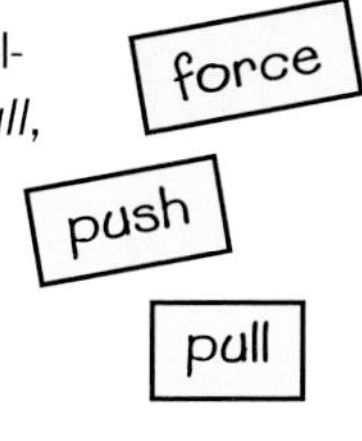

Technology Link

Children can learn more about force in *Push It or Pull It?* by Rozanne Lanczak Williams on **Harcourt Science Instant Readers CD-ROM.**

Guide the Learning continued

SCIENCE IDEAS

Have children read pages F6–F7. To help them **relate pictures to text**, ask the questions on both pages. Then discuss other pushes and pulls such as pushing a lawnmower, pulling someone on a swing to get it started, and pulling a wagon.

Critical Thinking Have children observe the truck towing the car. Ask:

▶ **What force would the car have to use to move on its own?** push

VISUAL LEARNING

Have students use the photo on page F7 to **predict outcomes**. Ask:

▶ **What force should the girl use to stop the ball?** push

USE PROCESS SKILLS

Compare Have children compare the amount of force the ballplayers use on pages F6 and F7.

▶ **Which player is using a hard push to change how the ball is moving?** the girl kicking the ball **Which is using a gentle push?** the child catching the ball

DEVELOP SCIENCE VOCABULARY

force Help children recognize that a force is always either a push or a pull. Have them collect or draw pictures that show objects being moved. Have them label the pictures to name the force being used. Children may put the pictures into a class book for display.

PUPIL'S EDITION OR BIG BOOK

Pushes and Pulls

Pushes and pulls make things move or stop moving. A tow truck pulls a car to the repair shop. A player pushes with a glove to stop a moving ball.

■ **Would the player use a push or a pull to throw the ball?** push

F6

Investigation Challenge

Hands-On Activity: Investigate Sources of Energy

Provide the following materials for children: disposable aluminum pie pans, paper fasteners, pencils, clay, and small paper cups.

Challenge children to make a waterwheel to investigate moving water as a source of energy. You may wish to provide a model for children to use to make their own waterwheel. Have children hold the waterwheel under a faucet of running water and describe what happens.

Social Studies Link

Putting Pushes and Pulls to Work Tell children that the class is going to take a walk around the school to look for machines people use to move things. Have them brainstorm what they might see. Help children make a list of different machines, and use it as a checklist as they walk. Remind them to stay with the class and follow all school rules. When you return, have children draw pictures and write about what they saw. Guide them to think about ways the machines help people get what they need to live.

A push or a pull can make something change direction. When you kick a ball, you are using a push. First the ball rolls to you. Your push makes it change direction. Then it moves away from you.

- **What will the ball do when the player kicks it?** change direction and move away from her

Think About It

1. What is a force?
2. What can pushes and pulls do?

3 Wrap Up and Assess

SUMMARIZE

Have children **summarize** what they have learned. Refer back to the web begun on page F5. Have children tell you what a force is. Write the words *push* and *pull* in the ovals connecting to the word *force*. Then have children help you fill in different things that pushes and pulls can do.

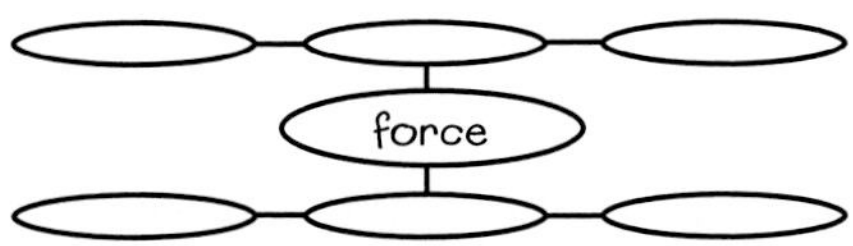

THINK ABOUT IT

1. A force is a push or a pull.
2. Pushes and pulls make things move or stop moving. They make things change direction.

Informal Assessment

Portfolio Provide children with the opportunity to draw pictures and write about examples of pushing and pulling forces. Have them show one example of each force and write a caption to explain how the force makes the object move. They may want to put their work in their science journals.

LESSON CONCEPT REVIEW/ASSESSMENT

Children can use **Workbook p. WB135** to review the lesson concepts.

Science Songs

The Science Songs CD provides original children's songs that can be used to reinforce chapter concepts. Use **Track 17** with this chapter.

Literature Connections

Harcourt Science Instant Reader
Push It or Pull It?
by Rozanne Lanczak Williams.
Also available on CD-ROM.

Read Aloud
Train Song
by Diane Siebert, HarperCollins, 1993.

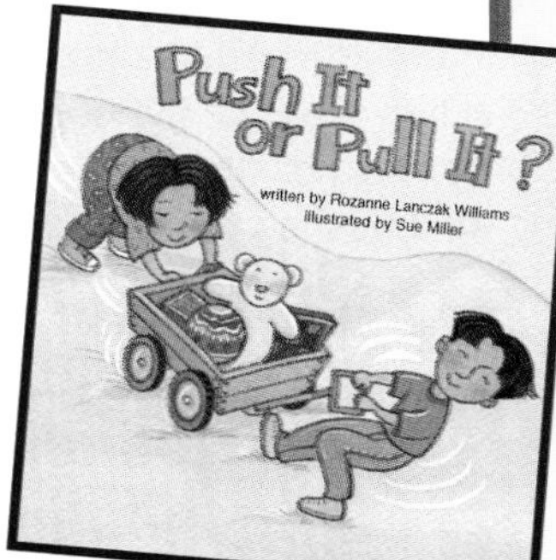

LESSON 2

What Are Some Ways Things Move?

Objectives

- Recognize that objects move in different ways.
- Observe and describe different kinds of movement.

Motivate

Play a Game Play a version of "20 Questions" where a child thinks of a moving object and others try to guess it by asking how it moves (Does it fly? Does it go round and round?) and where we find it.

Investigate

Time 20–30 min **Grouping** pairs

Process Skill classify

Preparation Tips and Expected Results See page F2e.

Center Activity Option Place this investigation or a copy of the Investigation, page TR72, in your science center.

Activity Tips

- Model how you want children to record their observations.
- Allow time for children to communicate to the class how they grouped the objects so they can compare results.

Children may record their results in their science journals.

Activity Questions

- Why did you group the objects the way you did?
- What questions do you have about how the objects moved?

When Minutes Count . . .

As a whole-class activity, have children observe how different objects move as you push or pull them. Have them help you group them by putting together those that move the same way.

PUPIL'S EDITION OR BIG BOOK

What Are Some Ways Things Move?

Investigate

Moving Objects

You will need

objects

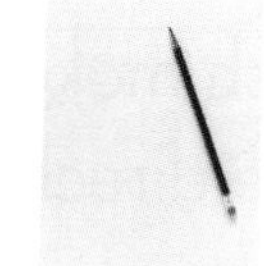

paper and pencil

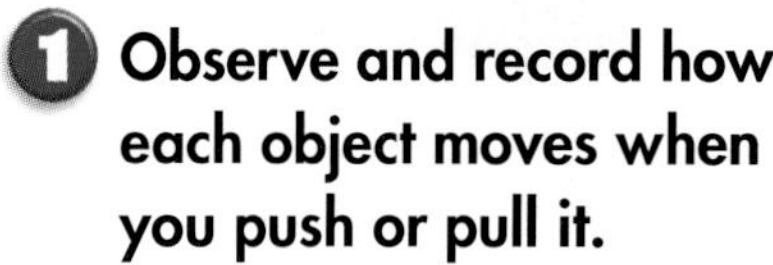

1. Observe and record how each object moves when you push or pull it.

2. Group objects that move the same way. Write how you grouped them.

Science Skill

To group the objects, put those that move in the same way together.

F8

Science Skills

Process Skill: Classify Display Process Skill Tip Transparency F1-2. Help children read the list of objects and talk about how they move when a strong wind pushes them. spin, flap, or spin and flap Guide them to sort the objects by how they move. Write their responses to fill in the diagram.

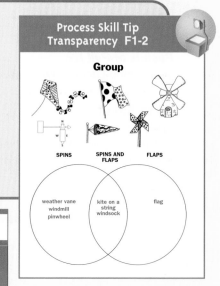

Process Skill Tip Transparency F1-2

Group

SPINS | SPINS AND FLAPS | FLAPS

weather vane, windmill, pinwheel | kite on a string, windsock | flag

PROCESS SKILLS PRACTICE

To practice and apply process skills, see **Workbook p. WB136.**

Learn About

Ways Things Move

Pushes and pulls make things move in different ways. Tell what you know about how these rides move.

F9

Learn About

1 Before Reading

PREVIEW/SET PURPOSE

Have children preview pages F9–F11. Make a chart on the board or on chart paper. Explain to children that they will help you fill in different objects that move and different ways that they move as the lesson progresses.

Object That Moves	How It Moves

2 Guide the Learning

SCIENCE IDEAS

Have children read page F9. Tell them to think about rides or playground equipment or toys that they might have been on. Ask them to tell how these things move. To help them **relate pictures to text** and **identify the main idea**, ask:

- ▶ **What rides go round and round?** Answers may include: merry-go-round, tilt-a-whirl.
- ▶ **What rides go back and forth?** Answers may include: swings, ships.

DEVELOP READING SKILLS

Recall Supporting Facts and Details Ask children to describe what forces are used to make the rides move, stop moving, and change direction.

BACKGROUND

Webliography

Keyword motion

www.harcourtschool.com

Different Ways Things Move As forces act upon them, different objects move in different ways. Marbles roll when pushed. Tops spin and eggs wobble. Rubber bands move back and forth very fast when pulled. Guitar strings vibrate. Some things, like falling rocks or diving hawks, move fast and make a straight path as they fall or dive. Others, like river barges or turtles, move slowly as they make a straight path. We can observe and describe how different objects move, and categorize their movements by the paths they take, or their speed, or whether they move the same over and over again.

SCIENCE WORD WALL

Words That Tell About Movement
Have children make word cards for *straight* and *curve*.

straight

curve

ESL Activity Have children identify pictures of machines or objects for each motion.

Technology Link

Visit the Harcourt Learning Site for related links, activities, and resources.
www.harcourtschool.com

Guide the Learning continued

SCIENCE IDEAS

Have children read pages F10 and F11. Help them **summarize** by asking:

▶ **What are two ways to tell how things move?** the path they make, if they move fast

VISUAL LEARNING

Have children use the photos to talk about their own experiences with each of the objects shown. Guide them to think about the forces that make the objects move in different ways.

USE PROCESS SKILLS

Observe and Compare Guide children to observe and compare how each of the objects shown is moving. Ask them to describe the object's path and its speed.

Critical Thinking Help children recognize that an object may move in several different kinds of ways, depending on the forces acting upon it.

▶ **What other words could be used to tell how the train is moving?** fast, slow

Repeat with the swing, top, and cyclists.

DEVELOP SCIENCE VOCABULARY

curve Lead children in a discussion about where they have seen curves and things they have seen move on curved paths.

PUPIL'S EDITION OR BIG BOOK

Telling How Things Move

There are different ways to tell how things move. One way is by the path they make. A train moves in a straight path. It may **curve**, or bend, along its path.

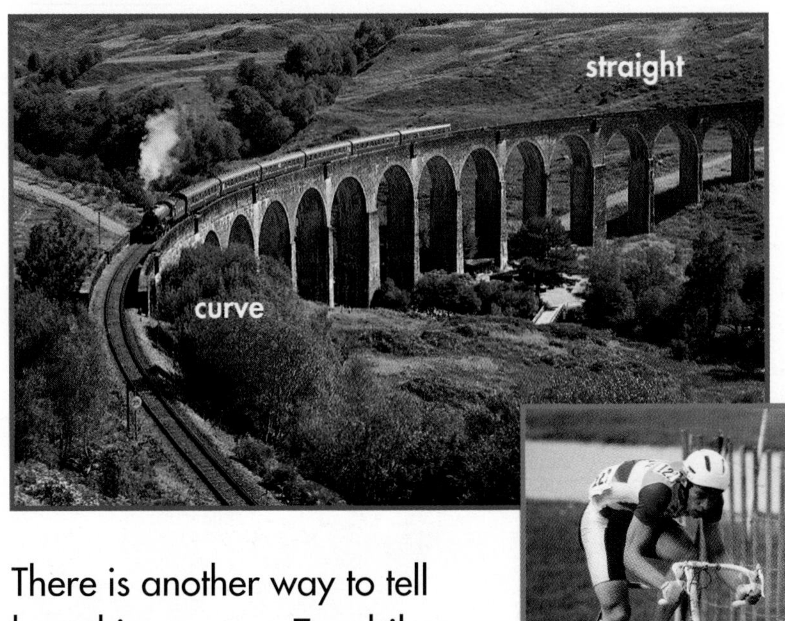

There is another way to tell how things move. Two bikers may start at the same time. If one moves ahead, he or she is moving faster.

F10

Reaching All Learners

Visually Impaired or Kinesthetic Learners
Children who are visually impaired or who learn better kinesthetically will benefit from using their hands and arms to make straight, curved, round, and other types of motions. They should also vary the speed of their movement to experience fast and slow.

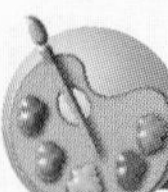

Art Link

Paper Pop-Ups Have children make spring-like pop-ups out of construction paper to observe stored and released energy. Have them tape the ends of two one-inch strips of construction paper at right angles as shown. Contrasting colors makes this more fun. Have children fold one strip over the other again and again until the remaining ends meet. Tape the ends. Children will enjoy pushing down on the pop-up and letting it go, releasing the stored energy, and watching the paper pop-up bounce.

Some things move the same way over and over. A top spins round and round. A swing moves back and forth.

- **What kind of force keeps a swing moving?**
  push

Think About It

1. What are some ways things move?
2. How can you tell if one thing is moving faster than another?

F11

3 Wrap Up and Assess

SUMMARIZE

Have children **summarize** what they have learned by helping you complete the chart begun on page F9. Have them suggest different objects that move, such as a merry-go-round, train, and sled. Then have them use words to describe how the objects move such as *round and round, straight, curve, fast, slow,* and *back and forth.*

Object That Moves	How It Moves

THINK ABOUT IT

1. Things move in different ways, such as straight, curved, back and forth, fast, slow, and round and round.
2. You can tell that one thing is moving faster than another when it moves ahead.

Informal Assessment

Performance Provide children with different objects that move. Have them demonstrate the different ways the objects move, including their path and speed.

LESSON CONCEPT REVIEW/ASSESSMENT

Children can use **Workbook p. WB137** to review the lesson concepts.

Literature Connections

Read Alouds

The Wheeling and Whirling-Around Book by Judy Hindley, Candlewick, 1996.

Forces and Movement by Peter D. Riley, Franklin Watts, 1998.

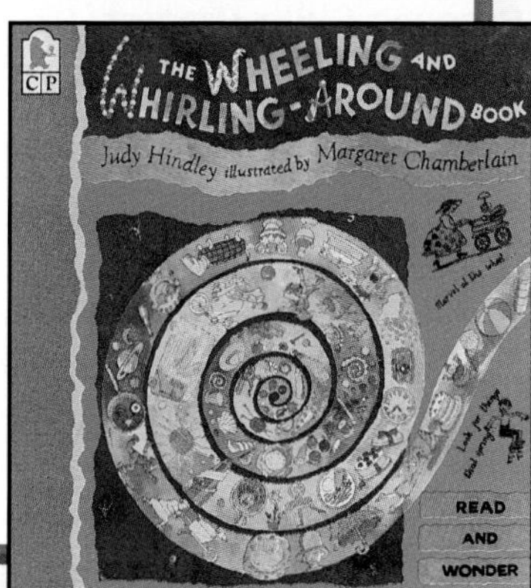

THE WHEELING AND WHIRLING-AROUND BOOK
Judy Hindley illustrated by Margaret Chamberlain
READ AND WONDER

LESSON 3

Why Do Things Move the Way They Do?

Objectives

- ▶ Recognize that motion involves moving from one place to another.
- ▶ Recognize that the amount of a change in motion is related to the strength of the push or the pull.

Motivate

Talk About Hard and Soft Pushes and Pulls

Ask children to identify times when they need to push or pull hard on something, and when they need to push or pull gently. Have them tell what happens when they do the opposite of what is needed.

Investigate

Time 20–25 min **Grouping** individuals

Process Skill predict

Preparation Tips and Expected Results See page F2e.

Center Activity Option Place this investigation or a copy of the Investigation, page TR73, in your science center.

Activity Tips

- ▶ Tell children not to push the ball down the ramp because the push will change how far it rolls.
- ▶ Model how to position the block so the ball will bounce off it.

Children may draw pictures in their science journals to show what happened.

Activity Questions

- ▶ What happened to the ball when it hit the block?
- ▶ What kind of force (push or pull) made the ball change direction?

When Minutes Count . . .

Use the Activity Video to preview and model how a force (a push or bounce off the block) can be used to change the ball's direction.

PUPIL'S EDITION OR BIG BOOK

Why Do Things Move the Way They Do?

Investigate

Predicting Motion

You will need

ramp

plastic ball

tape

block

1. Set up the ramp. Predict where the ball will stop. Mark that place with tape.
2. Let the ball roll down the ramp. Was your prediction right?
3. Now put the block where the ball will hit it. Do Step 2 again.

Science Skill

To predict where the ball will stop, think about how a ball rolls and bounces.

F12

Science Skills

Process Skill: Predict Display Process Skill Tip Transparency F1-3. Have children tell about how a penny and marble move when pushed on a desk top. Then ask them to predict what kind of push is needed to push the penny and the marble. Write their predictions in the space provided.

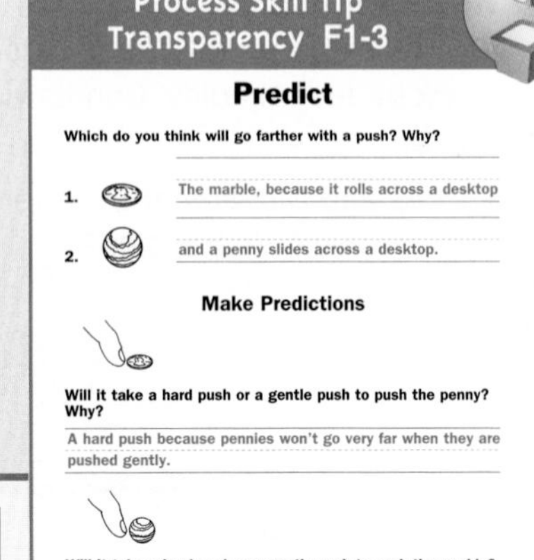

Process Skill Tip Transparency F1-3

Predict

Which do you think will go farther with a push? Why?

1. The marble, because it rolls across a desktop
2. and a penny slides across a desktop.

Make Predictions

Will it take a hard push or a gentle push to push the penny? Why?

A hard push because pennies won't go very far when they are pushed gently.

Will it take a hard push or a gentle push to push the marble? Why?

A gentle push because a marble would roll too far with a hard push.

PROCESS SKILLS PRACTICE

To practice and apply process skills, see **Workbook p. WB138.**

Why Things Move the Way They Do

Moving from one place to another is **motion**. You can observe the motion of an object. This will help you predict where it will move next.

F13

1 Before Reading

PREVIEW/SET PURPOSE

Have children preview pages F13–F17. Make a chart such as the one below. Tell children that they will help you fill it in as the lesson progresses.

What Is Moving?	How Can You Change How It Is Moving?

2 Guide the Learning

SCIENCE IDEAS

Read aloud page F13. To help reinforce the **main idea**, as well as **recall supporting facts and details**, ask:

▶ **What are two different ways to observe the motion of an object?** observe its path and how fast it moves

DEVELOP READING SKILLS

Relate Pictures to Text Guide children to observe and describe the path the marble in the photo will take as it moves. Have them talk about the pushes and pulls that act upon it as it moves.

BACKGROUND

Webliography
Keyword motion
www.harcourtschool.com
GO ONLINE

Why Things Move the Way They Do Motion, or moving an object from one place to another, is predictable when we understand the forces acting upon the object. Children have a wide variety of experiences with moving objects, including swings, balls, in-line skates, and jump ropes. Through experience, they have learned that a swing, for example, tends to return to its resting place unless it is pushed or pulled continuously. They know that a hard push helps them swing longer than a gentle push. By observing the forces required to control the motion of the swing, they become better able to predict how it will move.

SCIENCE WORD WALL

Motion Words Have children make word cards for *motion, path,* and *speed* to post on your Word Wall. Have children collect or draw pictures to show things in motion such as swings, balls, and jump ropes. Have them display these on the Word Wall.

motion

path

speed

Guide the Learning continued

SCIENCE IDEAS

Have children read aloud page F14. Guide them to **predict outcomes.**

▶ **What happens when the puck hits another hockey player's stick?** It changes direction and speed.

DEVELOP SCIENCE VOCABULARY

motion To help reinforce children's understanding of the word, have them look at the photos on pages F14 to F17 and identify what is in motion. Then have them identify the force that put the object or person in motion.

speed Emphasize that the word *speed* means how *quickly or slowly* something moves. Ask children to name things that move at a fast speed and things that move at a slow speed.

PUPIL'S EDITION OR BIG BOOK

Changing Motion

A push or pull can change the motion of something. A hockey puck moves straight ahead unless something changes its motion.

F14

ESL ACTIVITY

Show children pictures of things in **motion** such as a person jogging, a moving swing, a see-saw, a ball being rolled, and a child jumping or hopping. Ask children to describe what is happening in each picture. Then have them draw their own pictures of something that is in motion and talk about it.

Investigation Challenge

Hands-On Activity: Back-and-Forth Spinner

Help children cut 3-inch disks from stiff cardboard and poke two holes about one-half inch apart in the center of the disk. Have them draw an arrow as shown. Thread a length of string through the holes and tie the ends to make a loop. Have children rotate the disk, holding the loop between their hands, and pull the loop taut to watch the disk whirl as the string unwinds. Challenge them to use their pull to make the arrow change direction. Children will observe how the winding and unwinding string makes the disk change direction as they pull.

Different kinds of pushes change the **speed**, how quickly or slowly the puck moves. A hard push moves the puck quickly. A gentle push moves it slowly.

■ **What kind of push should the player use to move the puck slowly?**

gentle push

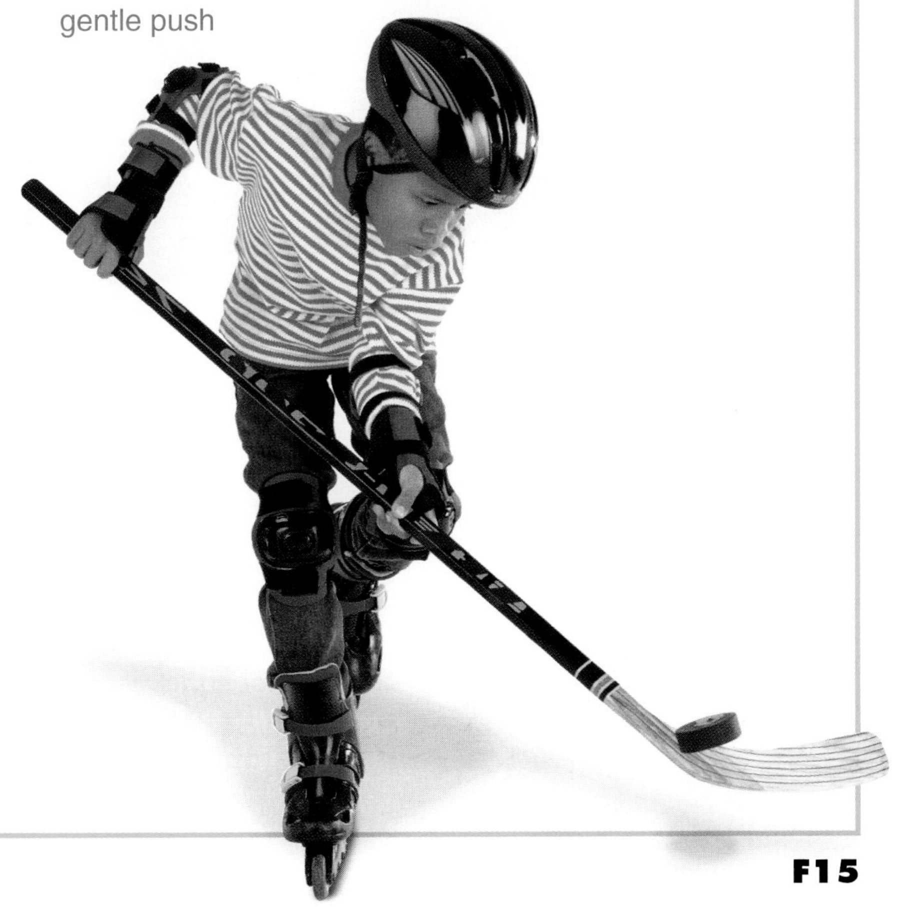

Guide the Learning continued

SCIENCE IDEAS

Have children read the text on page F15. To help them **identify cause and effect**, help them think about other examples of hard and gentle pushes used to change the motion of different objects. Examples might include hitting a nail with a hammer, launching a toy sailboat, playing on a seesaw, and playing baseball.

VISUAL LEARNING

Have children observe and describe a skater's motion such as fast, slow, spins, glides, moves straight, curves. Have them answer the question about the force the skater uses to stop. Ask what force the skater needs to go again.

Critical Thinking Use this question to help children **draw conclusions** about motion.

▶ **How could the skater use a push to slow or stop his motion?** push his skate brake

Cultural Connection

Make a Travois Tell children that Native Americans invented a device to help them move their belongings from place to place. Their invention, made of two tree branches with an animal skin stretched between them, could be dragged by a horse, a dog, or a person. French explorers called the invention a travois (tra-VWAH).

Have children make a travois by taping a piece of paper between two straws or pencils. They can use a toy horse to demonstrate how it works. Ask children why they think Native Americans moved some things with a travois instead of carrying them. The travois made it easier to move big or heavy things. It required less force than carrying them.

Guide the Learning continued

SCIENCE IDEAS

Have children read aloud pages F16 and F17. Then have them use the examples given in the photos to **draw conclusions** about how objects change direction.

- ▶ **Which people are about to make something change direction?** girl sitting on floor; boy playing table tennis; children in bumper boats
- ▶ **How can you tell?** They are ready to push the object moving toward them.

USE PROCESS SKILLS

Observe Have children look at each photo and give examples of different bumps and bounces about to take place. Have them use the words in sentences that tell what will bump or bounce. For example, "The girl will bump the table tennis ball and it will bounce back to the boy."

PUPIL'S EDITION OR BIG BOOK

Changing Direction

A force can change the direction in which an object moves. A ball will roll in one direction until something pushes it and makes it change.

pushes the ball to change its direction

■ **What does the paddle do to the ball in table tennis?**

F16

Language Arts Link

Concrete Poetry: Bumps and Bounces
Some poems can be written so that the words show what the poem says. Help children recall experiences they have had with bumps and bounces, and have them draw pictures to show what happened. Have them write about the experience. Then have them arrange their sentence in a picture that shows what took place.

I dropped the ball

Reading Mini-Lesson

Identify Cause and Effect Have children look at the photos on pages F16–F17. Ask them what causes the boats to change direction and what effect it has to cause both boats to move backward. List children's responses about their own experiences involving the effects of pushing and pulling.

READING SKILLS PRACTICE

To practice and apply this reading skill, see **Workbook p. WB145.**

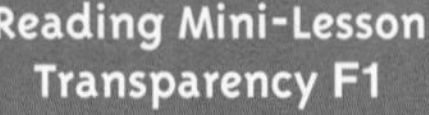

Identify Cause and Effect

Pushing and Pulling

Cause	Effect
Someone pushes you on a swing.	You go higher and faster.
You pull the rope on a bell.	The bell rings.

Bumps are the pushes that change the direction of bumper boats. When you bump your boat against another boat, your boat bounces back.

Think About It

1. What is motion?
2. What can change the motion of something?

F17

3 Wrap Up and Assess

SUMMARIZE

Have children **summarize** what they have learned. Return to the chart begun on page F13 and have children help you fill in different kinds of objects that move. ball, hockey puck, swing Then have them describe ways they can change how each moves. bounce the ball, hit the puck hard, push the swing gently

What Is Moving?	How Can You Change How It Is Moving?

THINK ABOUT IT

1. Motion is moving from one place to another.
2. Different kinds of pushes and pulls can change the motion of an object.

Informal Assessment

Performance Assess children's understanding of changing motion and changing direction. Give them a ball and have them show you ways to change its speed. Then have them roll it and change its direction. Have them tell you orally what is happening as they use pushes or pulls to change how the ball moves.

LESSON CONCEPT REVIEW/ASSESSMENT

Children can use **Workbook p. WB139** to review the lesson concepts.

Literature Connections

Read Alouds

The Science Book of Motion by Neil Ardley, Harcourt, 1992.

Doctor DeSoto by William Steig, Farrar, Straus & Giroux, 1990.

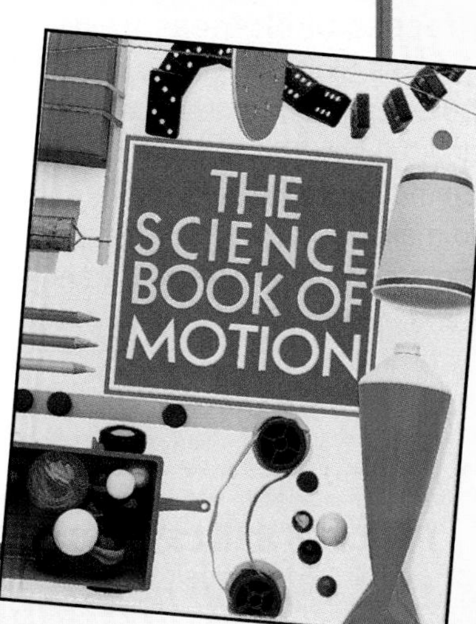

LESSON 4

How Do Objects Move on Surfaces?

Objectives

- ▶ **Recognize that friction is a force that makes it harder to move things.**
- ▶ **Observe that the motion of objects can be changed by the amount of friction acting upon them.**

Motivate

Dramatize Invite children to show what it is like to skate or in-line skate across a smooth, then rough surface. Ask:

- ▶ When do you go faster? on a smooth surface

Time 20–25 min **Grouping** pairs

Process Skill measure

Preparation Tips and Expected Results See page F2f.

Center Activity Option Place this investigation or a copy of the Investigation, page TR74, in your science center.

Activity Tips

- ▶ You may want to put parameters on the activity and give children more time to investigate during recess.
- ▶ Tell children not to push the truck down the ramp because that will change how far it rolls.
- ▶ Model how to measure the distance from the end of the ramp rather than the top.

Children may draw pictures in their science journals and record their measurements.

Activity Questions

- ▶ On which surface did the truck roll farther?
- ▶ Why do you think that happened?

When Minutes Count . . .

As a whole-class activity, roll the truck down a ramp onto smooth and rough surfaces. Have volunteers help you measure and record how far the truck rolls on each. Discuss how the surfaces affect motion.

PUPIL'S EDITION OR BIG BOOK

How Do Objects Move on Surfaces?

Investigate

Smooth and Rough Surfaces

You will need

ramp

toy truck

meterstick

paper and pencil

1. Set up a ramp on a smooth surface. Let the truck roll down.
2. Measure how far it rolls. Record the number. Do the same on a rough surface.
3. On which surface does the truck roll farther? Use your numbers to tell.

Science Skill

Measure how far the truck rolls from the end of the ramp to where the truck stops.

Science Skills

Process Skill: Measure Display Process Skill Tip Transparency F1-4. Guide children to observe the setups and tell how they are different. Have them help you record the ramps used to make the car roll. Have them count the paper clips to measure and record the distance the car rolled each time.

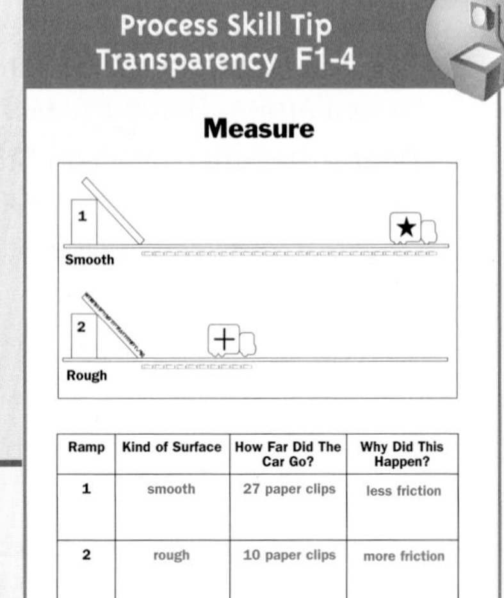

Ramp	Kind of Surface	How Far Did The Car Go?	Why Did This Happen?
1	smooth	27 paper clips	less friction
2	rough	10 paper clips	more friction

PROCESS SKILLS PRACTICE

To practice and apply process skills, see **Workbook p. WB140.**

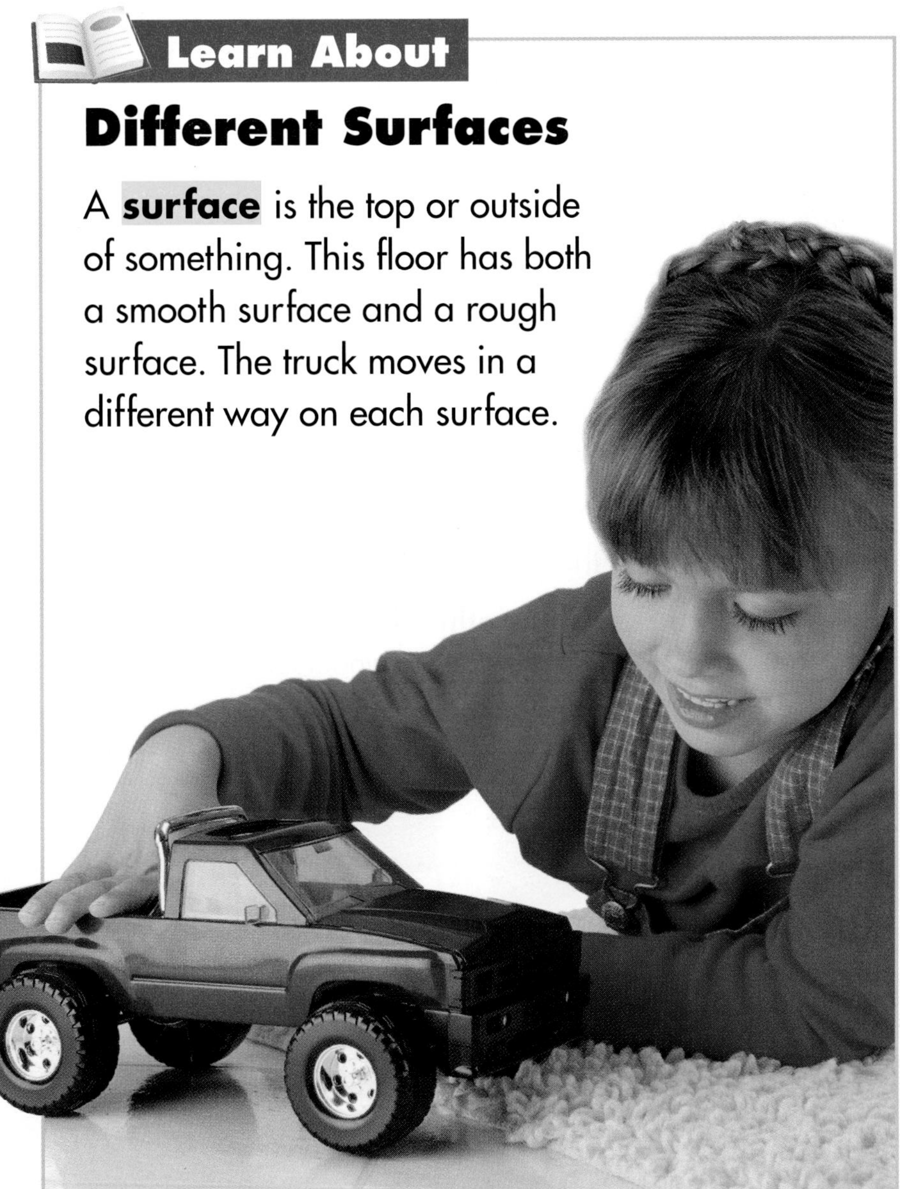

Learn About
Different Surfaces
A surface is the top or outside of something. This floor has both a smooth surface and a rough surface. The truck moves in a different way on each surface.
F19

1 Before Reading

PREVIEW/SET PURPOSE

Have children preview pages F19–F21. Make a K-W-L chart as shown. Have children help you fill in what they already know and what they want to know about friction. They will help you fill in what they learned at the close of the lesson.

K-W-L Chart		
What I Know	What I Want to Know	What I Learned

2 Guide the Learning

SCIENCE IDEAS

Read aloud page F19 with children. Be sure children understand the **main ideas**:

- ▶ **A surface is the top or outside of something.**
- ▶ **Surfaces can be smooth or rough.**

DEVELOP READING SKILLS

Relate Pictures to Text Have children identify the smooth and rough surfaces in the photo. Guide them to find surfaces that are like the surfaces shown. If possible, have them roll a toy car or truck on both surfaces to observe how the movement changes from one to the other.

BACKGROUND

Webliography
Keyword motion
www.harcourtschool.com
GO ONLINE

Surfaces and Friction A moving object can be acted upon by several forces, including **friction,** a pulling force that makes it harder to move things.

Friction occurs when two surfaces rub together. Children can rub their dry hands together and feel heat when friction makes it hard for their hands to move back and forth. When they put soap and water on their hands, they can rub back and forth more easily. There is less friction and they feel less heat.

Children experience different amounts of friction in many ways, including riding a bicycle or in-line skating on smooth surfaces and rough surfaces. They can go faster and use less push on smooth surfaces, and have to go slower and use more push on rough surfaces because of friction.

SCIENCE WORD WALL

Friction and Surfaces Have children make word cards for *friction* and *surface* to post on the Word Wall. Then help children make a list of words that describe different surfaces.

ESL Activity Have children identify materials that have different surfaces and collect them. Post the materials next to the word cards so that children can use their sense of touch to reinforce the meaning of the words.

rough
smooth
bumpy
friction
surface

Guide the Learning continued

SCIENCE IDEAS

Read aloud pages F20–F21. Help children **identify cause and effect** by asking them to indicate which surface makes it easier for the cyclist to go fast.

Critical Thinking Have children recall riding on smooth and rough surfaces.

▶ **Why is a wet or icy road harder to ride on than a dry road?** A wet road decreases friction and makes it more slippery.

USE PROCESS SKILLS

Observe Have children observe the photo of the sneaker bottom. Discuss why sneakers are helpful to wear on smooth surfaces. Tread gives the sneaker more friction to keep you from slipping or sliding. Have them compare the tread on the sneaker with treads on their own sneakers.

VISUAL LEARNING

Have children observe the caution sign. Ask volunteers to tell about experiences they have had when they saw this kind of sign. Help them **use graphic sources for information**.

▶ What tells you that the floor's surface may not have enough friction for safe walking? the symbol

DEVELOP SCIENCE VOCABULARY

friction Guide children in a discussion about what friction can do. Help them recall that when they rub their hands together, friction also makes their hands warm.

PUPIL'S EDITION OR BIG BOOK

More Friction, Less Friction

When two surfaces rub together, they make friction. **Friction** is a force that makes it harder to move things.

A rough surface makes more friction than a smooth one. On a rough road, a bike is harder to move. You have to push harder on the pedals.

■ **What surfaces rub together when you ride a bike over a road?** bike wheels and road surface

F20

THE QUESTIONS KIDS ASK!

What are some other forces besides friction?

Address Misconceptions Other forces besides friction are gravity, electric force, and the magnetic force you experience with magnets. Each of these forces can be used to make a push or a pull. Gravity pulls things down toward the center of Earth, for example. If you rub a balloon on your hair, electric force will pull your hair up to the surface of the balloon. Magnetic force pulls on some metals to make them stick to the magnet. You may want to use a balloon to demonstrate how electric force pulls hair toward the surface of the balloon.

Physical Education Link

Using Friction to Crabwalk Use a space such as a gymnasium with a smooth floor surface where children have room to move about. Have children line up on one side of the gym wearing just socks on their feet. Ask them to crabwalk to the other side of the gym. Then have them put their sneakers back on and try it again. Have them compare which way was easier. Talk about how wearing socks makes less friction, which makes it harder for them to push off.

You can change how much friction a surface makes. If you cover a surface with something wet, it makes less friction. If you cover a surface with something rough, it makes more friction.

Think About It

1. What is friction?
2. What kind of surface makes more friction? What kind makes less friction?

3 Wrap Up and Assess

SUMMARIZE

Have children **summarize** what they have learned. Refer back to the K-W-L chart you began on page F19. Have children help you fill in what they learned about friction.

K-W-L Chart		
What I Know	What I Want to Know	What I Learned

THINK ABOUT IT

1. Friction is a force that makes it harder to push or pull things.
2. Rough surfaces make more friction and smooth surfaces make less friction.

Informal Assessment

Classroom Observation Assess children's understanding of friction by observing their interactions as they investigate moving objects on smooth and rough surfaces. Have them tell how the different surfaces change how the object moves.

LESSON CONCEPT REVIEW/ASSESSMENT

Children can use **Workbook p. WB141** to review the lesson concepts.

Literature Connections

Read Alouds

Mrs. Toggle's Zipper by Robin Pulver, Aladdin, 1993.

Inclined Planes by Michael Dahl, Bridgestone Books, 1996.

LESSON

5 How Do Wheels Help Objects Move?

Objectives

- ▶ Recognize that a wheel is a roller that turns on an axle.
- ▶ Recognize that rollers and wheels can be used to make things easier to push or to pull.

Motivate

Dramatize Have children show what it is like to push or pull a box of heavy bricks across the floor. Then have them show what it is like to push or pull the same box of bricks when the box has wheels. Guide them in a brief discussion to compare the two experiences.

Time 20 min **Grouping** individuals

Process Skill draw a conclusion

Preparation Tips and Expected Results See page F2f.

Center Activity Option Place this investigation or a copy of the Investigation, page TR75, in your science center.

Activity Tips

- ▶ Model how to tape the wheels so the truck doesn't roll.
- ▶ Allow time for children to talk about their conclusions.

Children may draw pictures to show what happened and add them to their science journals.

Activity Questions

- ▶ What happens when you use wheels and rollers to move the book?
- ▶ How do you explain what happened to the truck when you taped the wheels?

When Minutes Count . . .

Use the Activity Video to preview and model how rollers and wheels make objects move.

PUPIL'S EDITION OR BIG BOOK

How Do Wheels Help Objects Move?

Investigate

Rollers

You will need

rollers

heavy book

toy truck

tape

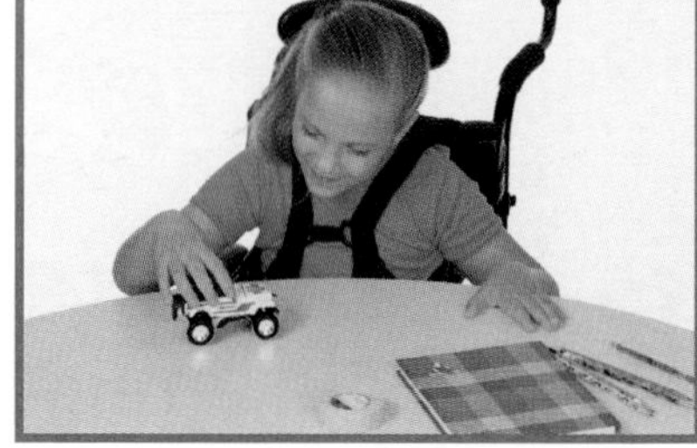

1. Push the book. Then put rollers under it. Push again. Which is easier?
2. Push the truck. Tape the wheels, and push it again. Which is easier?
3. Draw a conclusion about wheels and rollers.

Science Skill

To draw a conclusion about something, use what you have observed to explain what happens.

F22

Science Skills

Process Skill: Draw a Conclusion

Display Process Skill Tip Transparency F1-5. Record children's observations about how the two bicycles are different. One has a flat tire. Ask which is easier to ride. first bicycle Discuss experiences they have had with bicycle tires that helped them draw their conclusion.

Process Skill Tip Transparency F1-5

Draw a Conclusion

Which is easier to ride?

1

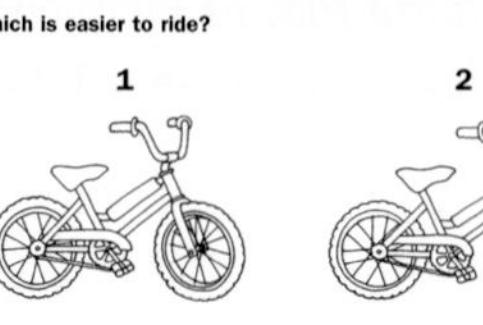

2

Bike	What We Observe	Is the bike easy or hard to ride?	Why?
1	It has two full tires.	easy	The tires will roll well.
2	It has a flat tire.	hard	The flat tire will cause friction.

PROCESS SKILLS PRACTICE

To practice and apply process skills, see **Workbook p. WB142.**

Learn About

What Wheels Can Do

A roller is any object that rolls. A **wheel** is a roller that turns on an axle. Rollers and wheels make things easier to push or pull.

F23

1 Before Reading

PREVIEW/SET PURPOSE

Have children preview pages F23–F25. Make a web as shown on the board or on chart paper. Tell children that they will help you fill in what wheels can do as the lesson progresses.

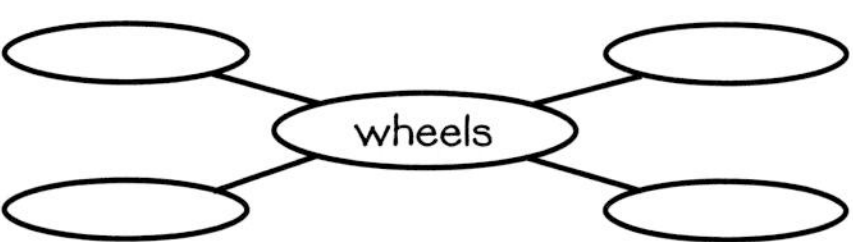

2 Guide the Learning

SCIENCE IDEAS

Read aloud page F23 with children. Make sure children understand the **main idea**.

- **A wheel is a roller that turns on an axle.**
- **Rollers and wheels can be used to make things easier to push or pull.**

DEVELOP READING SKILLS

Draw Conclusions Guide children to use the text to answer the following questions:

- **Does this machine use rollers or wheels to move?** wheels
- **If you took off the wheels, would it be harder or easier to move the machine?** harder

BACKGROUND

Webliography GO ONLINE
Keyword motion
www.harcourtschool.com

Wheels and Rollers Anything that rolls can be used as a roller. Smooth round marbles are rollers and can be used to play games or slide something heavy across a room.

Wheels are rollers. Wheels are useful when they turn on an axle. The axle keeps the wheels from wobbling and makes it possible to push and pull them in different ways, as with motors or pedals. Wheels and rollers change the effect of the push or pull we apply to an object.

When you push or pull on a heavy bag of cement at rest on the ground, it takes a lot of effort to make it move. But if you slide a dolly, which has wheels, underneath it, it takes much less effort to make it move. Wheels and rollers make it so much easier to move heavy loads, it is hard to think about what life would be like without them.

SCIENCE WORD WALL

Wheels, Rollers, and Axles
Have children make word cards for the words *wheel*, *roller*, and *axle*. Suggest children draw pictures of different things that use rollers, axles, or wheels. Display these on your Word Wall.

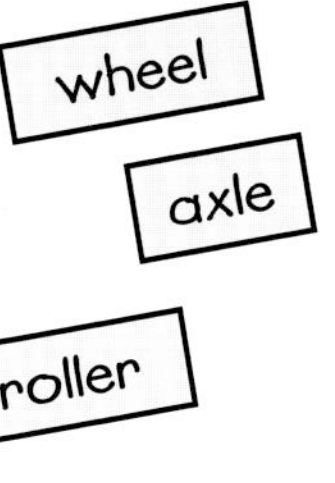

Have children read aloud pages F24 and F25. Help them **relate pictures to text** by having them identify which picture shows the "basket on wheels," the "chair on wheels," and the "wheels on boxes." Explain that "basket on wheels" helps describe how a shopping cart is used. Ask volunteers to describe a train and a bulldozer in the same way.

USE PROCESS SKILLS

Compare Have children compare the sizes of the wheels shown on the different objects and suggest reasons for why those sizes work best.

Critical Thinking Use this question to help children **draw conclusions** about the size of wheels.

▶ **What would happen if the wheels were bigger than those shown here?** They would change how fast the object moves, and how easily it could turn.

VISUAL LEARNING

Have children observe the number of wheels used on each object shown. Guide them to **predict outcomes** by asking what would happen if there were fewer wheels on each. The object would not move as easily, it might be less stable.

DEVELOP SCIENCE VOCABULARY

wheel Guide children in a discussion about wheels. Help them generate a list of things they have seen with wheels.

to Use Wheels

People use wheels in many ways. They use baskets on wheels to carry things when they shop. They use chairs on wheels to help them move around. Some children put wheels on boxes to make play cars.

F24

Math Link

How Many Wheels? Have children collect pictures of different machines such as cars, trucks, handcarts, bicycles, and conveyor belts that use wheels to make things easier to move. Have them group and sequence the pictures by the number of wheels used. Children can make a display or make collages to show their work, using numerals to represent each set of pictures. Challenge them to find examples of machines that use just one wheel (unicycle), or machines that use eighteen (tractor trailer trucks).

People use wheels to help them push or pull loads. A dolly's wheels make it easy to push heavy boxes. Many suitcases have wheels so that people can pull them along.

- **Why do people use things that have wheels?**
  They are able to move things easily.

1. What is a wheel?
2. What can wheels do?

F25

Literature Connections

Read Alouds

Wheels and Axles by Michael S. Dahl, Bridgestone Books, 1996.

The Wheels on the Bus by Maryann Kovalski, Little Brown & Co., 1990.

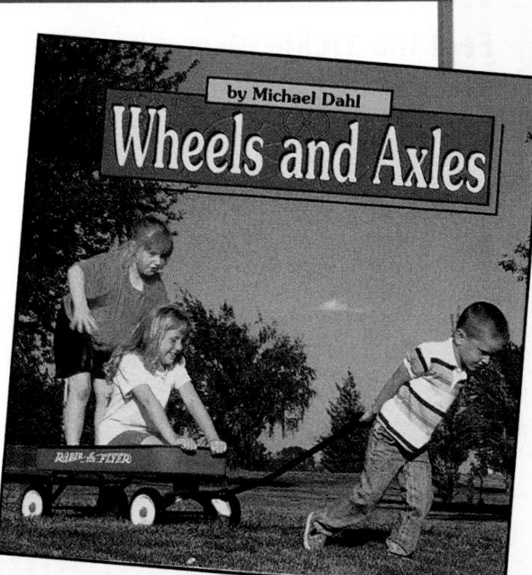

3 Wrap Up and Assess

SUMMARIZE

Have children **summarize** what they have learned. Refer back to the graphic organizer begun on page F23. Have children help you fill in examples of how wheels and rollers make it easier to push or pull different objects.

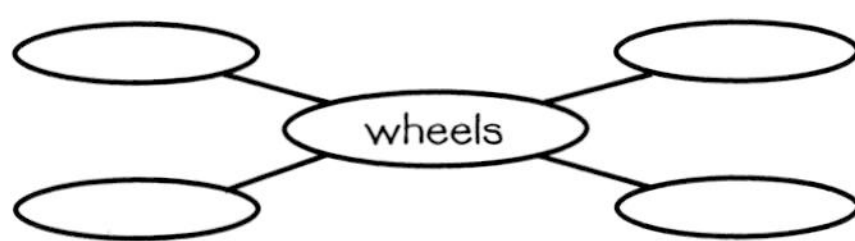

THINK ABOUT IT

1. A wheel is a roller that turns on an axle.
2. Wheels make it easier to push or pull heavy loads.

Informal Assessment

Performance Provide children with the opportunity to tell you how wheels and rollers make things easier to move. Give children a heavy object, such as a brick, and pencils or round blocks. Have them show you one way to make the objects easier to move. Have them tell you how they solve the problem as they do it.

LESSON CONCEPT REVIEW/ASSESSMENT

Children can use **Workbook p. WB143** to review the lesson concepts.

VOCABULARY REVIEW

Children can use **Workbook p. WB144** to review the chapter vocabulary.

Chapter 1 Links

Social Studies/ Career Link
An Architect Plans Buildings

Link Objective Recognize how understanding forces is necessary in some careers.

Talk about the photographs. Have children describe the shape of the pyramid and the materials from which it is made. Explain that this shape stands up to the downward pull of gravity or the sideways push of strong winds.

Link to careers. Explain that people hire architects to design buildings. Ieoh Ming Pei was born in China in 1917. At this museum in Paris, people needed an entrance to serve thousands of visitors but one that would not distract from the beauty of the buildings around it. Pei's design does the job.

THINK AND DO

Encourage children to make triangle shapes. They may use supports to hold the cards upright.

Informal Assessment

Portfolio Children may add pictures of their work to their portfolios.

PUPIL'S EDITION OR BIG BOOK

Links

Social Studies/Career Link

An Architect Plans Buildings

I. M. Pei designs buildings. He knows about forces that push and pull. He designs buildings that won't fall down.

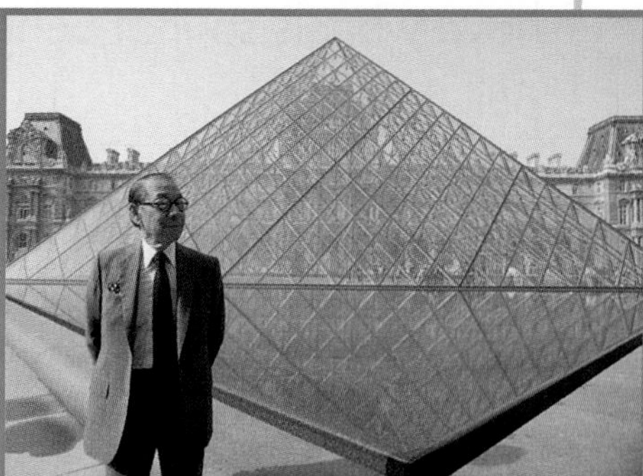

Think and Do

Use index cards to build a house. Then blow on your house of cards. Find different ways to make a house you can not blow down.

F26

More Link Options . . .

Art Link

Designing with Clay Help children recognize the effects of pushing and pulling on different shapes. Divide the class into small groups. Give each group a piece of clay. Ask each group to design small buildings that best withstand the pull of gravity and the push of strong winds. Encourage children to incorporate both form and function. Then have a contest between groups. Have the class vote on which building will be the strongest. Then test for strength. Also have children vote on which building looks the nicest.

Music Link

Feel the Tickle Help children recognize that musical pitches are caused by something moving back and forth very fast. Have children put three fingers on their larynx and hum. Have them hum so they can feel their lips vibrate, or tickle. At the same time, they should feel their throat vibrate against their fingers. Explain that they can make a sound when they hum because there are vocal cords in their throat that vibrate, or move back and forth very fast. Have them hum a high note and ask if they can feel the vibration as much as they do with a low note. They will feel less vibration. Explain that low notes are caused by slower vibrations than high notes.

Math Link

Add Pushes for Points

In some games, players use pushes to score points. Air hockey and bowling are two games like this.

Write

Make a game that uses pushes to score points. Use a box lid. Then use a pencil to flip a bottle cap ten times into the lid.

Add the number it lands on to your score each time. Then write about the kind of push you use to get the most points.

F27

Math Link
Add Pushes for Points

Link Objective Recognize how pushing and pulling can be used to score points in a game.

Talk about the photograph. Lead children in a discussion about strong and gentle pushes needed to compete for points.

Read aloud the text. Invite children to tell about experiences they have had with games where pushes were needed to score points.

WRITE

Remind children that the objective of this game is to push the bottle cap across a smooth surface to score points. For safety reasons, they should not flip the cap up into the air. Open the end of the box top so that the cap can be pushed into the scoring section. By holding the pencil between the thumb and index finger of one hand, they can use their other hand to gently flick the pencil so that it pushes the cap into the lid. For kinesthetic learners, you may wish to use a plastic coffee can lid on a linoleum floor and masking tape. Provide paper for children to write about the kind of push needed to get the most points.

Music/Physical Education Link

Rowing with Music Help children use the song "Row, Row, Row Your Boat" to demonstrate that motion is a change of position. Invite children to form a line and sing the song. As they sing, have them move around the classroom, acting out the rowing action. Stress that they have to push down in the water with the oars and pull them out of the water.

Drama Link

Guess What I'm Pushing, Guess What I'm Pulling Help children make a list of different activities that require pushing and pulling movements such as pulling a wagon, pushing a swing, sweeping the floor, and opening a jar of peanut butter. Have children take turns using pushes or pulls to act out activities from the list while others guess.

Chapter 

Review and Test Preparation

Tell What You Know

SUMMARIZE/RETELL

1. Have children use the words to tell about the picture. Use the following concepts to assess their understanding.

- ▶ A force is a push or a pull.
- ▶ Motion is moving from one place to another.
- ▶ A surface is the top or outside of something.
- ▶ Friction is a force that makes it harder for something to move.

Vocabulary

REVIEW SCIENCE VOCABULARY

TEST PREP Test-Taking Tips

Model this strategy with children to help them match the pictures with the words:

To match the word with the picture, first I match all the words I know. Then I go back and match the words I'm not sure of.

Children review chapter vocabulary by matching pictures with words.

2. b
3. d
4. a
5. e
6. c

GRAPHIC ORGANIZER FOR CHAPTER CONCEPTS

Children can use the graphic organizer to review the key concepts and ideas from each lesson. See **Workbook p. WB133** and **Transparency F1.**

PUPIL'S EDITION OR BIG BOOK

CHAPTER 1 REVIEW

Tell What You Know

1. Tell what you know about the picture. Use the words *force, motion, surface,* and *friction.*

Vocabulary

Tell which picture goes best with each word.

2. push
3. pull
4. curve
5. speed
6. wheel

a. 

b. 

c. 

d. 

e. 

F28

Graphic Organizer for Chapter Concepts

Transparency F1 • Workbook, p. WB133

Unit F, Chapter 1 Pushes and Pulls

LESSON 1 What Makes Things Move?	LESSON 2 What Are Some Ways Things Move?	LESSON 3 Why Do Things Move the Way They Do?
1. A force is a push or a pull.	**1.** Things move in many different ways.	**1.** Motion changes when you push or pull something.
2. When you push something, you press it away.	**2.** One way to tell how a thing moves is by the path it makes.	**2.** A hard push will move something quickly.

LESSON 4 How Do Objects Move on Surfaces?	LESSON 5 How Do Wheels Help Objects Move?
1. Friction makes it harder to move objects.	**1.** A wheel is a roller that turns on an axle.
2. A rough surface makes more friction than a smooth surface.	**2.** Wheels and rollers make things easier to push and pull.

Using Science Skills

7. **Measure** Pull a rock across rough and smooth surfaces with a rubber band. Measure how long the rubber band stretches each time. Make a chart. Record the numbers. Which makes more friction?

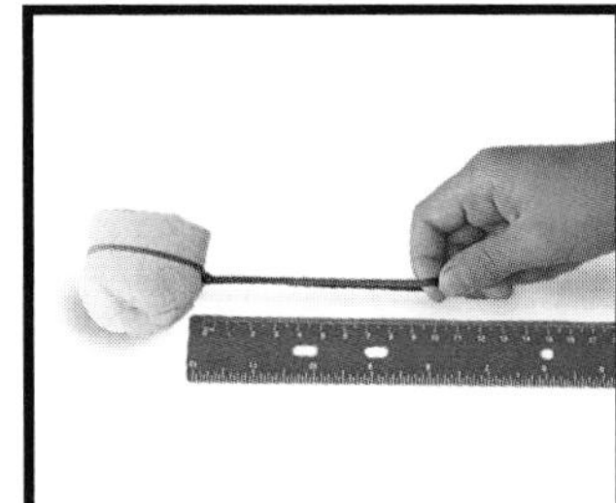

Friction on Surfaces	
Surface	How Long the Rubber Band Stretches
rough	
smooth	

8. **Draw a Conclusion** Rub your hands together. Feel the friction. Then put a few drops of oil on your hands. Rub again. Draw a conclusion.

F29

Using Science Skills

REVIEW PROCESS SKILLS

7. Measure Help children make the chart or have a duplicate prepared ahead of time. CAUTION: **Remind children to be careful with the rubber band as snapping it can hurt someone.** Identify smooth and rough surfaces to use. After children have recorded their measurements on the chart, ask children to use the numbers to tell which surface makes less friction. smooth Ask them to explain how they know. It takes less pull to make the rock move.

   Have children use their charts to predict what will happen if they try the same experiment using a heavy book on rollers. They may want to test their predictions if time allows.

PERFORMANCE ASSESSMENT

8. Draw a Conclusion Use hand lotion or baby oil on children's hands. Help children identify experiences they may have had oiling something to make it move more easily. CAUTION: **Check for allergies. Avoid using peanut oil. Protect clothes with safety apron so oil will not get on clothes.**

WRITING ABOUT SCIENCE

Have children write a composition that involves writing for a specific purpose. You may wish to use the prompt that is provided in the Workbook. The prompt is accompanied by a graphic organizer that will help children organize their ideas before writing. Models for writing are provided in the **Teaching Resources** book. You may wish to reproduce those for children or display them on a transparency.

WRITING ABOUT SCIENCE

A chapter writing prompt and a prewriting activity are provided on **Workbook p. WB146**.

CHAPTER TEST

See **Assessment Guide pp. AG87–90** for the Chapter Test. Assessment Options are provided on p. F2i.

TAKE-HOME BOOK

Use the **Take-Home Book** (described on p. F2h) to provide more chapter content and activities.

CHAPTER 2 Planning Guide Magnets

LESSON	PACING	OBJECTIVES	MATERIALS
1 What Are Magnets? F32–37	3 days	▶ Recognize that a magnet is a piece of iron that attracts objects with iron in them. ▶ Observe how the magnetic force works and its different uses.	**Investigate** bar magnet, objects, paper, pencil
2 What Are the Poles of a Magnet? F38–41	2 days	▶ Observe that a magnet has two different poles. ▶ Recognize that a magnet's pulling force is strongest at the poles.	**Investigate** bar magnet, paper clips, paper, pencil
3 What Can a Magnet Pull Through? F42–45	2 days	▶ Recognize that magnetic force can pass through some things to attract iron objects. ▶ Observe that magnetic force gets weaker as distance increases from the magnet.	**Investigate** bar magnet, paper clips, different materials
4 How Can You Make a Magnet? F46–49	2 days	▶ Recognize that a magnet can magnetize things it attracts. ▶ Compare the strength of different magnets.	**Investigate** magnet, 2 paper clips
End of Chapter F50–53 **Math Link: Measure Magnetic Force** **Social Studies Link: Compass Readings** **Chapter Review and Test Preparation**		▶ Recognize that different magnets have different strengths. ▶ Understand that magnets are essential tools for many travelers. ▶ Review chapter concepts.	

PROCESS SKILLS	VOCABULARY	RESOURCES AND TECHNOLOGY	REACHING ALL LEARNERS
Process Skill Tip gather and record data **Other Process Skills** compare, predict	**magnet** **attract** **strength**	**Workbook,** pp. WB147–149 **Vocabulary Cards,** pp. TR157–160 **Transparency** F2-1 **Harcourt Science Activity Video** **Harcourt Science Instant Readers CD-ROM**	**Advanced Learners,** p. F1g **Visually Impaired,** p. F35 **ESL Activity,** p. F36 **Investigation Challenge,** p. F35 **Informal Assessment,** p. F37
Process Skill Tip infer **Other Process Skills** plan a simple investigation	**repel** **poles**	**Workbook,** pp. WB150–151 **Transparency** F2-2 **Harcourt Science Activity Video** **Internet Site**	**Informal Assessment,** p. F41
Process Skill Tip plan an investigation **Other Process Skills** observe	**magnetic force**	**Workbook,** pp. WB152–153 **Transparency** F2-3 **Harcourt Science Activity Video**	**Informal Assessment,** p. F45
Process Skill Tip draw a conclusion **Other Process Skills** observe	**magnetize**	**Workbook,** pp. WB154–158 **Transparency** F2-4 **Harcourt Science Activity Video**	**ESL Activity,** p. F47 **Informal Assessment,** p. F49
		Take-Home Book, pp. TH45–46 *Hector's Magnet Gets the Job Done* **Activities for Home or School,** pp. TR108–109 **Chapter Test,** pp. AG93–96	**Informal Assessment,** p. F50 **Performance Assessment,** p. AG97 **Portfolio Evaluation,** p. AGxxiv

Prepare for Activities

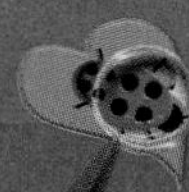

Use this page to help you organize and prepare materials for the Investigations, which begin each lesson of this chapter.

LESSON INVESTIGATION	MATERIALS

1 What a Magnet Can Do
F32

PURPOSE Gather and record data about magnets.

PREPARATION TIPS Collect objects that a magnet will and will not attract. Make a copy of the chart for the class (p. TR167).

TIME 20–25 minutes

EXPECTED RESULTS Children discover that a magnet only attracts objects with iron in them.

MATERIALS
- bar magnet
- objects such as jacks, paper clips, button, marble, nail, barrette, and rubber ball
- paper and pencil

2 A Magnet's Ends
F38

PURPOSE Infer that magnetic force is strongest at the poles of a magnet.

PREPARATION TIPS Use small paper clips.

TIME 15–20 minutes

EXPECTED RESULTS Children discover that they can make long chains of paper clips at the poles of the magnet.

MATERIALS
- bar magnet
- paper clips
- paper and pencil

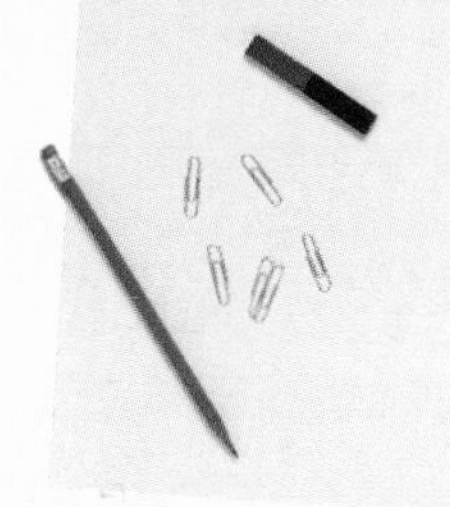

3 Things Magnets Pull Through
F42

PURPOSE Plan an investigation to find out different materials a magnet can pull through.

PREPARATION TIPS Have on hand different materials such as cardboard, paper, plastic, carpet, and wood.

TIME 20–25 minutes

EXPECTED RESULTS Children discover that a magnet can pull through some materials and not others.

MATERIALS
- bar magnet
- paper clips
- different materials such as a metal lunch box, carpet, plastic, paper clips, cardboard, and paper

4 Making a Magnet
F46

PURPOSE Conclude that a magnet can be used to magnetize a paper clip.

PREPARATION TIPS Try this activity ahead of time. Children may need help with Step 3.

TIME 15 minutes

EXPECTED RESULTS Children discover that they can use a magnet to magnetize a paper clip.

MATERIALS
- magnet
- 2 paper clips

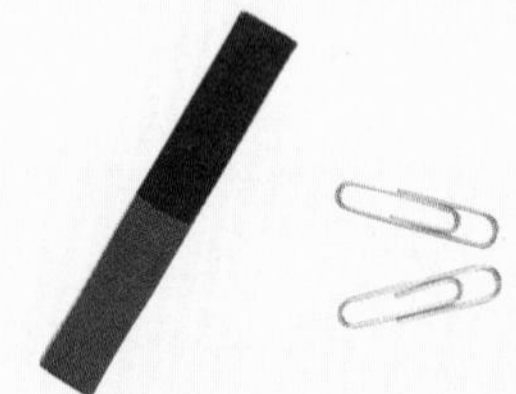

Harcourt Science Activity Videos

The Activity Video for this unit shows children doing the Investigations. You may wish to use the video for classroom management ideas or to model the investigation process for children.

Equipment Kits

Underlined items above are provided in the equipment kits (available separately).

Expanding the Learning

Providing More Depth

. . . with Trade Books

These books provide in-depth information about the unique properties of magnets and how to make magnets.

Electricity and Magnetism by Maria Gordon (Thomson Learning, 1996) uses activities to help children learn about magnetism first-hand.

Experiments with Magnets by Helen J. Challand (Children's Press, 1986) provides step-by-step instructions for simple investigations.

The Fisherman and His Wife by Brothers Grimm (Farrar, Straus and Giroux, 1987) is the classic tale of the fisherman who frees a fish, receives a reward, and then keeps returning to the fish to ask for more and more.

Magnetism by John Woodruff (Steck-Vaughn, 1998) uses easy activities that can be done at home to explain magnetism.

Magnets and Sparks by Wendy Madgwick (Steck-Vaughn, 1999) demonstrates the properties and uses of magnets and electricity.

The Science Book of Magnets by Neil Ardley (Harcourt Brace, 1991) is a simple book of experiments that demonstrate magnetism.

Science With Magnets by Helen Edom (EDC Publications, 1992) explains the properties and principles of magnetism and contains hands-on activities for children to do with magnets.

What Magnets Can Do (Rookie Read-Aloud Science) by Allan Fowler (Children's Press, 1995) helps children discover what magnets can do.

Trade books titles are current at time of publication but may go out of print without notice.

Visit The Learning Site for related links, activities, and resources.

www.harcourtschool.com

. . . with the Take-Home Book

Hector's Magnet Gets the Job Done
pages TH45–46, *Take-Home Books*

This take-home book provides reinforcement of science concepts and vocabulary presented in the chapter and provides an activity. See p. F53.

Hector's Magnet Gets the Job Done

Hector and Chris are playing with toy trains. The cars stick together because they have magnets on each end.

. . . with More Activities

. . . with the Harcourt Science Instant Reader

INSTANT READERS

Jeff's Magnet
written by Madge Alley

Jeff's Magnet by Madge Alley identifies familiar objects that can and cannot be picked up by a magnet. This nonfiction reader reinforces chapter science vocabulary and concepts, as well as high-frequency words. See p. F37.

The **Harcourt Science Instant Reader** is also available on **CD-ROM,** which includes science activities and investigations.

Assessment Options Chapter 2

Formal Assessment

- **Chapter Review and Test Preparation,** PE pp. F52–53
- **Chapter Test,** pp. AG93–96

Performance Assessment

- **Chapter Review and Test Preparation,** PE p. F53
- **Chapter Performance Task,** pp. AG97–98
- **Project Evaluation Checklist,** p. AGxviii

Ongoing Assessment

- ✓ **Questions,** PE pp. F33–37, F39–41, F43–45, F47–49
- **Lesson Review,** PE pp. F37, F41, F45, F49
- **Informal Assessment**
  - **Classroom Observation,** TE p. F49
  - **Performance,** TE p. F37
  - **Portfolio,** TE pp. F41, F45, F50
- **Observation Checklist,** AGxiv

Student Self-Assessment

- **Self-Assessment – Investigate,** p. AGxvi
- **Self-Assessment – Learn About,** p. AGxvii
- **Project Summary Sheet,** p. AGxix

Portfolio Assessment

- **Science Experiences Record,** p. AGxxii
- **Guide to My Science Portfolio,** p. AGxxiii
- **Portfolio Evaluation,** p. AGxxiv

Chapter Test AG93

Magnets

Part I Vocabulary 4 points each

Draw a line from the word to the picture it goes with.

1. poles
2. repel
3. attract

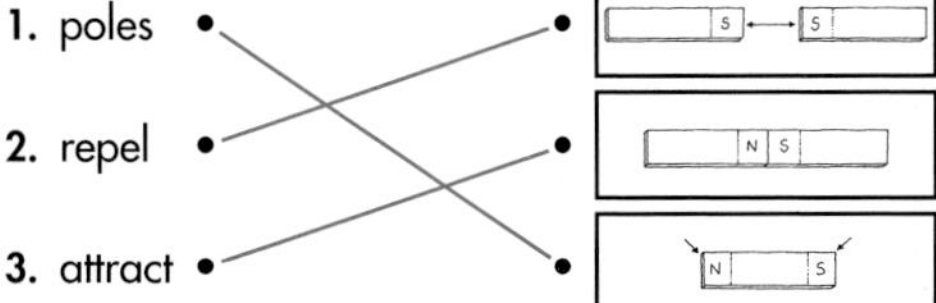

Circle the best answer.

4. A piece of iron that can pull things is a ___.

rock stone (magnet)

5. A magnet's ___ is how strongly it pulls.

pole (strength) plan

6. A ___ can pass through paper.

(magnetic force) natural force small force

Chapter Test AG94

7. A magnet can ___ the things it attracts.

(magnetize) repel push

Part II Science Concepts and Understanding

8. Circle things a magnet attracts. 6 points each

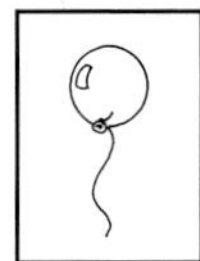

9. Which pole will attract the *S* pole of another magnet? Put an ***X*** on it.

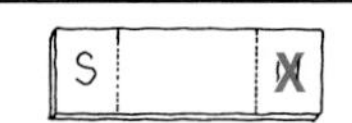

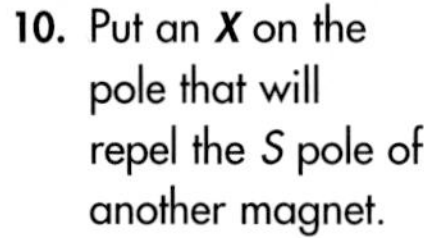

10. Put an ***X*** on the pole that will repel the *S* pole of another magnet.

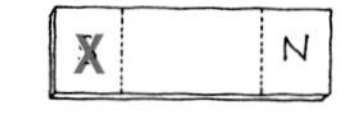

Chapter Test AG95

11. Write the word that completes *both* sentences.

All magnets have ___ in them.

Magnets attract objects that are made of ___. iron

Write the letter of the best answer.

A 12. Where is a magnet's pull the strongest?
- **A** at the poles
- **B** in the middle
- **C** above the magnet

H 13. What can you make a magnet from?
- **F** a crayon
- **G** a book
- **H** a paper clip

B 14. What kind of magnet is found in the ground?
- **A** a gem stone
- **B** a lodestone
- **C** a diamond

Chapter Test AG96

Part III Process Skills Application 15 points each

Process skills: infer, investigate

15. Put an ***X*** by the sentence that tells what you can infer from this picture.

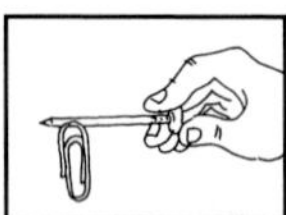

___ The nail repels the paper clip.

X The nail has been magnetized.

16. You plan to investigate whether you can make a magnet out of a nail. Write **1**, **2**, and **3** to show the order of the steps you would take.

1 See if the nail will pull paper clips.

3 Touch the nail to the paper clips again to see if it will pull them.

2 Stroke the nail with a magnet ten times in the same direction.

Performance Assessment AG97

PERFORMANCE TASK

Comparing Magnet Strength

Materials

1. Put a small piece of tape near the middle of each magnet. Write ***A*** on one piece of tape and ***B*** on the other.
2. How can you find out which magnet is stronger? Plan an investigation using the two magnets and some paper clips. Then follow your plan.
3. Draw a picture of your investigation. Put a star beside the stronger magnet in your picture.
4. Share with classmates what you found out.

Performance Assessment AG98

PERFORMANCE TASK

Teacher's Directions

Comparing Magnet Strength

Materials Performance Task sheets, a variety of magnets—two different ones for each pair of children, paper clips, masking tape, markers

Time 20–30 minutes

Suggested Grouping pairs or small groups

Science Processes investigate, gather data, record

Preparation Hints Each pair of children will need 10 to 20 paper clips, depending on the size and strength of the magnets.

Introduce the Task Ask three children to select one magnet each from the assortment you have gathered. Then ask these children to demonstrate that what they selected *is* a magnet. Have them show how it picks up or attaches itself to metal objects. Brainstorm with children how they might investigate which of the three magnets is the strongest. Have children compare how well each attracts the same metal object. Distribute the Performance Task sheets. Ask one volunteer to read the directions aloud. Ask other children to explain what they will be doing.

Promote Discussion When children finish, have the partners join others in a small group to compare their work. Have one partner in each pair describe the investigation they did and its outcome. Ask the groups to decide which of the magnets used by its members was stronger and how they know.

Scoring Rubric

Performance Indicators

___ Plans an investigation to determine which magnet is stronger.
___ Follows the investigation plan.
___ Draws a picture of the investigation.
___ Uses the picture to explain the investigation and its outcome to others.

Observations and Rubric Score

3 2 1 0

Workbook Support

Process Skills Practice WB148

Record Data

Gather and circle the things that are pulled by a magnet. Make an **X** on the things that are **not** pulled by a magnet.

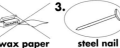

1.  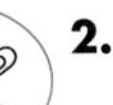 paper clips
2.  wax paper
3. steel nail
4. candle
5. scissors
6.  yarn

7. Record your data in this chart.

My Chart	
Pulled by a magnet	**NOT pulled by a magnet**
scissors nail paper clips	yarn candle wax paper

Lesson Concept Review/Assessment WB149

What Are Magnets?

Circle each object that a magnet would attract.

1.  leaf
2.  nail
3. pencil
4.  thread
5. key
6. staples

Match each magnet to the words that tell what the magnet does.

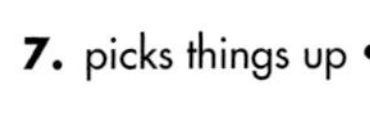

7. picks things up

8. holds things together

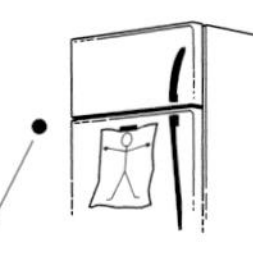

Process Skills Practice WB150

Infer

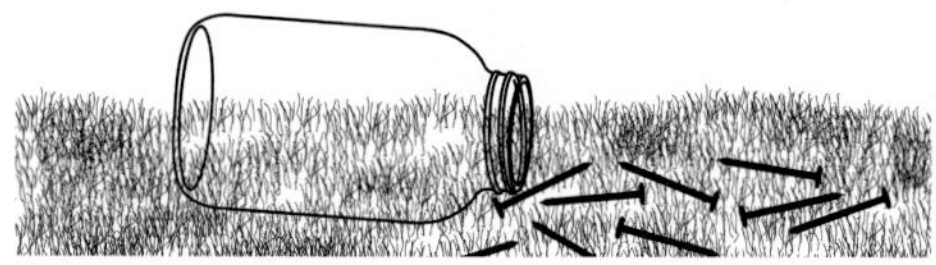

1. A man dropped a jar of nails in tall grass. What would you use to help him pick up the nails? Color the **best** answer. magnet

2. Tell why you would choose that item.

The nails are made from iron and are attracted by the magnet.

3. What kinds of things would a magnet pick up? Circle the **best** answer.

plastic wood iron

Lesson Concept Review/Assessment WB151

What Are the Poles of a Magnet?

1. Match each word to the picture it tells about.

repel • attract •

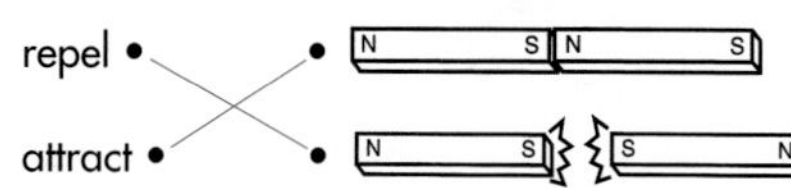

2. Write **S** and **N** to show how these magnets attract.

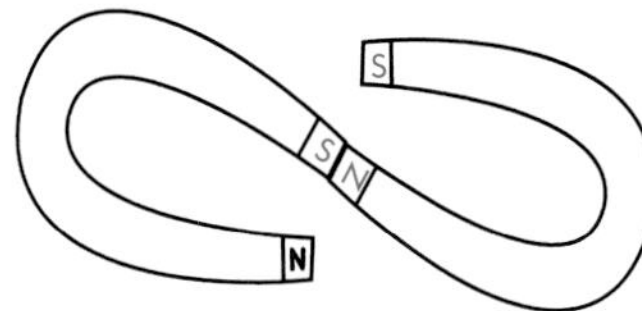

3. The magnet attracts iron bits. Color the parts of the magnet that have the strongest force.

The poles should be colored.

Process Skills Practice WB152

Plan an Investigation

How many paper clips can a magnet pick up?

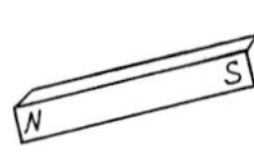

1. Tell how you could investigate this question.

Accept reasonable answers. Children may suggest sticking the end of the magnet in the pile. Or they may suggest holding the magnet and adding paper clips to it one-by-one.

2. Draw how your magnet looks as you investigate. Children should draw the magnet with several paper clips on it.

Lesson Concept Review/Assessment WB153

What Can a Magnet Pull Through?

1. Joey wants to move a nail with a magnet. Circle the picture that will work the **best** for Joey.

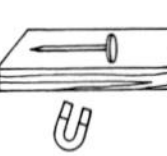  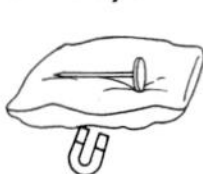

2. Circle all the things that the magnetic force of a small magnet can pass through.

  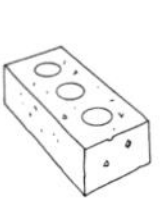 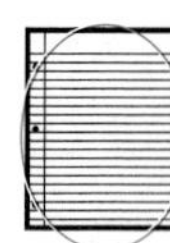

3. Circle the things that can be attracted with magnetic force.

   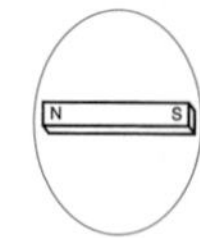

Workbook Support Continued

Process Skills Practice WB154

Draw a Conclusion

1. Edie and Harry are fishing with magnets. Edie's magnet does not lift the crayons. Tell why.

Crayons are not made of iron.

Magnet A Magnet B

2. Magnet A lifted paper clips. Magnet B did not. Tell why.

Magnet B is farther away from the paper clips than Magnet A.

Lesson Concept Review/Assessment WB155

How Can You Make a Magnet?

1. Color the objects that are magnetized.
Nail and scissors should be colored.

2. Circle the object you would use to magnetize a nail.

N S

3. How many paper clips have been magnetized?
one two (five)

Vocabulary Review WB156

Magnets

Circle **true** or **false**. If the sentence is false, change the underlined word to make it true.

1. Attract means to pull something.
(true) false
2. A pole is a piece of iron that attracts things.
magnet true (false)
3. How strongly a magnet pulls is its strength.
(true) false
4. A magnet is weakest at its poles.
strongest true (false)
5. To repel means to pull something.
push true (false)
6. A magnet can magnetize a paper clip.
(true) false

Reading Skills Practice WB157

Draw Conclusions

Magnets Magnets attract things made of iron. A magnet can magnetize, or give magnetic force, to the things it attracts. Mr. Smith ran a key over a magnet ten times the same way. Then he used the key to pick up some staples and paper clips.

1. What did Mr. Smith do to his key?

He used his magnet to magnetize the key.

2. Why did Mr. Smith's key pick up staples and paper clips?

Because the staples and paper clips have iron that attracts them to the magnet.

Writing Practice WB158

Write Directions

A. Make up a game or a toy that uses magnets. Draw your game or toy in the box.

B. Write directions for playing your game or using your toy. Tell what to do first, next, and last.

First

Next

Last

Chapter 

Magnets

Generate Questions

Did You Know?/*Fast* Facts

Before children open their books, guide them in a discussion about magnets. Ask:

- ▶ **How do people use magnets?** Possible answers: hold things to refrigerators, as door latches
- ▶ **How do magnets work?** Encourage all responses.

Have volunteers read aloud pages F30–F31.

Discuss the photographs. Ask questions such as this one to help children **relate pictures to text**:

- ▶ **Where are the magnets that run the Maglev train?** beneath the train cars and in the tracks

Explain that research is being done on Maglev trains in Germany and Japan. Maglev stands for "magnetic levitation." When the train is moving, the magnets make it levitate, or rise above the tracks.

The magnets shown on the pencil are pushing apart from each other like they do on the Maglev train.

Encourage children's questions. Write children's questions on the board, or have them write or draw in their journals.

PUPIL'S EDITION OR BIG BOOK

Reading Skills Checklist

Strategies for developing the following reading skills are provided in this chapter.

- ☑ use context *p. F35*
- ☐ recall supporting facts and details
- ☐ arrange events in sequence
- ☑ draw conclusions *pp. F44, F48*
- ☑ identify the main idea *pp. F33, F39, F43, F47*
- ☑ identify cause and effect *pp. F40, F44*
- ☑ predict outcomes *pp. F40, F44, F48*
- ☑ summarize *pp. F37, F41, F45, F49*
- ☐ use graphic sources for information
- ☑ relate pictures to text *pp. F30, F33, F35, F36, F43, F47*
- ☐ distinguish between fact and nonfact
- ☐ develop concepts of print
- ☑ build vocabulary *pp. F33, F34, F39, F40, F43, F44, F47, F48*

School-Home Connection

Distribute copies of the School-Home Connection, p. TR25.

Follow Up Have volunteers compare the results of the activity they did at home. Additional School-Home Connections are provided by the **Activities for Home or School** (pp. F54–55) and the **Take-Home Book** (p. F30d).

Teaching Resources, p. TR25

School-Home Connection

Harcourt Science

Chapter Content

Today we begin a new chapter in science. Your child will learn about magnets. We will be doing activities that help us understand what a magnet can do, where the poles of a magnet are located, and the types of things that can be magnetized.

Science Process Skills

Learning to **draw conclusions** is an important skill in science. Drawing conclusions is done after observations are made. Drawing conclusions based on observation is how we make sense of the world around us.

To give your child practice in making observations and drawing conclusions from those observations, observe and experiment with magnets around the house. Give your child an assortment of objects, such as paper clips, pencils, and various types of hardware. Make sure that some of the materials will be attracted to a magnet, and others won't. Have your child test the different objects, and observe what happens. Then help your child draw a conclusion about what types of things are attracted to magnets. (The objects that are attracted to a magnet contain the metal iron.)

Science Fun

Picture Magnets

What You Need

- strip of magnetic tape
- favorite photo
- glue
- cardboard
- cookie cutter
- scissors

What to Do

1. Trace the shape of the cookie cutter onto the cardboard and the photo, making sure to include the part of the photo you want on your finished magnet.
2. Cut out both shapes.
3. Glue the photo to the cardboard.
4. Glue the strip of magnetic tape to the back of the cardboard. Let dry.
5. Use your magnet to decorate the refrigerator or give to a friend!

Activity Materials from Home

Dear Family Member:

To do the activities in this chapter, we will need some materials that you may have around the house. Please note the items listed at the right. If possible, please send these things to school with your child.

Your help and support are appreciated!

- ___ **small objects such as buttons, barrettes, nails, marbles, balls, and jacks**
- ___ **piece of carpet**
- ___ **cardboard box**

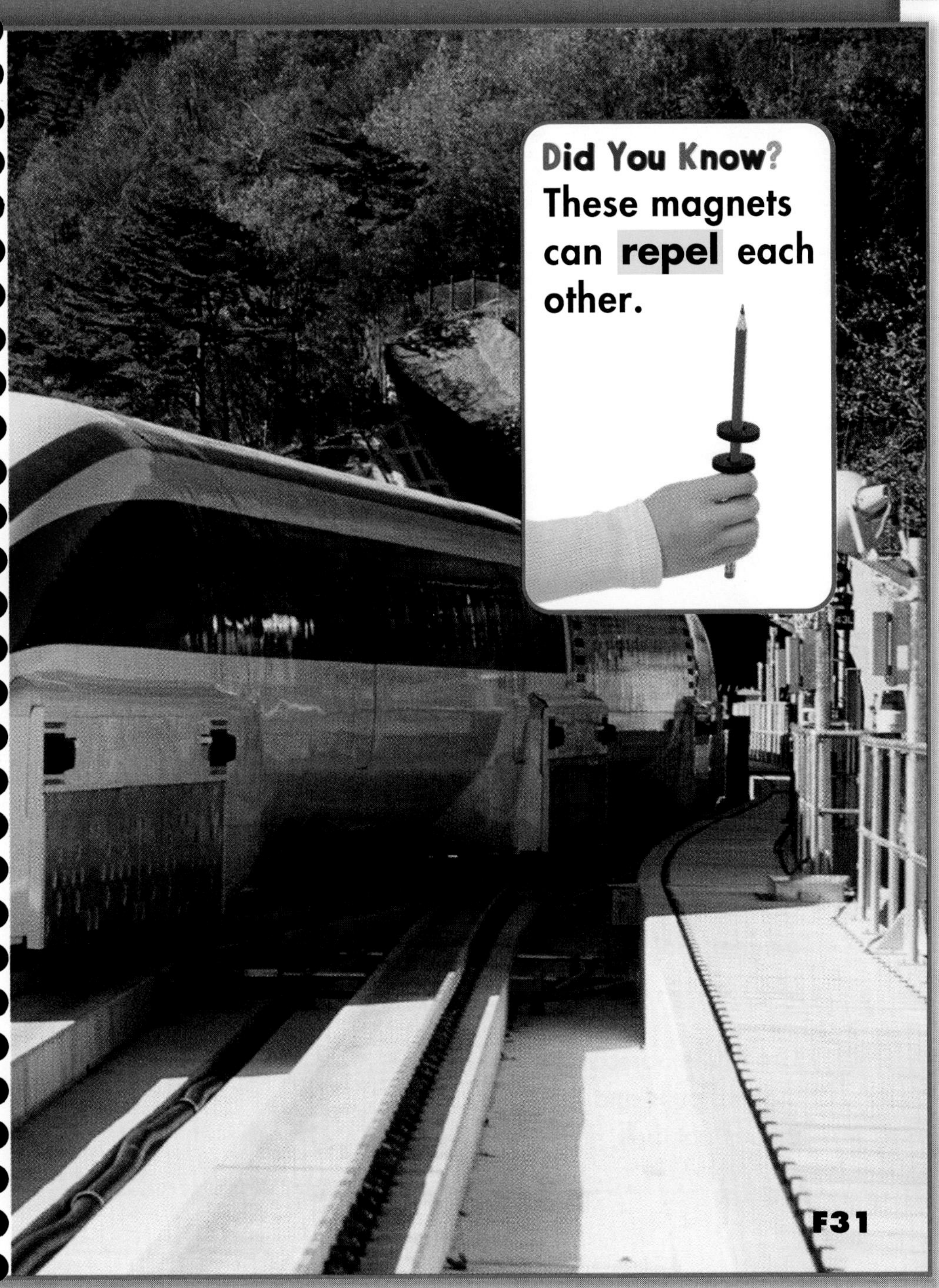

Did You Know?
These magnets can repel each other.
F31

Graphic Organizer for Chapter Concepts

Transparency F2 • Workbook, p. WB147

Unit F, Chapter 2 Magnets

LESSON 1 What Are Magnets?	LESSON 2 What Are the Poles of a Magnet?
1. Magnets are pieces of iron that attract things. **2.** Magnets can attract things made of iron. **3.** People use different kinds of magnets in different ways.	**1.** Poles are places on a magnet where the pull is the strongest. **2.** Every magnet has a north pole and a south pole. **3.** Two poles that are the same repel each other.
LESSON 3 **What Can a Magnet Pull Through?**	**LESSON 4** **How Can You Make a Magnet?**
1. The pull of a magnet is called magnetic force. **2.** Magnetic force can pass through paper, water, air, glass, and material.	**1.** A magnet can magnetize an object made of iron. **2.** You can make a magnet by stroking an iron object with a magnet.

Prereading Strategies

Preview the Chapter

Have children look through the chapter and read aloud the question headings for each lesson. Invite them to answer the questions. Use this to gain a sense of what children already know about magnets and what they want to learn.

Preview the Photographs

Have children look at the photos throughout the chapter. Use their comments to guide discussion about experiences they may have already had with magnets.

Preview the Vocabulary

Write the vocabulary words on page F30 on the board. Have children identify words they don't know or would like to know more about. Tell them they will find out about these words as they go through the lessons.

DEFINITIONS

magnet a solid that can attract iron

attract to pull closer to

strength how strongly a magnet can pull

poles places on a magnet where the pull force is strongest

repel to push away

magnetic force the pull of a magnet

magnetize to give magnetic force to something

VOCABULARY CARDS AND ACTIVITIES

Children can use the Vocabulary Cards to make their own graphic organizers or to add to an ongoing file of science terms. The Vocabulary Cards and a variety of strategies and activities are provided beginning on p. TR110 in the **Teaching Resources** book.

GRAPHIC ORGANIZER FOR CHAPTER CONCEPTS

Children can use the graphic organizer to record key concepts and ideas from each lesson. See **Workbook p. WB147** and Transparency F2. A completed graphic organizer is also shown on page F52.

LESSON 1

What Are Magnets?

Objectives

- ▶ **Recognize that a magnet is a piece of iron that attracts objects with iron in them.**
- ▶ **Observe how the magnetic force works and its different uses.**

Motivate

Talk About Magnets Have different kinds of magnets for children to observe and handle. Discuss ways the different magnets are used.

Time 20–25 min **Grouping** individuals or pairs

Process Skill gather and record data

Preparation Tips and Expected Results See page F30c.

Center Activity Option Place this investigation or a copy of the Investigation, page TR76, in your science center.

Activity Tips

- ▶ Model how to make the chart (p. TR167) or prepare one ahead of time.
- ▶ Allow time for children to tell how the objects they grouped are the same and different.

Children can place their charts in their science journals.

Activity Questions

- ▶ How are the objects that a magnet pulls similar? How are they different?
- ▶ What more would you like to know about magnets? How can you find out?

When Minutes Count . . .

As a whole-class activity, using an overhead projector, use a magnet to test different objects. Have children observe which are pulled and which are not. Record the results on a chart on the board. Then ask children to group the objects and tell how they are similar and different.

PUPIL'S EDITION OR BIG BOOK

What Are Magnets?

Investigate

What a Magnet Can Do

You will need

bar magnet

objects

paper and pencil

What a Magnet Can Do		
Object	Pulls	Does Not Pull

1. Gather data about the magnet. Hold it near each object.
2. Make a chart like this one. Record what you observe.
3. Group the objects the magnet pulls and those it does not pull.

Science Skill

To gather data about what a magnet can do, observe and record what it does.

F32

Science Skills

Process Skill: Gather and Record Data Display Process Skill Tip Transparency F2-1. Have children observe the magnets shown and describe how they are the same and different. Have them list one thing they think each magnet can attract and one it can't. Record their answers in the spaces provided.

Process Skill Tip Transparency F2-1

Gather and Record Data

How Magnets Are the Same and Different				
Magnet	How It Is the Same as Other Magnets	How It Is Different	It Can Attract	It Can't Attract
	Attracts objects with iron in them	Square shaped Bigger than two other magnets	nail	marble
	Attracts objects with iron in them	Shaped like a U Smaller than the square-shaped magnet	paper clip	pencil
	Attracts objects with iron in them	Shaped like a bar Long	pin	glass

PROCESS SKILLS PRACTICE

To practice and apply process skills, see **Workbook p. WB148.**

Learn About

Magnets

A **magnet** is a piece of iron that can **attract**, or pull, things. The things it pulls are usually made of iron. Iron is a kind of metal.

■ **How are magnets used here?** to hold things on the refrigerator; paper clip container; can opener

F33

Learn About

1 Before Reading

PREVIEW/SET PURPOSE

Have children preview pages F33–F37. Draw a chart. Tell children they will help you add to the chart as the lesson progresses.

Properties of Magnets	Different Kinds of Magnets	How People Use Magnets

2 Guide the Learning

SCIENCE IDEAS

Have children read page F33. Help them **identify the main idea: A magnet is a piece of iron that can attract things.**

▶ What is a magnet made of? iron

▶ What happens when you put a magnet next to something made of iron? The magnet attracts it.

Help children **relate pictures to text.**

▶ What things are magnets pulling in this photo? measuring cups, paper clips, can, refrigerator door

▶ What metal is in those things? iron

DEVELOP READING SKILLS

Build Vocabulary Have children find in the text the word that means to pull on things. Ask them to use the word in sentences.

BACKGROUND

Webliography
Keyword magnetism
www.harcourtschool.com
GO ONLINE

Magnets A magnet is a solid, such as a stone or a piece of metal, that attracts other objects made from iron, steel, nickel, or cobalt. Natural magnets, called *magnetite* or *lodestone*, are made inside the Earth. Magnets are used to produce electricity. They are also found in computers and varied appliances. They activate speakers in television sets, radios, stereos, and telephones. Their pulling force makes them useful as door catches or latches.

CAUTION **Magnets can damage the magnetic strips on credit cards and computer software, so avoid placing magnets near them. In addition, striking or heating magnets will cause them to demagnetize.**

SCIENCE WORD WALL

Magnets Attract Iron Make word cards for *magnet, attract,* and *iron*. Have children draw pictures to show different kinds of magnets and the things they attract.

magnet

iron

attract

Technology Link

Instant Reader CD-ROM Children can learn more about magnets in ***Jeff's Magnets*** by Madge Alley on **Harcourt Science Instant Reader CD-ROM.**

Guide the Learning continued

SCIENCE IDEAS

Have children read pages F34 and F35. Invite children to talk about their own experiences using magnets. Encourage them to use the words *attract* or *repel* to describe the magnets' force.

USE PROCESS SKILLS

Compare Have children compare the uses for magnets shown on these pages. Ask what are the similarities and differences between the uses. Guide children to understand that magnets are used to pull objects to them. Some are used to protect cows, others to help motors run.

DEVELOP SCIENCE VOCABULARY

magnet Use the photos of the cow magnet and lodestone to add to children's understanding of different kinds of magnets.

attract Have children use the word as they point to examples shown in the photos.

PUPIL'S EDITION OR BIG BOOK

How People Use Magnets

People use magnets to hold things closed and to lift things. They also use them in televisions and electric motors.

A farmer may put a magnet in a cow's stomach. The magnet attracts bits of metal that the cow may eat. This keeps the metal from hurting the cow.

Cultural Connection

The Fisherman and His Wife Tell children that Jakob and Wilhelm Grimm lived in Germany during the first half of the 19th century. They were brothers who collected and published folktales such as *Snow White*, *Cinderella*, and *The Fisherman and His Wife*. Have children use *The Fisherman and His Wife* as the basis for a simple play that demonstrates the use of a magnet attached to the end of a fishing pole. Read or tell the tale to children and help them decide which of the wife's greedy demands they want to include in their play. Help them make the flounder so that the fisherman can catch it using a magnet at the end of a pole. Have one child be the narrator and have other children act out the parts.

Social Studies Link

Sorting Trash Explain to children that recycling centers use giant magnets to sort metals with iron in them from metals that do not have iron. To show how this works, mix pieces of foil, soup cans, paper clips, soda cans, and other bits of metal trash in an open box. Make sure there are no sharp edges. Have children predict which materials a magnet will sort out. Then have them use a magnet to test their predictions.

Where Magnets Can Be Found

Some magnets are found in nature. Lodestone is a kind of magnet found in the ground.

lodestone

■ **How are the children using magnets in this fishing game?**

The magnets attract the iron washers that are attached to the fish.

Guide the Learning continued

SCIENCE IDEAS

Explain that *lodestone* means "leading stone." In the past, sailors used a lodestone to find *north*. They suspended the rock from a string and let it turn freely. One end of the rock always turned north. Children can suspend a bar magnet from a string and watch the ends seek north and south. This works best away from the iron or steel beams often found in buildings.

VISUAL LEARNING

Help children **use context** to identify the lodestone and **relate pictures to text**.

▶ **How can you tell which is the lodestone and which is a magnet made by people?** The lodestone looks like a rock.

Reaching All Learners

Visually Impaired Children who are visually impaired will benefit from using magnets and objects with iron in them to feel the magnetic force. You can also have them use two magnets to feel the pushes and pulls of like and opposite poles.

Investigation Challenge

Hands-On Activity: Separate Salt from Iron

Mix a teaspoon of iron filings with a teaspoon of salt in a small bowl. You can make iron filings by carefully cutting a piece of steel wool with scissors. Challenge children to use what they know about magnets to separate the iron filings from the salt.

Guide the Learning continued

SCIENCE IDEAS

Have children read pages F36 and F37. Provide different types of magnets for children to use with paper clips or other objects with iron in them. Challenge them to find the strongest magnet. If possible, use examples of the magnets shown.

Critical Thinking Have children use magnets of different sizes to observe how many paper clips each can lift.

► **Do you think larger magnets are always stronger than smaller magnets? Why?** No, because the size of the magnet doesn't determine its strength.

VISUAL LEARNING

To help children **relate pictures to text**, have them observe the different magnets shown and use size, color, and shape to describe each one.

USE PROCESS SKILLS

Predict Have children make a chart like the one shown on page F37. Have them use their own magnets and predict which will be the strongest. They should record what they find out after testing each magnet. Have them use their charts to communicate what they learned about how magnets can be different in strength.

PUPIL'S EDITION OR BIG BOOK

How Magnets Are the Same and Different

Magnets are the same in one way. They attract objects made of iron. They do not attract objects made of other materials.

Magnets may be different in other ways. They may be round or square, big or small, straight or curved. They may be different colors.

F36

Social Studies Link

Original Magnets Magnetite is an iron ore that often is magnetic. It was once commonly called lodestone, which means "*leading* stone," because early navigators used it as a compass.

ESL ACTIVITY

Magnets can be different shapes and are often named for the shape they represent. Help children make a list of the shapes shown on these pages, such as horseshoe, donut or ring, and bar. Encourage all descriptive responses. Make word cards for each shape, and have children talk about and sort the magnets to match the word cards.

Magnets may be different in **strength**, or how strongly they pull. One magnet may attract more paper clips than another.

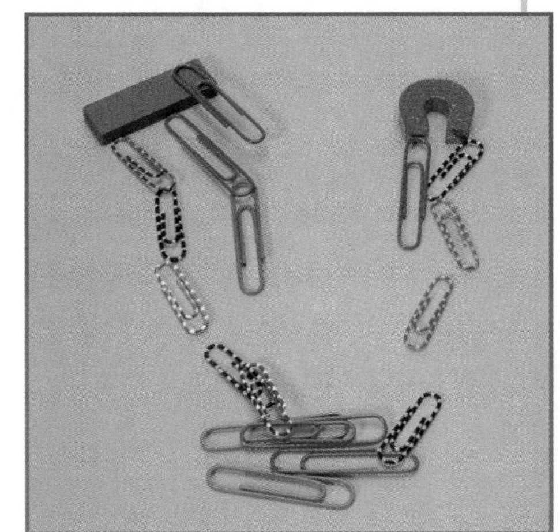

■ **Look at the chart. Which magnet has the greater strength?**

Magnet Strength	
Magnet	Number of Clips
bar magnet	6
horseshoe magnet	3

Think About It

1. What is a magnet?
2. What are some ways people use magnets?

3 Wrap Up and Assess

SUMMARIZE

Have children **summarize** what they have learned. Help them complete the chart begun on page F33. Discuss with them the properties of magnets, the different kinds of magnets, and the ways people use them.

Properties of Magnets	Different Kinds of Magnets	How People Use Magnets

THINK ABOUT IT

1. A magnet is a piece of iron that can attract things with iron in them.
2. People use different kinds of magnets to hold things closed, lift things, and help televisions and electric motors work. Farmers put magnets in cows' stomachs.

Informal Assessment

Performance To assess children's understanding of magnets, have them collect different objects and demonstrate which ones a magnet will attract and which ones it won't attract. Have children draw pictures to show how the objects can be grouped. You may wish to have them add their pictures to their science journals.

LESSON CONCEPT REVIEW/ASSESSMENT

Children can use **Workbook p. WB149** to review the lesson concepts.

Literature Connections

Harcourt Science Instant Reader
Jeff's Magnet
by Madge Alley.
Also available on CD-ROM

Read Aloud
Experiments with Magnets
by Helen Challand,
Children's Press, 1986.

LESSON 2

What Are the Poles of a Magnet?

Objectives

- ▶ **Observe that a magnet has two different poles.**
- ▶ **Recognize that a magnet's pulling force is strongest at the poles.**

Motivate

Dramatize Use two bar magnets to demonstrate like poles repelling and opposite poles attracting. Then have volunteers pretend they are magnets and dramatize how magnetic poles attract or repel.

Time 15–20 min **Grouping** individuals or pairs

Process Skill infer

Preparation Tips and Expected Results See page F30c.

Center Activity Option Place this investigation or a copy of the Investigation, page TR77, in your science center.

Activity Tips

- ▶ Model how to make the bar graph, or prepare one ahead of time for children to fill in.
- ▶ Show children how to add the paper clips one at a time, end-to-end, to make a chain.

Children may put their bar graphs in their science journals.

Activity Questions

- ▶ Which parts of the magnet are the strongest?
- ▶ How do the numbers on your bar graph tell you that?

When Minutes Count . . .

Use the Activity Video to preview and model which parts of a magnet are the strongest.

PUPIL'S EDITION OR BIG BOOK

What Are the Poles of a Magnet?

Investigate

A Magnet's Ends

You will need

bar magnet

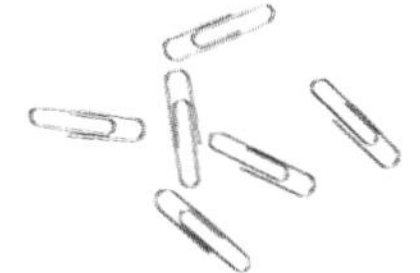
paper clips

paper and pencil

1. Pick up paper clips with one end of the magnet. Record the number. Then do the other end.
2. Pick up paper clips with the middle of the magnet. Record the number.
3. Make a bar graph. Infer which parts of the magnet are strongest.

Science Skill

To infer which parts of the magnet are the strongest, compare the numbers in your bar graph.

Science Skills

Process Skill: Infer Display Process Skill Tip Transparency F2-2. Explain to children that the letter *A* represents a chain of paper clips and the letter *B* a single paper clip. Have them infer which part of each magnet will attract the chain or the single paper clip, or both. Write the corresponding letter at the appropriate place on each magnet.

Process Skill Tip Transparency F2-2

Infer

What parts of the magnet might attract the chain of paper clips and the single paper clip?

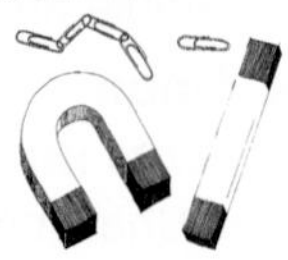

1. **What parts of the magnets will probably attract the chain of paper clips? Why?**
   The ends (poles) will attract the chain of paper clips because they are the strongest parts of the magnet.
2. **What part of the magnet may not attract the chain of paper clips? Why?**
   The middle part of the magnet may not attract the chain of paper clips because it isn't as strong as the ends.
3. **How many poles does a magnet have?**
   A magnet has two poles.

PROCESS SKILLS PRACTICE

To practice and apply process skills, see **Workbook p. WB150.**

Learn About

The Poles of a Magnet

A magnet has two **poles**. These are the places where its pulling force is strongest. Where are the poles of this bar magnet? How can you tell?

on the ends of the magnet; ends attracted paper clips

F39

Learn About

1 Before Reading

PREVIEW/SET PURPOSE

Have children preview pages F39–F41. Draw a K-W-L chart as shown. Help children fill in what they already know and want to know about the poles of a magnet. Tell them that they will complete the chart at the end of the lesson.

K-W-L Chart		
What I Know	What I Want to Know	What I Learned

2 Guide the Learning

SCIENCE IDEAS

Have children read page F39. Help them **identify the main idea**: **a magnet has different poles.**

▶ **How many poles does a magnet have?** two

▶ **What can you tell about the poles of a magnet?** A magnet's pull force is strongest there.

DEVELOP READING SKILLS

Build Vocabulary Help children identify the poles of the magnet shown. Explain that a magnet always has two poles. If you cut the bar magnet in half, each half would still have two poles. Then have children find the word *repel* in the lesson, and tell what it means. Explain that *repel* is the opposite of *attract.*

BACKGROUND

Webliography GO ONLINE
Keyword magnetism
www.harcourtschool.com

A Magnet's Poles Every magnet has a north or north-seeking pole and a south or south-seeking pole. The poles have different properties that can be observed when you put them close together. Poles that are alike (two north poles or two south poles) push apart, or *repel*, and poles that are different (a north and a south pole) pull together, or *attract.* People sometimes remember this with "likes repel; opposites attract."

Magnets always have two poles, although they are not always easy to find. Bar magnets have their poles at the end, but latch magnets have them on their sides. You can use iron filings (cut from a piece of steel wool and placed in a sandwich bag) to observe where the force of a magnet is strongest. The simplest way to find the poles is to observe which part of the magnet most repels or pushes away another magnet's like pole.

The Earth is a giant magnet and has two poles as well.

SCIENCE WORD WALL

North and South Poles
Have children make word cards for *north pole, south pole,* and *repel* to add to the Word Wall.

north pole

south pole

repel

GO ONLINE Technology Link

Sci Links Learn more about different magnets and the poles by visiting this Internet Site.
www.scilinks.org/harcourt

Guide the Learning continued

SCIENCE IDEAS

Have children read pages F40–F41. Help them **identify cause and effect.** Use two magnets with unmarked poles. Bring the poles together and describe whether you feel them attracting or repelling. Have children tell whether the poles are the same or different.

Critical Thinking Use these questions to help children reinforce their understanding of poles.

▶ **What would happen if you put two magnets on a table with a north pole facing a south pole and slid them together? with a south pole facing a south pole and slid them together?** They would attract each other and come together; they would force themselves apart.

USE PROCESS SKILLS

Plan a simple investigation Have children make a plan to find what happens when poles come together and **predict** what will happen when similar and different poles are put together.

VISUAL LEARNING

Have children observe the photo on page F41 and tell where the pull is strongest.

DEVELOP SCIENCE VOCABULARY

poles Ask children where else they can find a north pole and a south pole.

repel Ask children to tell the opposite of *repel*. Have them list opposites that mean the same or nearly the same as *repel/attract*.

What Poles Can Do

Every magnet has a north pole and a south pole. They are often called the *N* pole and the *S* pole.

Two poles that are different attract each other. An *N* pole and an *S* pole attract each other.

Two poles that are the same **repel**, or push each other away. Two *N* poles repel each other.

repel each other

■ **What do you think two *S* poles would do?**

F40

THE QUESTIONS KIDS ASK!

Why are the poles of a magnet called north and south?

Address Misconceptions A magnet's poles are often called north and south because they point to Earth's North and South Poles. A magnet's north pole is actually its north-seeking pole. Demonstrate this by suspending a magnet from a string and allowing it to turn freely (away from any iron or steel). It will come to a stop pointing to Earth's magnetic North Pole. The other pole points south.

Physical Education Link

A Magnetic Version of Musical Chairs Choose an area where children have space to move. Set up chairs in a line just as you would in the traditional game of Musical Chairs. Put an *N* or an *S* alternately on each chair to represent the poles of a magnet. Assign each child an *N* or an *S* as well. Explain to children that they are going to play Musical Chairs, but they can sit only if their pole is the opposite of the one on the chair nearest to them. If their pole is the same, they cannot sit and are "repelled" from that round of the game. Start and stop the music as you normally would, removing chairs as you go. Ask children to explain how they know whether or not they can sit on a chair.

Bits of iron can show where a magnet's pull is strongest. The iron bits make a pattern around the magnet. More bits go to the poles, where the pull is strongest.

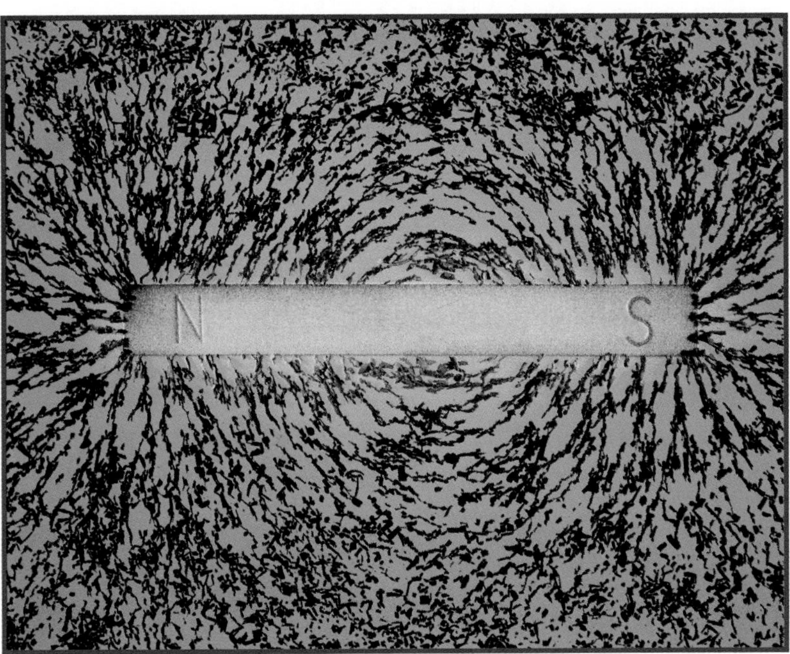

Think About It

1. What are poles?
2. What do poles do?

Literature Connections

Read Alouds

Magnetism by John Woodruff, Steck-Vaughn, 1998.

What Magnets Can Do (Rookie Read-Aloud Science) by Allan Fowler, Children's Press, 1995.

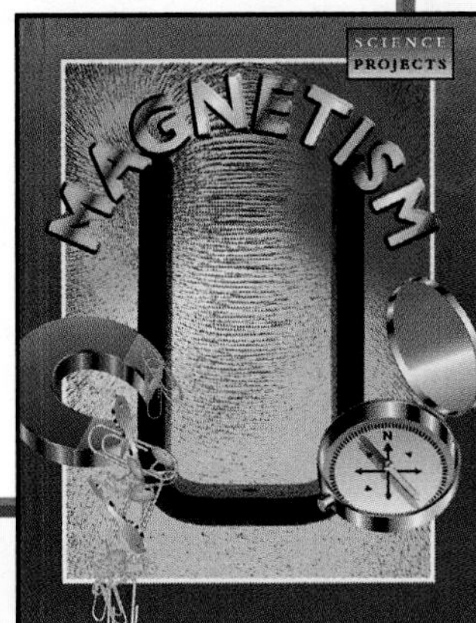

3 Wrap Up and Assess

SUMMARIZE

Have children **summarize** what they have learned as they help you complete the K-W-L chart begun on page F39. Invite them to use their experiences with a magnet's poles to fill in the last column.

K-W-L Chart		
What I Know	What I Want to Know	What I Learned

THINK ABOUT IT

1. Poles are two places on a magnet where the pull is strongest.
2. North and south poles attract each other. Two north or two south poles repel each other.

Informal Assessment

Portfolio Give each child the opportunity to demonstrate what a magnet's poles can do. Then have them write about what they did for their demonstration. They can add their writing to their portfolios.

LESSON CONCEPT REVIEW/ASSESSMENT

Children can use **Workbook p. WB151** to review the lesson concepts.

LESSON 3

What Can a Magnet Pull Through?

Objectives

- ▶ **Recognize that magnetic force can pass through some things to attract iron objects.**
- ▶ **Observe that magnetic force gets weaker as distance increases from the magnet.**

Motivate

Talk About Things a Magnet Can Pull Through Ask children to brainstorm things magnets can pull through. These include water, bowls, and air. As the lesson progresses, have children test these objects.

Investigate

Time 20–25 min **Grouping** individuals

Process Skill plan an investigation

Preparation Tips and Expected Results See page F30c.

Center Activity Option Place this investigation or a copy of the Investigation, page TR78, in your science center.

Activity Tips

- ▶ Model how you would like children to record their plans.
- ▶ Allow time for children to communicate what they observe.

Children can write their investigation plans in their science journals.

Activity Questions

- ▶ What things did the magnet pull through? What things did it not pull through?
- ▶ What questions do you have about what a magnet can pull through?

When Minutes Count . . .

As a whole-class activity, have children suggest things to find out what a magnet can pull through. Use a bar magnet and paper clips to test their ideas. Record and discuss what happens.

PUPIL'S EDITION OR BIG BOOK

What Can a Magnet Pull Through?

Investigate

Things Magnets Pull Through

You will need

bar magnet

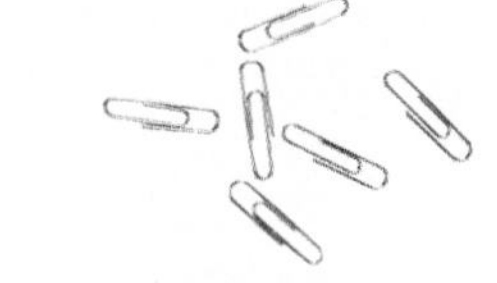

paper clips

different materials

1. Can a magnet attract paper clips through things? Plan an investigation to find out. Write your plan.
2. Follow your plan to investigate your ideas. Record what you observe.
3. Use your data to communicate what you find out.

Science Skill

To investigate what things a magnet can pull through, first make a plan and then try your ideas.

F42

Science Skills

Process Skill: Plan an Investigation Display Process Skill Tip Transparency F2-3. Ask children to read the question on the transparency. For each item mentioned have them plan an investigation to answer the question. Then ask them to predict the result and tell why they expect this result. Record their answers.

Process Skill Tip Transparency F2-3

Plan an Investigation

Can a Magnet Pull a Paper Clip Through This?

	Postcard	Rubber Ball	Pillow	Paper Towel
How to show	Put a paper clip on a postcard. Pull a magnet under the postcard.	Have one person hold a magnet on one side of the ball, and another hold a paper clip on the other side.	Put a paper clip on the pillow and move a magnet under it.	Put a paper clip on top of the paper. Have another person move a magnet under the towel.
Expected result	The magnet will pull through.	The magnet won't pull through.	The magnet won't pull through.	The magnet will pull through.
Why you predict this result	The post-card is thin enough for the magnet to pull through.	The rubber ball is too thick and big. The magnet isn't strong enough.	The pillow is too thick for the magnet to pull through.	The paper is thin enough for the magnet to pull through.

PROCESS SKILLS PRACTICE

To practice and apply process skills, see **Workbook p. WB152.**

Learn About

The Force of a Magnet

A magnet's pull is called **magnetic force**. This force can pass through some things to attract iron objects.

■ **What material is magnetic force passing through to attract these puppets?** cardboard

F43

Learn About

1 Before Reading

PREVIEW/SET PURPOSE

Have children preview pages F43–F45. Make a chart as shown below. Children will help you fill it in as the lesson progresses.

Materials a Magnet's Force Can Pass Through	Materials a Magnet's Force Can Not Pass Through

2 Guide the Learning

SCIENCE IDEAS

Read aloud with children page F43. Help **identify the main idea: Magnetic force can pass through some things to attract iron objects.**

▶ **What is magnetic force?** a magnet's pull

▶ **What can magnetic force do?** pass through some things to attract iron objects

DEVELOP READING SKILLS

Relate Pictures to Text Have children look at the photo and answer the question. Then ask them to think of what might be attached to the puppets to make a magnet attract them. something with iron in it Invite volunteers to tell what the girl might do with her magnets to make the puppets move.

BACKGROUND

Webliography
Keyword magnetism
www.harcourtschool.com

GO ONLINE

Magnetic Force Magnets can be used to make some things move, even without touching them, because magnetic force reaches beyond the magnet. This area where the force extends is called the *magnetic field*. How far the force reaches, or the size of the magnetic field, depends on a magnet's strength. Most magnets used by children have small fields extending an inch or less. Earth has a magnetic field that extends more than 37,000 miles into space.

Magnetic force happens in an iron object when groups of atoms, called *domains*, align. The domains cause an electromagnetic force that reaches beyond the object. The force is strongest within the magnet, and decreases as distance from the magnet increases.

Scientists hypothesize that Earth's magnetic force comes from its molten core of hot iron surrounded by a fluid outer core that moves around and around as Earth spins.

SCIENCE WORD WALL

Magnetic Force Have children make a word card for the words *magnetic force*. Then suggest they make word cards for each material a magnet can pull through such as *water* and *glass*. Arrange these word cards on the Word Wall.

magnetic force

water

glass

Guide the Learning continued

SCIENCE IDEAS

Have children read pages F44–F45 and **identify cause and effect** by asking the question on page F44. Have them test their predictions.

VISUAL LEARNING

Have children look at the photo on page F45. Help them recognize that the magnet has to pull through air to reach the clip.

▶ **How much air can the magnet pull through to make the clip move?** Answers will vary.

Children can put a paper clip and magnet on top of the clip and magnet in the photo to test their predictions. Have them slide the magnet toward the clip until it moves, then note the distance between the two.

USE PROCESS SKILLS

Observe Have children observe the photo of the glass of water and describe what material magnetic force is pulling through to hold the paper clip. glass

Critical Thinking Use this question to help children **predict** and **draw conclusions**.

▶ **What will happen to the paper clip if you slide the magnet down the glass? Why?** It will follow the magnet. The force can pass through water.

DEVELOP SCIENCE VOCABULARY

magnetic force Help children recognize that *magnetic force* can also be used to identify materials that a magnet attracts.

PUPIL'S EDITION OR BIG BOOK

Observing Magnetic Force

The magnetic force of a magnet can pass through paper or cloth. It can also pass through water and glass.

■ **What do you think might happen if the glass were thicker?**

The magnetic force might not pass through it.

F44

Math Link

Count the Pages Provide children with small squares of construction paper and different kinds of magnets. Have them put a paper clip on one side of the paper and a magnet on the other. Have them add paper squares, one at a time, until the magnet can no longer attract the clip. Have them count and record the number of squares for each magnet. Have them compare their results to see which magnet is the strongest.

Magnetic force is strong close to a magnet. It can pull a paper clip through the air. Farther away, it may not be strong enough to do this.

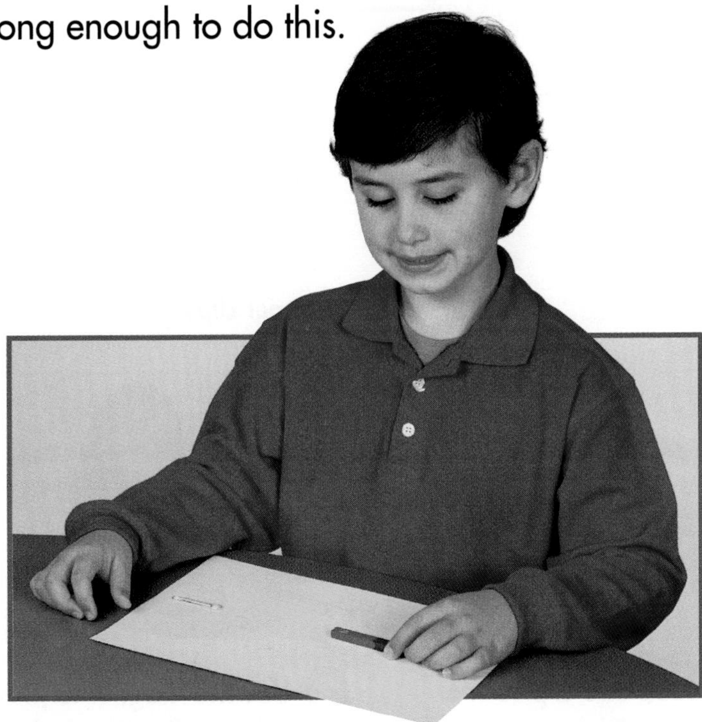

Think About It

1. What is magnetic force?
2. What are some materials magnetic force can pass through?

F45

3 Wrap Up and Assess

SUMMARIZE

Have children **summarize** what they have learned. Return to the chart begun on page F43, and help them fill in different materials a magnet does and does not pull through.

Materials a Magnet's Force Can PassThrough	Materials a Magnet's Force Can Not Pass Through

THINK ABOUT IT

1. A magnet's pull is called magnetic force.
2. Magnetic force can pass through paper, cloth, water, glass, and air.

Informal Assessment

Portfolio Have children draw pictures to show examples of magnetic force passing through different materials. Have them write captions to explain what is happening, using the expression "magnetic force." Place their drawings and captions in their portfolios.

LESSON CONCEPT REVIEW/ASSESSMENT

Children can use **Workbook p. WB153** to review the lesson concepts.

Literature Connections

Read Alouds

Science With Magnets by Helen Edom, EDC Publications, 1992.

Magnets and Sparks by Wendy Madgwick, Steck-Vaughn, 1999.

LESSON **4**

How Can You Make a Magnet?

Objectives

- ▶ **Recognize that a magnet can magnetize things it attracts.**
- ▶ **Compare the strength of different magnets.**

Motivate

Dramatize Place a magnet in contact with an iron nail. This will temporarily magnetize the object. Invite children to use it to pick up paper clips. Have them suggest ways the nail might have been magnetized.

Time 15 min **Grouping** individuals

Process Skill draw a conclusion

Preparation Tips and Expected Results See page F30c.

Center Activity Option Place this investigation or a copy of the Investigation, page TR79, in your science center.

Activity Tips

- ▶ You may need to touch the clip more than once to get it to magnetize.
- ▶ Model how to take away the magnet gently in Step 3.

Have children record what they observe in their science journals.

Activity Questions

- ▶ How does the magnet change the first paper clip?
- ▶ How can you make a paper clip act like a magnet?

When Minutes Count . . .

Use the Activity Video to preview and model the investigate process with children.

PUPIL'S EDITION OR BIG BOOK

How Can You Make a Magnet?

Investigate

Making a Magnet

You will need

magnet

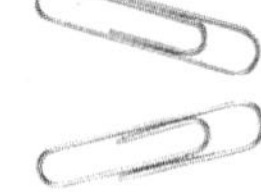
2 paper clips

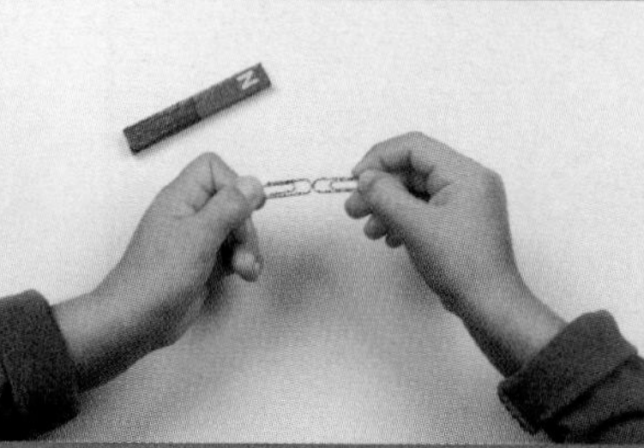

1. Touch one clip to the other. Observe.
2. Use the magnet to pick up one clip. Touch that clip to the other one. Observe.
3. Take away the magnet. Draw a conclusion. How can you make a magnet?

Science Skill
To draw a conclusion, use what you have observed to form an idea.

Science Skills

Process Skill: Draw a Conclusion
Display Process Skill Tip Transparency F2-4. Ask children to observe the three steps of the experiment and then answer the questions in detail. Record their answers on the lines provided.

Process Skill Tip Transparency F2-4

Draw a Conclusion

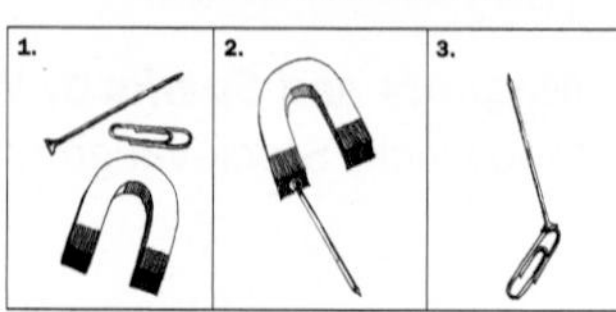

1. What objects are used in the experiment?
   a nail, a magnet, and a paper clip
2. What happened in Step 2? How and why?
   The magnet attracted the nail. The magnet was brought near the nail. The magnetic force attracted the nail.
3. What happened in Step 3? How and why?
   The nail attracted the paper clip. The magnet magnetized the nail in Step 2. You can magnetize an iron object by touching it with a magnet.

PROCESS SKILLS PRACTICE

To practice and apply process skills, see **Workbook p. WB154.**

Learn About

Making a Magnet

A magnet can **magnetize**, or give magnetic force to, things it attracts. The magnet on this crane has magnetized some pieces of metal. Their new magnetic force attracts more pieces.

F47

1 Before Reading

PREVIEW/SET PURPOSE

Have children preview pages F47–F49. Draw the following web. Have children help you fill it in as the lesson progresses.

2 Guide the Learning

SCIENCE IDEAS

Have children read page F47. Help them **relate pictures to text** and understand this **main idea**: **A magnet can magnetize something it attracts.**

- **Where is the magnet on the crane?** at the end of the cable
- **What are some pieces of metal doing?** Some are attracting other pieces of metal.
- **Why are some pieces of metal attracting other pieces of metal?** Because they have been magnetized.

DEVELOP READING SKILLS

Build Vocabulary Help children identify the root word in *magnetize*. Ask what other word they know that contains the word *magnet.*

BACKGROUND

Webliography
Keyword magnetism
www.harcourtschool.com
GO ONLINE

Making Magnets Placing a magnet in contact with an object that has iron in it will temporarily magnetize the object. This happens because the magnet's magnetic force affects some of the domains (groups of atoms aligned and facing the same direction) in the iron object. The longer the magnet touches the iron object, the longer its magnetic force will last.

Using a magnet to stroke the iron object in the same direction several times will affect the domains in the object so that they have a longer lasting magnetic force. Similarly, commercial magnets are even longer lasting because their domains have been processed (using heat) to organize them to produce maximum force.

SCIENCE WORD WALL

Magnet Words Have children make a word card for *magnetize* and add it to the Word Wall. Then review other "magnet" words that are on the Word Wall. They can use all the word cards to write sentences.

magnetize

ESL Activity Have children work in pairs to illustrate each word card. They can tape their drawings to the word cards on the Word Wall.

Guide the Learning continued

SCIENCE IDEAS

Read pages F48–F49. Explain that magnets are often made from iron heated with other materials so that their magnetic force lasts longer.

VISUAL LEARNING

To help children **predict outcomes**, have them observe the photo on page F48.

▶ **What would happen if the girl stroked the magnet ten times along a paper clip?** She would magnetize the clip. **(NOTE: Some nails may need more than 10 strokes to magnetize.)**

Critical Thinking Use this question to help children identify objects that can be magnetized:

▶ **What other objects can and cannot be magnetized?** Any objects with iron in them will magnetize; others will not.

USE PROCESS SKILLS

Observe Help children observe that the child in the photo is stroking the nail with the magnet and not the other way around.

CAREERS/PEOPLE IN SCIENCE

Many of the magnets we use every day are ceramic magnets. They are made from combining certain metals with oxygen. Ceramic engineers investigate ways to make these magnets stronger.

DEVELOP SCIENCE VOCABULARY

magnetize Have children use the word as they use magnets to magnetize different objects.

PUPIL'S EDITION OR BIG BOOK

Ways to Make a Magnet

You can magnetize an iron nail. Stroke the nail on the magnet ten times the same way. Then the nail will be magnetized for a short time.

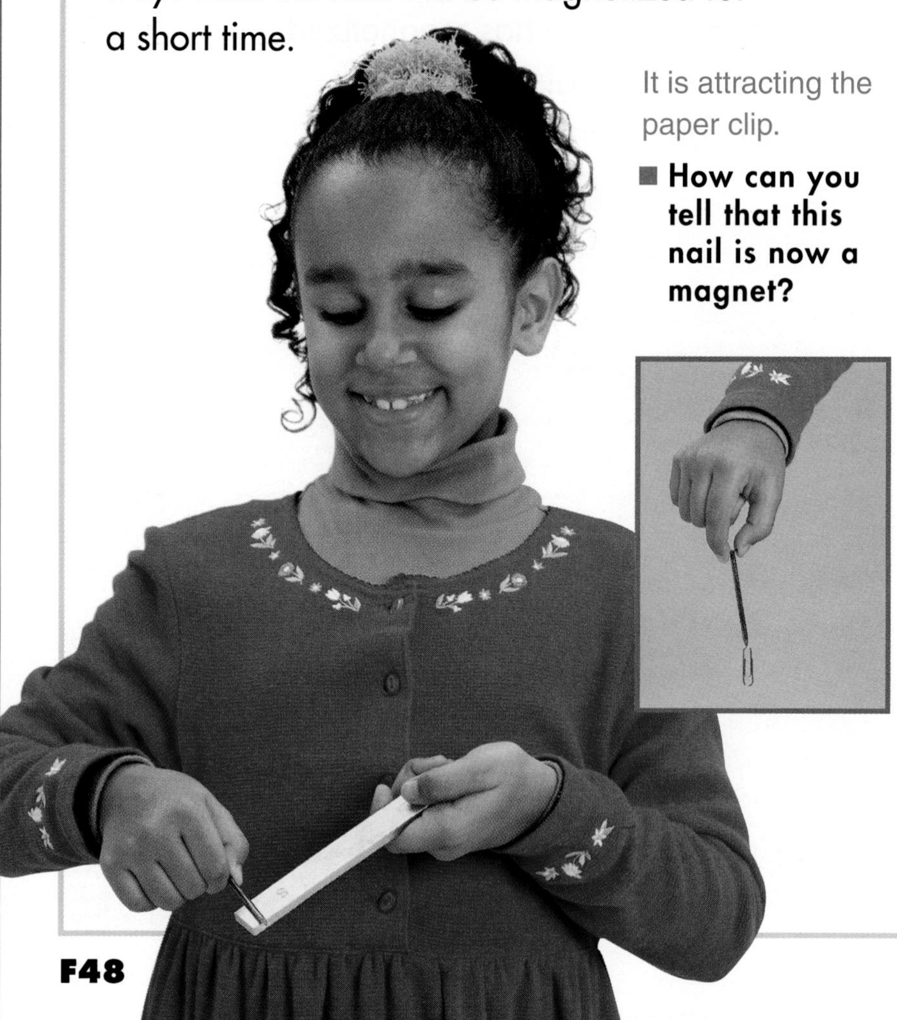

It is attracting the paper clip.

■ **How can you tell that this nail is now a magnet?**

F48

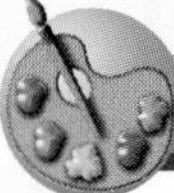

Art Link

Make a Magnet Animal Have children make small animal magnets. Use small square magnets available in quantity from electronic stores. Have children draw an animal shape on a piece of cardboard and then cut out the shape. Have children paint their animals and glue the magnet to the back of the cardboard. Children can use them as refrigerator magnets.

Reading Mini-Lesson

Draw Conclusions Have children read page F48 to draw conclusions about materials that can be magnetized. Point out the words *iron nail,* asking children what *iron* is. metal Display the transparency and have children draw conclusions.

READING SKILLS PRACTICE

To practice and apply this reading skill, see **Workbook p. WB157.**

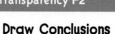

Reading Mini-Lesson Transparency F2

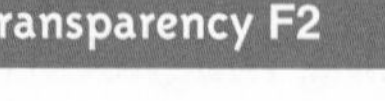

Draw Conclusions

Do you think a block of wood can be magnetized? Why or why not?

No, because it does not contain the metal iron.

Do you think a needle can be magnetized? Why or why not?

Yes, because it is made of iron.

What conclusion can you draw about materials that can be magnetized?

Possible conclusion: Materials that contain iron can be magnetized.

Some magnets are made from iron heated with other materials. These magnets are made in a factory.

Magnet Engineer

A magnet engineer finds new ways to make magnets. These magnets may be stronger or last longer than iron ones.

Think About It

1. What can you use to magnetize an object made of iron?
2. How can you make a magnet?

Literature Connections

Read Alouds

The Science Book of Magnets by Neil Ardley, Harcourt Brace, 1991.

Electricity and Magnetism by Maria Gordon, Thomson Learning, 1996.

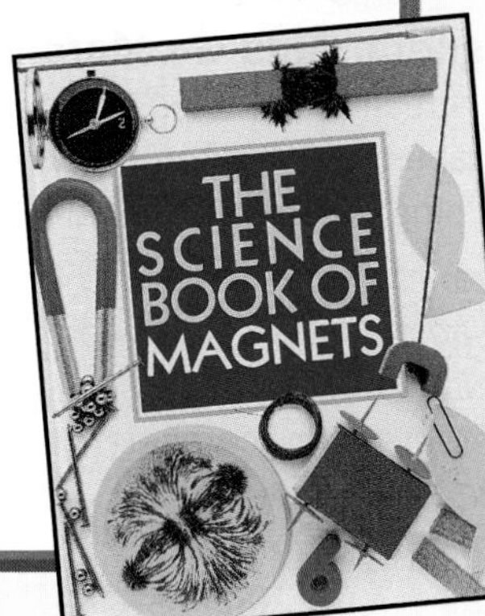

3 Wrap Up and Assess

SUMMARIZE

Have children **summarize** what they have learned by completing the web started on page F47.

THINK ABOUT IT

1. You can use a magnet to magnetize an object made of iron.
2. You can make a magnet by stroking an object made of iron with a magnet.

Informal Assessment

Classroom Observation Provide children with the opportunity to demonstrate one or more ways to make a magnet. Have them describe orally or in writing what is needed to give the object magnetic force. The object must have iron in it, and a magnet must be used.

LESSON CONCEPT REVIEW/ASSESSMENT

Children can use **Workbook p. WB155** to review the lesson concepts.

VOCABULARY REVIEW

Children can use **Workbook p. WB156** to review the chapter vocabulary.

Chapter 2 Links

Math Link
Measure Magnetic Force

Link Objective Recognize that different magnets have different strengths.

Talk about the photograph. Invite children to suggest other types of magnets they might test.

Read aloud the text. Have children compare this method with the method used on page F44.

WRITE

Have children mark the position of the paper clip and the magnet at the start of each test to ensure that the tests are the same. They can trace the clip and make a starting line for the magnet and then place both on their spots before they begin each test.

Model a way for children to collect and record their data, using a different color crayon for each magnet, so that they can compare results. Ask them to use words that compare, such as *stronger* and *strongest,* when they write about the activity.

Informal Assessment

Portfolio Children may add their paper strips to their portfolios.

PUPIL'S EDITION OR BIG BOOK

Links

Math Link

Measure Magnetic Force

You can compare the strengths of different magnets. To do this, you will need to record how far their magnetic forces reach.

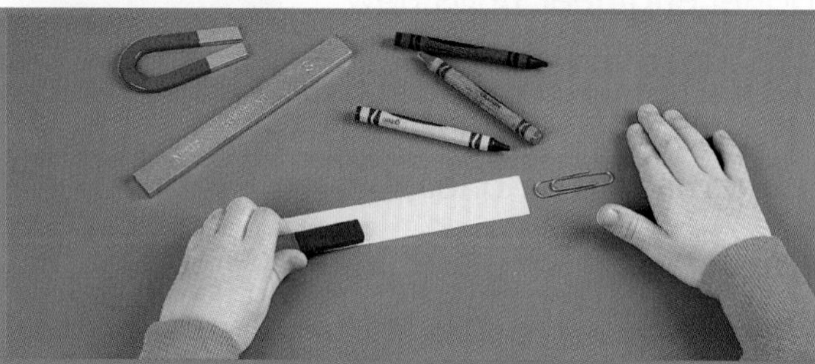

Write

Lay a paper clip at one end of a paper strip. Hold one magnet at the other end. Slide the magnet slowly toward the clip. Mark where the magnet is when the clip moves.

Do the same thing with each magnet. Write about the strength of each magnet.

F50

More Link Options . . .

Social Studies Link

Compass Points Help children use a bar magnet to decide where north is. (Suspend the magnet from a string. If there's too much steel around, use small compasses.) Then, have them decide where east, west, and south are, and label each wall of the classroom accordingly. Ask children to give the location of different places and things you name, using the labels they read on the walls. (The hall is west of the class. The plant is south of the class.)

Music/Math Link

Magnetic Ants Go Marching Help children make ants on paper and attach paper clips to the ants' backs. Have them use bar magnets to make the ants march rhythmically across a cardboard landscape as they sing the following to the tune of *Johnny Comes Marching Home.*

The ants go marching one by one, hurrah, hurrah! (repeat)
The ants go marching one by one,
The little one stops to suck his thumb
And they all go marching
down to the ground
to get out of the rain.

Repeat, using other verses:

Two . . . to tie his shoe.
Three . . . climb a tree.
Four . . . shut the door.
Five . . . wave good-bye.

Have children make up verses for higher numbers as needed.

Social Studies Link

Compass Readings

Long ago, travelers used compasses to find their way. Travelers still use them today. A compass has a magnetized needle that always points north.

Think and Do

Make your own compass. Float a plastic plate in water. Place a bar magnet in the center of the plate. Turn the plate. Which way is north?

F51

Social Studies Link
Compass Readings

Link Objective Understand that magnets are essential tools for many travelers.

Talk about the photograph. Encourage children to talk about any experiences they may have had with compasses. Introduce a working compass to the class prior to having children read the text. Then after completing the link, mark the points on a compass on large placards in the classroom.

Read aloud the text. Compare the compass needle with the lodestone shown on page F35. Discuss why people invented the needle to use instead of the stone.

THINK AND DO

Do this activity away from any iron or steel, including beams used in ceilings and walls of buildings. The bar magnet will rotate some before settling in its north-seeking position. You can also do this by dangling the magnet from a string. Repeat the test, rotating the magnet, to see how many times it seeks north.

Language Arts Link

Silly Magnetic Sentences Help children brainstorm lists of different naming words, action words, and describing words. Have them write each word on a different card. Attach paper clips to each card. Sort the naming words, action words, and describing words into separate piles. To make sentences, have children hold a bar magnet over each pile until the magnet picks up one word from each. Have them string their words together to make silly sentences, and put their sentences together to make even sillier stories.

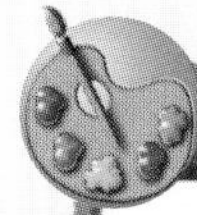

Art Link

Sail the Boat Have children stick paper clips through small pieces of plastic foam (cut from produce trays) so that the clip hangs down as shown. Have them draw and cut out paper boats to tape on top of the foam. They can sail their boats in cups of water, using a magnet beneath the cup to make the boat move.

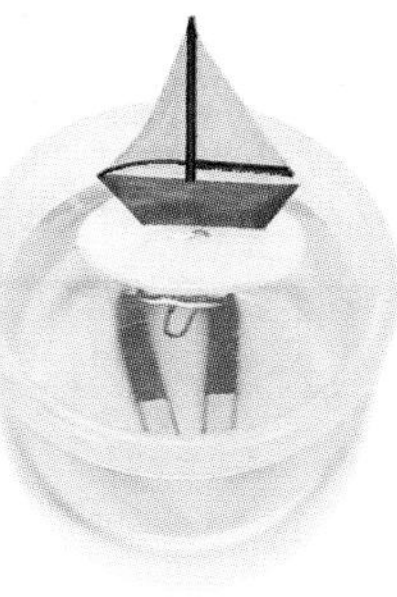

Chapter 

Review and Test Preparation

Tell What You Know

SUMMARIZE/RETELL

1. Children use the words provided to tell about the pictures. Check for the following concepts in their responses.
   - ▶ Magnets may be different in strength, or how strongly they pull.
   - ▶ A magnet has two poles.
   - ▶ Magnetic force can pass through things such as glass, air, water, and paper to attract an iron object.

Vocabulary

REVIEW SCIENCE VOCABULARY

Children review chapter vocabulary by matching pictures with words.

2. c
3. a
4. b
5. d

GRAPHIC ORGANIZER FOR CHAPTER CONCEPTS

Children can use the graphic organizer to record key concepts and ideas from each lesson. See **Workbook p. WB147** and **Transparency F2.**

PUPIL'S EDITION OR BIG BOOK

Tell What You Know

1. Use the words *strength, poles,* and *magnetic force* to tell about each picture.

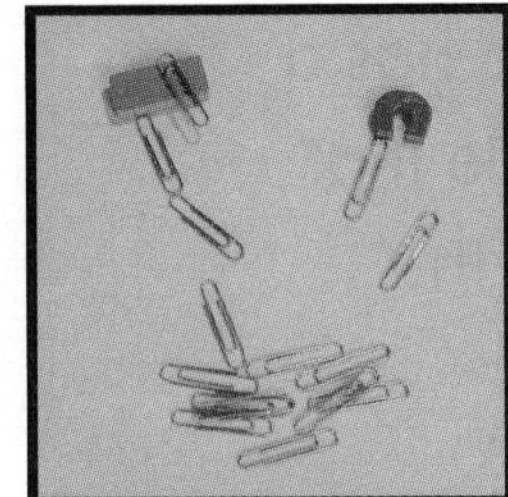

Vocabulary

Tell which picture goes with each word.

2. magnet
3. attract
4. repel
5. magnetize

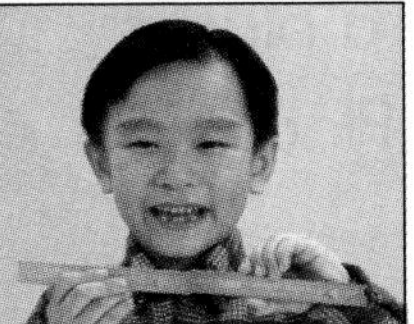

a.

b.

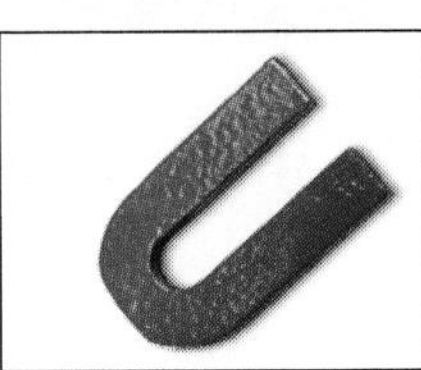
c.

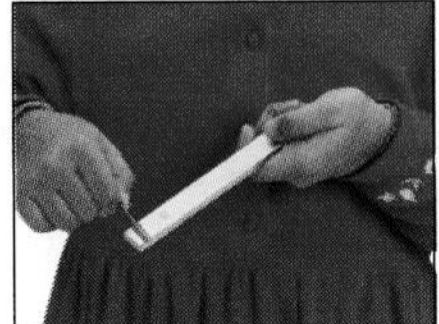
d.

F52

Graphic Organizer for Chapter Concepts

Transparency F2 • Workbook, p. WB147

Unit F, Chapter 2 Magnets

LESSON 1 What Are Magnets?	LESSON 2 What Are the Poles of a Magnet?
1. Magnets are pieces of iron that attract things. 2. Magnets can only attract things made of iron. 3. People use different kinds of magnets in different ways.	1. Poles are places on a magnet where the pull is the strongest. 2. Every magnet has a north pole and a south pole. 3. Two poles that are the same repel each other.
LESSON 3 **What Can a Magnet Pull Through?**	**LESSON 4** **How Can You Make a Magnet?**
1. The pull of a magnet is called magnetic force. 2. Magnetic force can pass through paper, water, air, glass, and material.	1. A magnet can magnetize an object made of iron. 2. You can make a magnet by stroking an iron object with a magnet.

Using Science Skills

6. Infer Look at the two patterns made by the bits of iron. Which magnet made each pattern? How do you know?

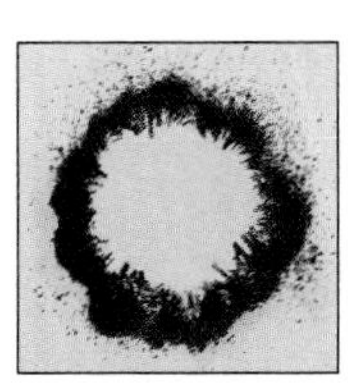

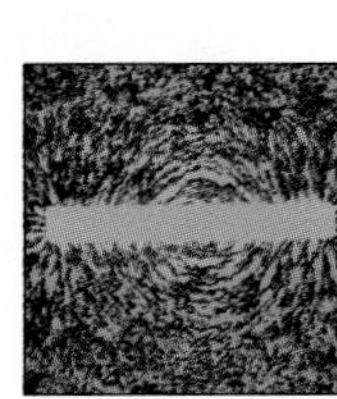

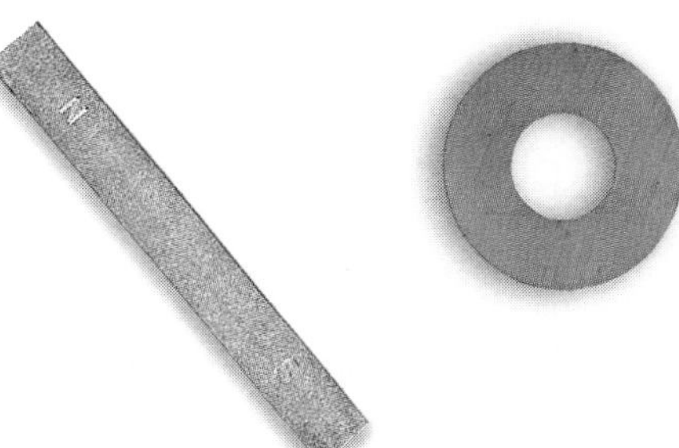

7. Investigate Some people use a metal detector to help them find things made of metal.

Play a metal detector game. Ask a partner to put three metal objects in a group of objects.

Predict which objects your magnet will attract. Investigate to find out.

F53

Using Science Skills

REVIEW PROCESS SKILLS

TEST PREP Test-Taking Tips

Model this strategy with children to help them infer which magnet made each pattern.

To tell which magnet made each pattern, first I think about what I know about a magnet's poles. Then I look at the patterns shown and draw a conclusion about which magnet made each pattern.

6. Infer Guide children to use the patterns made by the iron filings to locate the poles of the magnets. where the force is strongest They can then match the location of the poles with the magnets shown.

PERFORMANCE ASSESSMENT

7. Investigate Guide children to record their predictions before using the magnet to find the metal objects with iron in them. Then have them record what happens in their investigation. Have them construct reasonable explanations of why the magnet attracts some metal objects such as those with iron in them and not others. They can use their recorded observations to group the objects they try based on their magnetic properties.

WRITING ABOUT SCIENCE

Have children write a composition that involves writing for a specific purpose. You may wish to use the prompt that is provided in the Workbook. The prompt is accompanied by a graphic organizer that will help children organize their ideas before writing. Models for writing are provided in the **Teaching Resources** book. You may wish to reproduce those for children or display them on a transparency.

WRITING ABOUT SCIENCE

A chapter writing prompt and a prewriting activity are provided on **Workbook p. WB158**.

CHAPTER TEST

See **Assessment Guide pages AG93–96** for the Chapter Test. Assessment Options are provided on p. F30e.

TAKE-HOME BOOK

Use the **Take-Home Book** (described on p. F30d) to provide more chapter content and activities.

Activities
for Home or School

Magnetic Kite

Objective

▶ **Observe how magnetic force can pull an object through air.**

Suggested Time 30 minutes

Hints

▶ Provide children with large-sized, metal paper clips.

▶ You may wish to provide a kite pattern that children can trace onto tissue paper.

Safety Tip Tell children about the proper use of scissors to prevent any injury.

Draw Conclusions Children observe that magnetic force can pull a paper clip through the air for short distances.

Magnetic Race-Car Game

Objective

▶ **Observe how magnets can pull through cardboard.**

Suggested Time 45 minutes

Hints

▶ If possible, have children use bar magnets that are long enough to hold under the cardboard.

▶ If there are not enough magnets, children can "race" individually and have a partner time them.

Safety Tip Caution children not to place their magnets near any electronic device or computer.

Draw Conclusions Children observe that magnets can pull through some materials, such as cardboard.

Investigate Further In a sandbox, hide several small objects that magnets can attract. Provide children with strong magnets for them to use to pull out the buried treasure.

UNIT F

Activities
for Home or School

Magnetic Kite

1. Cut out a tissue paper kite.
2. Attach thread and a paper clip.
3. Tape the thread's tail to a table.
4. Use the magnet to pick up your kite without touching it.

Magnetic Race-Car Game

1. Draw a road on cardboard.
2. Put two paper clips on the road.
3. Put two magnets under the cardboard. Move the magnets to race your clips.

F54

School-Home Connection

These activities provide an excellent opportunity to assign hands-on activities for the children and their families. The materials are often easy to obtain and are safe to work with. For those activities that you do not wish to do in the classroom, encourage children to complete them at home. Remind them that communicating their results is always important, but especially so for home activities since you will not be there to observe their activities. Ask children to use sketches, graphs, or even photographs to show their results.

Make a Water Wheel

1. Push toothpicks into the ends of a piece of clay. *Be careful. Toothpicks are sharp.*
2. Push strips cut from a carton into the clay to make a water wheel.
3. Hold the wheel by the toothpicks. Place the wheel under running water.
4. Tell how the water makes the wheel turn.

Marble Fun Slide

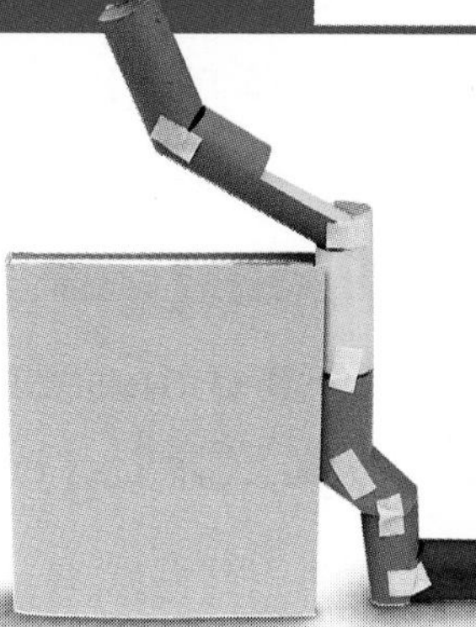

1. Tape together paper towel tubes to make a fun slide.
2. Use books to hold up the tubes.
3. Put a marble at the top, and listen to it race to the bottom. Talk about how it moves.

F55

Language Arts Link

Accordion Book Have children complete the following prompt.

Make a book that you pull open and push to close! On each page, write about a push or pull.

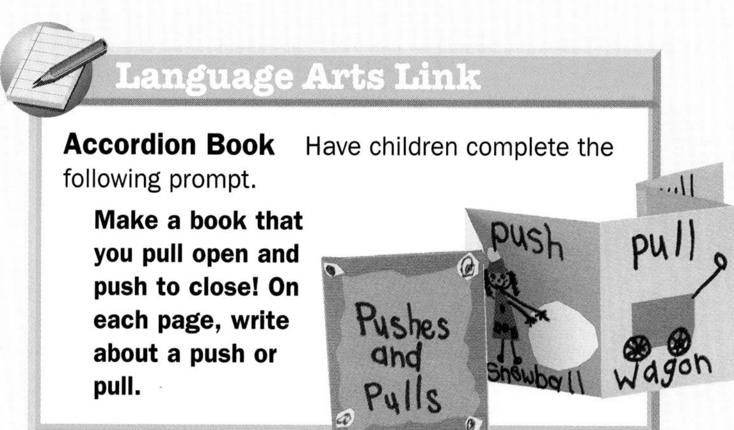

Make a Water Wheel

Objective

- **Use a model to observe how some forces work.**

Suggested Time 20 minutes

Hints

- You may wish to have children cut strips from a yogurt cup ahead of time.
- The water should run with a low to medium force out of the faucet. A stronger stream may break the wheel.

Safety Tip Caution children about handling scissors and toothpicks since both are sharp.

Draw Conclusions Children learn about forces as they observe how water pushes on the carton strips to make the wheel turn.

Marble Fun Slide

Objective

- **Draw conclusions about motion.**

Suggested Time 45 minutes

Hints

- You may need to demonstrate how to tape two tubes together.
- Children may wish to draw models of slides to help them formulate their ideas before making their models.

Safety Tip Caution children to pick up all marbles off the floor so no one will fall.

Draw Conclusions Children observe that marbles go down the slides and draw the conclusion that the joints make marbles change direction.

Investigate Further Children may visit a playground or an amusement park where there are slides. They can play the part of the marble and observe their own motions as they glide down differently-shaped slides.

ACTIVITIES FOR HOME OR SCHOOL

Reproducible copies of these activities are provided in the **Teaching Resources** book.

UNIT F Expeditions

Objectives

- Observe push and pull forces in action.
- Compare push and pull forces in magnets.

Hints

A field trip to Brookhaven National Laboratory Science Museum or a similar destination may not be feasible for your class. If so, consider visiting The Learning Site on the Internet. This site provides links to sites appropriate for student learning.

UNIT F Expeditions

PLACES TO VISIT

Brookhaven National Laboratory Science Museum, Long Island, New York

At this science museum, you can learn about magnets. You can predict, classify, and test the ways magnets work.

Plan Your Own Expedition

Visit a museum or science center near you. Or log on to The Learning Site.

F56

UNIT TEST

See **Assessment Guide pp. A99–102** for the Unit Assessment. The Unit Assessment includes items for all the chapters in this Unit.

References

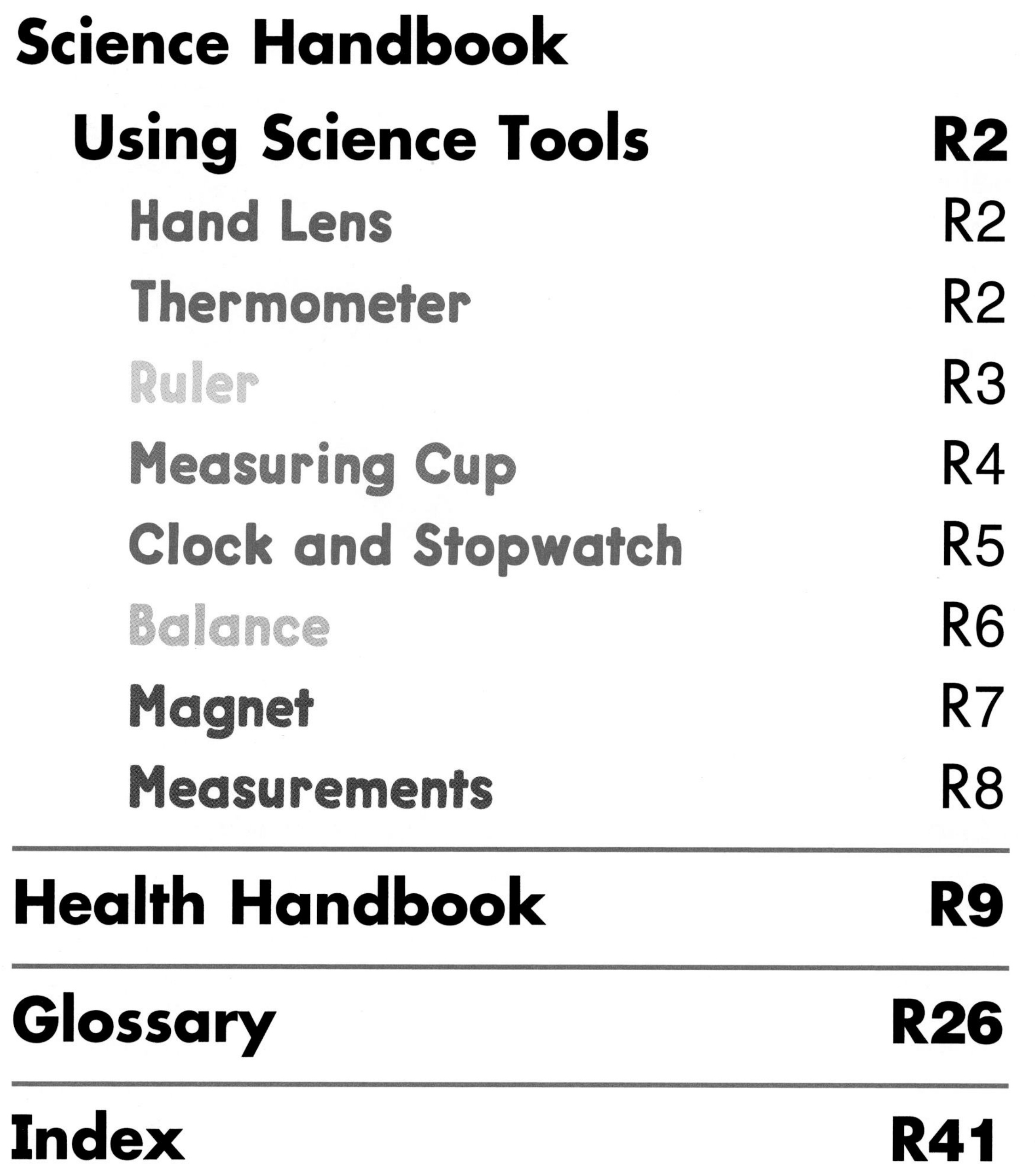

Using Science Tools

Hand Lens

1. Hold the hand lens close to your face.
2. Move the object until you see it clearly.

Thermometer

1. Place the thermometer.
2. Wait two minutes.
3. Find the top of the liquid in the tube.
4. Read the number.

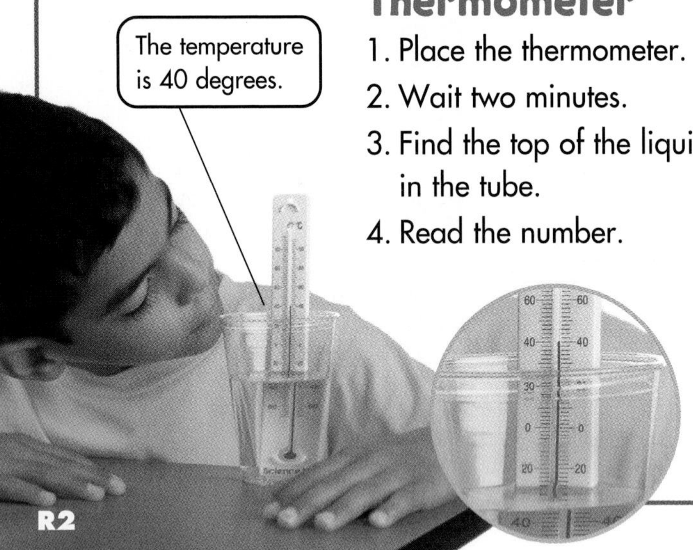

The temperature is 40 degrees.

R2

Ruler

1. Put the edge of the ruler at the end of the object.
2. Look at the number at the other end.
3. Read how long the object is.

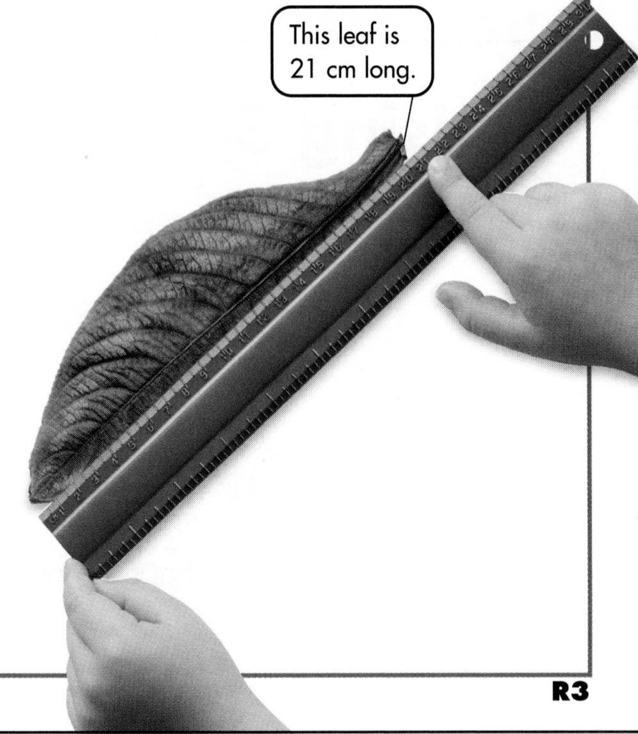

This leaf is 21 cm long.

R3

Science Handbook pages R2–R3

Making a Water-Drop Lens

Children can make a water-drop lens to use when a hand lens is not available. A water-drop lens is best used to make flat objects, such as leaves and pieces of paper, appear larger.

Materials: 2 erasers about 1 cm thick, piece of acetate, water, dropper

1. Place the object you want to see better on a table between two erasers that are the same size.
2. Place a sheet of acetate on top of the erasers, about 1 cm above the object.
3. Use the dropper to place one drop of water on the sheet over the object.
4. Move the object if you need to until you can see it well.

Making a Thermometer

Children can make this simple thermometer easily. It won't give an exact temperature reading, but children can tell if the temperature is going up or going down.

Materials: plastic soda bottle, clear plastic straw, ruler, clay, colored water, dropper, marker

1. Add colored water to the bottle until it is nearly full.
2. Place the straw in the bottle. Finish filling the bottle with water, but leave about 1 cm of space at the top.
3. Lift the straw until 10 cm of it sticks up out of the bottle. Use the clay to seal the mouth of the bottle.
4. Use the dropper to add colored water to the straw. Make the straw a little more than half full.
5. Mark the level of the water on the straw. This is the start level.

Children can get an idea of how the thermometer works by placing it in a bowl of hot water. They will see the level of water in the straw rise. If they put the bottle in a bowl of ice, they will see the level of water in the straw drop.

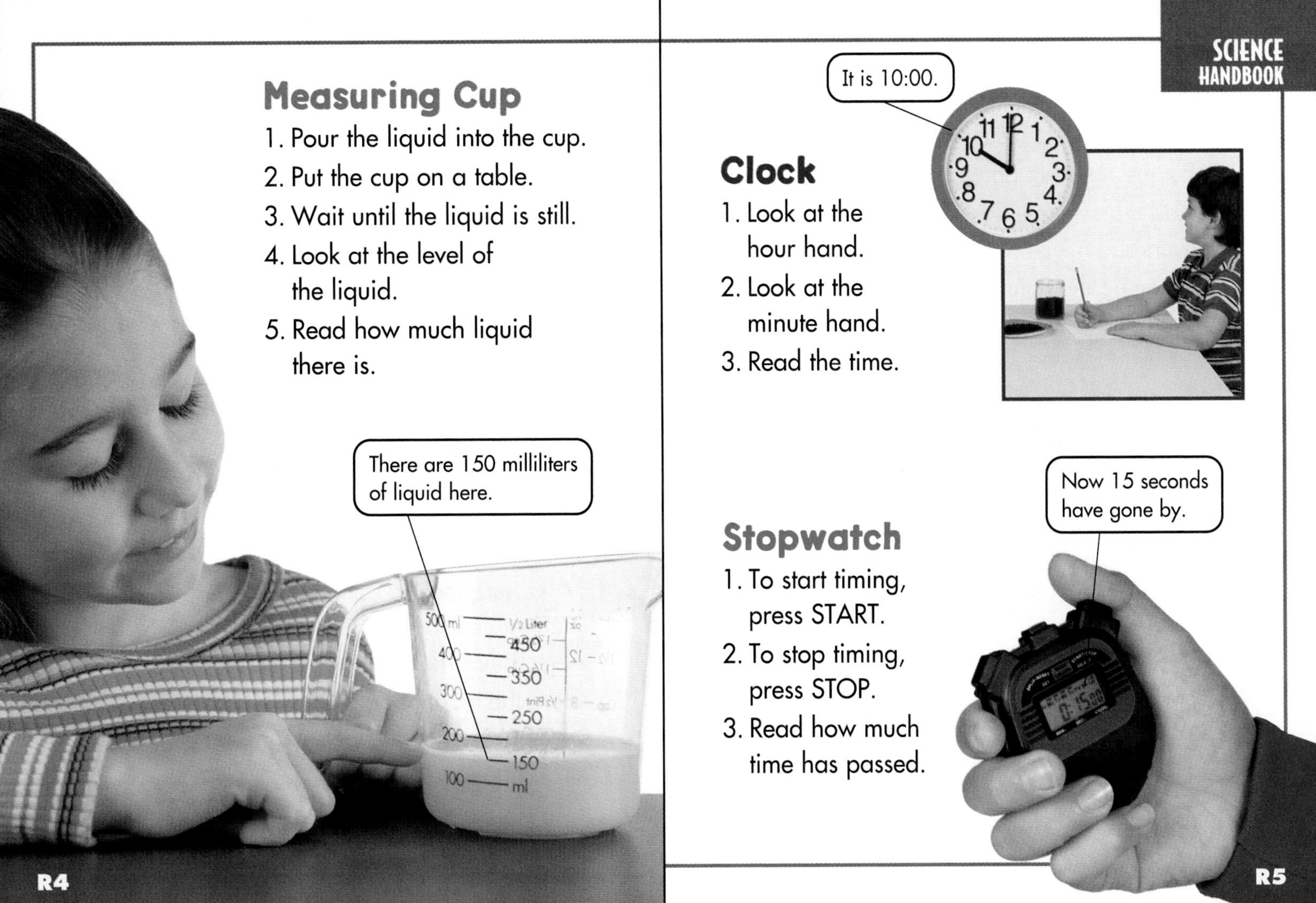

Measuring Cup
1. Pour the liquid into the cup.
2. Put the cup on a table.
3. Wait until the liquid is still.
4. Look at the level of the liquid.
5. Read how much liquid there is.
There are 150 milliliters of liquid here.
Clock
1. Look at the hour hand.
2. Look at the minute hand.
3. Read the time.
It is 10:00.
Stopwatch
1. To start timing, press START.
2. To stop timing, press STOP.
3. Read how much time has passed.
Now 15 seconds have gone by.
SCIENCE HANDBOOK
R4
R5

Science Handbook pages R4–R5

How to Use a Dropper

Children will need to know how to use a dropper for some investigations and also for constructing their own science tools.

Materials: dropper, container of liquid

1. With the dropper out of the liquid, squeeze the bulb and keep it squeezed. Then put the end of the tube into the liquid.
2. Stop squeezing the bulb. (You will see the liquid go into the tube.)
3. Take the dropper from the liquid, and move it to the place you want to put the liquid. (If you are putting the liquid into another liquid, don't let the dropper touch the second liquid.)
4. Gently squeeze the bulb until one drop comes out of the tube. Do this until you have added the right number of drops.

Tips for Measuring Around an Object

Children can use this fast method to measure around a circular object.

Materials: object to be measured, string, marker, scissors, ruler

1. Wrap a piece of string around the object you want to measure. Mark the place where the string comes together to make a circle.
2. Cut the string where you marked it.
3. Measure the length of the string.

SCIENCE HANDBOOK

Balance

1. Start with the pans even.
2. Put the object in one pan.
3. Add masses until the pans are even again.
4. Count up the number of masses.

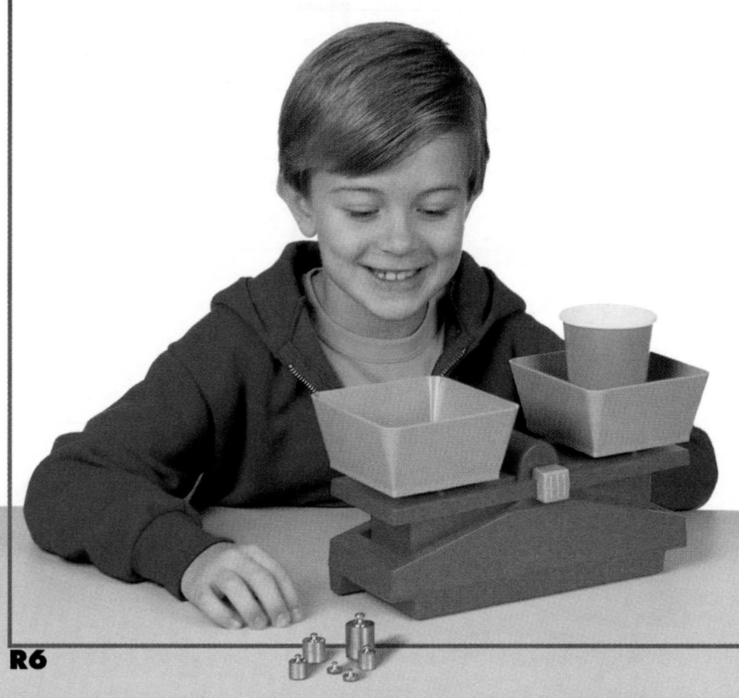

R6

Magnet

1. Put one of the poles of the magnet near the object.
2. Look at the object to see if the magnet attracts it.
3. Make sure that you don't drop or hit the magnet.
4. Make sure that you don't put the magnet near a computer or other objects that have a magnet inside.
5. Store the magnet by placing a piece of steel or another magnet on the poles.

R7

Science Handbook pages R6–R7

Making a Balance

Children can make this balance from a few simple materials. It is best used to measure small masses.

Materials: ruler, string, tape, 2 paper cups, 2 large paper clips

1. If the ruler has holes in it, tie the string through the middle hole. If it does not have holes, tie the string around the middle of the ruler.
2. Tape the other end of the string to a table. Let the ruler hang down from the side of the table. Make the ruler hang level.
3. Unbend the end of each paper clip a little. Push these ends through the sides of the paper cups. Hang the cups on the ruler by the paper clips.
4. Move the cups until the ruler is level.

Using and Caring for Magnets

The term magnetism comes from Magnesia, the name of a region in Asia where lodestone, a naturally magnetic ore, was first found.

Some children may have difficulty accepting that magnets exert a pull on an object. Help them feel what they can't see by having them bring a small metallic object, such as a steel paper clip, toward a magnet. Lead children to notice that when the paper clip comes very close to the magnet, they can feel the magnet's force pulling on it.

Magnets must be handled carefully if they are to keep their energy. The molecules of a magnet that has been dropped will be jarred out of line. Extreme heat will also upset the magnetic field of a magnet. Magnets should always be stored in a keeper, or with the north pole of one next to the south pole of another.

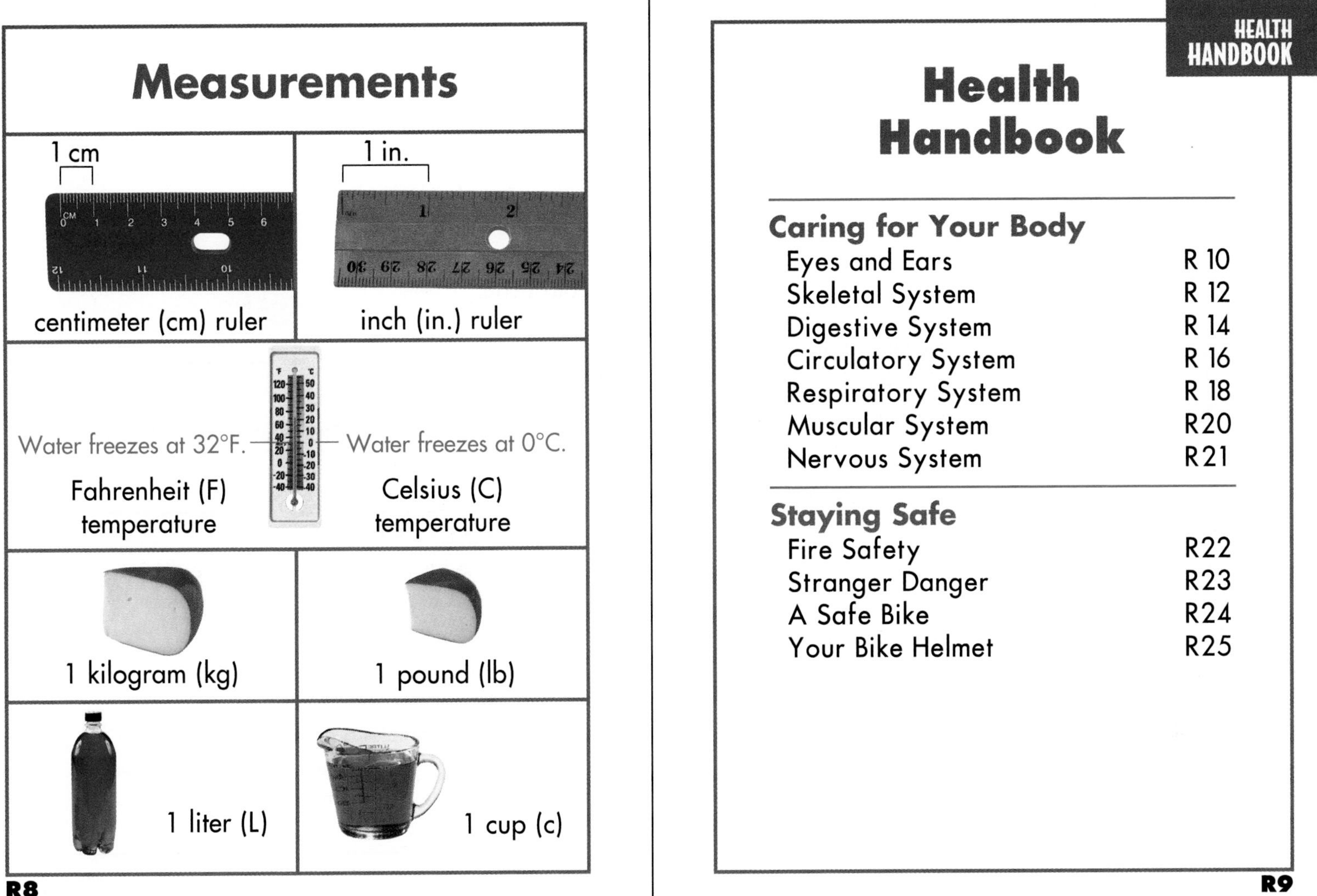

Measurements

1 cm

centimeter (cm) ruler

1 in.

inch (in.) ruler

Water freezes at 32°F.

Fahrenheit (F) temperature

Water freezes at 0°C.

Celsius (C) temperature

1 kilogram (kg)

1 pound (lb)

1 liter (L)

1 cup (c)

R8

HEALTH HANDBOOK

Health Handbook

R9

Health Handbook pages R8–R9

Using the Health Handbook

This section of the Student Edition provides information that addresses important health concerns of children. It also provides interesting and detailed information about the systems of the human body. The structure and function of each system is identified. Student activities and tips for caring for each system are also included.

The Health Handbook can be used as a reference section to support concepts presented in other chapters. It can also be used for a unit of study about health and the human body.

Eyes and Ears

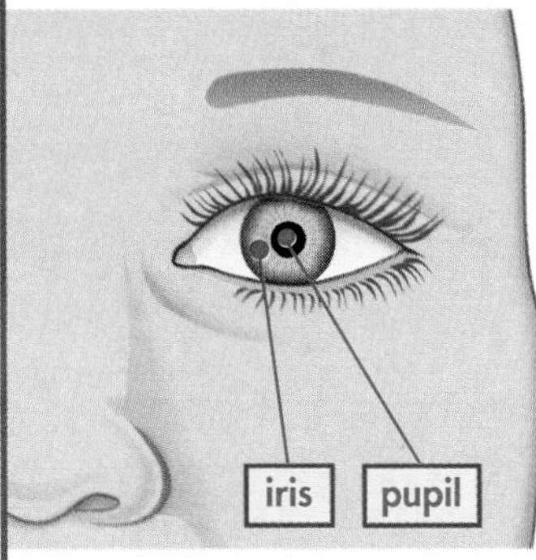

Outside of Eye

Caring for Your Eyes and Ears

- Some bright light can hurt your eyes. Never look at the sun or at very bright lights.
- Never put an object in your ear.

Eyes

When you look at your eyes, you can see a white part, a colored part, and a dark center. The colored part is the iris. The dark center is the pupil.

Inside of Eye

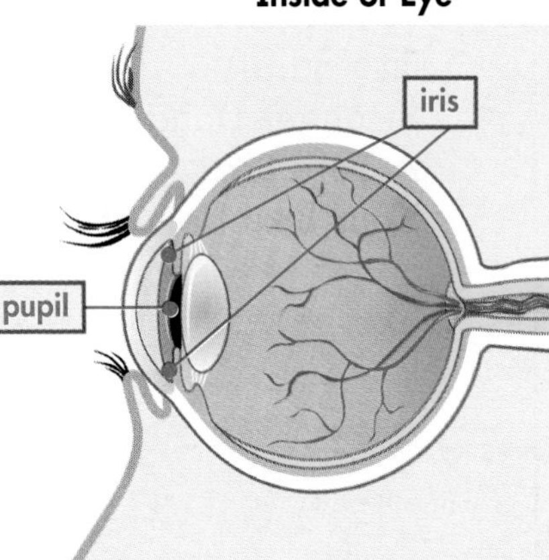

Ear

Your ears let you hear. Most of each ear is inside your head.

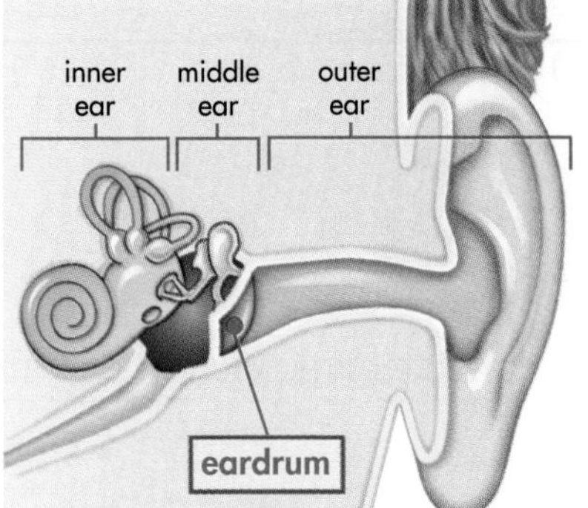

Inside of Ear   Outside of Ear

ACTIVITIES

1. The iris of the eye may be different colors. Look at the eyes of your classmates. How many colors do you see?
2. Ask a classmate to stand across the classroom from you. Have him or her say your name in a normal voice. Now put a hand behind each ear and have him or her say your name again in the same voice. Which time sounded louder?

R10   R11

Health Handbook pages R10–R11

Background

Ears The outer ear collects sound waves and funnels them into the ear. The sound waves make the eardrum, bones in the ear, and fluid in the inner ear vibrate. The vibrations are picked up by nerves that send signals to the brain. The brain sorts out the signals to identify what the sound is and where it is coming from.

Discussion

Why do you think most of each ear is inside your head? The bones and membrane of the ear are small and somewhat fragile. The heavier bones of the head help protect the inner ear. Explain to children that the skull also acts like an echo chamber, amplifying sound.

What kind of light can hurt your eyes? strong sunlight, bright artificial lights (especially halogen lamps)

Why should you not put anything into your ears? Explain that objects inserted into the ears can damage the inner ear or cause infections, leading to possible hearing loss. Children can clean their outer ears by using a washcloth, which should not be put in the ear. Soft rubber ear plugs may be worn for swimming if necessary.

Activities

Activity 1 Before they begin, be sure children can locate the iris. Caution children not to point to or put their fingers in another person's eye. Make a tally chart on the board to keep track of the different eye colors.

Activity 2 Have children speculate about why they heard more clearly when they cupped their hands around their ears. Explain that the purpose of the outer ear is to trap sound waves. Cupping the hand behind the ear increases this trapping ability.

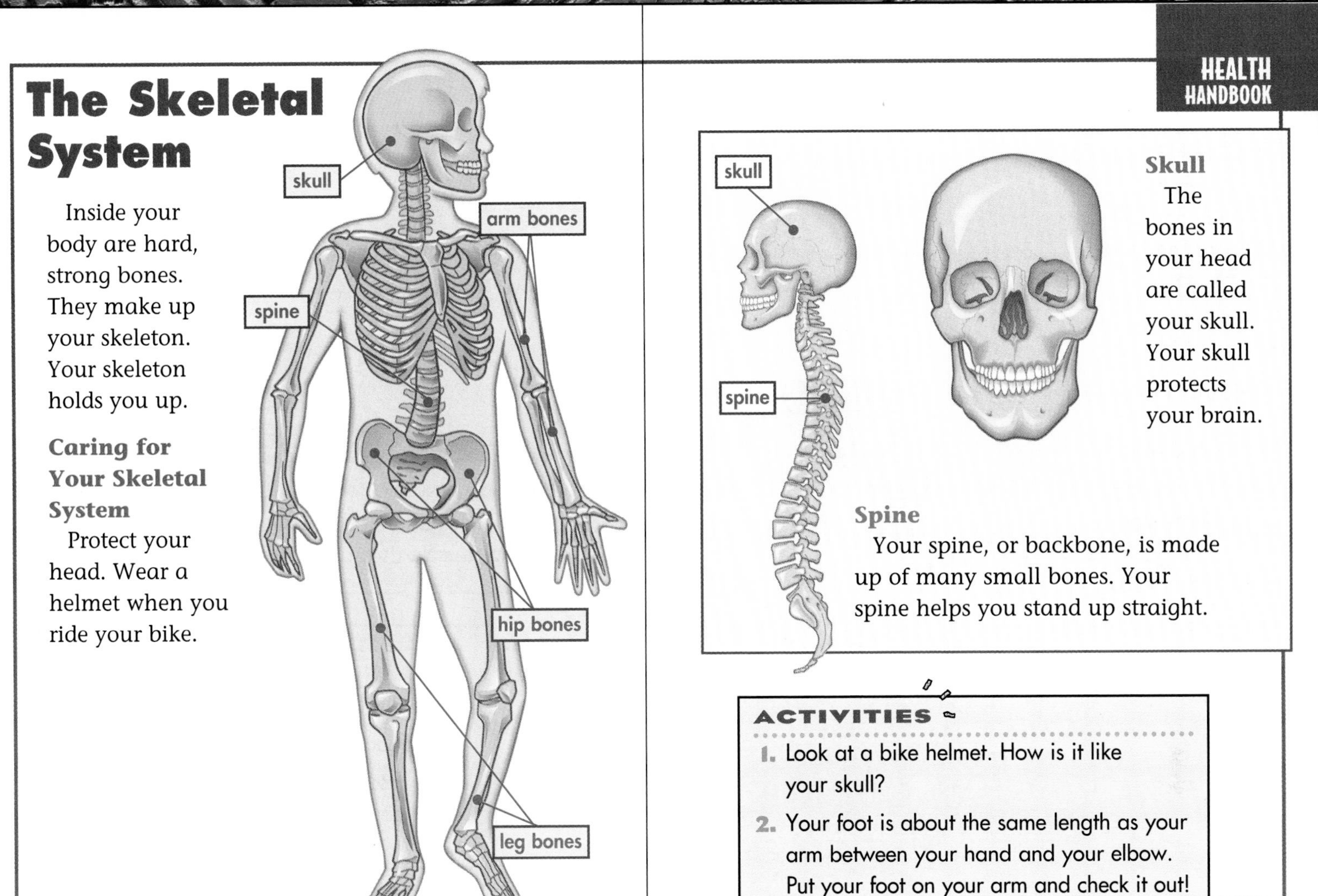

The Skeletal System

Inside your body are hard, strong bones. They make up your skeleton. Your skeleton holds you up.

Caring for Your Skeletal System

Protect your head. Wear a helmet when you ride your bike.

R12

HEALTH HANDBOOK

Skull

The bones in your head are called your skull. Your skull protects your brain.

Spine

Your spine, or backbone, is made up of many small bones. Your spine helps you stand up straight.

ACTIVITIES

1. Look at a bike helmet. How is it like your skull?
2. Your foot is about the same length as your arm between your hand and your elbow. Put your foot on your arm and check it out!

R13

Health Handbook pages R12–R13

Background

Skull The skull has openings for nerves to pass through. Besides the hole for the spinal cord, there are also holes for the eyes and ears. The hinged joint that forms the jaw exposes the tongue.

Long Bones Bones of the arms and legs are hollow, like a tube, and are filled with marrow. The marrow helps make blood cells.

Discussion

Have children feel the insides of their cheeks with their tongues.

Are cheeks hard or soft? Why? They are soft, because there are no bones in them.

Have children feel their faces with their fingertips to find the bones beneath the soft tissue.

How do bones feel? hard

What do you think your body would be like without your skeleton? Help children recognize that without the support of the skeleton, the body's soft tissues would not be strong enough to move, stand, or walk. To emphasize this idea, have children sit on a carpeted floor and act out being floppy rag dolls with no bones.

Activities

Activity 1 Have children compare the shapes of the bike helmets to the shape of the top of the skull, where the helmet is intended to be worn. The helmet protects the skull just as the skull protects the brain.

Activity 2 The easiest way for children to check this proportion is to sit with one ankle drawn up on the other knee (in an open cross-legged position) and lean forward slightly to align the forearms with the foot. Children may also trace around their feet and then lay their forearms on the tracings.

The Digestive System

Your digestive system helps your body get energy from the food you eat.

Caring for Your Digestive System

- Brush and floss your teeth every day.
- Don't eat right before you exercise. Your body needs energy to digest food.

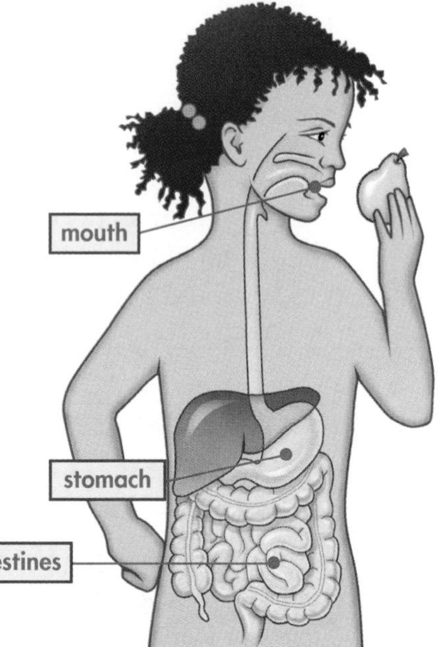

Teeth

Some of your teeth tear food and some grind it into small parts.

tongue
teeth

Tongue

Your tongue helps you swallow food. It is a strong muscle that also lets you taste.

ACTIVITIES

1. Bite into an apple and chew the bite. Which teeth did you use for these jobs?
2. Lick a salty pretzel and a lollipop. Compare how they taste.

R14 R15

Health Handbook pages R14–R15

Background

Teeth Teeth are living structures that grow and need nourishment in the same way as other parts of the body. The visible part of the tooth is made of a hard, shiny substance called *enamel*, which protects the tooth from damage and prevents bacteria from entering the tooth. Beneath the enamel is *dentin*, a slightly softer material that makes up most of the tooth. Inside the dentin is the *pulp* cavity, which consists of blood vessels and nerves. Both dentin and pulp extend into the root of the tooth.

Discussion

Ask children what they ate or will eat for lunch today. Have volunteers describe their favorite lunch foods.

Why do people eat? They eat because they get hungry. Explain to children that their bodies turn the food they eat into energy to do things, to grow, and to stay healthy. The parts of the digestive system work together to help carry out this process.

What are teeth used for? tearing and grinding food

What does the tongue do? It helps you taste and swallow food.

Activities

Optional Materials **mirror, apple slices, salted pretzels, lollipops**

Note: Check for food allergies or dietary restrictions before offering children food in class.

As an alternative, have children carry out the activities at home and then report their findings.

Activity 1 Children bite with their front teeth, called *incisors*, and chew with their back teeth, called *molars*. Have children look at their teeth in a mirror to note that the front teeth are sharp-edged and the back teeth are wide and dull. These shapes correspond to the functions of the teeth.

Activity 2 Human taste buds (the bumps on the tongue) can distinguish four general tastes: sweet, salty, sour, and bitter. The other elements that go into experiencing a food's flavor involve the sense of smell, texture, and other more subtle sense clues.

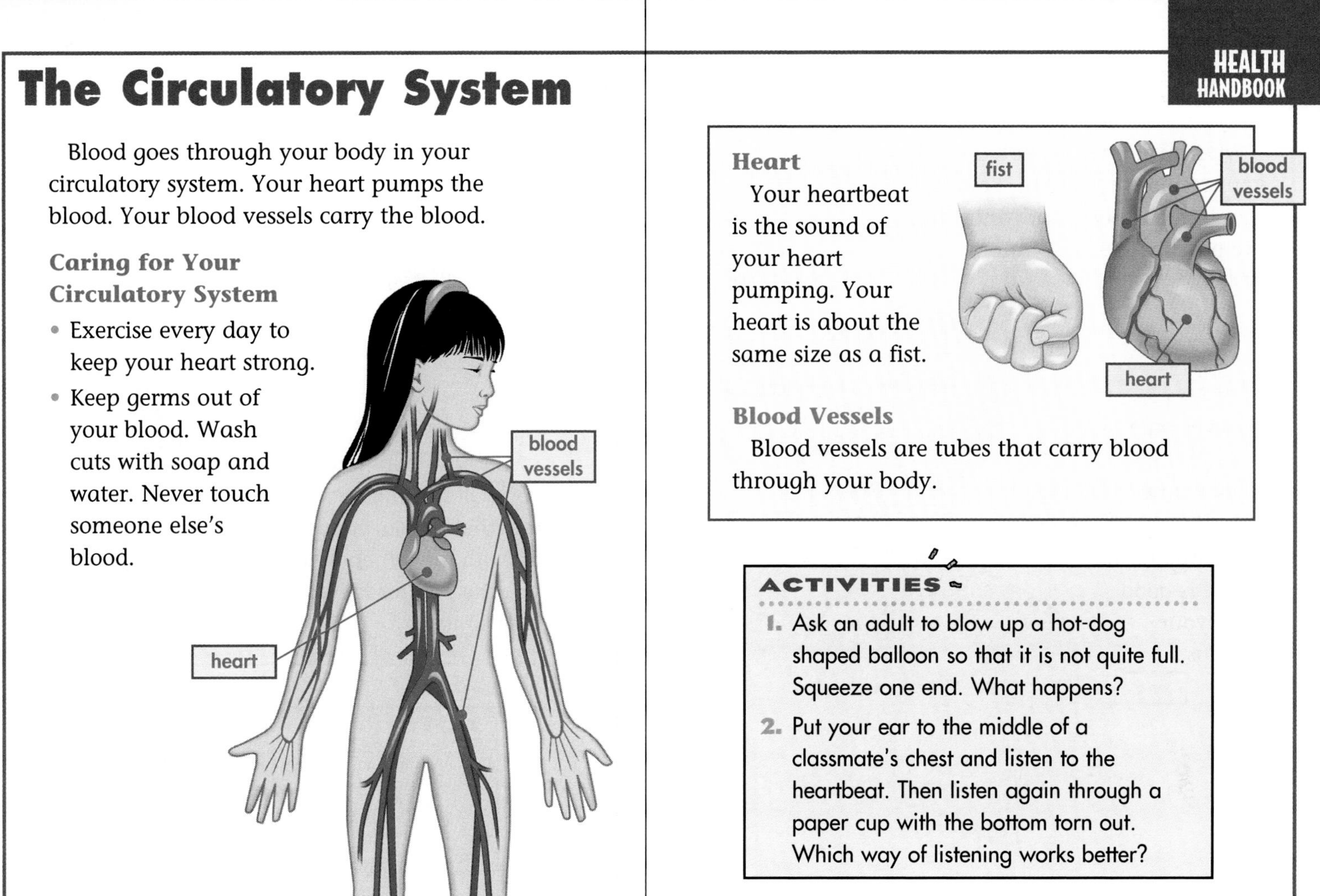

HEALTH HANDBOOK

The Circulatory System

Blood goes through your body in your circulatory system. Your heart pumps the blood. Your blood vessels carry the blood.

Caring for Your Circulatory System

- Exercise every day to keep your heart strong.
- Keep germs out of your blood. Wash cuts with soap and water. Never touch someone else's blood.

Heart

Your heartbeat is the sound of your heart pumping. Your heart is about the same size as a fist.

Blood Vessels

Blood vessels are tubes that carry blood through your body.

ACTIVITIES

1. Ask an adult to blow up a hot-dog shaped balloon so that it is not quite full. Squeeze one end. What happens?
2. Put your ear to the middle of a classmate's chest and listen to the heartbeat. Then listen again through a paper cup with the bottom torn out. Which way of listening works better?

R16 R17

Health Handbook pages R16–R17

Background

Circulatory System Blood is carried throughout the body by arteries, veins, and capillaries. Arteries deliver materials, such as oxygen and nutrients, to parts of the body. Veins pick up waste materials, such as carbon dioxide. Capillaries are microscopic blood vessels that allow needed substances to seep into the body's tissues.

Discussion

Have children look at the insides of their forearms to locate the blue lines that indicate blood vessels. Then show children how to place two fingers on the inside of the opposite wrists to feel the pulse.

What makes the pulse beat? Explain that the regular fluttering motion children feel at a pulse point is caused by the pressure of the blood being pumped through the blood vessels. The pulse beats at the same rate as the heart.

Activities

Optional Materials **hot-dog shaped balloon or rubber squeeze ball, paper cups**

As an alternative, have children carry out the activities at home and then report their findings.

Activity 1 Give children a partially inflated balloon or a rubber squeeze ball. When one end of the balloon or part of the ball is squeezed, air moves to the other part and fills it up. This squeezing motion is similar to the way the heart pumps blood.

Activity 2 Remind children that cupping something around the ear amplifies sound.

The Respiratory System

When you breathe, you are using your respiratory system. Your mouth, your nose, and your lungs are parts of your respiratory system.

Caring for Your Respiratory System

- Never put anything in your nose.
- Exercise makes you breathe harder and is good for your lungs.

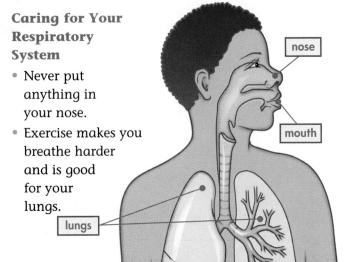

HEALTH HANDBOOK

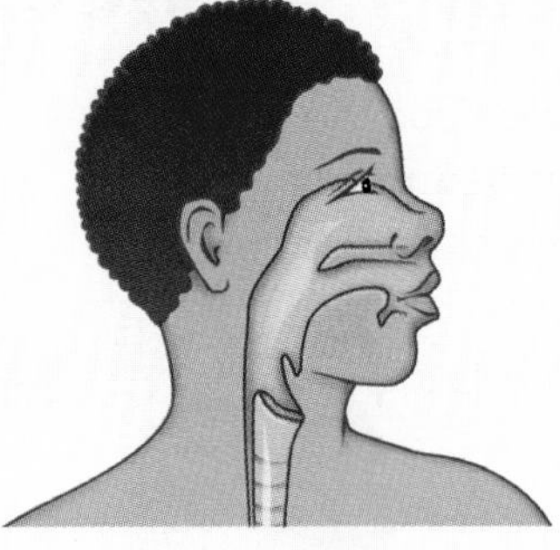

Mouth and Nose

Air goes in and out of your body through your mouth and nose.

Lungs

You have two lungs in your chest. When you breathe in, your lungs fill with air. When you breathe out, air leaves your lungs.

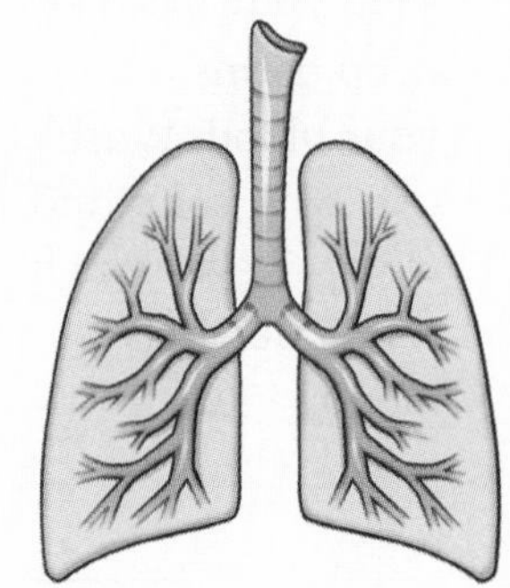

ACTIVITIES

1. Watch your chest and stomach muscles as you take a breath and let it out. Describe what happens.
2. Count how many breaths you take in one minute.

R18 R19

Health Handbook pages R18–R19

Background

The Respiratory System When a person inhales, air enters the mouth and nose and goes into the trachea. The nose helps warm the air and add moisture to it. The trachea connects the nose and mouth to the lungs. The trachea divides into two smaller tubes that go to the lungs. These tubes are called *bronchi.* The trachea and bronchi are lined with many small hairs and coated with mucus. The mucus traps germs and small bits of dust and dirt. The small hairs constantly sweep the mucus up and out.

Discussion

Have children cover their mouths and breathe in and out through their noses only. Then have them cover their noses and breathe only through their mouths. Finally, have children breathe in and out through their noses and mouths at the same time.

What were you doing? breathing

What do we take into our bodies when we breathe? air, oxygen

Why do you think we can breathe with just our noses, just our mouths, or both together? because all the parts of the respiratory system are connected

Activities

Activity 1 Have children place one hand on their chests below the breastbone while they inhale and exhale, to feel how the muscles of the chest expand to draw air into the lungs and contract to force it out again.

Activity 2 Explain that breathing is automatic; we can control our breathing to some degree, but we can't stop it entirely at will, and we don't have to consciously decide to take each breath. Have children count their respiration, both at rest and after exercising.

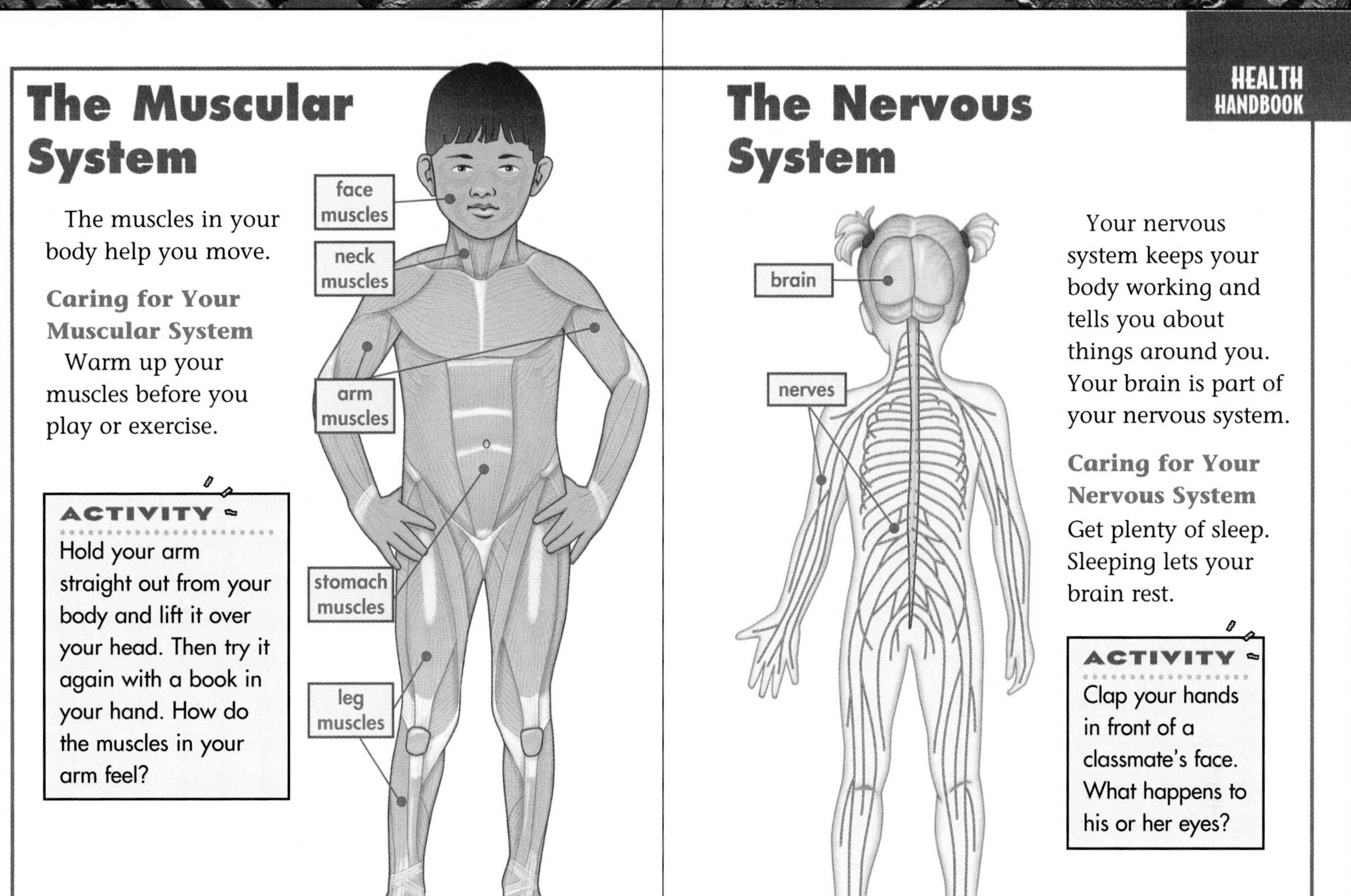

The Muscular System

The muscles in your body help you move.

Caring for Your Muscular System
Warm up your muscles before you play or exercise.

ACTIVITY
Hold your arm straight out from your body and lift it over your head. Then try it again with a book in your hand. How do the muscles in your arm feel?

R20

The Nervous System

Your nervous system keeps your body working and tells you about things around you. Your brain is part of your nervous system.

Caring for Your Nervous System
Get plenty of sleep. Sleeping lets your brain rest.

ACTIVITY
Clap your hands in front of a classmate's face. What happens to his or her eyes?

R21

HEALTH HANDBOOK

Health Handbook pages R20–R21

Background

The Nervous System The nervous system makes the heart beat and the lungs work. It allows a person to see, hear, smell, taste, and touch. It lets a person learn, remember, and feel emotions. It moves all of the muscles in the body.

Discussion

Write *muscles* and *nerves* on the board. Have children raise their arms over their heads.

What makes your arms move? muscles

Some children may think it is the bones that move the arm. Explain that while the bones provide structure and support, it is actually the muscles, stretchy bands of tissue, that move by stretching and contracting like rubber bands.

Then have children gently pinch the web of skin between the thumb and finger of their opposite hand. Explain that the sense of touch, which enables us to feel things, depends on nerves, tiny fibers running throughout the body and connected to the brain.

Activities

Activity 1 Explain that holding a book or other heavy object while raising the arm makes the muscles work harder. One way to exercise and increase muscle tone is to lift weights. Caution children never to lift weights without adult supervision.

Activity 2 Have children keep their hands at least 3 inches away from their partners' eyes. Explain that blinking is an automatic response, communicated by the nerves to the muscles of the eyelid, to protect the eye.

Staying Safe

Fire Safety

You can stay safe from fires. Follow these safety rules.

- Never play with matches or lighters.
- Be careful around stoves, heaters, fireplaces, and grills.
- Don't use microwaves, irons, or toasters without an adult's help.
- Practice your family's fire safety plan.
- If there is a fire in your home, get out quickly. Drop to the floor and crawl if the room is filled with smoke. If a closed door feels hot, don't open it. Use another exit. Call 911 from outside your home.
- If your clothes catch on fire, use Stop, Drop, and Roll right away to put out the flames.

❶ **Stop** Don't run or wave your arms.

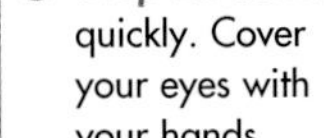

❷ **Drop** Lie down quickly. Cover your eyes with your hands.

❸ **Roll** Roll back and forth to put out the fire.

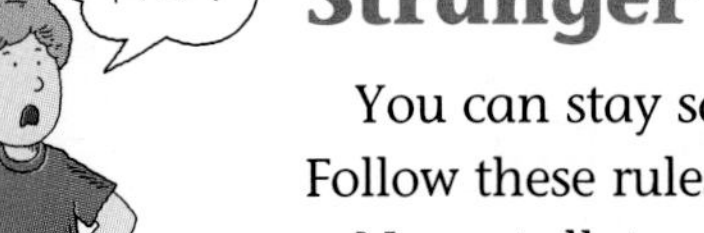

Stranger Danger

You can stay safe around strangers. Follow these rules.

- Never talk to strangers.
- Never go with a stranger, on foot or in a car.
- If you are home alone, do not open the door. Do not let telephone callers know you are alone.
- Never give your name, address, or phone number to anyone you don't know. (You may give this information to a 911 operator in an emergency.)
- If you are lost or need help, talk to a police officer, a guard, or a store clerk.
- If a stranger bothers you, use the Stranger Danger rules to stay safe.

❶ **Say no!** Yell if you need to. You do not have to be polite to strangers.

❷ **Get away.** Walk fast or run in the opposite direction. Go toward people who can help you.

❸ **Tell someone.** Tell a trusted adult, such as a family member, a teacher, or a police officer. Do not keep secrets about strangers.

R22 R23

Health Handbook pages R22–R23

Background

Fire Breakouts About three out of ten home-fire deaths occur between the hours of midnight and 4:00 A.M., when most people are asleep. Because fires can develop undetected, an early morning fire is likely to be fatal. Smoke detectors should be installed on every level of the home, including the basement and attic.

Discussion

What could happen if a child lights a match? The child could be burned; clothes, furniture, or even the house could catch fire if a match is dropped.

Why should you never play near stoves, fireplaces, heaters, or barbecue grills? These fire hazards could cause serious burns or fires if you get close enough to touch them or overturn them, or if your clothing catches on fire.

Who are some other people you could ask for help if you were lost or in danger? familiar teachers, guards wearing uniforms and badges, bus drivers at the wheel of their bus

If a stranger approaches you when a trusted adult is not around, what should you do? Tell children they should run away and yell "Help!" as loudly as they can. Some experts suggest that children shout, "This man (woman) is not my father (mother)!"

Activities

Language Arts Link—Choose a Code Word Explain that it is good for families to have a secret code word to use for identification when a parent or guardian must send an unknown person to pick up a child in an emergency. Have children think of code words to share with their families. Remind children never to share their code words with anyone outside the family.

Reading Mini-Lesson—Identify Compound Words Write the word *fire* on the board. Have children think of all the words they can that begin with the word *fire*. Tell children that when two words go together to make one longer word, the long word is called a compound word. Give these examples: *firefighter*, *fireplace*, and *firefly*. Explain that familiar two-word phrases, such as *fire engine*, are not compound words.

Staying Safe

A Safe Bike

To ride your bike safely, you need to start with a safe bike. A safe bike is the right size for you. When you sit on your bike with the pedal in the lowest position, you should be able to rest your heel on the pedal.

After checking the size of your bike, check to see that it has the right safety equipment. Your bike should have everything shown below.

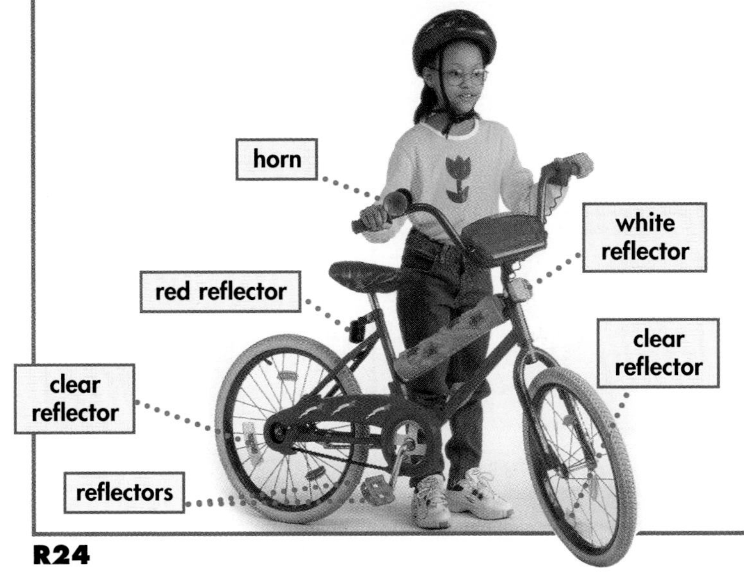

Your Bike Helmet

Always wear a bike helmet. Wear your helmet flat on your head. Be sure it is strapped tightly. If your helmet gets bumped in a fall, replace it right away, even if it doesn't look damaged.

Safety on the Road

- Check your bike for safety every time you ride it.
- Ride in single file. Ride in the same direction as traffic.
- Stop, look, listen, and think when you enter a street or cross a driveway.
- Walk your bike across an intersection.
- Obey all traffic signs and signals.
- Don't ride at night without an adult. Wear light-colored clothing and use lights and reflectors for night riding.

R24 R25

Health Handbook pages R24–R25

Background

The Importance of Helmets Each year in the United States, more than 300 children are killed in bicycle-related accidents. About 400,000 children require emergency room treatment as a result of bicycle injuries. Eighty percent of fatal bike injuries and seventy-five percent of disabling injuries could have been prevented if the rider were wearing a well-fitting helmet. In states where laws requiring mandatory use of bicycle helmets by children have been enacted, the number of fatalities is on the decline.

Discussion

Guide children on an imaginary bike ride. Have them follow your movements as you pantomime bike safety practices.

What do we do before we get on our bikes? Pantomime tying shoes and putting on a bike helmet.

Now we're riding. We have both hands on the handlebars. We're facing the same way as the traffic. Lead children around the room in single file.

Here's a street we need to cross. What do we do? Pantomime getting off a bike and walking it across an intersection.

After circling the room a few times, pantomime stopping, putting down the kickstand, and removing the helmet.

Activities

Art Link - Bicycle Safety Review basic equipment and safety rules for riding a bicycle. Have children create posters depicting the proper safety steps for bicycling.

Physical Education Link - Bicycle Obstacle Course Set up an obstacle course on which children can test their ability to steer and brake when riding a bicycle. Invite children to bring their bicycles to school and have a few bicycles handy for children who do not own bikes or who are unable to bring them. Demonstrate the correct way to wear a bicycle helmet. Then let children take turns testing their skills on the course.

A

air
What people breathe but can not see, taste, or smell. It is a natural resource. (C29)

attract
To pull something. (F33)

algae
Plantlike living things found in water. (B40)

amphibian
An animal with smooth, wet skin. (A52)

C

change
To make different. (E25)

condense
To change from water vapor into tiny drops of water. (D18)

curve
To bend along a path. (F10)

D

desert
A dry place. (B31)

dissolve
To mix a solid with a liquid completely. (E17)

E

enrich
To make better. (B12)

evaporate
To change from water into water vapor. (D18)

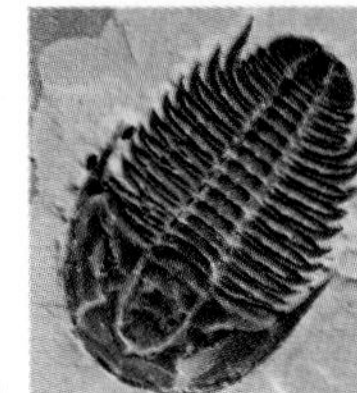

extinct
Kinds of plants or animals that are no longer living. (C14)

F

fall
The season that follows summer. (D43)

fossil
Parts and imprints of a plant or an animal that lived long ago. (C9)

float
To stay on top of a liquid. (E13)

force
A push or a pull. (F5)

flowers
The parts of a plant that make seeds. (A27)

forest
A place where many trees grow. (B27)

fresh water
Water that is not salty. It is a natural resource. (C33)

gills
Body parts that help a fish take air from water. (A47)

friction
A force that makes it harder to move things. (F20)

H

hatch
To break out of an egg. (A60)

G

gas
Matter that does not have a shape of its own, such as air. (E21)

I

insect
An animal that has three body parts and six legs. (A55)

L

lake
A body of water with land all around it. (C34)

liquid
Matter that flows to take the shape of its container. (E9)

larva
A caterpillar. (A66)

living
Needing food, water, and air to live and grow. (A11)

leaves
The plant part that makes food for the plant. (A26)

M

magnet
A piece of iron that pulls things made of iron. (F33)

magnetic force
The pulling force of a magnet. (F43)

matter
Everything around you. (E5)

magnetize
To give magnetic force to something a magnet attracts. (F47)

mineral
One kind of nonliving thing that is found in nature. (C27)

mammal
An animal that has hair or fur and feeds its young milk. (A50)

moon
The brightest object in the sky at night. (D28)

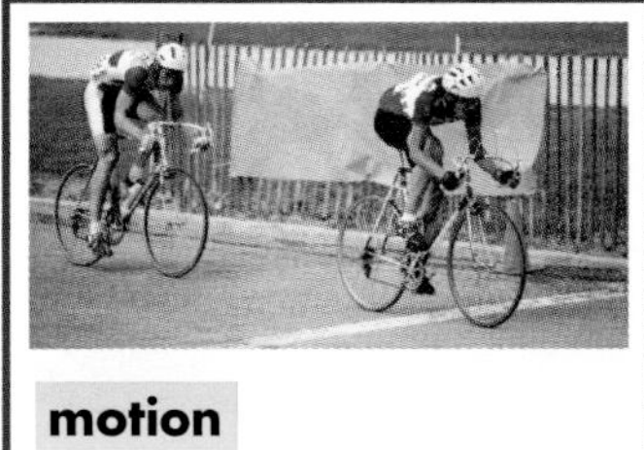

motion
Movement from one place to another. (F13)

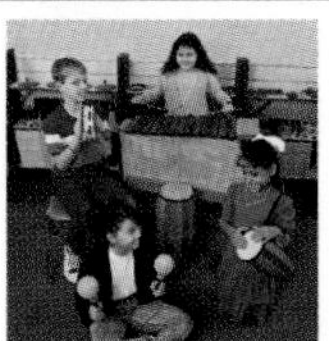

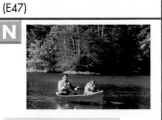

musical instrument
Something used to make music. (E47)

N

natural resource
Something found in nature that people can use. (C23)

nonliving
Not needing food, water, and air and not growing. (A11)

O

ocean
A large, deep body of salt water. (B39)

P

pitch
How high or low a sound is. (E44)

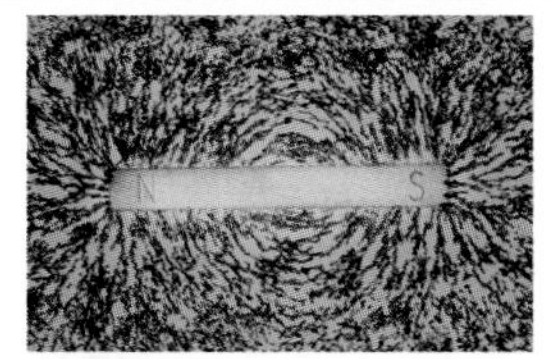

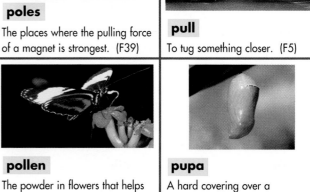

poles
The places where the pulling force of a magnet is strongest. (F39)

pollen
The powder in flowers that helps flowers make seeds. (B13)

product
Something that people make from other things. (B16)

pull
To tug something closer. (F5)

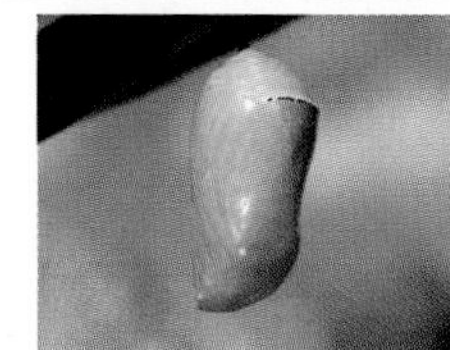

pupa
A hard covering over a caterpillar. (A67)

push
To press something away. (F5)

rain forest
A forest that is wet all year. (B35)

repel
To push away. (F40)

recycle
To collect things so they can be made into new things. (C40)

reptile
An animal with rough, dry skin. (A52)

reduce
To use less of a natural resource. (C38)

reuse
To use things again. (C39)

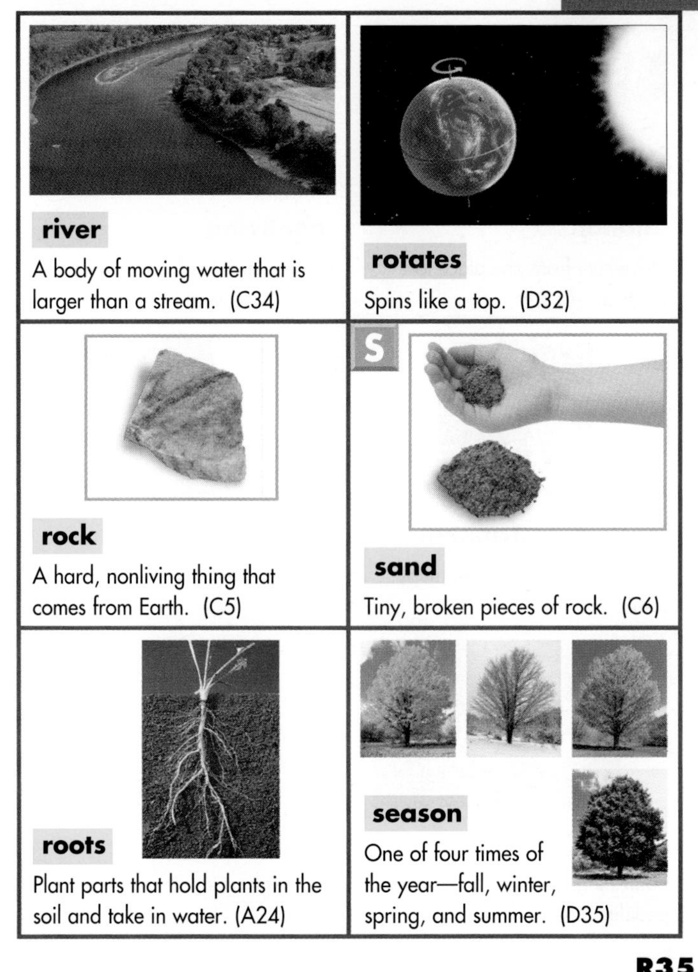

river
A body of moving water that is larger than a stream. (C34)

rotates
Spins like a top. (D32)

rock
A hard, nonliving thing that comes from Earth. (C5)

sand
Tiny, broken pieces of rock. (C6)

roots
Plant parts that hold plants in the soil and take in water. (A24)

season
One of four times of the year—fall, winter, spring, and summer. (D35)

seed
What most plants grow from. (A29)

shelter
A place where an animal can be safe. (B8)

seed coat
Covering a seed may have. (A29)

sink
To drop to the bottom of a liquid. (E13)

senses
Touch, sight, smell, hearing, and taste. (A5)

solid
Matter that keeps its shape. (E6)

sound
Everything you hear. (E35)

stars
Objects in the sky that give off light. (D28)

speed
How quickly or slowly something moves. (F15)

stem
Plant part that helps hold up the plant and moves water to the leaves. (A25)

spring
The season that follows winter. (D35)

stream
A body of moving water smaller than a river. (C34)

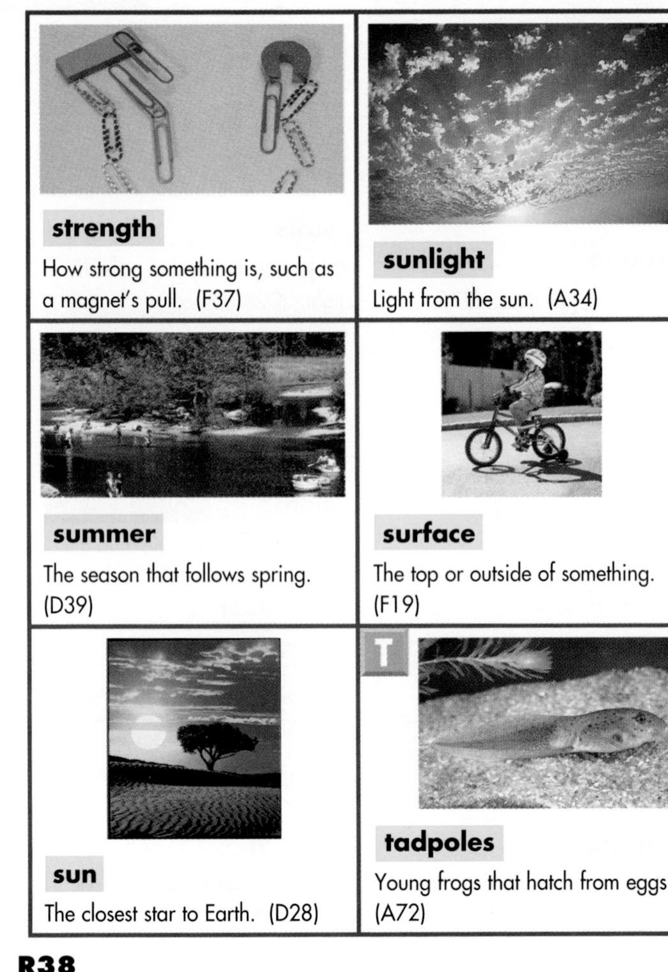

strength
How strong something is, such as a magnet's pull. (F37)

sunlight
Light from the sun. (A34)

summer
The season that follows spring. (D39)

surface
The top or outside of something. (F19)

sun
The closest star to Earth. (D28)

T

tadpoles
Young frogs that hatch from eggs. (A72)

R38

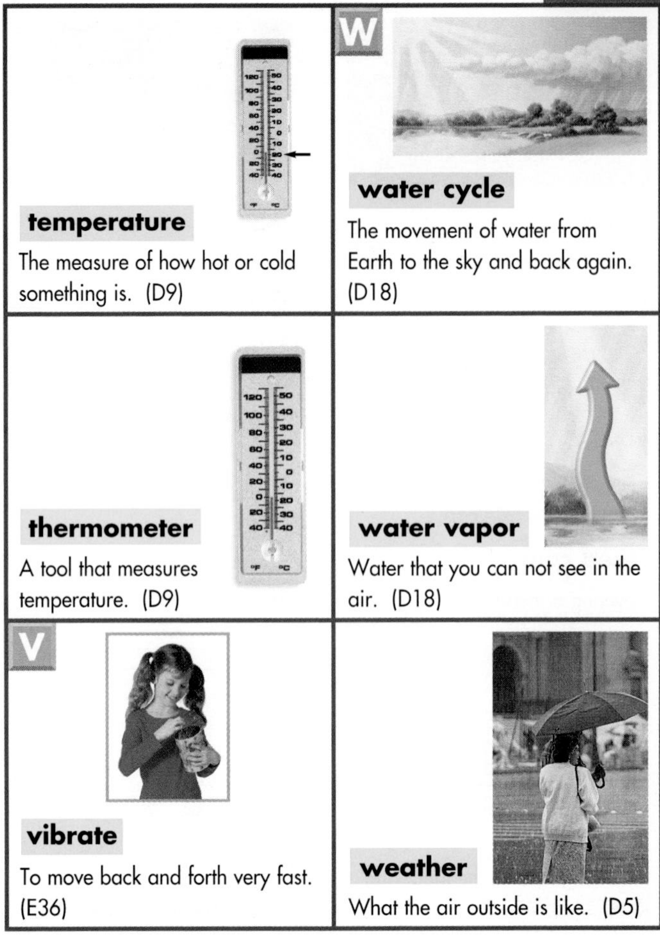

temperature
The measure of how hot or cold something is. (D9)

W

water cycle
The movement of water from Earth to the sky and back again. (D18)

thermometer
A tool that measures temperature. (D9)

water vapor
Water that you can not see in the air. (D18)

V

vibrate
To move back and forth very fast. (E36)

weather
What the air outside is like. (D5)

R39

wheel A roller that turns on an axle. (F23)	
wind Moving air. (D13)	
winter The season that follows fall. (D47)	

SEASONS OF SCIENCE

Fantastic Fall

As an option, use these topics and lessons to teach seasonal science during the fall months.

TOPICS	LESSONS	SPECIAL DATES*
AUGUST – SEPTEMBER		
► **Weather** ► **Living Things**	**UNIT D Chapter 2, Lesson 5** What Is Fall? **UNIT A Chapter 1, Lesson 2** What Are Living and Nonliving Things?	**Aug. 7 NATIONAL MUSTARD DAY** Have children use their senses to tell about the color, smell, and texture of mustard. **Aug. 31 NATIONAL LEMONADE DAY** Have children help you make lemonade. They can use their senses to tell about lemons. Check for food allergies.
SEPTEMBER – OCTOBER		
► **Measuring Temperature** ► **The Five Senses**	**UNIT D Chapter 1, Lesson 2** What Is Temperature? **UNIT A Chapter 1, Lesson 1** How Do My Senses Help Me Learn?	**Sept. 8 INTERNATIONAL LITERACY DAY** Have children select favorite books about seasons for you to read aloud. **about Sept. 22 FIRST DAY OF FALL** Talk about the weather. Children can draw pictures that show how they dress in colder weather. **Sept. 26 FALL HAT WEEK** Children can make and decorate paper hats that tell about fall.
OCTOBER – NOVEMBER		
► **Exploring Sounds** ► **Wind**	**UNIT E Chapter 2, Lesson 1** What Are Sounds? **UNIT E Chapter 2, Lesson 2** How Are Sounds Different? **UNIT D Chapter 1, Lesson 3** What Is Wind?	**Oct. NATIONAL POPCORN POPPIN' MONTH** Children can observe and describe corn seeds. Then make and share popcorn. **Nov. PEANUT BUTTER LOVERS MONTH** Have children use their senses to observe peanuts and peanut butter. Check for allergies. **Nov. 25 THANKSGIVING**

*Check a calendar. Some dates may vary slightly from year to year.

Fall Activities

Weather Tracking

Objective Observe daily weather changes.

Materials construction paper, scissors, markers, glue, large calendar

1. Have children decide as a group what types of weather they will track—hot, cold, rainy, snowy, windy, for example.
2. Ask them to agree on cutouts that will be used to designate each of the weather categories. For example, they might use an orange sun, a blue coat, a yellow umbrella, a white snowflake, a blue wind face.
3. Each day have children place a cutout on the calendar to show the weather for the day.
4. Ask them to make a graph to show how often each type of weather occurs. Repeat the activity throughout the year. Display the information to have a record of seasonal changes.

Sunday	Monday	Tuesday	Wednesday	Thursday	Friday	Saturday

Surprising Sounds

Objective Identify sources of sounds.

Materials various items from home and school to produce sound; tape recorder; tapes; index cards; quiet, secluded area for recording

Encourage children to bring in items that produce sound. Have them place their items on a table.

1. Tell children to select two or more items from the collection. They should make a recording of the sounds produced from those items. Suggest that they move to a secluded area to make their recording. They should take an index card and write or draw on it the items they have selected. Have them write their name on the back of the card.
2. Children take turns coming to the table, listening to a tape, and making a list of those items they think made the sound on the tape. Then they find the index card that most closely matches their guesses.
3. Have children ask the person whose name is on the back of the card if their guesses are correct.

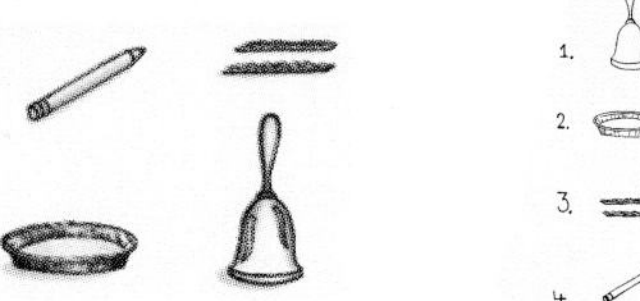

Funny Fall Stories

Objectives Observe and make models of fall objects.

Materials pictures of fall objects such as a pumpkin, an apple, a sweater, leaves; index cards; crayons

1. Divide the class into small groups. Give one of the objects to each group. Tell the children to observe and then to draw and label it on the index cards.
2. Collect a card from each group. As you tell the fall story below, pause and hold up each card noted in parentheses. Ask children to fill in the word.
3. Mix up the cards and tell the story again. Get ready for lots of laughter!

One fall evening. I put on my (sweater) and went outside. I walked through the (leaves) and ate an (apple). In a garden I saw a huge orange (pumpkin). Suddenly, something flew by my head. Was it an (owl)?

Using Our Senses

Objective Use the senses to observe objects from nature.

Materials fall nature items; five bins, each marked with one of the senses; hand lenses; grid paper

Take children on a walk to collect seasonal nature items or have them bring in seasonal items from home. Assemble these items on a classroom table.

1. Ask children to use their senses to observe the items. They should sort them into bins according to which sense they used the most to observe each item.
2. Tell children to make a picture graph to show their results.
3. When finished, they should place all of the items back on the table for other children to observe and sort.

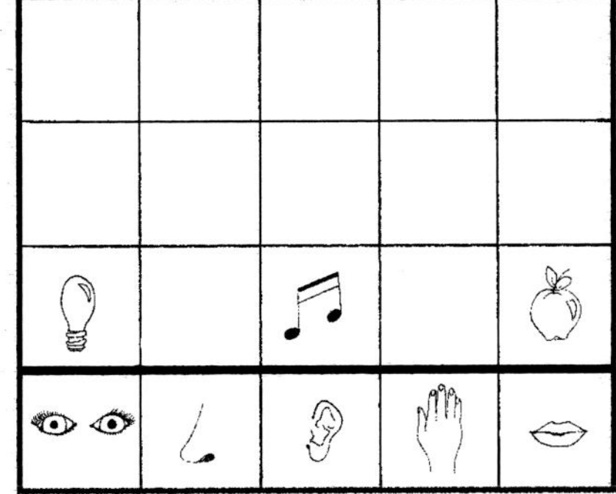

SEASONS OF SCIENCE

Wonderful Winter

As an option, use these topics and lessons to teach seasonal science during the winter months.

TOPICS	LESSONS	SPECIAL DATES*
	NOVEMBER – DECEMBER	
▶ Winter	**UNIT D Chapter 2, Lesson 6** What Is Winter?	**Nov. 10 NATIONAL YOUNG READERS DAY** Have children select books about winter for you to read aloud. Children can act out or draw a winter scene.
▶ Day and Night	**UNIT D Chapter 2, Lesson 2** Why Do We Have Day and Night?	**about Dec. 21 FIRST DAY OF WINTER** Help children make welcome cards for winter. **Dec. 25 CHRISTMAS DAY** **Dec. 26 KWANZAA** *Note: Check a calendar for dates of holidays such as Hanukkah.*
	DECEMBER – JANUARY	
▶ Kinds of Animals	**UNIT A Chapter 3, Lesson 2** What Are Some Kinds of Animals? **UNIT B Chapter 2, Lesson 1** What Lives in a Forest?	**Jan. NATIONAL SOUP MONTH** Tell or read aloud the story *Stone Soup*. Talk about water as an ingredient. **Jan. 11 NATIONAL THANK-YOU DAY** Talk about this form of politeness. Together, write a class thank-you letter to someone whom children recognize as helping them with science activities, such as a volunteer.
▶ Plants	**UNIT A Chapter 2, Lesson 2** How Do Plants Grow? **UNIT B Chapter 1, Lesson 1** How Do Animals Need Plants?	**Jan. 18 DR. MARTIN LUTHER KING, JR.'S BIRTHDAY**
	JANUARY – FEBRUARY	
▶ Deserts	**UNIT B Chapter 2, Lesson 2** What Lives in the Desert?	**Feb. NATIONAL WILDBIRD FEEDING MONTH** Children can make winter bird feeders.
▶ Oceans	**UNIT B Chapter 2, Lesson 4** What Lives in the Ocean?	**Feb. 2 GROUNDHOG DAY** Tell about this animal. Then discuss. the coming season and the many signs of spring children can look for. **Feb. 14 VALENTINE'S DAY** **Feb. 15 PRESIDENTS' DAY**

*Check a calendar. Some dates may vary slightly from year to year.

Winter Activities

Shorter Days, Longer Nights

Objectives Observe the sky at night and record observations in a crayon-resist picture.

Materials white paper, white or yellow crayons, diluted black tempera paint, thick paintbrushes

During clear weather and a full-moon phase, ask children to observe the night sky at home. The next day, make a list on the board of what children observed. Tell them they will make night sky pictures.

1. Demonstrate how to press hard with the crayons to draw stars and a moon. Point out that the objects are hard to see on the white paper, just as the stars and the moon are hard to see in the sky during the day.
2. Have children predict what will happen when you paint over your entire paper with the diluted black paint. Model the procedure. Then let them make their own night skies.

Home Sweet Home

Objective Identify animals and their biomes.

Materials paper plates, brass fasteners, construction paper scraps for spinners, various animal magazines that can be cut, rulers, scissors, glue, teacher-made biome pictures of the forest, rain forest, desert, and ocean

1. Ask children to use a ruler to draw lines on their plates, dividing the plate into four sections like a pie. Tell them to cut animal pictures from magazines and to glue one animal in each section of the paper plate.
2. Show children how to make a spinning pointer for the center of the plate by using a brass fastener and an arrow cut from scrap construction paper.
3. Tell children to spin the pointer on their plate to each of the four different animals. They will name each animal and tell where it lives, matching it to biome pictures. Suggest that they give one detail as to how each animal has adapted to life in its biome.
4. Suggest that children trade their plates.

Terrific Terrarium

Objective Make a model of a biome.

Materials 2-liter plastic bottles, soil, rocks, small plants, glue, shells, small pieces of materials from nature

In advance, cut off the tops of the bottles.

1. Tell children to pour a small amount of soil into the bottom of a bottle and to place small plants in the soil.
2. Suggest that they add small items such as rocks or twigs.
3. Have children spray water onto the plants and soil.
4. Let them glue colorful shells or other natural items to the outside to personalize and decorate their container.
5. Ask children to record changes in plant growth in their journals.

Using the Text to Make a Mural

Objectives Gather and record information about the forest, rain forest, desert, and ocean.

Materials long strips of butcher paper; art materials; straw, twigs, leaves, shells, and other items from nature; textbook

Tell children they will make murals of the four biomes (forest, rain forest, desert, and ocean). List the biomes on the board.

1. Divide the class into four groups, one for each biome.
2. Tell children they will be making a mural. Twigs, leaves, and other items from nature can be glued to the murals to make them three-dimensional.
3. Encourage children to modify their murals throughout the year to show the animal families growing and the landscape changing.

SEASONS OF SCIENCE

Spectacular Spring

As an option, use these topics and lessons to teach seasonal science during the spring months.

TOPICS	LESSONS	SPECIAL DATES*
FEBRUARY – MARCH		
▶ **Spring**	**UNIT D Chapter 2, Lesson 3** What Is Spring?	**Feb. 5 WEATHERPERSON'S DAY** Discuss what weatherpeople do. Help children monitor sky conditions and temperature three times during the day.
▶ **Plant Parts**	**UNIT A Chapter 2, Lesson 1** What Are the Parts of a Plant?	**Feb. 15 PRESIDENTS' DAY** Have children observe your school's flag to find out how hard the wind blows. Children can make their own flags in class. **about Mar. 21 SPRING BEGINS** Help children make paper decorations for a spring parade.
MARCH – APRIL		
▶ **Investigating Water**	**UNIT A Chapter 2, Lesson 3** What Do Plants Need? **UNIT B Chapter 2, Lesson 3** What Lives in a Rain Forest?	**Mar. 11 JOHNNY APPLESEED DAY** Have apples for a snack. Children can observe and tell about the parts and different kinds they observe. Check for allergies.
▶ **Weather** 	**UNIT D Chapter 1, Lesson 1** What is Weather? **UNIT D Chapter 2, Lesson 1** What Can We See in the Sky?	**Apr. 5 EGG SALAD WEEK** Have children observe and tell whether eggs, celery, bread, and green peppers come from plants or animals. Then make egg salad sandwiches. Check for allergies.
APRIL – MAY		
▶ **Animals and Plants**	**UNIT B Chapter 1, Lesson 2** How Do Animals Help Plants?	**Apr. 11 WEEK OF THE OCEAN** Help children find out about salt water and how ocean plants and animals help us. List children's ideas, and have them draw pictures.
▶ **Rocks**	**UNIT C Chapter 1, Lesson 1** What Can We Observe About Rocks?	**Apr. 18 SKY AWARENESS WEEK** How does air help us? What do we see in the sky? Help children make mobiles that show their answers.

*Check a calendar. Some dates may vary slightly from year to year.

Spring Activities

Water Race

Objectives Predict and observe how water moves through different kinds of paper.

Materials varieties of paper such as newsprint, stationery, computer paper, paper towels, writing paper, drawing paper; water; plastic cups; hand lenses

Explain to children that inside the trees are tubes that carry water. The tubes move water from the roots to the tip of every branch. Remind children that paper comes from trees. Tell them they will have a race to see which kind of paper lets water move fastest.

1. Have children use a hand lens to examine the different kinds of paper. Children should note that the paper with the largest air spaces is the most porous and absorbs water the fastest.
2. Cut each kind of paper into strips about 1 inch by 5 inches. Put about one inch of water in each cup.
3. Have children place two different strips of paper in each cup. Have them predict in which kind of paper water will move faster and compare their prediction with the results.

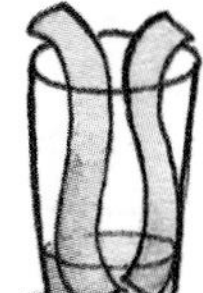

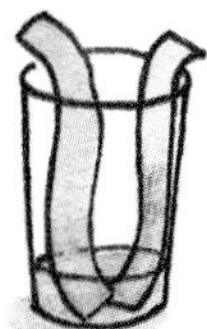

Observing Flowers

Objectives Observe and record the characteristics of different spring flowers.

Materials variety of real, silk, or plastic spring flowers; pencils; crayons or markers; drawing paper

1. Have children sit in small groups and appoint a leader for each group. Give each leader one flower.
2. Explain that the leader tells one fact about how the flower looks, feels, or smells and then passes the flower to the next person in the group. Each child takes a turn telling a new fact about the flower.
3. Have children draw a picture of their flower when they are done. Children can color their flowers and label the flowers' parts.
4. Put the drawings in a display next to the flowers.

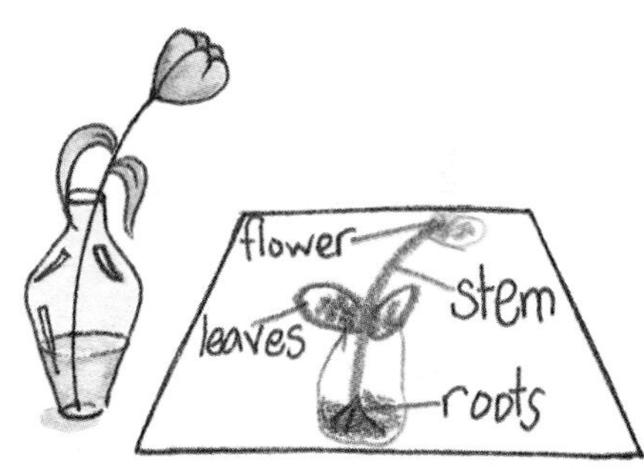

Soil Investigation

Objective Observe the components of different soils.

Materials different types of soil (rich topsoil, rocky soil, clay, sand) in plastic cups, pans, spoons

1. Ask children to take a cup of each soil, pour it in a pan, and examine it. They can use a spoon as a tool to help them observe the components of each type of soil.
2. Ask children to find the soil that would be best for growing plants and the soil that would be best for molding into a shape. Have them explain the reasons for their answers.

Colors of the Rainbow

Objective Predict and observe how different colors of clay will mix.

Materials red, yellow, and blue modeling clay; covered containers; cardboard; rainbow model

In advance, draw a rainbow showing the colors in the correct order.

1. Tell children to take a small sample of each color of clay and a small piece of cardboard.
2. They should mix some of the colors of clay together to make the colors of the rainbow. Other colors (red, yellow, and blue) can be used as they are.
3. Show children how to roll a small rope of each color. They place each of their ropes on their own piece of cardboard to make their clay rainbow.

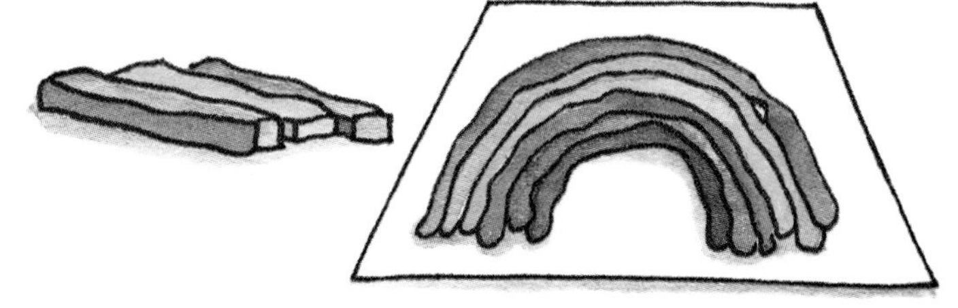

SEASONS OF SCIENCE

Super Summer

As an option, use these topics and lessons to teach seasonal science during the summer months.

TOPICS	LESSONS	SPECIAL DATES*
MAY – JUNE		
▶ **Movement** 	**UNIT F Chapter 1, Lesson 1** What Makes Things Move? **UNIT F Chapter 1, Lesson 3** Why Do Things Move the Way They Do?	**May 5 CINCO DE MAYO** **May 21 INTERNATIONAL PICKLE WEEK** Have children help you plan a summer picnic. Include pickles and cucumbers. Talk about how one is made from the other. Check for allergies.
▶ **Growing Plants**	**UNIT A Chapter 2, Lesson 2** How Do Plants Grow?	**June 21 FIRST DAY OF SUMMER** Children can fold paper accordian style and decorate to make fans. Talk about the warm weather coming and other ways to stay cool.
JUNE – JULY		
▶ **Magnets**	**UNIT F Chapter 2, Lesson 1** What Are Magnets? **UNIT F Chapter 2, Lesson 4** How Can You Make a Magnet?	**June 20 CARPENTER ANT AWARENESS WEEK** Find out and share information about ants and how they live in soil. **July 4 INDEPENDENCE DAY**
▶ **Water**	**UNIT E Chapter 1, Lesson 2** What Can We Observe About Liquids? 	**July 18 SPACE WEEK** Answer the frequently asked question "Why is the sky blue?" (Answer: Earth's air breaks up sunlight and makes it look blue. On the moon, where there is no air, the sky looks black.)
JULY – AUGUST		
▶ **Gravity and Other Forces**	**UNIT F Chapter 1, Lesson 2** What Are Some Ways Things Move?	**July 1 INTERNATIONAL JOKE DAY** Share these water jokes and riddles with children: • What can run but cannot walk? (water) • Why did the boy spill a glass of water? (He wanted to see a waterfall.) • When is the ocean the friendliest? (When it waves.)
▶ **Changes in Matter**	**UNIT E Chapter 1, Lesson 6** How Can We Change Objects?	

*Check a calendar. Some dates may vary slightly from year to year.

Summer Activities

Corn-y Riddles

Objective Draw conclusions from classmates' clues to identify corn products.

Materials picture of a corn plant; items containing corn, such as popcorn, corn chips, corn muffin mix, corn tortillas, canned corn, corn on the cob, cornhusk doll

1. Ask children to identify several of the items from the display.
2. Ask what the items have in common. Explain that every item comes from, or is made from, the corn plant.
3. Encourage a volunteer to be a riddler. He or she looks at all the items and asks a riddle about one of them. Keep the items in sight as children listen and respond to the clues. Remind the speaker not to look at the item and to give challenging clues.

Water Mazes

Objectives Plan and make models to observe the effect of gravity on flowing water.

Materials variety of materials through which water can flow, such as tubes, cardboard or vinyl pipes, straws, paper towel rolls; clay; water; washtubs

1. Divide the class into teams and give each team a washtub. Tell children they may use up to five of the available materials to construct a water maze. The object is to have water flow from the beginning of their maze to the end. Explain that there is no right or wrong solution to the problem.
2. After children have tested their maze with water, they can invite classmates to watch them demonstrate how it works.
3. Before teams dismantle their maze, have them record their work with sketches or diagrams and tell about problems they had and how they solved them.

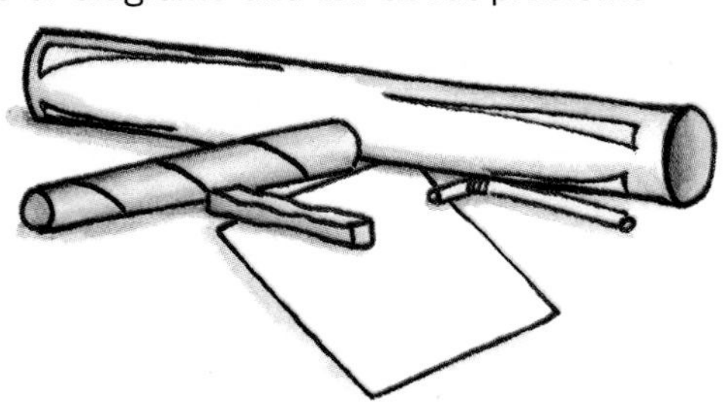

Magnet Fun

Objectives Gather and classify a variety of magnets.

Materials large magnetic board, various magnets, index cards, pencils

1. Tell children they will build a collection of magnets and classify them.
2. Ask children to think of a number they will use as their goal for the magnet collection. They will then try to collect that many magnets. They can use magnets from the classroom and, with permission, magnets from home.
3. Suggest that children sort the magnets each week as time permits. Have them write the method they used for sorting on an index card and place it on the table for others to use. Encourage them to develop new rules for sorting—for example by sizes or shapes.
4. Have children decide where the magnet board will be placed in the classroom so everyone can enjoy watching the collection grow.

Soil Layers

Objective Observe the layers of soil.

Materials soil, plastic jar with lid, water, drawing paper, pencils, crayons

1. Have children fill a plastic jar halfway with soil.
2. Ask children to add water to fill the jar.
3. Children should put the lid on the jar and shake the jar until the water and soil are mixed well.
4. Explain that they will need to place the bottle on a table and wait for the soil to settle.
5. Ask children to draw a picture to show what they observe.

Bibliography

Science Trade Books

Animals in Winter by Henrietta Bancroft (HarperCollins, 1997) describes the ways animals cope with winter. *NSTA Trade Book*

Apples, How They Grow by Bruce McMillan (Houghton Mifflin, 1979) explains the development of the apple. *NSTA Trade Book*

Autumn Across America by Seymour Simon (Hyperion, 1993) uses photos of trees to show autumn changes.

Balloons: Building and Experimenting with Inflatable Toys by Bernie Zubrowski (William Morrow, 1990) tells how to use inflatable balloons to power different homemade toys.

Be a Friend to Trees by Patricia Lauber (HarperCollins, 1994) describes many ways that plants and animals use trees to meet their needs.

Beautiful Bats by Linda Glaser (Millbrook, 1997) describes the habits and characteristics of bats.

The Big Balloon Race by Eleanor Coerr (HarperCrest, 1992) tells of a historic flight of balloonist Carlotta Myers.

Big Band Sound by Harriett Diller (Boyds Mills, 1996) tells how a young girl makes her own drum set from recycled materials.

Cactus by Carol Lerner (HarperCollins, 1996) details the concept of food chains and shows how plants and animals need one another. *NSTA Trade Book*

Cactus Hotel by Brenda Z. Guiberson (Henry Holt, 1991) describes the saguaro cactus and its role as a home for desert animals. *NSTA Trade Book*

Cars and Trucks and Other Vehicles by Claude Delafosse (Cartwheel Books, 1996) explains the important parts of cars and other vehicles.

The Cloud Book by Tomie dePaola (Holiday House, 1985) introduces the common types of clouds and what they can tell us about weather changes.

Cloudy With a Chance of Meatballs by Judi Barrett (Aladdin, 1982) tells of "delicious" weather words and what they mean. *Children's Choice*

Coral Reef: A City That Never Sleeps by Mary M. Cerullo (Cobblehill, 1996) explains how ocean plants and animals are adapted to live in these "cities in the sea."

Crab Moon by Ruth Horowitz (Candlewick Press, 2000) tells of a young boy who observes horseshoe crabs coming ashore to lay eggs on a June night.

The Crazy Quilt by Kristin Avery (Addison-Wesley, 1994) is an easy picture book that can be used to foster discussion on recycling.

The Desert Fox Family Book by Hans Gerold Laukel (North-South, 1999) follows a mother desert fox and her young in the desert. *NSTA Trade Book*

Doctor De Soto by William Steig (Farrar, Straus & Giroux, 1990) explains how to use simple machines to do dental work on larger patients when you are a mouse.

Dwight and the Trilobite by Kelli C. Foster and Gina C. Erickson (Forest House, 1994) tells about Mrs. Knight and her son Dwight who take a desert walk to find a trilobite.

Electricity and Magnetism by Maria Gordon (Thomson Learning, 1996) uses activities to help children to learn first-hand about magnetism.

Everybody Needs a Rock by Byrd Baylor (Aladdin, 1987) provides rules for finding the perfect rock to have fun with.

Experiments with Magnets by Helen J. Challand (Childrens Press, 1986) provides step-by-step instructions for simple investigations.

Feel the Wind by Arthur Dorros (Turtleback, 2000) describes conditions needed to make different kinds of wind, from light breezes to hurricanes. *NSTA Trade Book*

The Fisherman and His Wife by Brothers Grimm (Farrar, Straus & Giroux, 1987) is the classic tale of the fisherman who frees a fish, receives a reward, and then keeps returning to the fish to ask for more and more. *ALA Notable*

***The Flower: An Ecology Story Book* (The Ecology Series)** by Chris Baines (Crocodile Books, 1998) features two children who plant a flower and learn how it grows.

***Flowers, Trees, and Fruits* (Young Discoverers: Biology Facts and Experiments Series)** by Sally Morgan (Kingfisher, 1996) provides basic information about the structure, uses, and growth of plants, accompanied by a variety of experiments.

Forces and Movement by Peter D. Riley (Franklin Watts, 1998) tells about pushing and pulling forces that make things start, stop, slow down, stick, and slip.

Fossils Tell of Long Ago by Aliki (HarperTrophy, 1990) explains how fossils can give us clues about the past, and tells how they are formed. *NSTA Trade Book*

Fox by Mary Ling (Dorling Kindersley, 1992) follows every stage of a fox's development from its birth to its independence.

Frogs by Gail Gibbons (Holiday House, 1994) describes frogs, how their bodies change, the sounds they make, and how they are different from toads.

From Caterpillar to Butterfly by Deborah Heiligham (HarperCollins, 1996) explains the metamorphosis of caterpillar to butterfly. *NSTA Trade Book*

The Goat in the Rug by Charles L. Blood and Martin Link (Simon & Schuster, 1976) describes the steps, including clipping, dyeing, and weaving of mohair, in making a Navajo rug. *NCSS Trade Book*

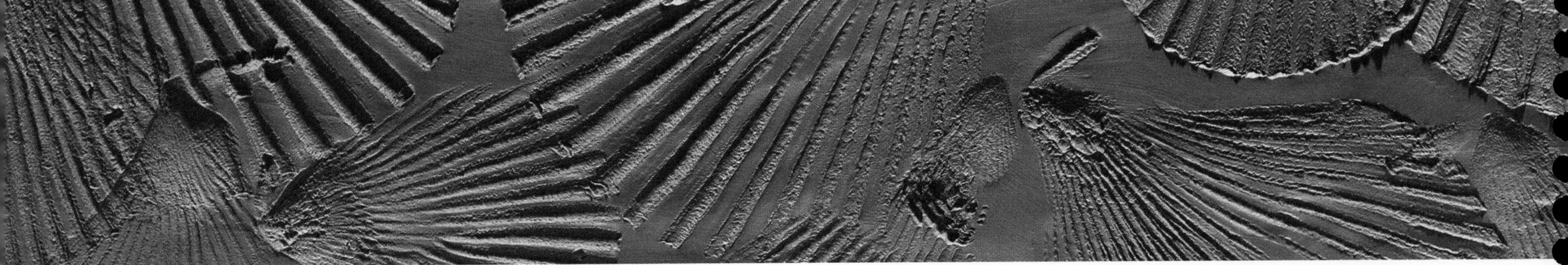

Grandpa's Soup by Eiko Kadono (Eerdmans Books for Young Readers, 1999) tells about the making of Grandpa's soup and the sharing of it with friends.

The Great Trash Bash by Loreen Leedy (Holiday House, 1991) has the animals of Beaston learning how to recycle and control their trash.

The Grumpalump by Sarah Hayes (Clarion, 1990) tells how a small group of animals roll, shove, pull, whack, and finally inflate the Grumpalump to change it into a hot air-balloon.

Hearing Sounds by Gary Gibson (Aladdin, 1994) explains interesting sound facts and suggests easy scientific activities.

The Honey Makers by Gail Gibbons (William Morrow, 1997) describes honeybees, their colonies, and how they produce honey.

How Animals Care for Their Babies by Roger B. Hirschland (National Geographic Society, 1996) provides information about the ways in which animal parents care for their young.

How Do You Know It's Fall? by Allan Fowler (Childrens Press, 1992) includes key observations to help readers answer the question.

I Wonder Why Trees Have Leaves and Other Questions About Plants by Andrew Charman (Kingfisher, 1997) is a resource that answers children's everyday questions.

If You Are a Hunter of Fossils by Byrd Baylor (Aladdin, 1984) describes how a mountain looked when it was an ancient sea.

Inclined Planes by Michael Dahl (Bridgestone Books, 1996) uses photos and simple text to show different examples of inclined planes and how they help things move.

The Insect Book: A Basic Guide to the Collection and Care of Common Insects for Young Children by Connie Zakowski (Rainbow, 1997) provides simple information for keeping insects for observation.

Insect Metamorphosis: From Egg to Adult by Ron and Nancy Goor (Atheneum, 1991) illustrates examples of both complete and incomplete metamorphosis.

Jody's Beans by Malachy Doyle (Candlewick, 1999) Tells how, with the help of her grandfather, Jody learns about seeds and plants in her garden. *Notable Social Studies Trade Book*

June 29, 1999 by David Wiesner (Clarion, 1992) tells of a child who tries to grow her class-project seeds in a most unusual way. *ALA Notable*

Just a Dream by Chris Van Allsburg (Houghton Mifflin, 1990) tells how Walter finally understands the importance of caring for the environment. *NSTA Trade Book*

Lemonade for Sale by Stuart J. Murphy (HarperCollins, 1998) tells how the Elm Street Kids' Club makes lemonade to make money. This book can also be used as a springboard to discuss math concepts such as graphing.

Look at the Moon by May Garelick (Mondo, 1996) Does the same moon shine on all parts of the world? This journey in verse explains.

Machines We Use by Sally Hewitt (Childrens Press, 1998) provides information about simple machines and experiments for children to try.

The Magic School Bus at the Waterworks by Joanna Cole (Scholastic, 1986) describes the different processes that are used to make water drinkable.

Magnetism by John Woodruff (Steck-Vaughn, 1998) uses easy activities that can be done at home to explain magnetism.

Magnets and Sparks by Wendy Madgwick (Steck-Vaughn, 1999) demonstrates the properties and uses of magnets and electricity.

Mary Anning: Fossil Hunter by Sally M. Walker (CarolRhoda Books, 2001) is the story of Mary Anning who found many fossils in nineteenth-century England.

Max Found Two Sticks by Brian Pinkney (Simon & Schuster, 1997) finds a young boy responding to questions by drumming on various objects.

The Mitten by Jan Brett (Putnam, 1996) is an adaptation of a Ukrainian folktale about a mitten that is lost in the snow and becomes home for woodland creatures.

Moon Rope by Lois Ehlert (Harcourt, 1992) is an adaptation of a Peruvian folktale in which the animals try to climb to the moon.

Mrs. Toggle's Zipper by Robin Pulver (Aladdin, 1993) tells how Mrs. Toggle's zipper gets stuck and traps her inside her coat.

Mushroom in the Rain by Mirra Ginsburg (Aladdin, 1997) explains how a mushroom can shelter many woodland creatures. *ALA Notable*

My Five Senses by Margaret Miller (Simon & Schuster, 1994) is a simple introduction to the five senses and how they help us. *NSTA Trade Book*

Nature's Green Umbrella: Tropical Rain Forests by Gail Gibbons (William Morrow, 1995) explains the tropical rain forests' ecosystems and discusses preservation and protection. *Children's Choice*

Oceans by Seymour Simon (Mulberry, 1997) contains clear, concise text and excellent photos that explore our enormous ocean world.

Paper, Paper Everywhere by Gail Gibbons (Voyager, 1997) explains how paper is made. *Children's Choice*

Planting a Rainbow by Lois Ehlert (Raintree, 1999) introduces children to seeds and flowers. *NSTA Trade Book*

Pond Year by Kathryn Lasky (Candlewick, 1995) describes how two girls explore a pond and discover tadpoles in summer and ice in the winter.

The Puddle by David McPhail (Farrar, Straus & Giroux, 2000) explains the water cycle and what happens to a puddle when the sun comes out.

A Raindrop Hit My Nose by Ray Butrum (Multnomah, 1998) explains where the raindrop came from and where it is going.

Rainsong/Snowsong by Philemon Sturges (North-South, 1995) describes with illustrations and rhyming text the joys of playing in the rain and snow.

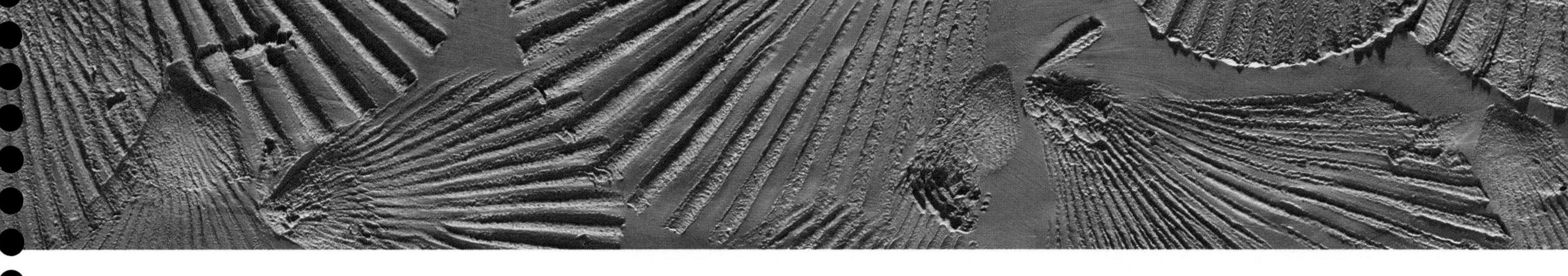

Recycle! A Handbook for Kids by Gail Gibbons (Little, Brown, 1992) explains from start to finish the process of recycling materials into new products. *NSTA Trade Book*

The Rose in My Garden by Arnold Lobel (Greenwillow, 1984) explains ways animals rely on plants. *School Library Journal*

The Salamander Room by Anne Mazer (Knopf, 1991) explains how a child reinvents a forest environment for his salamander as he thinks about what it needs to survive.

The Science Book of Air by Neil Ardley (Harcourt, 1991) uses colorful photos and illustrations to provide background information and activities that enhance important concepts.

The Science Book of Magnets by Neil Ardley (Harcourt, 1991) is a simple book of experiments that demonstrate magnetism.

The Science Book of Motion by Neil Ardley (Harcourt, 1992) offers a variety of different activities that help explore how things move.

Science with Magnets by Helen Edom (EDC Publications, 1999) explains the properties and principles of magnetism and contains hands-on activities for children.

Solids and Liquids by David Glover (Kingfisher, 1993) looks at the makeup of solids and liquids and includes experiments.

Song and Dance Man by Karen Ackerman (Knopf, 1992) tells of the relationship between children and their grandfather, a former vaudevillian. *ALA Notable*

Sounds All Around by Wendy Pfeffer (HarperCollins, 1999) explains how sound waves travel through the air and are picked up by tiny bones in the ear.

The Squirrel and the Moon by Eleonore Schmid (North-South, 1996) describes a young squirrel's fascination with the moon.

Stop, Look & Listen by Sarah A. Williamson (Williamson Publishing, 1996) provides simple text and activities that focus on using the senses.

Storms by Seymour Simon (Morrow Junior Books, 1989) describes conditions in the atmosphere that cause storms such as hurricanes, tornadoes, and hailstorms.

Summer by Ron Hirschi (Cobblehill, 1991) is one of four books by the author that use photographs to describe each of the four seasons.

Sunken Treasure by Gail Gibbons (HarperCollins, 1988) looks at why ships sink and explores ways to recover them as well as their cargo.

Sunshine Makes the Seasons by Franklyn M. Branley (HarperCollins, 1985) explains why sunlight and the Earth's tilted axis cause seasons. *NSTA Trade Book*

Those Amazing Ants by Patricia B. Demuth (Macmillan, 1994) describes those fascinating insects, the ants, in simple text and pictures. *NSTA Trade Book*

Thump, Thump, Rat-a-Tat-Tat by Gene Baer (HarperCollins, 1989) has the sounds of a distant marching band growing larger and louder as it approaches.

Thunder Cake by Patricia Polacco (Putnam, 1990) tells about thunderstorms and shows how to overcome fear of them. *Notable Trade Book for the Language Arts*

The Tiny Seed by Eric Carle (Picture Book Studio, 1987) tells the story of the life cycle of a flower in terms of the adventures of a seed.

Train Song by Diane Siebert (HarperCollins, 1993) provides a nostalgic look at trains. *ALA Notable*

Tropical Rain Forests by Emilie U. Lepthien (Childrens Press, 1993) provides an overview of rain forest ecology.

Twilight Comes Twice by Ralph Fletcher (Houghton Mifflin, 1997) tells in beautiful, poetic prose some activities that occur at dusk and dawn.

The Ugly Duckling by Hans Christian Andersen (Greenwillow, 1985) is the classic fable of how an ugly duckling grows into a swan.

The Velveteen Rabbit by Margery Williams (Camelot, 1996) describes how a boy's love for his stuffed rabbit turns the rabbit into a living thing.

Very Last First Time: An Inuit Tale by Jan Andrews (Simon & Schuster, 1998) tells how an Inuit girl explores a cave of sea ice formed at low tide on the seacoast of Northern Canada.

Water by Diane McClymont (Garret Educational, 1991) tells about where our water comes from and how we use it, including problems we may face in the future and possible ways to solve them.

Weather Forecasting by Gail Gibbons (Simon & Schuster, 1993) describes weather forecasting tools and the people who use them. *NSTA Trade Book*

Weather Words and What They Mean by Gail Gibbons (Holiday House, 1990) explains basic weather words and what they mean.

What Is the World Made Of? by Kathleen Weidner Zoelfeld (HarperCollins, 1998) provides hands-on examples to show how matter can change.

***What Magnets Can Do* (Rookie Read-Aloud Science)** by Allan Fowler (Childrens Press, 1995) helps children discover what magnets can do.

What Makes Day and Night by Franklyn M. Branley (HarperCollins, 1996) is an easy-to-follow description of how the rotation of Earth causes day and night.

The Wheeling and Whirling-Around Book by Judy Hindley (Candlewick, 1996) explains the things in our world that go round and round.

Wheels and Axles by Michael S. Dahl (Bridgestone Books, 1996) describes uses of wheels.

The Wheels on the Bus by Maryann Kovalski (Little, Brown, 1990) discusses moving parts.

Who Eats What? by Patricia Lauber (HarperCollins, 1995) explains food chains and shows how plants, animals and humans need one another. *NSTA Trade Book*

Wonderful Worms by Linda Glaser (Millbrook, 1992) describes the vital role worms play in the planet's ecosystem. *NSTA Trade Book*

Soaring Into Space

Bernard A. Harris, Jr., M.D.

Dr. Bernard Harris, a **Harcourt Science** *advisor, tells how his boyhood dream of exploring space became a lifelong adventure. Through his efforts to reach the stars, he became a medical doctor and an astronaut. He served on two space shuttle missions and holds the distinction of being the first African American to "walk" in space. In this article, Dr. Harris tells his story of pursuing his dream, and he invites students to participate in space exploration so they can share in the excitement and challenges it brings. He also stresses how important science education is to the future of our nation.*

Pursuing My Dream

I was born in Texas, but at the age of seven I was transported to the Navajo Indian reservation in New Mexico and Arizona. My mother was an educator who taught at the boarding schools on the reservation. She was a wonderful teacher who instilled in her students and her own children the value of a good education.

It was out there, under starry skies on the great plains of the Navajo nation, that I conceived my dream of becoming an astronaut. On television I watched the American space program develop before my eyes and was fascinated by what I saw. Young men were risking their lives for their country in order to win the crown of being the first person on the moon. The space program provided an outlet for my imagination. I watched every television program and read every book about space that I could. I explored the future through the creative writings of authors like H.G. Wells, Isaac Asimov, and Jules Verne.

Science is a natural vehicle for inspiring children to learn. For me as a child, studying how humans transcended earthly bounds to get into space inspired me to learn more about many fields of science. When I took imaginary trips through space, I was inspired to learn about astronomy. I sought answers to questions such as "How do the astronauts use the positions of the stars to navigate their vessels?" I learned about the human body after asking questions such as "How do people survive in the harsh environment of space?" I learned about advances in technology through questions such as "How do the basic requirements for survival in space lead to scientific discoveries?" These questions and others inspired me to look deeper into the science of the universe.

While I was in middle school, I set my goal to become an astronaut. In high school, I discovered that I could pursue two of my interests—medicine and spaceflight. I chose to follow in the footsteps of medical doctors who worked in space medicine. I obtained a bachelor's degree and an M.D. degree, completed a residency in internal medicine at the Mayo Clinic, and then set my sights on space.

I joined NASA as a flight surgeon in 1987 and became an astronaut in 1990. I am a veteran of two spaceflights, having logged more than 438 hours in space and traveled more than 7.2 million miles.

The Role of Educators

The role of educators has been critical in my life. They assisted me in my personal development and in my preparation for a career in medicine and space. Just as the teachers of my past helped me to reach my goals, the

During both of my missions, I conducted research in life science, materials science, and astronomy. The shuttle crews and I completed over 150 investigations during three weeks in space. The results of our investigations contributed to the ever-growing pool of knowledge about space and the world in which we live. ▼

NASA photo

My view from space was incredibly beautiful. I could see Earth as our home planet and appreciate its position in our galaxy. The unique vantage point of space enhances our understanding of who we humans are and helps us learn about our place in the universe. ▶
NASA photo

teachers of today have the power to shape the scientific future of our nation. Among today's students are the scientists, physicians, and astronauts of tomorrow. For those students, education is the passport to their future.

As an astronaut who is concerned about the education of our youth, I utilize every opportunity to highlight the importance of space and science education. I continue to rely on education to reach my goals by seeking additional advanced college degrees. My belief in education has come from the educators in my life. A teacher has the power to open a child's mind to life's possibilities. Once a child's mind is opened, the sky is the limit!

The STARS Academy™

One way to open children's minds to science and all areas of learning is to get them involved in a hands-on, interactive education program. The STARS Academy, presenting space-based and earth-based multidisciplinary adventures via the Internet, is such a program.

Students participate in experiments on the International Space Station and the Space Shuttle through pictures, interactive activities, and video. Comparing information from the weightless environment of space, they conduct classroom experiments and form hypotheses about what they think will happen in space. STARS Academy students have studied orb spiders, butterflies, ladybugs, and most recently, an entire aquatic ecosystem.

Academy members also explore problems here on Earth – tracking and protecting endangered species, for example – and the role space technology plays. By exchanging research ideas and cultural information online, STARS Academy students throughout the world work together to create solutions for the future. The STARS Academy online program also makes today's technologies more accessible and exciting for students and teachers alike.

For more information visit the STARS Academy website.

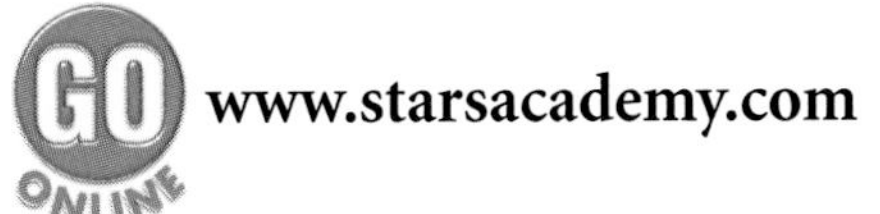

Students from Beijing, China, study silkworms in preparation for the STS-107 space shuttle mission.

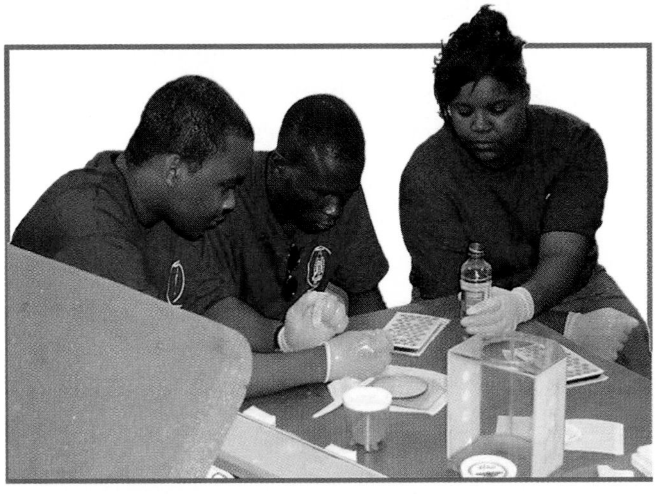

Students from Albany, Georgia, prepare their butterfly experiment for the STS-93 space shuttle mission.

Student photos courtesy of SPACEHAB, Inc.

Tips and Trash-Pile Treasures

By Carol Valenta

When materials for science activities are difficult to obtain or too expensive for your budget, you can find acceptable and less expensive substitutes in unlikely places. You may want to include the following list of tips, activity ideas, and trash-pile "treasures" as a supplement to your file of materials and ideas.

Activity Place Mats

Have students make large place mats out of newsprint to help them organize and account for materials during activities. Provide each team with a large sheet of newsprint and a marker. As you show students a sample of each item they will receive, have them draw and label on the newsprint a box where they can place the item.

Plastic Bottles

Make a terrarium from a 2-liter bottle by removing the label and cutting off the top. Fill a clean butter tub with soil, and plant seeds or small plants. Cover the plants by inserting the clear plastic "dome" into the soil.

Other ways to use 2-liter bottles include these:

Funnel	Save the top that was cut off while making the terrarium.
Aquarium	Place the bottle on its side, and stabilize with clay or cutout boxes.
Planter	Place the bottle on its side, stabilize with clay or cutout boxes, and cut out the new "top half."
Bird Feeder	Cut out windows around the side, and push disposable chopsticks through the bottle to serve as perches.

Disposable Microscope Slides

Cut an index card into five strips that are each 3 inches long. Use a paper punch to make a hole in the middle of each strip. Place transparent tape over each hole. The adhesive on the opposite side can be used to hold small crystals, tiny insects, hairs, and so on. Place these "slides" on the microscope or hold them up for viewing with a hand lens.

Disposable Spoons

When you need to conserve materials and avoid contamination of substances, use large wooden tongue depressors as disposable spoons. Mark a line to indicate how far to "fill."

Substitute Droppers

Oil, soap, and acids are often hard to remove from droppers and leave them contaminated. When precision in measuring is not necessary, substitute drinking straws for droppers. Put one end of the straw into the liquid, and cover the other end with a finger. Move the straw to the desired location, and remove the finger. Students need practice to perfect these movements.

Standard Masses

When multiple standard masses are needed for weighing, use the following: paper clips (plastic or metal), individual staples (ends folded), toothpicks, small uniform tiles, full aluminum soft drink cans, milliliters of water (1 mL to 1 g), or coins.

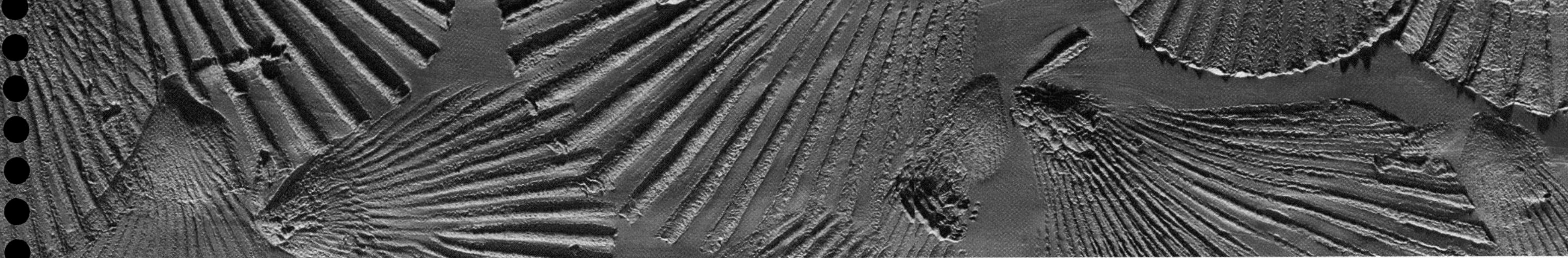

Saturated Solutions

Many household substances are fine crystals or salts that can be dissolved in water to form saturated solutions. Some examples are table salt, Epsom salts, alum crystals, and sugar.

To make a saturated solution, heat water in a coffee maker and store in a thermos until ready to use. Pour the hot water into a large plastic foam cup until it is half full. Using a small spoon, stir in one spoonful of crystals at a time until no more will dissolve. The solution is saturated at that temperature when no more will dissolve. Since hot water dissolves more of the solid than cool water, crystals form as the solution cools.

Soap-Bubble Solutions

Soap-bubble solutions may need to be used with care in the classroom but can be explored with great abandon outdoors. In a large plastic dishpan, mix the following:

4 parts water

2 parts liquid detergent

1 part corn syrup

1 part glycerine

Use plastic coat hangers, small plastic-mesh fruit and vegetable baskets, or the plastic holders from six-packs of canned drinks as frames for making bubbles.

Crystal Snow Scenes

Make a saturated solution of Epsom salts (magnesium sulfate) to create crystal snow scenes that form while you watch. Paint snowflakes and snow scenes on dark-colored paper with an old paintbrush dipped in the solution. Set the drawings aside to dry. Although the crystals that form are easily visible, it is better to view them through a hand lens.

Shapely Crystals

Make a saturated alum solution. (Alum can be purchased at a pharmacy.) Pour the solution into a glass jar.

Use a 15-cm length of colored chenille stick to create an interesting shape, and suspend it from a pencil with a piece of sewing thread. Then completely submerge the shape in the saturated alum solution. As the solution cools, crystals will form. A faint tint of the color from the chenille stick will show through the crystals.

Salt-Crystal Fantasies

Make a saturated solution of table salt. Place the solution in a small open plastic tub, and set it aside where it will be exposed to air. Check frequently. Fluffy salt crystals form as evaporation takes place. These crystals are similar to those that form on wood near the ocean.

Amorphous Starch Stuff

There are many ways to make this amazing goo that acts like a liquid one minute and a solid the next. The following version allows students to observe the changes.

Fill paper cups or empty yogurt containers approximately one-third full with cornstarch. Have students slowly add water colored with food coloring to the cornstarch, one small spoonful at a time, and stir the mixture. Have them stop adding water when the mixture first has liquid properties. When their mixture is about 2 parts cornstarch and 1 part colored water, it should be runny but thick enough to roll into a ball.

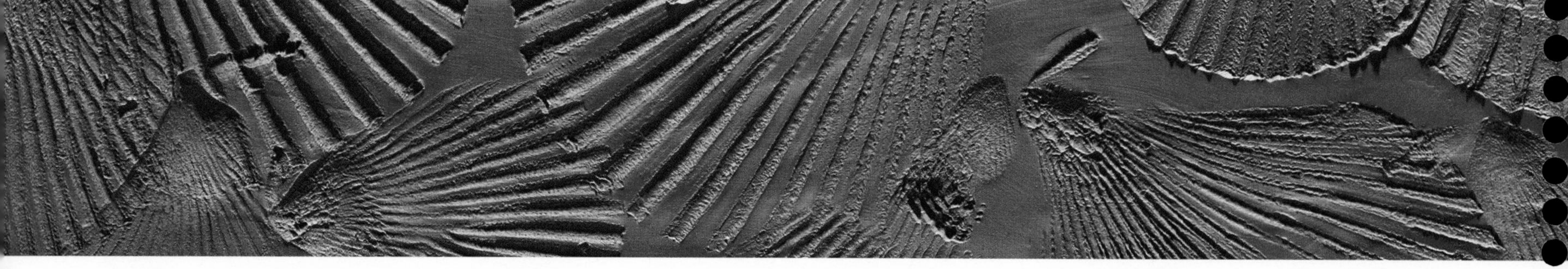

Kitchen Indicators

Tea is an indicator for acids and bases. Adding lemon juice, an acid, to tea lightens the color of tea. Adding any base, such as baking soda, darkens the color.

Red cabbage juice and grape juice can also be used as indicators for acids and bases. Make an indicator with cabbage juice by chopping up several red cabbage leaves and soaking them for an hour in very hot water. The juice turns red in an acid and blue in a base.

Testing for Starch

A dilute iodine solution can be used to test for starch. Slowly add tincture of iodine, available at drugstores, to about 250 mL of water. Stop adding drops when the solution is about the tint of filtered apple juice. This works with any strength of iodine. Store this solution in dark dropper bottles or away from the light. Have students wash their hands after use.

Starchy Papers and Vanishing Art

Use a dilute iodine solution to test and classify paper scraps for starch. Collect a wide variety of papers—notebook and typing paper, napkins, and so on.

Place a small sample of paper on foil or wax paper and test with a drop of dilute iodine solution. A change to bluish-black indicates the presence of starch.

Make two more iodine solutions of different strengths that are stronger than the first solution. Paint them on paper containing starch. Hang this monochromatic "artwork" in a brightly lighted place.

Substitutes for Iron Filings

Plain, unsoaped steel wool can be used as a substitute for iron filings. Cover the table with newspaper, and cut the steel wool into fine shreds using yard clippers or old scissors. Pour these shreds into storage containers.

For larger-size pieces, use a stapler to punch out individual staples until you have a large supply. These have a small enough mass to be attracted by a magnet and align with the magnetic field.

Magnet Sources

Small magnets, such as refrigerator magnets, are used in electromagnets. Electronics supply stores are excellent sources for small, inexpensive magnets.

Lemon Lights

Lemons can function as chemical cells. Push a probe made from a steel paper clip into the lemon. About 1 cm away from the first probe, push in a second probe made from a brass thumbtack. Attach a very fine insulated copper wire to the probes to complete the circuit. Students can try other combinations of metal to explore the changes in potential energy. To test the circuit, use a holiday cool light or bring a compass close to it.

Little Lights

Strings of holiday lights are a good source of cool lights for activities. An old string of lights can be cut apart to provide enough lights for the whole class. This is an easy item for families to donate.

To separate the bulbs, simply cut the wire midway between each light. Then use wire cutters or scissors to carefully remove about 1 cm of insulation from the ends of the wires coming from each bulb.

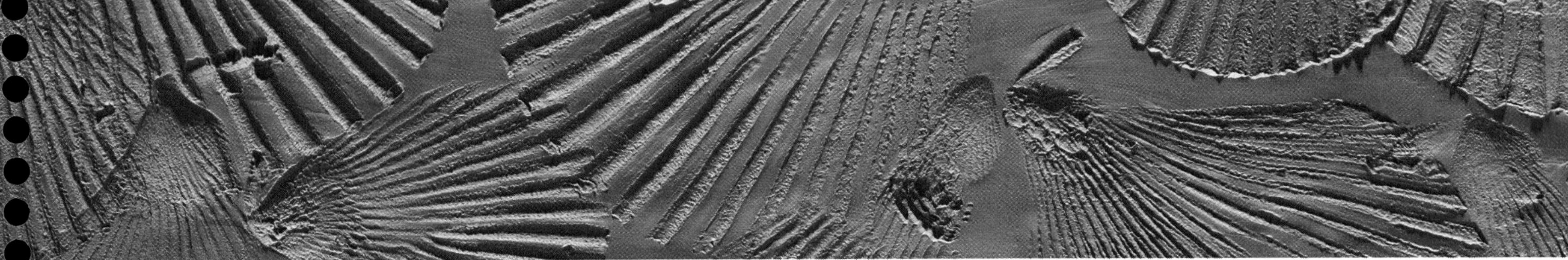

Circuit Stand-Ins

The following items can be used to substitute for parts of circuits:

Wire	Place a narrow transparent tape down the center of a 2.5 cm by 30 cm strip of aluminum foil. Fold the foil over the tape to form as narrow a strip as possible.
Bulb Holder	Wooden spring-clip clothespins can be used to attach wire and bulbs together and to hold the bulbs.
Batteries	Wide rubber bands make good battery holders, securing wires to the cells and offering flexibility.
Clips	Small metal clips for holding hair can be used in place of alligator clips in making circuits.

Great Gears

Glue strips of corrugated paper, with the "bumps" out, around the outside edges of plastic lids from jars or plastic tubs to model gears for experimentation. Other strips of corrugated paper can be used as pulleys when the ends are fastened together to form a ring. Old-fashioned soft-drink bottle tops can also be used as gears.

Pendulum Patterns

A liquid detergent bottle half-filled with sand and suspended can be used as a pendulum to demonstrate patterns of motion.

"Eggciting" CO_2

Place several eggshells in a zip-type clear plastic bag. Use a can, rolling pin, or dowel to crush the shells. Pour the shells into a 1-liter plastic bottle. Add vinegar, and cover the bottle opening with a balloon. Carbon dioxide will form and inflate the balloon. Seashell chips and small pieces of broken chalk will work also.

Terrific Timers

Place an aluminum pie plate in a plastic dishpan. From a string over the pie plate, suspend a large plastic bottle filled with water. Find the lowest part of the bottle. Use a thumbtack or T-pin to make a hole at this low point. Enlarge the hole as necessary until one drop at a time falls to hit the pan. Count the drops in a given period of time to establish a benchmark unit of time, such as 10 drops in 15 seconds.

Colored Light Gels

Gelatin can be used to create brightly colored gels for light experiments. Dissolve one envelope of unflavored gelatin in 3 tablespoons of boiling water in a heat-resistant glass bowl. Stir until the gelatin is dissolved, and then add 2 or 3 drops of food coloring. Pour into margarine tub lids or other similar lids, to a depth of about 1 cm. Allow the gels to dry several days until hard.

Index

Note: Page numbers in boldface indicate pages in the *Teacher's Edition*. All other page numbers refer to pages in the *Student Edition*, which are reproduced in this guide.

N

O

P

S

National Science Education Standards

The Science Content Standards, which are within the National Science Education Standards, outline what students should know, understand, and be able to do in the natural sciences for grades Kindergarten through 8. The Standards are broken into two grade-level sets: standards for grades K-4, and standards for grades 5-8. The following chart shows where in *Harcourt Science* Standards are met at grades K-3. Some of the K-4 standards are met in *Harcourt Science,* Grade 4. Please consult the Teacher's Editions for grades 4-6 for correlations to the Standards for other grade levels of *Harcourt Science*. For more information about the Standards, please see pages T8-T9.

National Science Education Standards, Grades K-4		Harcourt Science Teacher Edition pages, Grades K-3
PHYSICAL SCIENCE		
Properties of Objects and Materials	Objects have many observable properties, including size, weight, shape, color, temperature, and the ability to react with other substances. Those properties can be measured using tools, such as rulers, balances, and thermometers.	**Grade K:** B45-B47, E18-E23 **Grade 1:** *22, A4, C4-C7, C17, C46, E8, E24-E28, R2-R8 **Grade 2:** *16, *22, A14-A17, A21, A23-A24, E7, E9-E24, R2-R8, R16 **Grade 3:** xxii, B43. C5-C8, C12-C15, D28-D29, E4-E5, E6-E12, E20-E28, E33, E44-E48, E53, R2-R8
	Objects are made of one or more materials, such as paper, wood, and metal. Objects can be described by the properties of the materials from which they are made, and those properties can be used to separate or sort a group of objects or materials.	**Grade K:** E8-E9, E10-E17, E18-E25 **Grade 1:** E5-E10 **Grade 2:** E31-E36, E45-E47 **Grade 3:** C7, E4-E5, E33, E38-E41, F28-F29
	Materials can exist in different states—solid, liquid, and gas. Some common materials, such as water, can be changed from one state to another by heating or cooling.	**Grade K:** E18, E32, E35, F30-F36, F38-F43 **Grade 1:** C29-C31, E5-E10, E16-E18, E20-E23, E24-E28 **Grade 2:** E5-E6, E9-E25, E38-E43, E55-E56 **Grade 3:** C14-C15, E11-E12, E14-E18, E33
Position and Motion of Objects	The position of an object can be described by locating it relative to another object or the background.	**Grade K:** E26-E31 **Grade 1:** E51 **Grade 2:** D8-D11, D16-D17, D20-D21, D62-D63 **Grade 3:** D74-D77, F67, F72-F73
	An object's motion can be described by tracing and measuring its position over time.	**Grade K:** E26, E46-E53 **Grade 2:** D1, D20-D21, D62-D63, F18 **Grade 3:** D74-D77, F67
	The position and motion of objects can be changed by pushing or pulling. The size of the change is related to the strength of the push or pull.	**Grade K:** E26, E46-E53 **Grade 1:** F4-F21, F22-F25, F29 **Grade 2:** F5-F11, F18-F23 **Grade 3:** F28-F29, F64-F69, F72-F73, F76-F80
	Sound is produced by vibrating objects. The pitch of the sound can be varied by changing the rate of vibration.	**Grade 1:** E34-E53 **Grade 2:** F28-F45 **Grade 3:** F19, F31
Light, Heat, Electricity, and Magnetism	Light travels in a straight line until it strikes an object.	**Grade K:** E40 **Grade 1:** D30, D32 **Grade 2:** D4, D16-D17 **Grade 3:** D70, D78-D81, D85, F8
	Light can be reflected by a mirror, refracted by a lens, or absorbed by the object.	**Grade K:** E38-E45 **Grade 3:** F18
	Heat can be produced in many ways, such as burning, rubbing, or mixing one substance with another.	**Grade 1:** F19 **Grade 2:** B41, B44, C11, D14-D15 **Grade 3:** F36-F37, F41
	Heat can move from one object to another by conduction.	**Grade 3:** F40, F46, F56-F57
	Electricity in circuits can produce light, heat, sound, and magnetic effects.	**Grade 3:** F10-F11, F21, F22-F23, F28-F29
	Electrical circuits require a complete loop through which an electrical current can pass.	**Grade 3:** F21, F22-F23

National Science Education Standards, Grades K-4		Harcourt Science Teacher Edition pages, Grades K-3
	Magnets attract and repel each other and certain kinds of other materials.	**Grade K:** E54-E59 **Grade 1:** F32-F51, F54, F56 **Grade 2:** *14, F11-F17, F54, R8 **Grade 3:** E10, E11, F30
LIFE SCIENCE		
The Characteristics of Organisms	Organisms have basic needs. For example, animals need air, water, and food; plants require air, water, nutrients, and light.	**Grade K:** A10-A15, A18, A32-A41, A56-A63, B10-B15, B18-B23, B38-B43, B44-B49, C46 **Grade 1:** A23-A27, A32-A35, A42-A48, B4-B9, B14-B23, B46 **Grade 2:** *12, A1, A9-A10, A12, A70-A71, D14-D15 **Grade 3:** A4-5, A28-A30, A42-A45, B50-B52, B54-B58, B62-B64, C70, F9
	Organisms can survive only in environments in which their needs can be met.	**Grade K:** A10-A15, A16-A25, A32-A41, A43-A47, A48-A55, A56-A63, B10-B15, B38-B43, C46, C50 **Grade 1:** A35, A42-A48, A70-A73, B4-B9, B27-B42, B46-B48, D48-D49 **Grade 2:** A1, A12, A17, B1, B41-B45, B62 **Grade 3:** A4-A5, A69-A72, B6-B7, B15-B18, B24, B30-B31 B35-B38, B54-B58, B62-B64, C70
	The world has many different environments, and distinct environments support the life of different types of organisms.	**Grade K:** A10-A15, A16-A25, A26-A29, A32-A41, A48-A55, A56-A63, B24-B29, B50-B53, C10-C13 **Grade 1:** A35, A47, A52-A53, A70-A73, D48-D49 **Grade 2:** A15-A17, B34-B35 **Grade 3:** A69-A72, B6-B7, B15-B18, B24, B30-B31, B35-B38, B54-B58, B62-B64
	Each plant or animal has different structures that serve different functions in growth, survival, and reproduction. For example, humans have distinct body structures for walking, holding, seeing, and talking.	**Grade K:** A10-A15, A16-A25, A26-A29, A32-A40, A56-A63, B10-B15, B18-B23, B30-B37, B44-B49 **Grade 1:** A17, A22, A23-A27, A29, A37, A64-A69, A70-A73, B11-B13 **Grade 2:** A1, A9, A16-A18, A21, A24-A29, A48-A52, A54-A58, A61-A63, A70-A71, B20-B27 **Grade 3:** A7-A10, A18, A19-A24, A28-A30, A46-A47, A52, B48-B49, B64
	The behavior of individual organisms is influenced by internal cues (such as hunger) and by external cues (such as a change in the environment).	**Grade K:** A10-A15, A16-A25, A32-A41, A56-A63 **Grade 1:** B4-B9 **Grade 2:** A12, B20-B27, B40-B45 **Grade 3:** A4-A5, A68-A72, C70
	Humans and other organisms have senses that help them detect internal and external cues.	**Grade K:** A10-A15, A16-A25, A32-A40, A43-A47, B10-B15 **Grade 1:** A5-A9, A78 **Grade 2:** *12, A54, A60 **Grade 3:** A68-A73, E3, R29, R40-R41
Life Cycles of Organisms	Plants and animals have life cycles that include being born, developing into adults, reproducing, and eventually dying. The details of this life cycle are different for different organisms.	**Grade K:** A12-A15, A16-A25, A56-A63, B30-B37, B38-B43, B44-B49 **Grade 1:** A17, A30, A59-A61, A64-A69, A70-A73, A79 **Grade 2:** *13, A9-A12, A30-A35, A42-A46, A69 **Grade 3:** A18, A19-A24, A28-A30, A58-A59, A61
	Plants and animals closely resemble their parents.	**Grade K:** A12-A15, A16-A25, A43-A47, A56-A63, B10-B15, B18-B23, B44-B49 **Grade 1:** A30, A58, A59-A61 **Grade 2:** A32-A35, A44-A45, A71 **Grade 3:** A48-A49, A52-A53
	Many characteristics of an organism are inherited from the parents of the organism, but other characteristics result from an individual's interactions with the environment.	**Grade K:** A12, A16-A25, A43-A47, A56-A63, B10-B15, B18-B23, B44-B49 **Grade 1:** A30, A58, A59-A61, A75 **Grade 2:** A10-A11, A32-A35, A40, A44-A45, A47, A71 **Grade 3:** A48-A49, A53, A68

National Science Education Standards, Grades K-4		Harcourt Science Teacher Edition pages, Grades K-3	
	Inherited characteristics include the color of flowers and the number of limbs of an animal.	**Grade K:**	A12-A15, A16-A25, A26-A29, A43-A47, A56-A63, B10-B15, B18-B23, B44-B49
		Grade 1:	A30, A58, A59-A61
		Grade 2:	A32-A35, A44-A45
		Grade 3:	A48-A49
	Other features, such as the ability to ride a bicycle, are learned through interactions with the environment and cannot be passed on to the next generation.	**Grade K:**	A12-A15, A16-A25, A43-A47, A56-A63
		Grade 1:	A62-A63
		Grade 2:	A40d, A47
		Grade 3:	A53, A68
Organisms and Their Environments	All animals depend on plants. Some animals eat plants for food. Other animals eat animals that eat the plants.	**Grade K:**	A36-A40
		Grade 1:	A80, B4-B9, B14-B23
		Grade 2:	B29-B33
		Grade 3:	A44, B50-B52, B62-B64
	An organism's patterns of behavior are related to the nature of that organism's environment, including the kinds and numbers of other organisms present, the availability of food and resources, and the physical characteristics of the environment.	**Grade K:**	A16-A25, A26-A29, A32-A40, A56-A63, C22-C27
		Grade 1:	A70-A73, B27-B42, D48-D49
		Grade 2:	A12-A13, B4-B9
		Grade 3:	A68-A72, B6-B7, B14-B18, B22-B24, B30-B31, B35-B38, B43, B62-B69
	When the environment changes, some plants and animals survive and reproduce, and others die or move to new locations.	**Grade K:**	A16-A25, A32-A40, A56-A63, C22-C27, C46-C53, C54-C61
		Grade 1:	B11-B13, D48-D49
		Grade 2:	A12-A13, B20-B23, B25-B27, B41-B45
		Grade 3:	A4-A5, A24, A68-A72, A76-A80, B8, B30, B40-B41, C74-C75
	All organisms cause changes in the environment where they live. Some of these changes are detrimental to the organism or other organisms, whereas others are beneficial.	**Grade K:**	A36-A40, C22-C27, C46-C53, C54-C61
		Grade 2:	B1, B47-B52, B53-B58c
		Grade 3:	B78-B80, B40-B41, B50-B52, C74-C75
	Humans depend on their natural and constructed environments.	**Grade K:**	A36-A40, C16-C19, C22-C27
		Grade 2:	C4-C7, C8-C13, C14-C17
		Grade 3:	A78-A80, B9-B10
	Humans change environments in ways that can be either beneficial or detrimental for themselves and other organisms.	**Grade K:**	A36-A40, C22-C27, C46-C53, C54-C61
		Grade 2:	B1, B47-B52, B53-B58
		Grade 3:	A78-A80, B9-B10, B40-B41
EARTH AND SPACE SCIENCE			
Properties of Earth Materials	Earth materials are solid rocks and soils, water, and the gases of the atmosphere.	**Grade K:**	C28-C33, C34-C37, C40-C43
		Grade 1:	C4-C7, C25, C29-C31, C33-C35, D17-D19
		Grade 2:	B34, C7, C15-C18, D43-D45
		Grade 3:	C6-C8, C10-C16, C34-C36, C62-C64, C68-C70, C88-C90, D6-D12, D16-D18, D28-D33
	The varied Earth materials have different physical and chemical properties, which make them useful in different ways, for example, as building materials, as sources of fuel, or for growing the plants we use as food.	**Grade K:**	C28-C33, C34-C37, C40-C43
		Grade 1:	C7, C22-C25
		Grade 2:	C4-C18
		Grade 3:	C4-C5, C16, C60-C64, C88-C90, D6-D12, E6-E12, E48
	Earth materials provide many of the resources that humans use.	**Grade K:**	C28-C33, C34-C37, C40-C43, C46-C53
		Grade 1:	C7, C22-C27, C47
		Grade 2:	C10-C13, C15-C18
		Grade 3:	C7, C16, C62, C88-C90, C94-C97, F25
	Soils have properties of color and texture, capacity to retain water, and ability to support the growth of many kinds of plants, including those in our food supply.	**Grade K:**	C28-C33
		Grade 1:	D17-D19
		Grade 2:	A1, C1, C7
		Grade 3:	C60-C64, C68-C70
	Fossils provide evidence about the plants and animals that lived long ago and the nature of the environment at that time.	**Grade 1:**	C2-C3, C8-C16, C48
		Grade 2:	C22-C33, C33-C35, C37-C43
		Grade 3:	A76, C18-C23, F8, F25

National Science Education Standards, Grades K-4		Harcourt Science Teacher Edition pages, Grades K-3
Objects In the Earth and Sky	The sun, moon, stars, clouds, birds, and airplanes all have properties, locations, and movements that can be observed and described.	**Grade K:** A12-A15, A16-A25, A26-A29, A43-A47, A56-A63, B10-B15, B18-B23, B44-B49 **Grade 1:** A30, A58, A59-A61 **Grade 2:** A32-A35, A44-A45 **Grade 3:** A48-A49
	The sun provides the light and heat necessary to maintain the temperature of the Earth.	**Grade K:** D10-D15, D18-D21, D24-D27, D30-D33, D36-D39, D42-D45 **Grade 1:** D30-D32 **Grade 2:** D14-D23 **Grade 3:** D36, D59, F7, F9, F24, F48
Changes in the Earth and Sky	The surface of the Earth changes. Some changes are due to slow processes, such as erosion and weathering, and some changes are due to rapid processes, such as landslides, volcanic eruptions, and earthquakes.	**Grade K:** C10-C13, C16-C19, C22-C27, D10-D17, D18-D23, D30-D34, D36-D39, D42-D45 **Grade 1:** D6, D21 **Grade 2:** B41-B45 **Grade 3:** C14-C15, C46-C50, D16-D18
	Weather changes from day to day and over the seasons.	**Grade K:** D10-D17, D18-D23, D24-D27, D30-D34, D36-D39, D42-D45, D48-D52 **Grade 1:** D4-D6, D17-D19, D24-D25 **Grade 2:** B34, D19-D23, D34-D41, D47-D49, D56-D57, D61 **Grade 3:** D16-D18, D32-D33, D36-D40, D44-D47, D70-D71, D72-D73
	Weather can be described by measurable quantities, such as temperature, wind direction and speed, and precipitation.	**Grade K:** D10-D17, D24-D27, D30-D34, D36-D39, D42-D45, D48-D52 **Grade 1:** D4-D7, D12-D15, D20, D56 **Grade 2:** B34, D43-D45, D47,-D49, D61 **Grade 3:** D9, D16-D18, D32-D33, D36-D40, D42-D47
	Objects in the sky have patterns of movement. The sun, for example, appears to move across the sky in the same way every day, but its path changes slowly over the seasons.	**Grade K:** D18, D24, D30, D36, D42 **Grade 1:** D26, D28 **Grade 2:** D12-D13, D19-D23, D25-D29 **Grade 3:** D68-D69, D72-D73, D85
	The moon moves across the sky on a daily basis much like the sun.	**Grade 1:** D28 **Grade 2:** D12-D13, D28-D29 **Grade 3:** D76
SCIENCE IN PERSONAL AND SOCIAL PERSPECTIVES		
Personal Health	Safety and security are basic needs of humans. Safety involves freedom from danger, risk, or injury. Security involves feelings of confidence and lack of anxiety and fear. Student understandings include following safety rules for home and school, preventing abuse and neglect, avoiding injury, knowing whom to ask for help, and when and how to say no.	**Grade K:** AB1, AB2 **Grade 1:** *24, D28, E38-E42, R9-R25 **Grade 2:** *24, D56-D57, E25, R14-R23 **Grade 3:** xxiv, R8-R11, R16-R17, R26-R27
Characteristics and Changes in Populations	Human populations include groups of individuals living in a particular location. One important characteristic of a human population is the population density—the number of individuals of a particular population that lives in a given amount of space.	**Grade K:** C59 **Grade 3:** B4-B10
	The size of a human population can increase or decrease. Populations will increase unless other factors such as disease or famine decrease the population.	**Grade K:** C59 **Grade 3:** A74-A80, B9-B10
Type of Resources	Resources are things that we get from the living and nonliving environment to meet the needs and wants of a population.	**Grade K:** A32-A40, B50, C25, C40, C28-C33, C40-C43, C46-C53, C54-C61 **Grade 1:** B14-B23, C22-C27 **Grade 2:** C2-C7, C10-C13, D15, D52-D55 **Grade 3:** B50-B52, C7, C16, C64, C70, C88-C90, C94-C97, C100-C104, D6-D12, F7-F12, F25
	Some resources are basic materials, such as air, water, and soil; some are produced from basic resource, such as food, fuel, and building materials; and some resources are nonmaterial, such as quiet places, beauty, security, and safety.	**Grade K:** A32-A40, C25, C28-C33, C40-C43, C46-C53 **Grade 1:** B14-B23, C22-C27, C29-C31, C33-C35 **Grade 2:** A64-A65, C2-C7, C10-C13, C15-C18, D52-D55 **Grade 3:** A28-A30, B50-B52, C7, C62-C64, C68-C70, C88-C90, C94-C97, C100-C104, D6-D12, D16-D18, F8-F12, F25

National Science Education Standards, Grades K-4		Harcourt Science Teacher Edition pages, Grades K-3
	The supply of many resources is limited. If used, resources can be extended through recycling and decreased use.	**Grade K:** A32-A40, C28-C33, C34-C37, C40-C43, C46-C53, C54-C61 **Grade 1:** C36-C41 **Grade 2:** B53-B58, C8 **Grade 3:** C88-C90, C94-C97, C100-C104, D16-D18, F25
Changes in Environments	Environments are the space, conditions, and factors that affect an individual's and a population's ability to survive and their quality of life.	**Grade K:** A32-A40, B38-B43, B50-B53, C46-C53, C54-C61 **Grade 1:** C25 **Grade 2:** A15, B40-B45, B46-B51 **Grade 3:** A78-A80, B6-B7, B14-B18, B22-B24, B28-B30, B35-B38, B64, C70, D6-D12
	Changes in environments can be natural or influenced by humans. Some changes are good, some are bad, and some are neither good nor bad. Pollution is a change in the environment that can influence the health, survival, or activities of organisms, including humans.	**Grade K:** A32-A40, C22-C27, C46-C53, C54-C61 **Grade 2:** B39, B47-B52, B52-B58 **Grade 3:** A78-A80, B9-B10, B40-B41, C46-C50, C74-C76
	Some environmental changes occur slowly, and others occur rapidly. Students should understand the different consequences of changing environments in small increments over long periods as compared with changing environments in large increments over short periods.	**Grade K:** A32-A40, B38-B43, C22-C27, C46-C53, C54-C61 **Grade 2:** D56-D57 **Grade 3:** A74-A75, B25, B40-B41, C46-C50, D16-D18, D37-D40
Science and Technology in Local Challenges	People continue inventing new ways of doing things, solving problems, and getting work done. New ideas and inventions often affect other people; sometimes the effects are good and sometimes they are bad. It is helpful to try to determine in advance how ideas and inventions will affect other people.	**Grade K:** B50-B53, C22-C27, C46, C54-C61, D51 **Grade 1:** E43 **Grade 2:** A19, B38, B53-B58, C13, C17, D47-D49, E25, F25 **Grade 3:** B9-B10, B40-B41, C76, C94-C95, C100-C104, D20-D21, D32, D44-D45, E48, F10-F11, F28-F29, F30, F42, F52-F54, F79-F70, F82-F83
	Science and technology have greatly improved food quality and quantity, transportation, health, sanitation, and communication. These benefits of science and technology are not available to all the people in the world.	**Grade K:** B50-B53, C25, C46, C54-C61 **Grade 1:** A16 **Grade 2:** A64-A65, B38, B53-B58, C13, E25, F25 **Grade 3:** C76, C94-C95, C100-C104, D20-D21, D44-D45, E48, E53, F8, F10-F11, F21, F28-F29, F30, F42, F54, F79-F80, F82-F83
HISTORY AND NATURE OF SCIENCES		
Science as a Human Endeavor	Science and technology have been practiced by people for a long time.	**Grade K:** B50, C25, E35 **Grade 1:** C16 **Grade 2:** C19, F25 **Grade 3:** D44-D45, F29, F30, F82-F83
	Men and women have made a variety of contributions throughout the history of science and technology.	**Grade K:** B50, C25, C46, E15, E35 **Grade 1:** B43, C16 **Grade 2:** A19, A67, B35, C19, C27, E25, F25 **Grade 3:** B41, F29, F30, F82-F83
	Although men and women using scientific inquiry have learned much about the objects, events, and phenomena in nature, much more remains to be understood. Science will never be finished.	**Grade K:** C25, C46, D51, E15 **Grade 3:** D20-D21, D32, D44-D45, F30
	Many people choose science as a career and devote their entire lives to studying it. Many people derive great pleasure from doing science.	**Grade K:** E15 **Grade 1:** A16 **Grade 2:** A19, A35, A67, C27-C29 **Grade 3:** B41, D20-D21, D32, F29, F30

Stanford Achievement Test

Harcourt Science prepares students to perform successfully on a variety of standardized tests, especially the Stanford Achievement Test. The following charts show how *Harcourt Science* Grades K-3 correlate to the objectives of the various levels of the Stanford Achievement Test. Please consult the Teacher's Editions for other grades of *Harcourt Science* for correlations to other levels of the Stanford Achievement Test.

Stanford Achievement Test Objectives for SESAT 1		Harcourt Science Teacher Edition pages
Earth and Space Science	Associate the sun with its functions	**Grade K:** B38-B42, D18, D30-D35
	Apply an understanding of pollution	**Grade K:** C54-C61
	Identify a source of water	**Grade K:** C40-C45, C46-C53, F10-F13
	Evaluate methods of helping the environment	**Grade K:** A32, A39, C54-C61
Life Science	Classify living things	**Grade K:** A10-A15, A17-A18, A42-A47, B17-B18, B24-B29
	Sequence growth patterns of organisms	**Grade K:** A56-A63, B32-B35, B44-B49
	Identify an animal by its environment	**Grade K:** A21, A26, A32-A41, A49-A55
	Relate the structures of living things to their functions	**Grade K:** A20, A26-A31, A42-A47, B18-B23
	Use observations to group organisms	**Grade K:** A10-A15, A16-A25, A42-A47, B24-B29, B50-B55
	Determine cause and effect of health relationships	**Grade K:** T30-T31
	Understand what is needed for proper nutrition	**Grade K:** T30-T31
	Sequence stages of animal development	**Grade K:** A56-A63
Physical Science	Understand the states of matter	**Grade K:** E18, E32, F10, F30, F38-F45
	Use observations to analyze shadows	**Grade K:** C11, E38-E45
	Apply an understanding of light	**Grade K:** E38-E45
	Apply an understanding of measurement	**Grade K:** A56-A63, B22, B38-B43, B44-B45, D10-D17, D43-D44, E44
	Draw a conclusion about heat	**Grade K:** B38-B43, D30-D35
Science Processes	Analyze simple graphs	**Grade K:** A24, A30, A40, B16, B28, B44-B45, B54, C60, D16, D22, D24-D25, E16, F36

Stanford Achievement Test Objectives for SESAT 2

Life Science	Evaluate relative importance of good health habits	**Grade K:** [illegible]
		Grade 1: [illegible]
	Use observations to group organisms	**Grade K:** A10-A1[illegible]
		Grade 1: A40-A41, A4[illegible]
	Identify senses used to gather data	**Grade K:** T26-T37
		Grade 1: A2-A3, A4-A9, A19, E20
	Sequence the growth patterns of organisms	**Grade K:** A56-A63, B44-B49
		Grade 1: A17, A29-A31, A37-A39, A58, A64-A69, [illegible]
	Identify living and non-living things	**Grade K:** A10-A15, C34-C39
		Grade 1: A4, A10-A15, A19, A40-A41, A55-A57, B27-B42
	Identify organs by their function	**Grade K:** T26-T37
		Grade 1: A2, A4, A5-A9, A23-A27
	Determine cause and effect of health relationships	**Grade K:** T30-T31
		Grade 1: A12, A62, B21
	Evaluate the relative value of different foods to meet nutritional needs	**Grade K:** T30-T31
		Grade 1: B21
Earth and Space Science	Evaluate methods of helping or harming the environment	**Grade K:** A32, A39, C54-C61
	Use observations to compare organisms	**Grade K:** A10-A15, A16-A25, A42-A47, B24-B29, B50-B55
		Grade 1: A55-A57, A58
	Identify sources of water	**Grade K:** C40-C45, C46-C53, F10-F13
		Grade 1: C33-C35, D18-D19
	Associate water with its characteristics	**Grade K:** F10-F15, F16-F21, F22-F29, F30-F37, F38-F45
		Grade 1: C33-C35, D17-D19
Physical Science	Associate objects with their state of matter	**Grade K:** E18, E32, F10, F30, F38-F45
		Grade 1: D17-D19, E4, E5-E10, E12-E15, E20-E23, E34-E28
	Deduce relative amounts of heat energy in objects	**Grade K:** D30-D35
		Grade 1: D8-D11
Science Processes	Analyze graphs	**Grade K:** A24, A30, A40, B16, B28, B44-B45, B54, C60, D16, D22, D24-D25, E16, F36
		Grade 1: *17, C43, D51, E7
	Predict the results of an experiment	**Grade K:** A33, A37, B40, E55-E56, F16, F22-F24, F30-F31
		Grade 1: B10, E16, E29, E31
	Evaluate an experimental design	**Grade K:** A40
		Grade 1: *10-*11, A54, A64, A74, B10, B26, B30, B34, B38, C28, C32, D4, D16, E31, F4

...nt Test Objectives for PRIMARY 1		Harcourt Science Teacher Edition pages
	Associate products with their sources	**Grade K:** B50-B55 **Grade 1:** A32, B14-B18 **Grade 2:** A10, C10-C13
	Comprehend the effects of processing on food nutrition	**Grade K:** B50-B55
	Associate organisms with their characteristics	**Grade K:** A10-A15, A16-A25, A42-A47, B24-B29, B50-B55 **Grade 1:** A4, A19, A20-A21, A22, A23-A27, A55-A57, A75, B42 **Grade 2:** A9, A48-A52, A54-A59, C34-C35, C40
	Classify animal groups	**Grade K:** A10-A15, A16-A25, A42-A47, B24-B29, B50-B55 **Grade 1:** A40-A41, A48-A53, A55-A57, A58 **Grade 2:** *13, A4, A70
	Draw a conclusion based on a graph of data from an experiment	**Grade K:** A24, A30, A40, B16, B28, B44-B45, B54, C60, D16, D22, D24-D25, E16, F36 **Grade 1:** *17, A64 **Grade 2:** A37, A52, B43, D58
	Determine the relative needs of an organism	**Grade K:** A32-A41, B38-B43 **Grade 1:** A23-A27, A32, A42-A47, A71-A73, B4-B9, B27-B42 **Grade 2:** *12, A1, A6-7, A9, A61-A63, A70-A71, B4, B6-B13, B14-B19, B20-B28, B33, B40, B45
	Sequence the growth patterns of organisms	**Grade K:** A56-A63 **Grade 1:** A17, A29-A31, A34-A39, B58, A64-A69, A70-A73, B42 **Grade 2:** *13, A6-A9, A30-A35, A39, A42-A46
	Apply an understanding of growth and development of organisms	**Grade K:** A56-A63 **Grade 1:** A17, A29-A35, A39, A58, A64-A69, A70-A73 **Grade 2:** A1, A6-A8, A9, A30-A35, A39, A42-A46, A70-A71
Physical Science	Apply an understanding of heat sources	**Grade K:** B38-B43, D30-D35 **Grade 1:** D8-D11 **Grade 2:** D1, D14-D15, D44, E38-E39, E41
	Draw a conclusion about forces needed to move objects	**Grade K:** E46-E53, E54-E59 **Grade 1:** D13, F4-F21, F22 **Grade 2:** F1-F4, F5-F11, F12-F17, F18-F23, F54
	Deduce the relative mass of objects	**Grade K:** E18-E25 **Grade 1:** E8, F8, F22 **Grade 2:** E8, E12, E35
	Make an inference about the effects of force	**Grade K:** E18-E25, E46-E53, E54-E59 **Grade 1:** D15, F4-F21, F22, F32-F51 **Grade 2:** *14, F1, F5-F11, F12-F17, F18-F23
Earth and Space Science	Deduce the relative effects of actions on the environment	**Grade K:** A32, A39, C54-C61 **Grade 1:** D12-D15, D17-D19 **Grade 2:** D47-D52
	Apply an understanding of seasonal characteristics	**Grade K:** D18-D23, D24-D29, D30-D41, D42-D47 **Grade 1:** D24-D25, D34-D53 **Grade 2:** B1, B46-B51, B52-B57, B62, D18-D23, D33, D52-D55
	Identify characteristics of objects	**Grade K:** E10-E17, E18-E25, E32-E37, E38-E45, E46-E53, E54-E59 **Grade 1:** C4-C7 **Grade 2:** E5-E7, E31-E36, E38-E43, E55
	Analyze light and shadows	**Grade K:** C11, E38-E45 **Grade 1:** D30-D32 **Grade 2:** D13, D17-D18, D24, D28-D29, D62-D63
Science Process	Draw a conclusion based on structure and function relationships	**Grade K:** A26-A31, A42-A47, B18-B23, B24-B29, B50-B55, C16-C21, C46-C53, E46-E53, E54-E59, F22-F29 **Grade 1:** A10, A58, A71-A73, B10, B14, B26, B30, B34, B42, C4, C28, C32, D4, D8, E29, F4, F22 **Grade 2:** A7, B40, C4, C24, D42, E9, F18, F30

Stanford Achievement Test Objectives for Primary 1		Harcourt Science Teacher Edition pages
	Associate objects with their characteristics	**Grade K:** E10-E17, E18-E25, E32-E37, E38-E45, E46-E53, E54-E59 **Grade 1:** A4, A22, A28, A32, A54, A58, A64, A70-A73, B10, B26, B42, C4-C7, D8 **Grade 2:** *10, A4, A36. D33, E8, E9, E31-E36, E38-E43
	Interpret a bar graph	**Grade K:** A24, A30, A40, B16, B28, B44-B45, B54, C60, D16, D22, D24-D25, E16, F36 **Grade 1:** *17, D51, E7 **Grade 2:** *17, A37

Stanford Achievement Test Objectives for Primary 2		Harcourt Science Teacher Edition pages
Earth and Space Science	Analyze patterns of light and shadows	**Grade 1:** D30-D32 **Grade 2:** D13, D17-D18, D24, D28-D29, D62-D63 **Grade 3:** D66-D67, D70-D71, D72-D73, D74-D75, D85
	Estimate relative temperatures	**Grade 1:** D8-D11, D20, D34, D38 **Grade 2:** D34-D41, D46 **Grade 3:** D34-D36
	Use observations to relate a structure to its function	**Grade 1:** C32 **Grade 2:** D58 **Grade 3:** A72, C34, C70, C90
Physical Science	Apply an understanding of the effects of gravity	**Grade 2:** A11, E3, F11, F19 **Grade 3:** D85, F28-F29, F70
	Determine the supporting evidence for physical changes	**Grade 1:** D17-D19, E16-E19, E24-E28 **Grade 2:** E38-E43, E55-E56 **Grade 3:** C33, C102-C103, D14-D18, D51, E16-E18, E40
	Identify a substance in a given state of matter	**Grade 1:** E4, E7-E15, E20-E23 **Grade 2:** E38-E43, E45-E47 **Grade 3:** C7, D16, E11-E12, E14-E18, E38-E39
	Predict the effect of force on objects	**Grade 1:** D13-D15, F4-F21, F22, F32-F51 **Grade 2:** *14, F1, F5-F11, F18-F23, F54-F55 **Grade 3:** C12-C15, F64-F65, F68, F76-F77
Life Science	Apply an understanding of food chains	**Grade 1:** B4-B9, B15, B17-B18 **Grade 2:** B29-B33 **Grade 3:** B50-B52, B54-B58, B60-B64
	Sequence the patterns of growth in an organism	**Grade 1:** A17, A29-A31, A34-A39, A58, A64-A69, A70-A73, A79 **Grade 2:** *13, A6-A7, A39, A42-46 **Grade 3:** A19-A24
	Use observation skills to determine plant relationships	**Grade 1:** A23-A27, B26 **Grade 2:** A9 **Grade 3:** A4-A5, A18, A26-A27
	Use observations to group organisms	**Grade 1:** A40-A41, A48-A53, A55-A57, B38 **Grade 2:** A4, A21, A70 **Grade 3:** A40-A41, A54, A56, A58-A64
	Apply an understanding of structures and their functions	**Grade 1:** A2-A3, A20-A21, A22, A23-A27, A29, A36, A39, A55-A57, A71-A73, B10 **Grade 2:** A1, A8-A9, A48-A52, A54-A59, A61-A63, A71, C34-C35, C40 **Grade 3:** A7-A10, A18, A19-A24, A46-A47, A50-A51, A72, B48-B49
	Associate an organism with its energy source	**Grade 1:** B4-B9 **Grade 2:** A1, A9, A61-A63, C10-C13 **Grade 3:** A4-A4, A28-A30, B58, C70, C90, C95, F7, F9, F24
	Associate animals with their habitat	**Grade 1:** A40, A42-A47, A70-A73, A80, B27-B29, B38, D48-D49 **Grade 2:** B4, B5-B19, B62 **Grade 3:** A4-A5, A69-A72, B6-B7, B15-B18, B24, B30-B31, B35-B38, B63, C64

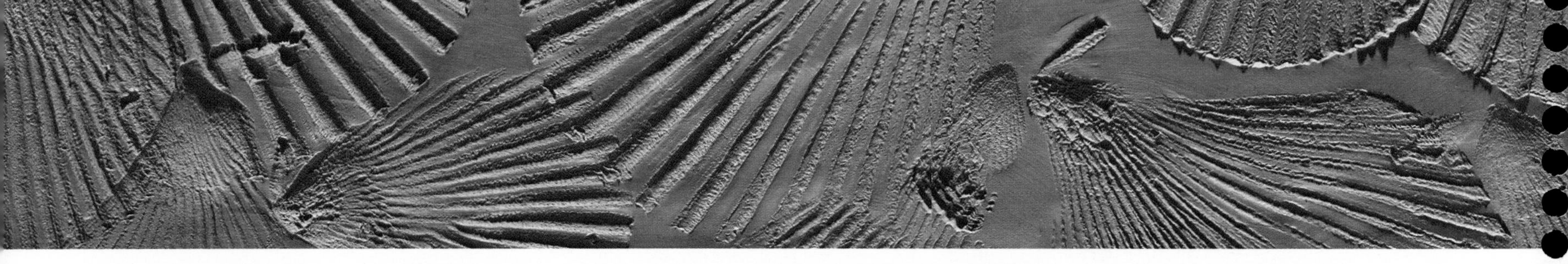

Stanford Achievement Test Objectives for Primary 2		Harcourt Science Teacher Edition pages
	Associate parts of a plant with their functions	**Grade 1:** A23-A27, A29, A32, A39, B10
		Grade 2: A1, A9, A70-A71, B40
		Grade 3: A7, A9, A18, A19-A24, A28-A30
Science Processes	Read a circle graph	**Grade 3:** A39, C59, C70
	Evaluate experimental designs	**Grade 1:** *10-*11, A1, A54, A74, B1, B10, B26, B30, B34, B38, C1, C32, D1, D4, D8, D20, E1, E29, E31, F1, F4
		Grade 2: A1, B1, C1, C4, C36, D1, D46, E1, F1, F30
		Grade 3: A1, A50-A51, B1, B23, B43, B61, C1, C47, C61, C67, C73, D1, D14-D15, E1, E15, E39, F1, F45
	Analyze bar graphs	**Grade 1:** *17, D51, E7
		Grade 2: *17, A37
		Grade 3: A22, A55, A74-A75, B28, B31, B39, C45, C98-C99, C100, E25, F23